# Theology

## A
## Course
## for
## College
## Students

---

VOLUME I

CHRIST AS PROPHET
AND KING

\*

JOHN J. FERNAN, S. J.

*"Philip, he who sees me*
*sees also the Father."*
*John 14:9*

*IMPRIMI POTEST*
JOHN J. McMAHON, *S.J.*
Praep. Prov. Neo Eboracensis

*NIHIL OBSTAT*
ROBERT E. DILLON, *J.C.D.*
Censor Librorum

*IMPRIMATUR*
✠ WALTER A. FOERY, *D.D.*
Episcopus Syracusensis

20 Junii 1952

*BX 904*
*F4*
*vol 1*
*cp 2*

PRINTED FOR LE MOYNE COLLEGE, SYRACUSE, N.Y.
BY THE GEORGIAN PRESS INC., 175 VARICK STREET, NEW YORK, N. Y. 1956

# CONTENTS

## *PART ONE*

### INTRODUCTION TO THE GOSPELS

## *PART TWO*

### BACKGROUND TO THE LIFE OF CHRIST

# PART THREE

## THE PUBLIC LIFE OF CHRIST

# PART FOUR

## DOGMATIC SUMMARY

# ACKNOWLEDGMENT

FATHER JOHN COURTNEY MURRAY, *S.J.* originally sketched the general outlines of this Theology Course for College Students. In 1941 he issued an incomplete manual, privately printed, for the use of Freshman students at Georgetown University, Washington, and Loyola College, Baltimore.

In recent years the Theology Departments at Canisius College, Buffalo, Le Moyne College, Syracuse, and St. Peter's College, Jersey City, have worked together on an adaptation of Father Murray's original plan. At the conclusion of five years of class-room experimentation, Father John J. Fernan, S.J., of Le Moyne College, was commissioned to write the new and complete text for Freshman year.

In this new text, much of Father Murray's original text has been used without alteration. This was done with his kind permission. On the other hand, many of the chapters in the present book are completely new additions. Hence, we wish to avoid any claim that Father Murray sponsors the present work. But on the other hand, we gratefully acknowledge that this work was inspired by Father Murray and much of its content can be found in his original notes.

Father John V. Curry, *S.J.,* of LeMoyne College, composed the entire index for this volume.

# THEOLOGY TEXTBOOKS

The following textbooks, comprising a four-year course in College Theology, may be ordered from
LeMoyne College Bookstore,
LeMoyne Heights,
Syracuse 3, N. Y.

*Vol. I*    Christ as Prophet and King

*Vol. II*   Christ Our High Priest

*Vol. III*  The Mystical Christ

*Vol. IV*   Christ in His Members

# PREFACE

The main purpose of this preface is to show the rationale of the whole college course in Theology and specifically of the First Year of this particular course. The following remarks are addressed more directly to the teacher than to the student but it is hoped that the student will also find in them a helpful explanation of the course which he is about to begin.

## THEOLOGY AND THE AIM OF CHRISTIAN EDUCATION

FROM THE OUTSET, the student must endeavor to understand that the college course in theology cannot truthfully be regarded as occupying a minor and marginal place in the total curriculum. It is not just a little pious embroidery loosely attached to an educational pattern woven of secular subjects. On the contrary, if its objective is viewed in relation to the total objective of Christian education, it emerges clearly as the *central* course, that gives intelligibility to the whole pattern of education as it is conceived by Christian educators.

A simple argument should suffice to convince anyone of the fact. If the supreme objective of a Christian education is to form a Christian man, and if a Christian man can be formed only by vital contact with Christ, and if the proper objective of the course in Christian theology is precisely to bring the college student into vital contact with Christ, then, obviously, the course in Christian theology must be considered the very soul of the college curriculum.

Some development of this argument must at least be suggested. First of all, the following statement of the goal of Christian education must be laid down as definitive:

"The proper and intimate meaning of Christian education is this: it is a form of co-operation with divine grace towards the formation of a *genuine* and *finished Christian man*. That is, it aims at fashioning the lineaments of Christ Himself in those who have been reborn by baptism. The Apostle Paul vividly stated this aim when he said: 'My little children, with you I am continually in labor *till Christ be formed in you*' (Galatians 4:19). For the genuine Christian must live a supernatural life in Christ: 'Christ is your life' (Colossians 3:4); and he must show forth this supernatural life *in each single phase* of his activity: 'that the life of Christ may be manifested in our mortal flesh' (2 Corinthians 4:11). For precisely this reason Christian education embraces the *totality* of human life, sc. physical and spiritual, intellectual and moral, individual and domestic and civil life. Its purpose is *not* in any way to *diminish* human life, but to elevate, order and *perfect* it in accordance with the example and teaching of Christ. Hence, the true Christian man, product of a Christian education, is the supernatural man, who thinks and acts and judges constantly and consistently in accordance with right reason, as illumined by the supernatural light of the example and teaching of Christ. In other words, to use a current term, he is the true and finished man of character" (Pius XI, "Divini Illius Magistri").

This magnificent paragraph suggests four intimately related ideas that lie at the very basis of the whole concept of Christian education.

1. There is at work in the world a divine power (which is called "grace"), whose energies are directed at one goal, the formation of "Christian men." In the process of education the energies of both educator and student must ally themselves with that divine power and work toward the same goal. In that alliance is their major hope of success.

2. Consequently, as its end-product, a Christian education should have that noblest of created things, a man, a being who is fully human, ready for the whole of human life, and equipped to be a force for human living in the world, because he realizes the dignity of human personality and the meaning of human life, and strongly wills to realize them in himself and in society.

3. A Christian education aims to make its subjects fully human by making them fully Christian. This is the cardinal principle which inspires the whole program of the Christian school or college, namely, that to be a "whole man" one must be a "whole Christian." It is too narrow a view of the function of Christianity to say that it aims at saving individual men from this world and guaranteeing their happiness in the next. Rather, that function must be conceived as the salvation of *humanity* in the fullest sense, both in this world and in the next. Of its essence it is a humanizing force, that desires not to diminish human life, but to make it more perfectly human in all its phases, personal and social. It flatly identifies itself with all things that are genuinely human; it asserts boldly that what is un-Christian is by that very fact inhuman; and it attacks incessantly, as hostile to itself, all the forces that are inimical to full human life.

4. Finally, a Christian education aims to make its subjects both men and Christian by bringing them into vital contact with Christ. For this is its other cardinal principle, namely, that a life that is Christian and therefore human, is a supernatural life in Christ, the life of a son of God, guided

and controlled in his every activity by the Spirit of Christ. The peculiarity of Christianity consists in this, that it is a way of being human, divinely. It asserts the impotence of humanity to be fully human out of its own resources and energies; it asserts the consequent need of a higher, divine energy in order that humanity may achieve itself; in a word, it asserts that the salvation of humanity is in Christ, that to be human is the grace of Christ.

Consequently, the major effort in a program of Christian education is to bring the student into vital contact with Christ: to open his intelligence to the meaning of Christ, to frame his affections to the doctrine of Christ, to develop in him the full potentialities of the grace of Christ that was given to him in baptism. This effort is the thing that distinguishes Christian education from purely secular education; and it is made specifically in the courses of theology proper to a Christian college.

Consequently, upon the success of this course, the case for Christian education chiefly rests. If the Christian college fails in the secular part of its program (arts, sciences, etc.), it fails partially; but if it fails in the theological part, then its failure is complete. There can be no disguising this fact. For the secular subjects are, of their nature, limited in their influence upon the student's life. But the influence of theology should be pervasive, intimately penetrating, creative of the whole personality—in a word, instrumental beyond all other courses in the humanization of the student because effective of his Christianization. And if it fails to exert this influence, nothing else can redeem the failure. The student may emerge something of a man, but not a whole man, because not a Christian man.

## The General Objective of the College Course in Theology

This is immediately suggested by the title itself: a course in *theology*. First of all, the supposition is that the student comes to college with at least an elementary knowledge of essential Christian truths, moral precepts, and devotional practices. If, for some reason or other, this supposition is not verified in individual cases, the deficiency must by all means be supplied. At any rate, the religious instruction given in college ought to proceed on a specifically college level. And this means that it must be not catechetical but rather theological in character. It should not aim merely at a knowledge of the individual truths and precepts that constitute Christian faith and morality, nor at a knowledge of the individual "means of grace" that are essential to a Christian life. Such is the purpose of catechetical instruction: to teach the Creed, the commandments, and the use of the sacraments.

On the college level, religious instruction pursues a higher, more scientific, and more profoundly religious purpose. It recognizes the fact that the college man is expected to have a more fully intelligent possession of Christian truth, and a keener vision of the splendor of the Christian ideal of life, both personal and social, in order that the power of his Christian convictions and the strength of character they have fashioned in him may equip him to fulfill the function of intellectual, moral, and spiritual leadership in the community that is his proper responsibility. In a word, it recognizes his need of theology, vital theology.

For theology is something more than simple faith; it is faith that has been scientifically studied. And vital theology is faith that has not only been scientifically studied, but has also been brought into vivifying contact with all the problems of life, and with all the spheres of thought or activity in which the Christian layman may choose, or be obliged, to move.

Consequently, the college course in theology has two things to do. First, inasmuch as it is a science, it cannot content itself with merely studying individual doctrines, etc.; rather, it must search out the "idea" of Christianity, what the thing is in its essence, what is its center, its core, its most intimate meaning. Then, around this center it must construct in organic fashion the whole of Christian theory and practice, showing the necessary and vital relation of part to part, and of each part to the center. Concretely, it must show that at the center of Christianity, giving it its whole meaning and expressing its "idea," stands the figure of Christ. It must show, too, that He is the source of all Christian truth, the sanction of all Christian morality, the inspiration of all Christian worship, both private and public, personal and sacramental.

For precisely in this respect does the simple Christian differ from the Christian theologian (such as, in his measure, the college man is expected to be): the former possesses his faith as a more or less heterogeneous collection of beliefs, moral habits, and devotional practices, to all of which he may, of course, be intensely devoted; the latter possesses his faith as a consistent whole, intelligently grasped as a whole, in the consciousness of its inner harmony and of the organic relation of truth with truth, of moral precept and devotional practice with dogmatic fact. In a word, the Christian theologian has accomplished in his own mind a work of reflection, of organization, of synthesis. He has made his faith properly intelligent, and proportionately strong. And in the process he has come to realize how complete is the satisfaction that it brings to all his human needs, and how adequate is the answer that it gives to the whole problem of human life, his own and that of humanity.

Secondly, in addition to this work of synthesis and unification (his supreme task as a scientist), the theologian has another important duty: he must systematically trace his faith to its origins in history. He does not evolve his idea of Christianity out of thin air, but out of hard fact. He does not construct his system of belief and practice while splendidly isolated in himself and in the present. Rather, his effort is always to attach himself to his roots in the past, to feel himself part of a history and a tradition, to convince himself that he possesses today, faithfully transmitted to him, the same living word that Christ and His Holy Spirit gave to the twelve men whom He chose as His apostles. In a word, he makes himself the historian of his own faith.

These two things, then, the college course in theology must do: a work of history and a work of synthesis. Both are works of science, but both, too, have a religious purpose, namely, a new enlightenment of faith, that it may in turn illuminate the whole of life, and direct and control its living. For though theology is primarily concerned with the search for Christian truth and with its intelligent organization, nevertheless, it has not achieved its total purpose if it stops at mere academic knowledge and does not become the inspiration of a way of *life*.

## General Outline of This Particular Course

The application of these general principles to a course for college students is necessarily limited by many practical factors, the most important of which are 1) the average ability of the students and 2) the number of class hours available. No single course can hope to exhaust the rich treasures of knowledge and inspiration contained in the body of Christian truth as it is in itself. Since, therefore, many equally effective college courses might be designed to achieve the same general objective, it is necessary that we here sketch briefly the key idea and general outline of this particular four-year course. Then we can go on to discuss the particular year of the course for which this textbook was written.

It is assumed throughout this course that the essence of the good news of the Gospel is the *new life we have in God*. This, then, is the core, the unifying principle of this course and all individual theological truths will be studied in relation to this central fact. This over-all unity may be stated generically in the following steps:

1. The Life that is in Christ.

2. The Life of Christ Communicated to the Church.

3. The Life of Christ Communicated to the Individual by the Church.

4. Asceticism—the means of developing the Life.

The following is a restatement of the same thing with a general indication of how the matter divides into four years:

*First Year*—Christ as Prophet and King.

(Studied from the concrete history of the four Gospels as interpreted by the Church.)

*Second Year*—Christ the Priest.

(Studied from the history of the Passion and Resurrection and then summed up dogmatically from the Epistle to the Hebrews, Councils of the Church and teaching of the Theologians.)

*Third Year*—Christ in His Mystical Body.

(Studied historically from the Acts of the Apostles and then summed up dogmatically from the Epistles of St. Paul and the Encyclicals on the Holy Spirit and Mystical Body.)

*Fourth Year*—Christ in the Individual Member of His Body.

(The historical data have already been seen in the previous years. The literary-dogmatic summary of the data is studied now from the Epistle to the Romans. And finally, a complete dogmatic study of all the elements of Justification is made from the Councils of the Church and the analysis of the Theologians.)

The final half-term of the course is devoted to a summary of the moral implications of all the dogma that was seen in the four years.

*Asceticism*. Perhaps a few words of explanation are in order as to why this aspect of Christianity is chosen, in preference to any other, as the concluding study of the whole course. It is assumed, in this final stage, that the student has deepened his understanding and intensified his love for the Life which has come down from Christ to the Church—to himself. The student's first desire and practical aim should be to develop to the fullest his own *personal* status as a member of the Mystical Body. The course in Asceticism is designed to help him fulfill this primary objective.

We have said, however, that the function of Christianity is not merely that each individual man might save his own soul, but that each might work for the salvation of humanity as a whole. This wider objective implies the whole social program of the Church as an answer to humanity's problems of today.

And yet, in a college theology course of two hours a week, it is impossible to include the social encyclicals. Personal asceticism was chosen in preference to specific social programs, not because the latter are considered as isolated from our objective, but because time-limits make a choice necessary and personal sanctification is the absolutely necessary foundation for the social apostolate. However, the general outline of this course with its emphasis on the Mystical Body should make it clear that we do not consider personal sanctification in a narrow, isolated sense. The student must constantly be made aware that he is part of a whole and even the most personal elements of his own sanctity, or lack of it, have direct social implications.

But granted that this course is social minded from beginning to end, it is true that we exclude from it a formal study of Catholic teaching applied to particular social problems. The answer to this pressing problem must be found, it seems to us, either by extending the scope of Ethics or by taking some of these subjects out of the course in Special Ethics and teaching them in a separate course of Catholic Social Morality.

Aside from some such practical solution, it must be remembered that what has been said about the objectives of Christian Education (pg. ix-xi) applies, not merely to the theology course, but to the *whole* college. It is not the function of Theology, which is a minor course in the number of hours assigned to it, to take over the detailed application of Christian principles to every specific problem treated in the other departments of the college.

## THE PARTICULAR OBJECTIVE OF FRESHMAN YEAR

The starting point of the course, and the particular objective of Freshman year ought to be clear from the foregoing remarks. We must begin with Christ. For Christianity *is* Christ. And any intelligent attempt to search out the "idea" of Christianity must necessarily begin by an intensive study of the life of its Divine Founder, as it is narrated in the four Gospels. To understand His life is to begin to understand what Christianity is. Hence the general objective of Freshman year is the acquisition of a thorough knowledge of the life of Christ, with the purpose of seeing into its meaning for the life of humanity. The course falls naturally into two main parts.

*PART I: A study of the four individual histories of the life of Christ, our four Gospels.* The idea is to acquire a complete and solid knowledge of the content, build, characteristics, etc., of each of the Gospels. They are the authentic historical sources of all our knowledge of Christ, and must be mastered.

This textbook is not meant to be a substitute for studying the Gospels themselves. Rather, the first two parts of this manual are meant to help the student appreciate more fully the human and divine worth of the Gospels and to give him some background for understanding their meaning. Perhaps the following remarks will clarify how the manual may be used in conjunction with the Gospels during the first term.

While the student is reading the four Gospels individually, those chapters of Part I (of this volume) which deal with the literary characteristics of the Gospels may be applied to each Gospel as it is being read. It would be well, for example, if the teacher outlined the literary characteristics of Matthew in a single lecture before the student begins his reading assignments. Then, as the student reads this Gospel in weekly assignments of several chapters, he should find detailed verification of what was given in the lecture.

While the student is engaged in this work, the teacher will have opportunity to lecture on such general features of the Gospels as their "Credibility", "Inspiration", etc., and, eventually, on the historical background of the chapters in Part II. But rather than having these extraneous topics supplant the main work of becoming familiar with the gospel texts, it would be better, if necessary, to omit discussion of some of them and assign them for private reading.

*PART II: A study of the life of Christ as an organic whole.* The task here will be to gather up and put in order the material furnished by the individual Evangelists, with the idea of seeing the life of Christ in its structure and plan, and in its progressive development through various periods and phases. But we limit our study to the Public Life of Christ, since the history of His Passion, Death and Resurrection will be examined in detail in Sophomore year.

Moreover, since our aim is to detect the basic significance of the life of Christ, we take a particular standpoint in our study of it. As a matter of fact, our Lord had a threefold mission or office: He was humanity's Prophet (*i.e.,* Teacher), Priest and King. And in accord with this threefold office, He came to earth to do three things. First, He came to *teach* mankind, secondly to *redeem* it by offering sacrifice for its sins, and thirdly to *unify* it by founding a Church, a visible community animated by the Holy Spirit, in which men would be united to God and to each other. In Freshman year, we study the prophetic and kingly mission of Christ.

*Christ as Prophet.* At the outset of His Public Life, Christ appeared among men primarily as a Prophet, a Preacher. And the chief lesson He had to teach was simply Himself, who He was. He was the Son of God, sharing equally with the Father and Holy Spirit in the one divine nature. He had been sent into the world, true Man, born of the Virgin Mary, to be the Saviour, the "Messias", or Anointed One, who would redeem the world. This was the primary lesson He had to present to men for their acceptance.

And in everything that He did or said, He was revealing, teaching Himself, the God-Man. Hence we shall study His Public Life primarily from the standpoint of His self-revelation. It forms the basic significance of His life. Moreover, we shall pay particular attention to the marvelous pedagogical skill with which He sought to convey this tremendous lesson.

We shall see how carefully He prepared the minds and hearts of His contemporaries for it, how abundantly He attested its truth, how patiently and manfully He struggled to win its acceptance by the Jews. There is no more fascinating study than this.

*Christ as King.* In revealing Himself as God-Man, Christ revealed that He is humanity's King. An essential characteristic of His preaching was that He came, not merely to persuade men to a better life in imitation of Himself, but with *authority* and *power* to give them the life as subjects of His Kingdom. It is for this reason that, simultaneously with the revelation of His own Person, Christ revealed His Kingdom—its nature, its characteristics, its whole juridical structure. He did not merely reveal it in the sense that He outlined the plan of it, but the plan had the force of His decree as King.

Consequently, in studying the Public Life of Christ, we shall observe carefully those to whom His teaching was particularly directed, namely, the Twelve Apostles. For in order to understand His Public Life as an organic whole, and to grasp its significance, it is essential to realize the fact that during it He occupied Himself above all else with the education of the Twelve. He chose them to be the cornerstones of His Church. He chose Peter to be their Head. He was going to hand over to them His own mission of teaching, ruling and sanctifying mankind. They were to be His witnesses. And so upon them He lavished His attention, His pedagogical genius, and His invincible love. His fullest self-revelation was made to them, the fullness of His power was given to them, that they might in turn teach others who He was and rule and sanctify them in His name.

These, then, are the two principal ideas we shall pursue in studying the life of Christ: His own self-revelation as Messias and Son of God, and His formation of the Twelve. They give us an insight into the whole "idea" of His life. They explain the title of our study: "The Prophetic and Kingly Mission of Christ".

*Foundation for Further Study.* In conclusion, it should be noted that the Freshman course is designed to furnish the foundation and the background of the courses to be given in future years.

First of all, it is designed to give the student a familiarity with the Gospels, and a love for them. "These sacred writings", as Leo XIII pointed out, "should influence the whole study of theology, and be, as it were, its very soul". All Christian theology is founded on the one great fact of Christ, God-Man. It is the Gospels that tell us of Him. And hence a thorough knowledge of their contents has always been regarded in the Church as the indispensable preliminary to any systematic and intelligent study of Christian truth and morality. Unless one understands *Him,* one cannot fully understand the Church He founded, her doctrines, her Sacraments, her laws.

Hence, this course should help to fulfill the desire expressed by another great Pontiff, Benedict XV: "Our one desire for all the Church's children is that, being saturated with the Bible, they may arrive at the all-surpassing knowledge of Jesus Christ". That knowledge, and the life that it inspires, is the ambition of every Christian, and especially of every Christian theologian.

The fundamental value of the Freshman course, lies, therefore, in the fact that it situates Christ in His proper position, namely, at the very center of Christianity. It shows Him forth as "perfect God, and perfect Man", humanity's Prophet and King, to whom all men must turn, that they may learn the answer to life's basic question: Who is God? and what is His plan for mankind?

The purpose of future years will be simply to show how from Christ as from its center the whole harmonious body of Christian dogma, with its corresponding scheme of Christian morality and worship, grows out in natural, organic fashion.

*PART ONE*

# INTRODUCTION TO THE GOSPELS

## Chapter 1

# THE BIBLE IN GENERAL

## 1. THE NAME

OUR TERM "Bible" is derived from the Latin, biblia, bibliae, meaning "book". The term is used to designate the collection of books which Jews and Christians have traditionally recognized as divine and sacred. These sacred writings were simply referred to as "The Books". There was no need of identifying them any further; these are *The* Books of all books by reason of their origins, their authorship, their content and their purpose. Other names for the Bible are Scripture ("the writing"), Sacred Scripture, Holy Writ.

*Testament.* The Bible is divided into two main portions with our Lord as the dividing point; the first part is called the Old Testament and the second part, the New Testament. The original Hebrew word which we translate as "testament" meant an alliance, a covenant, a pact between God and man. Thus, the Old Testament was the covenant which God made with the Jewish people whereby He promised them many blessings provided that the nation, on its part, was faithful to certain religious and moral conditions. Our word "testament" also means a man's "last will". This sense of the word is also implied in the Old and New Testaments because the temporal and spiritual blessings promised by God to His people as His part of the contract came to be regarded in the light of an inheritance or "heritage", as in the case of children inheriting the property of their father.

In the Jewish-Christian religious history there are two such alliances; first, the alliance made by God with the Jewish people through their religious leaders beginning with Abraham; then the contract made by God with the whole human race in and through His own Son, our Lord, Jesus Christ. The latter, as our Lord Himself says at the Last Supper, is the "new and eternal" covenant. Thus there are two "testaments" between God and man, the Old Testament made between God and the Jewish nation, and the New Testament made with the human race in and through our Lord.

In the very early Christian times, the word "Testament" came to be transferred from the alliance itself to the sacred books which treat of it. Although nowadays the word Old or New Testament calls to mind a book or collection of books, it should not be forgotten that these names refer primarily, not to the books, but to the central theme that runs through the books, namely, the "economy of salvation" instituted by God in the two Covenants.

The fact that the Bible includes both Testaments and the fact that the Church has always been careful to safeguard the entire Bible, indicates that the Old Testament was a preparation for and a foreshadowing of the New and Eternal Covenant. Thus, a fundamental unity links the two dispensations; the religious history of the Jewish nation and the Catholic Church is basically one; both represent different phases in the unfolding and development of a single divine plan.

## 2. Books of the Old Testament

According to the enumeration of the Council of Trent (Denz.784) there are forty-five books in the Old Testament.

a.] *Twenty-one Historical Books;* Genesis, Exodus, Leviticus, Numbers, Deuteronomy, Josue, Judges, Ruth, Kings (4), Paralipomenon (2), Esdras (2), Tobias, Judith, Esther, Machabees (2).

The first five of these books were written by Moses and are called "The Pentateuch" (five books). The Jews called them the Law (Torah).

b.] *Seven didactic books;* Job, Psalms, Proverbs, Ecclesiastes, Canticle of Canticles, Wisdom.

They are called didactic (teaching) books because they teach doctrine and give wholesome admonitions for leading a good life.

c.] *Seventeen Prophetical Books;* Isaias, Jeremias, Baruch, Ezechiel, Daniel (these, except Baruch, are Major Prophets); Osee, Joel, Amos Abdias, Jonas, Micheas, Nahum, Habacuc, Sophonias, Aggeus, Zacharias, Malachias (Minor Prophets).

In our edition of the Bible, the Lamentations of Jeremias are counted as a separate book of prophecy; in the above list, they are included as part of the Book of Jeremias.

## 3. Books of the New Testament

Trent enumerates twenty-seven books of the New Testament.

a.] *Five Historical Books;* Four Gospels of Matthew, Mark, Luke, John: The Acts of the Apostles—a short history of the early Church written by St. Luke.

b.] *Twenty-one Letters or didactic books;* Fourteen Letters of St. Paul; the seven "Catholic" letters—so-called because they are addressed to the Church in general rather than to any particular Church or individual. St. Peter (2), St. John (3), St. James, St. Jude.

c.] *One Prophetical Book;* the Apocalypse, written by St. John the Apostle.

## 4. THE LANGUAGE OF THE BIBLE

The language in which the books of the bible were originally written are Hebrew, the Aramaic, and the Greek. Hebrew is a Semitic language spoken by the original inhabitants of Chanaan and transmitted by them to Abraham and his descendants. Aramaic is a branch of the Semitic that was spoken in Assyria and Babylonia. After the Jews returned from captivity in Babylon, Aramaic began to be spoken in Palestine instead of Hebrew. Aramaic is the language our Lord used. A Greek dialect known as Koine (common) Greek began to be spoken throughout the civilized world after Alexander the Great; most of the New Testament is written in this language.

Most of the Old Testament was written originally in Hebrew. A few books or portions of books, notably Tobias and Judith, were written in Aramaic. The Book of Wisdom and Machabees were written in Greek.

All of the New Testament, except St. Matthew, was written in Greek. Matthew was originally written in Aramaic.

## 5. ANCIENT BOOKS

*Materials used for Books.* Archeological discoveries of the twentieth century have unearthed abundant specimens of writings that date as far back as 3,000 B.C. and contain texts which claim to have been written at a much earlier period. Men have used many kinds of material for writing; stone, wood, metals, linen, baked clay, animal skins, papyrus and parchment. But as far as the Scriptures are concerned, the last three are of principal importance.

*Leather,* was used at a very early date. We have specimens from Egypt of writing done on dried skins around 2,000 B.C. In the Talmud it is laid down that all copies of the Law must be written on skins and in roll form. This rule still continues in force and many examples of such leather rolls are in existence.

*Papyrus,* was also used in very ancient times in Egypt. It was made from the inner pith of the papyrus plant, a perennial, rush-like plant, six to ten feet high, which grew in abundance along the banks of the Nile river. Strips of this fiber were laid close together and then a second layer was placed on top with the strips running at right angles to those underneath. After being moistened with glue, the whole was subjected to pressure and a smooth writing surface resulted. Papyrus was in general use until the invention of paper in the eighth century. It was much cheaper and handier than any other writing material. But it was easily torn or worn away; hence it is not surprising that the original biblical manuscripts and earlier copies, which were written on it, lasted only a short time.

*Parchment,* was made from the skin of animals—goats, sheep, calves. This is not the simple animal skin or leather mentioned above. Parchment is the result of a special process by which the skins are dried, the hair removed, and the skin scraped and polished smooth with pumice on both sides. The finest parchment, usually from calfskin, is called *vellum.* Parchment was invented in the second century before Christ, but, because it was costly, it did not come into general use until the first part of the fourth century. In 350 A.D. Constantine ordered fifty copies of the Scriptures to be made on vellum for the churches of Constantinople.

*Form of Books.* Originally, leather and papyrus books were written in the form of a scroll. Individual sheets of papyrus or leather were fastened together to make a strip and rolled around a cylinder to make them manageable; this produced the volume (Latin, "volumen", a roll). Each book of the Bible, then, would be in a separate volume or if it were long, in several volumes. The Gospel of St. Matthew alone would require a scroll of thirty feet (which was the normal length). But in the early part of the second century (100-150 A.D.) Christians began to copy the Scripture on separate sheets which were bound together in book form (codex, codices). The advantage of the codex form was that a much greater amount of matter could be included than was possible in a scroll of normal length. For example, we now have substantial portions of a codex containing the four Gospels and the Acts written before 250 A.D. and another containing Paul's Epistles of 200 A.D.

*The Writing.* All ancient documents had to be written by hand; printing was not invented until 1450. At first, all manuscripts were written in "uncials", capital letters. The word probably means "inch-high"; but it is now used for all writing done in capital letters. It was not until the tenth century that small letters were used ("minuscule" or "cursive writing"). The uncial manuscripts of the Bible are written in columns—from one to four on a page—without accents or punctuation, without spacing between words and only a small space between columns.

## 6. Ancient Manuscripts of the Bible

The original manuscripts (autographs) of the various books of the Bible have perished. But we possess many very ancient copies, the most ancient of which are written in Hebrew, Greek and Syriac, and these are known as biblical manuscripts (hand-writing).

*Hebrew Text.* The oldest extant Hebrew manuscripts of the Bible date from the tenth century and after. They were preceded by a continuous line of copies, no longer existing, which went back to the originals. Before the time of Christ, there were many (mostly unimportant) variations in the multitude of Hebrew manuscripts that were spread throughout the world. But, at the beginning of the Christian era, Jewish scholars began more and more to eliminate these differences by comparison of copies and to lay down very strict rules for copying and preserving the text without mistakes. Thus, the Talmud tells us that in early Christian times there were three *slightly* different Hebrew texts in the Temple and from these, a new text was formed by selecting readings found in two texts against one. Gradually, the Jewish authorities withdrew from use all other texts and guarded the pure ones with great zeal. As new copies were handed down, an abundance of tradition was handed down with them; for example, the scholars went to such length as to compute and record the number of verses, words and even letters in each book in order to make the book, as far as is humanly possible, unchangeable. Hence, despite the fact that our present Hebrew copies are of a late date, we have assurance that they were handed down in a carefully preserved line of succession.

As a matter of fact, it is partly due to the scrupulous care exercised over the text by the Jews in early Christian times, that the older manuscripts have perished. When a manuscript had been copied with the exactitude required and had been duly verified, it was accepted as authentic and regarded as of equal value with any other copy. Age in a manuscript, far from being an advantage, was considered a disadvantage since it was liable to become defaced or damaged in the lapse of time. A damaged or imperfect copy was condemned as unfit for use. Such condemned copies naturally perished from neglect. Add to these causes, the persecutions to which the Jews, and later the Christians, were subjected and it is no wonder that the earlier Hebrew manuscripts no longer exist.

*Greek Manuscripts.* The oldest complete biblical manuscripts still extant are written in Greek. It is sufficient for our purpose to mention only four of them, all of which are written in codex (book) form in uncial (capital) letters on parchment. There are still more ancient partial manuscripts but we shall speak of them later when treating the Gospels (*cf.* Ch. 8. Pg. 63).

a.] *Codex Sinaiticus* (Sinaitic Manuscript). This copy was made in the fourth century. It has four columns to a page. It still contains most of the Old and all of the New Testaments. It was discovered in 1844 by Constantine Tischendorf, a great German biblical scholar, in the monastary of St. Catherine, at Mt. Sinai. For a long time this manuscript was kept in the Imperial Library at St. Petersburg, but it was sold in 1933 by the Soviet Government to the British Museum, where it is now preserved.

b.] *Codex Vaticanus* (Vatican Manuscript). It is the oldest and best complete manuscript that we have. It was written in the early part of the fourth century. It contains all of the Bible except for a few gaps. It is written with three columns to a page. There is a legend that St. Athanasius the Great brought it to Rome in 342 A.D. It is preserved in the Vatican library at Rome.

c.] *Codex Alexandrinus* (Alexandrine Manuscript). It dates to the first half of the fifth century and contains most of the Bible. It has two columns to a page. Originally it was brought by the Patriarch of Alexandria to his new see of Constantinople. In 1627, the Patriarch of Constantinople made a gift of this manuscript to Charles I, King of England, and it is now preserved in the British Museum.

d.] *Codex Ephraemi* (Parisian Manuscript). This manuscript, now preserved in Paris, is known as that of St. Ephraem because the original text had been partially erased to make way for some writings of St. Ephraem of Syria. Manuscripts like this which were used a second time for other purposes, are known as "palimpsests" (rewritten). Only part of the original writing of this manuscript could be restored. Most of the leaves of the Old Testament have been lost—sixty-four pages have been preserved as well as most of the New Testament. It dates to the fifth century and is written with one column to a page.

## 7. EARLY TRANSLATIONS OF THE BIBLE

The Old Testament was translated from the original Hebrew into Greek in the third and second centuries before Christ. The New Testament was translated into Latin, Syriac and other languages as early as the second century after Christ. These translations are of great value for the light they throw on the text. They were made from manuscripts which go much further back than the manuscripts which we have of the Old Testament in Hebrew and the New Testament in Greek. We shall consider only two of the most important translations, the Septuagint and the Latin Vulgate.

a.] *The Septuagint* is a Greek translation of the Bible which was begun around 285 B.C. At this time there were about 200,000 Jews living in and around the city of Alexandria in Egypt. These exiles had long since forgotten the Hebrew language and felt the need of a translation of the Scriptures into the language (Greek) which was their native tongue. A number of Jewish scholars went down from Jerusalem to begin the work of translating; legend has it that they numbered seventy-two, hence the name Septuagint (seventy). These men translated the Pentateuch in the third century before Christ and the rest of the Books of the Old Testament were done at different times by various translators down to about 100 B.C., when the work was completed.

This is the oldest of the translations and from it copies were made which were the predecessors to our Greek manuscripts, four of which are mentioned above (no. 6). It was through this translation that many Greek-speaking pagans came to a knowledge of the Old Testament and were thus prepared for the preaching of the Gospel. It was usually this Septuagint version which the Apostles quoted in their preaching and writing, thus bearing witness to its fidelity in rendering the sense of the Hebrew text.

b.] *The Latin Vulgate.* There were many early Latin translations of the Scripture in the early Christian centuries; some of them date back before the year 200 A.D. Among these is the "Itala" (made in Europe) and the "Afra" (made in Africa); both were made from the Greek text. Most of the scripture texts in the Missal are taken from the Itala version.

But the early translations were unsatisfactory in many respects and by the fourth century there was such diversity among them that Pope St. Damasus (A.D. 360-384) commissioned St. Jerome to issue a corrected text. In the course of fifteen years (390-405), St. Jerome made a new Latin translation of the Old Testament from the Hebrew text and revised the Latin text of the New Testament from the Greek. This new translation of the Bible gradually became the only Latin version of the Scriptures that was used in the Western Church. For this reason, it is called the Vulgate (common—or widely used).

In the course of centuries, many other translations of the Septuagint were made into Latin; at the time of the Protestant Reformation, the Reformers rejected the Vulgate and used their own translations. Catholics had also come to use many different Latin translations. Finally, to avoid endless confusion in Latin quotations of Scripture, the Council of Trent (1546) declared the Vulgate to be the "authentic" (official) Latin translation and the one to be used in public worship by the Western Church. This does not mean that the Church prefers this version to the original texts or to the Septuagint version. But, as far as Latin translations are concerned, the Vulgate has been declared to be in substantial conformity with the original texts especially where faith and morals are concerned. In 1907, Pope Pius X commissioned the Benedictine Fathers to study the Vulgate text, eliminate any errors which have crept into it, and restore it as far as possible to the original purity of St. Jerome's day. So far, a few revised books of the Old Testament have been published (Vatican Press) and the work is still going on.

## 8. ENGLISH TRANSLATION

*Douay Version.* Because of the suppression of Catholic worship in England under Elizabeth (1559), a group of English Catholic scholars under the protection of William Cardinal Allen, established a seminary for English candidates to the priesthood at Douay, in northeastern France. For political reasons, the seminary was later moved to Rheims and then, at a still later date, moved back to Douay again. These scholars translated the Bible from the Vulgate into English. The New Testament was published at Rheims in 1582 and the Old Testament at Douay in 1609. Actually, it is the Rheims-Douay version, but when the Old and New Testaments were combined into one book, it went by the name of the Douay version.

The chief aim of the translators was scrupulous exactness. They also tried to avoid, and succeeded in avoiding, all dogmatic bias to such an extent that, in this respect, their work has been praised by Protestant scholars. Moreover, in spite of certain defects (such as excessive literalness, stilted phraseology, lack of rhythm), their work had positive literary value and did much to enrich the English language. Protestant authors used the Douay version considerably in translating the King James Bible in 1611.

*Douay revised.* Richard Challoner, Bishop of London, published a revision of the Douay version in 1749. His aim was to render the English text more intelligible by eliminating cumbersome expressions which sounded more like Latin than English. He succeeded to a considerable extent but the text still contains grammatical errors, awkward constructions and needless obscurities. It is this Challoner revision which is used today in the Douay version.

*Confraternity text of New Testament.* The New Testament of the Rheims-Douay version was recently revised by a group of more than thirty American biblical scholars with the approval of the American Bishops. The purpose was to bring the Challoner revision up to date by using modern expressions for English words which have lost the meaning or usage which they had in the eighteenth century. Because this revision, published in 1941, was done under the patronage of the Episcopal Committee of the Confraternity of Christian Doctrine, it is called the "Confraternity" edition. The "Confraternity group" has also revised the Book of Psalms and is now at work on the remainder of the Old Testament. The latest Catholic edition of the whole Bible is called the "New Catholic Edition"; it contains the Douay version of the Old Testament as revised by Challoner, except for a new translation of the *first eight books* and of the *Psalms,* done recently by the "Confraternity" scholars. It also contains the Confraternity edition of the New Testament.

*Other English Translations.* Msgr. Ronald Knox (England) published (1948-49) an English translation made from the Vulgate; it is written in beautiful English although it sometimes sacrifices exactness of translation for beauty of style. The "Westminster" is another version recently done by a group of English Catholic scholars; it is a translation from the original Hebrew and Greek and aims more at exactness of meaning.

*Protestant English Translations.* The most widely known English Protestant translation of the Bible is the King James Version, printed in 1611 and dedicated to King James I. This version is also noted for its beauty of style for which exactness is often sacrificed. The most recent revision of this translation is called the American Revised Standard Version.

## TEST QUESTIONS

1. Explain the words "Bible", "New Testament", "Old Testament".
2. Name the three general classes of books in the Old Testament and the number of books in each class. Explain "Pentateuch", "Torah".
3. Name the three general classes of books of the New Testament. Name the author of each book in each class.
4. Describe three types of material used in ancient manuscripts of the Bible.
5. Explain "codex", "uncials", "minuscules", "autograph", "manuscript", "version".
6. Mention briefly several reasons why the early Hebrew manuscripts of the Bible were lost.
7. Name and describe briefly four ancient Greek manuscripts of the Bible which are still extant.
8. Explain the "Septuagint"—name, date, circumstances.
9. Explain the "Vulgate"—name, date, circumstances.
10. Explain the history and characteristics of the "Douay" version and the "Confraternity" edition.
11. Name two other modern Catholic versions of the Bible done in England.

## Chapter II

# THE ORIGINS OF THE GOSPELS

IN ORDER to understand any literary work it is necessary to know the circumstances that led to its composition. In the origins of our Gospels, three stages must be distinguished: first, the initial oral Gospel, the preaching of Christ and His Apostles; secondly, the formation of the "apostolic catechesis", a fairly standardized sum of instruction given orally to Christians and to prospective converts; thirdly, the actual writing of the four Gospels under the pressure of the needs of the time, to which was joined the inspiration of the Holy Spirit.

*The Oral Gospel.* When we hear the word "Gospel" we spontaneously think of a book; not so the early Christians. Before being a book, the Gospel was a spoken message of Christ to men, the word of gladness that He brought them. In the New Testament the word "evangelium" (Gospel) never refers to a book, but always to the Glad Message of Christ, given in His words and deeds. In the sense of a written record the word occurs for the first time in the "First Apology" of Justin Martyr, written toward the middle of the second century; therein he refers to "the memoirs of the Apostles, which are called gospels (evangelia)".

Christ Himself wrote nothing. He appeared as a Prophet, a Teacher: "Jesus came into Galilee, preaching the gospel of the kingdom of God" (Mk 1:14). And it was His own living word that He offered for acceptance, on His own personal authority. He was a sower, casting the seed of His living word into the hearts of those who heard Him (Lk 8:11).

Furthermore, it was as sowers of His word that He trained the Apostles (*cf.* Acts 13:49). During His own lifetime they were given a brief experience of preaching, proposing His doctrine on His authority. And after Pentecost it was essentially a task of preaching that they took up. The gift of Pentecost, brought them by the descent of the Holy Spirit, was the gift of eloquence, clear, bold, impassioned, authoritative. After the tongues of fire had rested on them we read that "they began to speak" (Acts 2:4), and that they gave themselves to "the ministry of the word" (Acts 6:4). It was as "ministers of the word" (Lk 1:2) that they were regarded by the faithful.

Moreover, their teaching centered about two points: "the things that were 'said' and 'done' by the Lord". Christ Himself in His final instructions (Lk

24:48; *cf.* Acts 1:8, 21-22; 10:40-43) had ordered them to make these things the burden of their preaching. For after He had reviewed His own life in the light of the Old Testament prophecies, He said to them: "You are witnesses of these things". Consequently it was for them to set forth the facts of His life and to interpret their meaning. They were to show men that the totality of His life manifests Him as truly the Son of God, made Man for the salvation of the world. And they were to bring men to Him. They were to persuade men that all their hope of happiness lay in a free and complete adherence to the adorable Person of Christ, in an unqualified acceptance of His words and deeds as the one unchallengeable standard and rule of their own.

So the Apostles preached Christ, what He did and said (Acts 1:1). Their primary concern was faithfully to relate the facts about Him (1 Jn 1:1), and insistently to make known to men "whatever had to do with Jesus" (Acts 18:25; *cf.* 8:35; 28:31). They did not know the word Christianity. They thought in personal terms: Christianity was to them the Person of Christ, God-Man, Master and Lord, the object of their highest love; as it was also the concrete community of living men and women, the Church, in which they found themselves one with each other through the common confession that "Jesus is Lord" (1 Cor 12:3).

*The Apostolic Catechesis.* Realizing the fact that Christ was the living and glowing center of the faith of the earliest Christians, we can understand that one of the first needs experienced by the Church was for an adequate survey, in some manageable form, of His words and deeds. This survey was needed primarily for the nourishment of the spiritual life of those within the Church; the facts of our Lord's life were the proper food on which Christian faith and hope and love might grow strong. Moreover, this survey was needed as an instrument for winning new converts; the early Church well knew that a sincere and prayerful study of the life of Christ was the surest way of bringing men to faith in Him.

Naturally, the drawing up of this survey (or a collection of surveys) devolved on the men who had been the authoritative witnesses of the life of Christ. Thus in the course of a comparatively brief space of time the Apostles were led to make a selection from the deeds and words of Christ, ordering them into discourses of greater or less length, and gradually giving them a fairly stereotyped form, as an aid to memory. Consequently there arose a form of oral teaching, uniform in its major outlines and commonly adopted, learned and repeated from mouth to mouth, to which the name "catechesis" has been given. Some of these catechetical discourses were apparently recitals of various facts of the life of Christ; in others, certain of His sayings were grouped together.

Of the former type, the factual discourse, we have reminiscences preserved

[11]

in two places in Paul's First Letter to the Corinthians: in 11:23-25 (the institution of the Eucharist), and 15:1-6 (the fact of the Resurrection). These are the most ancient specimens. Paul must have received this catechesis some two or three years after the death of Jesus, and some twenty years later He taught it to the Corinthians.

Of the latter type of catechesis, the more doctrinal discourse, we doubtless have examples in the five discourses that form, as we shall see, the framework of Matthew's Gospel. In Matthew, of course, these sermons have been amplified; but portions of them must certainly go back to the earliest days of apostolic preaching.

In the determination of the content of the apostolic catechesis, Peter, the leading figure among the Twelve, played a most important role. The Acts of the Apostles make it clear that he was the chief spokesman of the Church. And one of his discourses is particularly significant, since we have in it a sketch of the primitive catechesis (Acts 10:37-41, an instruction given in the house of Cornelius, the first pagan convert). It is built on quite the same lines that Mark will later follow in the construction of his Gospel. The same four divisions are discernible: 1) the preaching of John the Baptist and the Baptism of Jesus; 2) the preaching of Jesus in Galilee, His assumption of authority and the hostility aroused by it; 3) the passage to Judea and Jerusalem, following the swivel-point of Christ's ministry, namely, the Confession of Peter; 4) the Passion, Death and Resurrection.

Naturally, these first standardized recitals of the words and deeds of Christ were cast in Aramaic, the common language of Palestine. It was our Lord's own mother tongue; in it He formed His thoughts, and doubtless even during His lifetime certain of His sayings or sermons circulated among His followers, treasured in their memories. Very soon, however, translations of the catechesis in Greek became necessary, for the benefit of converts from paganism, and of those Hellenized Jews, not residents of Palestine, who spoke only Greek.

The essential point is that this oral catechesis, formulated by the Apostles, rather standardized in form, and consisting of longer or shorter collections of our Lord's sayings and deeds, was the original form in which Christian instruction was given. It preceded the writing of the Gospels, and was an effective preparation for this later work.

*The Written Gospels.* In the absence of historical documents it is not possible for us to describe in detail just how the oral catechesis passed into written form. However, one important point should be kept in mind, namely, that for some years no real need was felt for written documents. In this regard our modern ideas deceive us. Today the dissemination of ideas is accomplished by the printed word. But in ancient times instruction was communicated by word of mouth; in those days "a man's book was his memory".

Consequently the early Jewish and pagan converts received their religious instruction through rhythmic recitations, that covered the main points of the life, work, and teaching of Christ. In these oral, memorized discourses, especially of the words of Christ, they loved to catch the very accents of the Master's voice. Uniformly they shared the conviction of Papias: "I judged that I could never derive from books a fruit comparable to that which I get from the living and abiding word."

However, this state of affairs could not endure for very long. The Christian religion was spreading rapidly; Christian instruction was passing into the hands of those who were not themselves witnesses of the life of Christ, nor even immediate disciples of those who had seen and heard and lived with Him. Moreover, an increasing number of catechists and converts were not mentally trained, as were the Jewish scribes, to hold in their memories lengthy recitations. Hence it became desirable to get the oral catechesis fixed in writing.

Written documents would serve a *triple purpose*. First, a collection of the Old Testament prophecies that were fulfilled in Christ would be useful in making converts from Judaism. Secondly, collections of the words and deeds of Christ would furnish what we would call spiritual reading, material for meditation and prayer, to increase the knowledge and love of Christ in the hearts of Christians. Thirdly, excerpts from these documents could be read during the celebration of the Eucharist, along with excerpts from the Old Testament. In this connection it is interesting to note that Justin Martyr, for example, first mentions written Gospels when speaking of the early Christian liturgy. Evidently, the reading of the Gospel at Mass, so familiar to us, goes back to the very earliest times.

Though the fact is not certain, we have reason to suppose that certain portions of the life of Christ and of His teaching were put in writing by unknown authors within a relatively short time after the Ascension of our Lord. At any rate, we know for certain that between the years 40 and 100 A.D. our four Gospels made their appearance in writing. They are the four "forms" of the Gospel that have been received in the Church as having been written under the inspiration of the Holy Spirit, and as containing the faithful record of what Christ did and said, and what the first Apostles preached.

*The order of their composition was the following:* The most ancient tradition, preserved in the testimony of the earliest ecclesiastical writers, makes it scientifically certain that the Apostle Matthew was the first to compose a written edition of the primitive oral catechesis. He wrote in Aramaic for the Jews of Palestine, and an unknown translator put his work into Greek. The second in order was Mark, who wrote down in Greek the catechesis as Peter was wont to give it. In the third place comes Luke, the companion of Paul; he undertook a more literary revision of the catechesis, compiling it from a number of previously existing sources. Last of all, toward the end of the first century, John wrote his account.

The first three Gospels, Matthew, Mark, and Luke, are called the "Synoptic Gospels", a name that has been current since the eighteenth century. The reason for the name is that an arrangement of their contents in parallel columns would give at a glance (in Greek, "synopsis") a view of the Public Life and Passion of our Lord that reveals very striking similarities. For in spite of many differences, these three Gospels resemble one another quite closely in content, order, and even style. On the other hand, if John's Gospel be compared with them, it reveals many important differences, that put it in a class by itself.

*Significance*. The written Gospels are, then, just a summary of the oral instruction that was previously given for thirty years or so after the Ascension of Christ. The four Gospels which were eventually written had the Apostolic Catechesis as their source; they are really different versions of the one Gospel. Thus, in the third century, Origen says that "The Gospel recorded by four is one alone" and Augustine speaks of the "Four books of the one Gospel". The early Church has preserved the titles "Gospel *according to* St. Matthew" etc., to indicate that the Gospel is only one but it is written in four different ways according to Matthew, Mark, Luke and John.

*Church Has Whole Gospel*. The fact that the Church taught the Gospel for thirty years before it was written helps to explain the Catholic attitude toward the written Gospels which non-catholics find so difficult to understand. The Catholic attitude is that the Church and the Church alone was entrusted with the "Glad-tidings" of Christ and His message. St. Peter and the apostolic college were the sole depositories and interpreters of Christ's doctrine. It was to them and their successors that Christ promised His Holy Spirit who would make them witnesses of Him and give them the power to teach all that He had taught. In this work, Christ promised to be with them until the "consummation of the world". (Mt. 28:18; Mk. 16:15)

Since the Apostles began by spreading the Gospel orally, the earliest neophytes had to gather around them in order to receive the Christian teaching. No one could pretend to their knowledge of the story of Christ; there was no book which could give anyone the same knowledge. Consequently, by God's design, there grew up under the authority of the Apostles a visible society known as the Church; it was a community of living persons grouped about living leaders. As in the beginning, so now, the sole authority on Christ and His teaching is this Church which lives and teaches men from generation to generation by the power of Christ's Holy Spirit. The Tradition that has been handed down and is taught today by the living voice of the Church contains the complete message of Christ. The Scripture contains only part of it and if all the scriptures in the world were burned tomorrow, the message of Christ would still be carried on to the end of time by this living voice.

*Gospels Belong to Church.* When the Gospels were finally written, they were written under the authority of the Church as a sketch or digest of what the Church taught orally. These Scriptures do not contain the whole message (*cf.* John 21:25). And because the Gospels were written under the authority of the Church which preceded them, the Church alone has the right to judge them, interpret them and check departures in individual versions of them.

It is wrong then to suppose that one must go to the written Gospels to find the pure, unadulterated Christianity. It is wrong to suppose that all the teaching of the Church in addition to what is explicitly contained in the Scriptures, or that all the teaching about the meaning and application of the Scriptures, is just so much excrescence added to the pure, primitive, Christianity that is contained in the written word. Primitive Christianity is not to be found in any written word.

*Providence.* It is good to see the hand of Providence in this arrangement of things. Suppose that Christ had written a résumé of His doctrine and of His life before departing from this visible world. In that case, the establishment of a living, unified society of Christians would have been impossible. When a great man leaves a written compilation of his ideas, we are led to believe that in it he has given out the whole of his secret. If Christ had done this, the first Christians would have been inclined to seek the pure doctrine, not in the teaching of the disciples, but in the book left by the Master. Each would have interpreted it in his own fashion and each would have made his own little religion for himself. From the outset, the universal spirit would have been weakened; instead of a great disciplined and hierarchic body, we would have seen the fragmentation and scattering of the sects. This is what happened in the sixteenth century when the Reformers rejected the living authority of the Church and turned to Scripture as the only source of revelation.

## TEST QUESTIONS

1. Explain "Gospel".
2. Give evidence that the Gospel was oral in the beginning.
3. Explain what is meant by "Apostolic Catechesis".
4. Name some examples of the Apostolic Catechesis a) with regard to facts of Christ's life; b) with regard to Christ's sayings.
5. Cite an example from Scripture to show that the Apostolic Catechesis followed the same general outline as the three synoptic Gospels.
6. Why were the Gospels eventually written?
7. Explain "synoptic" as applied to the Gospels.
8. Explain the significance of the fact that the oral Gospel preceded the Written Word.
   What is the relationship between the Church and the Scriptures?

*Chapter III*

# THE GOSPELS AS A TYPE OF LITERATURE

⫸⫸⫸⫸⫸⫸⫸⫸⫸⫸⫸⫸⫸⫷⫷⫷⫷⫷⫷⫷⫷⫷⫷⫷⫷⫷⫷

I N THE LIGHT of what has been said about the origins of the Gospels we are now able to answer an important question, namely, to what type of literature do these books belong? The question is important for an obvious reason. If one is to read a book intelligently, one must know what kind of a book it is, what the author's purpose was, and how he conceived his task. Different types of literature, for example, fiction, history, the essay, poetry, drama, etc., have different aims and different forms, and each requires a particular attitude on the part of the reader. One cannot read a lyric poet as if he were a philosophical essayist, nor a scientific historian as if he were a poet.

Now, Christian tradition has always regarded the Gospels as genuine historical documents, dealing with the facts of Christ's life and work. On the other hand, it has also regarded them as a unique type of history, that stands alone in its class. Here, then, is our concrete question: just exactly what kind of history did the evangelists write? We must answer that question if we are to read them intelligently. And to proceed properly, we must first consider the Synoptic Gospels as a group, and then John's Gospel by itself.

## THE SYNOPTIC GOSPELS

*Purpose.* The particular type of history that the Synoptists wrote was determined by their purpose. As we shall see later, each of them had his own special purpose in writing. Nevertheless, they all shared the same general purpose, namely, each of them wished to give a sort of written edition of the traditional oral catechesis. In general, therefore, the Synoptists aimed at the same three objectives at which the "ministers of the word" aimed in their spoken instructions.

First and foremost, they wished to put before their readers the facts about Christ, what He did and said. Their fundamental purpose had to be to write good, *objective history,* the sheer story of "what happened". And to do so, they effaced themselves completely before their subject; nowhere do they intrude their own personalities, ideas or emotions. They allow the figure of Christ to dominate the whole narrative.

Secondly, they wrote their histories for a definitely *religious purpose*. They set down the facts about Christ in order to enlighten the faith of Christians and to strengthen their personal love of their Lord and Master. They wished to stimulate their readers to a more profound Christian life, based on a more complete and intelligent knowledge of Him, their Way, Truth and Life.

Finally, they had an *apologetic purpose*. That is to say, in writing down the facts about Christ they had in mind the winning of converts to Him and they knew that the surest way of setting any man of good will on the road to belief in Him would always be through a sincere, open-minded and prayerful study of His life. For everything that He did and said proved conclusively that He was the Son of God, made Man for the salvation of humanity.

Consequently, in the light of their relations to the apostolic catechesis, we may define the Synoptic Gospels as biographies of Christ, written as a means of religious instruction and formation, and written, too, as means of spreading Christian faith in Christ. And it is to be emphasized that the three purposes of the Synoptists are intimately linked; they wished to write good history precisely in order to make men better Christians, or to make them Christians if they were not such already. Finally, it is to be noted that the religious purpose was the dominant one: the Gospels were written primarily for Christians, to lead them deeper into the knowledge and love of the central object of their faith, the Person of Christ, the God-Man.

*Peculiarities*. Now, having in mind the general purpose of the Synoptists, we can understand the peculiarities of the history they wrote. They are not scientific biographies of Christ, written with modern completeness and exactness; and yet, they are, nevertheless, good biographies, relatively complete and ordered and properly faithful to historical facts. These peculiarities must be briefly developed.

*Selective history*. The information which the Synoptists give about their "hero" is relatively incomplete. For instance, they say little about the ministry of our Lord in Jerusalem and Judea. We would gather the impression from them that our Lord's public ministry lasted little more than a year; it is only because John fills in the details that we know that the Public Life lasted for more than two years. Again, the Synoptists make practically no attempt to sketch in the background of our Lord's life; they contain no formal characterization of Him, no explicit estimate of His grandeur or virtue, not even a description of His physical appearance. In these details they differ widely from modern biographies. Moreover, though they are always careful to preserve the sense of His words, yet at times they permit themselves a certain freedom in quoting Him (compare, for example, Mt. 8:25 with Mk. 4:38 and Lk. 8:24).

This incompleteness must be explained in terms of the authors' religious purpose. They wished to write the history of Christ but with the idea of giving it to their readers as the solid nourishment of faith and hope and love and as a lesson in the kind of life they should themselves lead. For this reason they make only a selection of our Lord's deeds and words. They were not writing merely to satisfy curiosity or for the purely scientific purpose of recording all the historical facts about Christ. Their history was for catechetical purposes and a catechism is not concerned with minutiae; rather, they selected enough events and sayings to show the main "sweep" of Christ's life up to the climax of His Crucifixion and Resurrection.

It is this religious purpose also which explains the remarkable similarity between the first three gospels not only in the events they record but in their manner of recording them. The Apostles in their preaching maintained a substantial uniform instruction in the essentials of their common faith. When the Evangelists wrote a digest of this teaching they not only utilized the content and form of the oral catechesis but each succeeding writer made use of the previously written Gospels to maintain, as far as possible, this uniformity of narrative. And yet, they did not slavishly copy from one another; each of them wrote with his own personality for a different audience with a different particular purpose in mind and consequently their narratives are as notably different as they are similar in both content and expression.

*Chronology neglected.* What is more important, the Synoptists do not share the concern of the modern scientific historian for precision in dating events, noting the place and circumstances of their occurrence, situating them in their correct chronological sequence and carefully identifying the actors in them. Consequently, when we compare the triple synoptic account of our Lord's life we find certain variations in order, in the manner of recounting events, etc. The Evangelists may use such expressions as "and then" or "then it came to pass" to link together different deeds or sayings; as the narrative thus flows along from one event to another we naturally get the impression that these things happened in the precise order in which they are narrated. As a matter of fact, events so connected in the narrative may have happened a year apart and in widely separated places.

Again, this unconcern for precise chronology is often the result of the religious purpose of the author. He may be following a logical rather than a chronological order—i.e., he may group together events or sayings that teach a similar lesson regardless of when or where they happened or were said. Sometimes, too, the Evangelists seem to follow the order of memory, getting down events as they come to mind, much after the fashion of an oral narrator. This is very disturbing to the scientific historian who ignores the religious purpose of the Evangelist. But from the Evangelist's point of view, the chronology is of no consequence; the important thing is that what he records are facts regardless of when or where they happened.

*Relative Completeness and Order.* Though the method of the Synoptists was not strictly scientific, as we understand the term, nevertheless they did write good objective history, relatively complete, ordered and accurate. They did not simply put together a helter-skelter collection of our Lord's deeds and words. On the contrary, they arranged their material in unmistakable order. Their books cover the major phases and incidents of our Lord's life and succeed in presenting it as an organic whole. A detailed chronological framework is discernible in the division of our Lord's life into certain clearly marked periods:

1. Christ's Preparation for His Ministry.
2. His Preaching in Galilee.
3. His Journey to Jerusalem.
4. His Passion, Death and Resurrection.

This is the standard division which Peter followed in his preaching (*cf.* Acts 10:37-41) and which Mark follows in his Gospel. Matthew and Luke follow the same general outline though they give more space to the sermons of Christ and add some events of their own. The Evangelists took over this standard division of the oral catechesis; it is simple, flexible and easily remembered. And then, within this framework they allowed themselves freedom in the arrangements of individual events.

## JOHN'S GOSPEL

The Fourth Gospel differs from the three Synoptics in so many respects that it cannot be classified with them as belonging to exactly the same type of historical literature. For while the Synoptists give a simple history of Christ, John gives at once a history and a theology. Since these two characteristics of His Gospel will be studied more fully later, this brief statement of them will suffice for the present.

*History.* It is clear that John wished to write an historical document. He presents himself as a witness of that which he records and he evidently expects his readers to accept his testimony as true. Moreover, in some respects he is more accurate than the Synoptists. For instance, he fills in certain indications of topography, and he makes it clear that the Public Life of our Lord must have occupied at least two years and a half, whereas from the Synoptics alone we might have concluded that it lasted but little more than a year. On the other hand, his book as a whole is a far less complete biography of Christ. And his order shows that he depended less explicitly on the form of the apostolic catechesis. John wrote long after the other Gospels were in circulation and his purpose was to fill in and complete the picture which they had given.

*Theology*. However, John chiefly differs from the Synoptists in that he is definitely a theologian and not merely an historian. They were content simply to narrate what Christ did and said, letting the facts speak for themselves. But John is constantly interested in interpreting the deeds and words of Christ, and in explaining who He was. He was writing for an elite among the Christians, and he wished to give them a deeper intelligence of the mystery of Christ, the Word of God Incarnate, the Light and the Life of men. For this reason he reports the doctrinal discourses of Christ at great length. For this reason, too, he selects certain events and miracles that are of special value in illuminating various facets of the mystery of Christ.

Evidently, then, John's Gospel belongs to a mixed type of literature; it is both theological and historical. For this reason it was called by Clement of Alexandria "the spiritual Gospel", that is, the Gospel that searches down into the meaning of Christ, hid beneath the material facts of His life.

## TEST QUESTIONS

1. What is the threefold general purpose common to the Synoptic Gospels?
2. How do the synoptic Gospels differ from modern biographies with regard to historical content; with regard to chronology?
   Give examples of the peculiarities of the Gospels in both these respects.
3. Explain the reason for these peculiarities. How can the Gospels be called good history?
4. Give the main chronological outline of the synoptic Gospels.
5. How do you account for the minute similarities and differences between the synoptic Gospels?
6. How does John's Gospel differ from the others as an historical book.
7. Explain the main difference between John's Gospel and the others as a type of literature.

## Chapter IV

# THE GOSPEL ACCORDING TO MATTHEW

❧❧❧❧❧❧❧❧❧❧❧❧❧❧❧❧❧❧❧❧❧❧❧❧❧❧

## AUTHOR

THE TESTIMONY to the authorship of the first Gospel is thus summarized by St. Jerome (d. 420): "Matthew, also called Levi, first a publican and later an apostle, was the first to commit to writing the gospel of Christ; he wrote in Hebrew; it was later translated into Greek, but the translator is unknown" (de vir. ill. c. 3).

Matthew is first met in the Gospel as "Levi" or "the son of Alphaeus" (Mk. 2:4; Lk. 5:27). He was a publican, a tax collector for the Roman government, who apparently operated around the Lake of Genesareth (Mk. 2:14), probably in the neighborhood of Capharnaum. The publicans were hated by the Jews for their venality and extortions, and were despised by the government that employed them. Whether Levi was any better than his fellows is a matter of conjecture; at any rate it is certain that he was not inwardly at peace in his employment, since at the mere invitation of Christ (Mk. 2:14) he abandoned it instantly. Apparently he was a man of some wealth, as we may judge from the banquet he tendered to celebrate his adoption as a disciple of Christ. This is the sum of our information about him. Tradition has it that after preaching in Judea and writing his Gospel he became a missioner in Ethiopia, Arabia, Persia and Media, and died a martyr, in a place and at a time unknown.

## DATE OF COMPOSITION

The evidence shows that Matthew must have written his Gospel sometime between the years 40 and 70 A.D. On the one hand he could hardly have written it before the year 40 or so, since he mentions that the perjury of the soldiers about the theft of Christ's body was current among the Jews "even to the present day" (28:15), and that the field of Judas' burial is "even to this day" called the "field of blood"; these expressions suppose the lapse of some years from the death of Christ. On the other hand he could not have written it after 70 A.D. (the year of the destruction of Jerusalem), since it is clear from his account of the prophecy of that event (24:1-51) that it had not yet taken place. All things considered, we are safe in assigning the composition of the book to the decade 40 to 50 A.D.; both internal and external evidence point to this conclusion.

## AUDIENCE

Evidently Matthew wrote his Gospel for the Jews of Palestine. For he wrote in Aramaic; he begins with a genealogy, joining Christ to the whole history of Israel, and he constantly supposes his readers to be familiar with the Old Testament, with the terminology of the prophets, with the very form of Hebrew letters (5:21), likewise with Jewish customs, attitudes of mind, forms of rhythmic speech, etc. Matthew's Jewish audience is also indicated by the fact that he concerns himself greatly with the peculiarly Jewish charge that Christ could not have been the promised Messias because His Kingdom was not accepted by the Jewish people.

## CHARACTERISTIC FEATURES

*The Order* or general pattern of Matthew's Gospel is distinctive. It begins with the story of the Infancy of Christ, in which Matthew gives prominence to Joseph. The general chronology of the Public Life is that of the apostolic catechesis. But a characteristic feature of the order is his grouping of the "sayings of the Lord" into five discourses, each of them provided with an introduction and with a stereotyped conclusion. The five discourses (which were not necessarily preached as units) are:

1. Moral Character of the Kingdom (Sermon on the Mount) ........................ *ch.* 5:1-7:29.
2. Instruction of the Twelve: the Missionary Life ............................ *ch.* 10:5-11:1.
3. The Parables of the Kingdom (Lake Sermon) *ch.* 13:1-13:53.
4. The Practice of the Christian Virtues...... *ch.* 18:1-19:1.
5. The Last Things ...................... *ch.* 24:1-26:1.

Each of these discourses is followed by a series of the "works of Christ" which in more or less direct fashion are a commentary on the foregoing discourse; *e.g.*, the prediction of the Apostles' persecution is followed by incidents showing Christ's own persecution by the Pharisees (compare ch. 10:22ff with ch. 12). The general purpose of introducing these "works" of Christ is to show Him to be the Messias, the King of the new Kingdom. One can see how, from the viewpoint of this logical unity, it mattered little whether or not the incidents collected to illustrate the same point happened in the order of their narration.

*The Content* of Matthew's Gospel was greatly influenced by the fact that he wrote for the Jews of Palestine. His characteristics in this regard may best be considered under the following headings:

1. *Emphasis on Christ as Messias*—rather than on His divinity as in the other Gospels. (Mt. 1:21; 12:23, 21:9, 15.)

The Divinity of Christ shines clearly enough through Matthew's account of His deeds and discourses but his first concern is to bring out that Christ is the King whom the Jews expected.

2. *New Law a Continuation of the Old.* The Jews had great reverence for the law of Moses as coming from God; they were inclined to be suspicious of the New Law because it seemed to contradict the Old. Matthew takes great pains to show that Christ also reverences the Old Law; He came to fulfill and complete it—not to destroy it. Thus, in reporting the Sermon on the Mount (Mt. 5:17ff) Matthew records Christ's comparisons between the two Laws. The Old Law forbids murder—the new law perfects it by forbidding anger and revenge; the Old Law forbids adultery, the New forbids impure thoughts; the Old forbids perjury, the New teaches such perfection in truth-telling that there will be no need of swearing at all; the Old permits divorce, the New forbids divorce and even separation in most cases. When Luke gives his account of the same sermon he is speaking to Pagans and he does not compare the New with the Old Law but merely outlines the perfection of the New Law (Lk. ch. 6).

3. *Abuses and extremes of Pharisaic traditions* and Christ's castigations of the Pharisees are emphasized in Matthew (9:10-17; 12:1-13; 15:1-20; c. 13). The other Gospels do not highlight this because the Pagans, for whom they were written, were ignorant of the conditions and traditions in Palestine. Matthew feels the necessity of explaining to the Jews that Christ is opposed to the human abuses that grew up around the Law while He is not opposed to the real spirit of the Law as it came from God.

4. *Chosen people.* The Jews, who for centuries had been chosen out of all the nations to be God's people, were scandalized at the fact that the Kingdom is for all—even the Gentiles. Matthew, as well as the other Gospels, preaches the universality of Christ's Kingdom. But he is very careful to show that Christ does recognize the Jews to be the chosen people. The Kingdom is offered to them first (15.24; 10:5-6). It is offered to the Gentiles only after Israel rejects it (8:12; 21:28ff.).

5. *Old Testament prophecies fulfilled in Christ.* Mark and Luke are content to record the prophecies which Jesus applies to Himself. But Matthew writing for people who will measure the Messias by what the prophets foretold of Him, seizes every opportunity to search out on his own and apply to Christ's life the words of the Prophets. For this reason, his Gospel is called the "Gospel of Messianic Prophecy". The following are ten instances where Matthew applies prophecy to the life of Christ; none of them are found in the other Gospels;—Virginal Conception (1:23); Birth at Bethlehem (2:6); Return to Egypt (2:15); Slaughter of Innocents (2:18); Preaching in Galilee (4:16); Working of Miracles (8:17); Avoidance of Publicity (12:18); Teaching in Parables (13:35); Triumphal Entry into Jerusalem (21:5); Price of Judas' Treason (27:9).

. *The Style* of Matthew's books is thoroughly semitic. It is full of the artifices which were commonly employed by the Jewish scribes as an aid to memory in oral recitation. It will suit our purpose to point out two of these tricks of Hebrew oral style as found in Matthew; the student can search out examples for himself if a more detailed study is desired.

1. *Symmetry by numerical arrangement, i.e.,* the disposition of incidents or sayings in groups of two, three or seven. For example, in chapters eight and nine we find three miracles, two questions, three miracles, two questions, three miracles. Again, there are seven parables in the Lake Sermon, seven woes pronounced against the Pharisees, seven petitions in the Lord's prayer.

2. *Parallels, i.e.,* repetition of the same idea under different forms of similarity or contrast. Thus, in Mt. 7:7-10 we have an example of parallelism in its simplest form; in v. 7 we are told to ask, seek, knock; v. 8 tells what happens to those who ask, seek, knock; v. 9 contrasts asking for a loaf, being handed a *stone,* asking for a *fish* and receiving a *serpent.* (*cf.* 16:19; 16:25). These parallelisms are developed into longer strophes, sometimes with several responding to one another (*cf.* Mt. 7:24-27; Mk. 9:42-47).

### TEST QUESTIONS

1. Outline briefly what we know of Matthew's life.
2. Explain why Matthew's Gospel must have been written after 40 and before 70 A.D.
3. What internal evidence shows that Matthew wrote for a Jewish audience?
4. Name the five discourses which form the framework of Matthew's Gospel and indicate the Chapters in which each is found.
5. Name and explain five characteristics of Matthew's Gospel as regards content.
6. Name and explain two Hebrew characteristics of style found in Matthew's Gospel.

# THE GOSPEL ACCORDING TO MATTHEW

I.    1:1 – 2:23: The Infancy

II.    3:1 – 4:16: The Beginnings of the Public Life
    a. Ministry of John the Baptist
    b. Baptism of Jesus; fast in the desert
    c. Departure for Galilee

III.    4:17 – 9:34: Jesus, the Messias, offers Himself and His
               doctrine to the people
    a. Preamble: call of the four brothers, tour     4:17-25
    b. *First discourse:* Sermon on the Mount,
       the doctrine of Christ         5:1 – 7:29
    c. Miracles: the person of Christ      8:1 – 9:34

IV.   9:35 – 12:50: Jesus is rejected by the leaders of the people
    a. Preamble tour, call of the Twelve     9:35 – 10:4
    b. *Second discourse:* Instruction to the
       Twelve; the Apostolic Life      10:5 – 11:1
    c. Unbelief and opposition      11:2 – 12:50

V.   13:1 – 16:12: Jesus withdraws from the crowd
    a. *Third discourse:* Lake Sermon, parables
       of the Kingdom           13:1-53
    b. Failure in Galilee, retirement with the
       Twelve          13:54 – 16:12

TURNING-POINT: the Confession of Peter, the founding of
               the Church          16:13 – 20

VI. 16:21 – 20:34: Jesus initiates His Apostles into the mys-
               tery of the Cross, the meaning and
               consequences of discipleship
    a. First prediction of the Passion, Trans-
       figuration, second prediction of the
       Passion         16:21 – 17:26
    b. *Fourth discourse:* on Christian virtue    18:1 – 19:1
    c. Various instructions, journey to Jeru-
       salem, third prediction of the Passion   19:2 – 20:34

VII.    21:1 – 26:1: Jesus' last conflicts with His enemies in
               Jerusalem
    a. Palm Sunday: the Messianic entrance     21:1-17
    b. Triumphant debates, denunciation of
       the Pharisees       21:18 – 23:39
    c. *Fifth discourse:* God's judgment on
       Jerusalem and on the world      24:1 – 26:1

VIII.   26:1 – 28:20: Jesus' defeat, and victory: the Kingdom
               opened to all nations

*Chapter V*

# THE GOSPEL ACCORDING TO MARK

⇛⇛⇛⇛⇛⇛⇛⇛⇛⇛⇛⇛⇛⇚⇚⇚⇚⇚⇚⇚⇚⇚⇚⇚⇚⇚⇚

## AUTHOR

TRADITION reports the following words of John the Apostle about Mark's Gospel: "Mark, the interpreter of Peter, wrote down accurately, though not in order, all that he remembered of the words and deeds of the Lord. For he had not heard the Lord nor followed Him, but later . . . he followed Peter. The latter gave his teaching according to the needs of the moment, but did not make an ordered collection of the sayings of the Lord. As a result Mark is not at fault in having written things as he remembered them; for he had only one preoccupation: not to leave out anything that he had heard, and not to make any false statements in his recital." (Papias d. 165).

The life of Mark is tolerably well known to us from the Acts of the Apostles. His name is variously given: John, John Mark, or Mark (Acts 13:5; 13:13; 12:25; 15:37; 15:39). His family was prominent in the first Christian community in Jerusalem; we know that his house was the refuge of Peter after his miraculous deliverance from prison (Acts 12:12), and that it was a meeting place for prayer. It would seem that Peter was linked to the family by special ties of affection: he speaks of Mark as "my son" (1Pr 5:13). However, Mark's first apostolic work was done in the company of Barnabas, his cousin (Col. 4:10) and Paul; they took him with them on their return to Antioch from Jerusalem (Acts 12:25), whither they had brought alms to the people suffering from famine (Acts 11:27-30). And he accompanied them on their first missionary journey as an "assistant" (Acts 13:5). However, after they had traversed the isle of Cyprus, and sailed up to Perge in Pamphylia, John Mark left the company and returned to Jerusalem (Acts 13:13). No reason is assigned for his departure; but if it be remembered that he must have been quite young at the time, many might be conjectured. At any rate, it is clear from the sequel that Paul was much displeased. Several years later, when he proposed to revisit the churches they founded, and Barnabas suggested that Mark be taken along. Paul absolutely refused, giving as his reason the lad's previous defection. The result was something of a quarrel, that seems to have dissolved the partnership of Paul and Barnabas. The fact is that Paul went off with Silas,

[26]

and Barnabas took Mark with him to Cyprus, Barnabas' native place (cf. the story in Acts 15:36-41).

It was some years after this (between 53 and 58) that Mark worked in Rome with Peter, as his "interpreter", i.e., he translated into Greek the sermons that Peter (who doubtless knew no Greek), preached in Aramaic, much after the fashion in which Rabbis in the synagogue had their sermons, preached in biblical Hebrew, translated into Aramaic for the common people. When Peter left Rome (about 58) he sent Mark to Alexandria as Bishop. About 62, Mark returned to Rome, this time as the coworker of Paul. It is pleasant to record that in his old age, Paul regained complete confidence in the young man. In 63, he sends Mark's regards to Philemon in Colosse (Phm 24); in the same year he sends Mark to Colosse in person with warm recommendations. Later, in 66, conscious of his own approaching death, he summons Timothy from Ephesus, and bids him "take Mark and bring him with you, for he is useful to me in the ministry" (2 Tim 4:11). Thus it was that Mark once again saw Peter, his father in Christ, not long before the latter's martyrdom, in 67. Of Mark's own last days and death nothing is known. As a man Paul characterized him well: "useful". He was not highly gifted, but he learned to be a good "second", and in subordinate offices he served two Apostles well.

## TIME AND PLACE OF COMPOSITION

It is certain that Mark wrote his Gospel while with Peter in Rome; tradition guarantees that fact. Moreover, certain fragments of a lost work of Clement of Alexandria suggest some of the circumstances. It seems that the Roman audience of Peter, captured by his preaching, wished to possess it in writing as an aid to memory. They were insistent in their requests, and finally Mark undertook the work, Peter himself being apparently reluctant to do it. Moreover, to Mark's enterprise Peter showed himself quite indifferent, doing nothing either to prevent it or encourage it. Later however he gave his approval, and permitted the public reading of the document. Such seems to have been the circumstances surrounding the composition of the Gospel. The available evidence from tradition, etc., fixes the date of its writing about the year 58 A.D., certainly between 53 and 58.

## AUDIENCE

Even apart from the external testimony already cited, it is clear that the readers Mark had in view are not inhabitants of Palestine, nor even, for the most part, of Jewish origin, but rather Christian converts from pagan-

[27]

ism. He is at pains to explain to them that the Jordan is a river (1:5), that Nazareth is in Galilee (1:9), that Bethany is near Mount Olivet (11:1). Moreover he translates for them Aramaic words: "Boanerges" means "sons of thunder" (3:17), "Bartimaeus" means "son of Timaeus" (10:46; *cf.* 5:41; 7:11; 9:43; 10:46; 14:36; 15:22). Furthermore he feels it necessary to explain the ceremonial customs "of the Pharisees and of all the Jews" (7:1-4). Finally, on two occasions he even gives Latin synonyms for Greek words (12:42; 15:16) indicating a Roman Audience, whose Greek had been influenced by Latin.

## CHARACTERISTIC FEATURES

*The order* of Mark's Gospel follows more closely than any other the catechesis of Peter. The following comparison with the outline of Peter's preaching will illustrate the point:—

*Peter's Sermon* (Acts 10:36-42)

    A. 36: (God) sent His word to the children of Israel, preaching peace through Jesus Christ, Who is Lord of all.

    B. 37: You know what took place throughout Judea; for He began in Galilee after the baptism preached by John:

    C. 38: How God anointed Jesus of Nazareth with the Holy Spirit and with power, and He went about doing good and healing all who were in the power of the devil; for God was with Him.

    D. 39: And we are witnesses of all that He did in the country of the Jews and in Jerusalem: 40: and yet they killed Him, hanging Him on a tree.

    E. 41: But God raised Him on the third day and caused Him to be seen plainly, not by all the people, but by witnesses designated beforehand by God, that is, by us, who ate and drank with Him after He had risen from the dead.

    F. 42 After He charged us to preach to the people and to testify that He it is Who has been appointed by God to be judge of the living and of the dead.

*Outline of Mark's Gospel*

    A.     1:1: Beginning of the Gospel of Jesus Christ, the Son of God.

    B.     1:2-13: Inauguration of the Public Life after the preaching of John the Baptist.

    C. 1:14 – 9:49: Ministry in Galilee: powerful teaching, many miracles of healing.

    D. 10:1 – 12:14: Ministry of Jerusalem.
       13:1 – 15:47: Passion and Death.

    E.     16:1-14: Resurrection and apparitions.

    F.     16:15-20: Commission of the Apostles to preach to all men.

Within this general framework Mark orders the narration of particular events according to different patterns. Though at times he groups events according to their chronological sequence, at other times he seems to group them according to the place of their occurrence (*e.g.* 11:1-13,37: events in Jerusalem), or according to a similarity of content (e.g. 2:15-3:6: conflicts with the Pharisees). Moreover, at times he seems to wish to trace the development of ideas (*e.g.* 1:39-3:35: the growth of hostility to Christ).

*Content.* The Romans, to whom Peter's preaching and Mark's Gospel were addressed, were the rulers of the world; as such, they had great respect for the power of which their legions were a proud symbol. Consequently, Mark presents to them a picture of Christ the Son of God, the King Who has complete power over the visible and invisible world; for this reason, His Gospel is called the Gospel of the power of Christ.

Hence, despite the fact that his Gospel is notably shorter (677 verses) than that of Matthew (1068 verses) and Luke (1149), Mark includes all except four of the miracles found in the First Gospel and adds two of his own (the deaf mute 7:31-37 and the blind man 8:22-26). Mark shows Christ's power over the crowd by detailing the impression of astonishment, wonderment, admiration etc., produced by Christ on those who heard Him (*cf.* 1:22; 1:27; 2:12; 4:40; 5:20; 10:24). In addition to his descriptions of Christ's power over the forces of nature and over the people, Mark puts special emphasis on His power in the invisible world as manifested in the expulsion of demons. Mark narrates ten instances of this driving the devil out of possessed persons. The first miracle recorded is of this nature (1:23) and it is accompanied by the demon's testimony to Christ's identity: "the Holy One of God", while similar testimony is had from other demons (1:34; 3:11-12; 5:7).

To achieve this fast-moving narrative of one act of power after another, Mark omits many important things that are found in Matthew and Luke; *e.g.,* the stories of Christ's childhood, most of the accounts of John the Baptist, most of the Old Testament prophecies concerning the Messias (the Romans did not know the Scriptures), the Sermon on the Mount, most of the sermons at the first mission of the Apostles, several of the best parables.

Mark's narrative is simply a series of concrete facts, linked by the conversational (and semitic) "and" or "immediately". No attempt is made to explain incidents or sayings with a view to preventing possible misinterpretations (*e.g.* 8:12; 10:18; 13:32). Instead, the narrative hurries on. Moreover, at times, afterthoughts are added out of their logical place (6:44; 10:22; 16:4). At other times the narrative receives startling abridgements (1:13; 1:20; 4:26 etc.).

*Style.* With modern readers (though not with the ancients, who were fonder of Matthew) Mark is in some respects the most popular of the Gospels. He lacks the literary polish and charm of Luke, but he surpasses him in vividness, homeliness, picturesqueness in the depiction of tableaus (1:23-28; 5:40-43; 10:35, where John and James begin their request in childish fashion). Moreover, he particularly delights the modern reader by his characteristic habit of noting details of our Lord's conduct,—notably His looks (3:5; 7:34; 10:21). He notes, too, His emotions of indignation (3:5), of tenderness (10:16), "taking them (the children) into his arms"); of astonishment (6:5-6), of resolution (10:32-33).

In general, Mark achieves his remarkable vividness by giving definite numbers, names of people, places and the time—in short, by adding all the concrete details which an eyewitness (Peter) would note. The relative brevity of Mark's Gospel results from his omissions (mainly, discourses). In stories that are common to the three Gospels, Mark is usually the richest in details. This graphic quality of his narrative, as compared with those of Matthew and Luke, may be illustrated by comparing the following narratives common to the three Synoptic Gospels:

Healing of the Paralytic; Mk. 2:1-12—Mark has 12 verses, Mt. 9, Luke 10.
Calming of Storm; Mk. 4:35-41—Mk. 7 verses, Mt. 5, Lk. 4.
Devils in Gerasa; Mk. 5:1-21—Mk. 21 verses, Mt. 7, Lk. 15.
Jairus' Daughter; Mk. 5:21-43—Mk. 23 verses, Mt. 9, Lk. 17.
Death of Baptist; Mk. 6:14-29—Mk. 16 verses, Mt. 12, Lk. 3.
Multiplication of Loaves; Mk. 6:30-44—Mk. 15 verses, Lk. 8.
Epileptic Child; Mk. 10:14-29—Mk. 16 verses, Mt. 8, Lk. 7.

The following arrangement of the Raising of Jairus' Daughter in parallel columns will illustrate what such comparisons reveal about Mark's vivid style:

| Matt. 9:18-26 | Mark 5:21-43 | Luke 8:40-56 |
|---|---|---|
| 18. As He was saying this to them, | 21. And when Jesus had again crossed over in the boat to the other side, a great crowd gathered together with Him; and He was at the water's edge. | 40. Now it came to pass when Jesus had returned, that the crowd welcomed Him, for they were all waiting for Him. |
| behold a ruler came up and worshipped Him, | 22. And there came one of the rulers of the synagogue named Jairus. And seeing Jesus, he fell at His feet. | 41. And behold, there came a man named Jairus, and he was ruler of the synagogue; and falling at the feet of Jesus, he entreated Him to come to his house, 42. for he had an only daughter about twelve years of age, and she was dying. |
| saying, "My daugther has just now died; but come, lay Thy hand upon her, and she will return to life". | 23. and entreated Him much saying: "My daughter is at the point of death; come, lay Thy hands upon her, that she may be saved and live. | |

| Matt. 9:18-26 | Mark 5:21-43 | Luke 8:40-56 |
|---|---|---|
| 19. And Jesus arose and followed him, and so did His disciples. | 24. And He went away with Him, and a great crowd was following Him and pressing upon Him. | And it happened as they went that He was pressed upon by the crowds. |
| 20. Now a woman who for twelve years had been suffering from hemorrhage | 25. And there was a woman who for twelve years had had a hemorrhage, 26. and had suffered much at the hands of many physicians, and had spent all that she had, and found no benefit, but rather grew worse. | 43. And a certain woman who for twelve years had had a hemorrhage and had spent all her means on physicians and could not be cured by anyone. |
| came up behind Him and touched the tassel of His cloak, | 27. Hearing about Jesus she came up behind Him in the crowd and touched His cloak. | 44. came up behind Him and touched the tassel of His cloak; and at once her hemorrhage ceased. |
| 21. saying to herself "If I touch but His cloak I shall be saved". | 28. For she said, "If I touch but His cloak, I shall be saved." | |
| | 29. And at once the flow of blood was dried up, and she felt in her body that she was healed of her affliction. | |
| | 30. And Jesus, instantly perceiving in Himself that power had gone forth from Him, turned to the crowd and said, "Who touched My cloak?" | 45. And Jesus said, "Who touched Me?" But as all were denying it, Peter, and those who were with Him, said, "Master the crowds throng and press upon Thee, and dost Thou say, 'Who touched Me?' " |
| | 31. And His disciples said to Him, "Thou seest the crowd pressing upon Thee, and dost Thou say, 'Who touched Me?' " 32. And He was looking around to see her who had done this. | 46. But Jesus said, "Someone touched Me; for I perceived that power had gone forth from Me." |
| 22. But Jesus turning and seeing her, said "Take courage, daughter, thy faith has saved thee." And the woman was restored to health from that moment. | 33. But the woman, fearing and trembling, knowing what had happened within her, came and fell down before Him, and told Him all the truth. 34. But He said to her, "Daughter thy faith has saved thee. Go in peace and be thou healed of thy affliction." | 47. But the woman, seeing that she had not escaped notice, came up trembling, and falling down at His feet, declared in the presence of all the people why she had touched Him, and how she had been healed instantly. |

| Matt. 9:18-26 | Mark 5:21-43 | Luke 8:40-56 |
|---|---|---|
| | | 48. And He said to her, "Daughter thy faith has saved thee; go in peace." |
| | 35. While He was yet speaking, there came some from the house of the ruler of the synagogue saying, "Thy daughter is dead. Why dost thou trouble the Master further? 36. But Jesus hearing what was being said to the ruler of the synagogue, said, "Do not be afraid, only have faith". | 49. While He was yet speaking, there came one from the house of the ruler of the synagogue saying to him, "Thy daughter is dead; do not trouble Him." 50. But Jesus on hearing this word answered the father of the girl, "Do not be afraid; only have faith and she shall be saved." |
| 23. And when Jesus came to the ruler's house and saw the flute players and the crowd making a din, He said, 24. "begone, the girl is asleep, not dead. "And they laughed Him to scorn." | 37. And He allowed no one to follow Him except Peter and James, and John, the brother of James. 38. And they came to the house of the ruler of the synagogue and He saw a tumult, people weeping and wailing greatly. 39. And going in He said to them, "Why do you make this din and weep? The girl is asleep, not dead". 40. And they laughed Him to scorn. But He, putting them all out, took the father and mother of the girl and those who were with Him, and entered in where the girl was lying. 41. And taking the girl by the hand, He said to her, "Talitha cumi," which is interpreted, "Girl, I say to thee, arise". 42. And the girl rose up immediately and began to walk; she was twelve years old. And they were utterly amazed. | 51. And when He came to the house. He allowed no one to enter with Him, except Peter and James and John, and the girl's father and mother. 52. And all were weeping and mourning for her. But He said, "Do not weep; she is asleep, not dead". 53. And they laughed Him to scorn, knowing that she was dead. |
| 25. But when the crowd had been put out, He went in and took her by the hand; and the girl arose. | | 54. But He, taking her by the hand, cried out, saying, "Girl, arise!" 55. And her spirit returned and she rose up to eat. And her parents were amazed, but He charged them to tell no one what had happened. |
| 26. And the report of this spread throughout all that district. | 43. And He charged them strictly that no one should know of it, and directed that something be given her to eat. | |

*Comparison with Matthew.* It is clear from the above example that the general quality of Mark's narrative is that of an eyewitness, a man of no literary gifts, plain and direct and even rude in speech but with a remarkable eye for details. Matthew, the tax collector, was used to giving only essentials in his reports; his gospel narrative too is only interested in essential facts. Peter, as a fisherman, was used to noting contours of shoreline, signs of fish in the water, signs of weather in the sky. It was natural then, that in relating the story of Christ, Peter produced spontaneously the picturesque features, the slight particulars which, without being necessary to the understanding of the story or the moral lesson, made the personalities of the gospel beings of flesh and blood. Mark, in his Gospel, follows the visualization of the scenes as they happened in the concrete even at the cost of seeming to contradict Matthew's account (compare Mt. 9:18 with Mk. 5:23, 35).

*Comparison with Luke.* Luke, as a man of literary ability, follows much of Mark's vividness (he used Mark's Gospel in writing his own) but he omits many slight details. Luke manifests artistic ability in selecting these vivid details and ordering them into a well-rounded narrative; Mark's vividness comes, not so much from literary skill but from having heard so often Peter's narration of the real-life story. Thus, for instance, Luke inserts the girl's age in its logical place at the beginning of the story; Mark tosses it in at the end, being reminded of it as he visualized the girl rising up from death and walking. Instead of preparing his stories like one who commands his recollections, Mark seems to follow the events as if they were unrolling themselves before his eyes. Thus, a man presents himself before Jesus to ask Him what he must do to obtain life everlasting. While Luke qualifies him as a man of parts at the beginning of the story, in Mark we do not know his social position until the moment when he becomes saddened at the Saviour's call: "For he had great possessions." Similarly, Mark does not tell us the size of the stone which closed Jesus' sepulchre until the very moment when the women are astounded to see it rolled aside: "For it was very great". This style of narration necessarily introduces recapitulation and repetition. Having narrated the crucifying of Jesus and the dividing of His garment by the soldiers, Mark notices that he has not indicated the time. He goes back: "And it was the third hour and they crucified Him." Hence, Mark's remarkable liveliness of style is not to be explained by any creative genius on his part; the explanation lies rather in the fact that he has transmitted to us the eyewitness recollections of Peter. "Here," Renan notes, "everything is taken from life; we feel that we are in the presence of actual recollections."

*Portrait of Peter.* A final feature of Mark's Gospel is the fact that Peter is the most sharply-defined figure in it, after our Lord Himself, of course. This is natural, since Mark is really describing Peter as Peter described himself, namely, as the unworthy disciple. Consequently the privileges of

Peter are omitted. Mark narrated neither the walking on the waters nor the promise of the primacy, that are told by Matthew. He omits the prayer of Christ for Peter, included by Luke. Finally, he omits the conferring of the primacy, narrated by John. On the other hand he tells of Peter's incoherence on the Mount of the Transfiguration, his sleeping in the Garden, his warming himself at the fire in the courtyard of Caiphas (whereas Matthew and Luke simply state that he was seated there). It is evident that Peter's "son" respects the humility of his father in Christ.

## TEST QUESTIONS

1. Summarize the life of St. Mark in chronological order indicating the time and place of composition of his Gospel.
2. Give the general outline of Mark's Gospel. What influenced him to follow this order; give the source of our knowledge on this point.
3. To whom did Mark address his Gospel primarily? How did the audience influence the content of his Gospel?
4. Mention some of the notable omissions in Mark's Gospel as compared with the other synoptists.
5. How, in general, does Mark achieve more vividness than the other synoptists? Give some examples of this from the Raising of Jairus' Daughter.
6. From the narrative concerning the daughter of Jairus, point out an apparent contradiction between the account of Matthew and Mark. How do you explain it?
7. Explain, giving examples, Mark's lack of literary ability compared to Luke.
8. What is distinctive about Mark's picture of Saint Peter? Give examples.

## THE GOSPEL ACCORDING TO MARK

I.       1:1-13: Introduction: John the Baptist and Jesus
        a. Ministry of the Baptist
        b. Baptism of Jesus, His fast in the desert

II. 1:14 – 9:49: Jesus' ministry in Galilee, the Lake region, the north
        a. Call of the four brothers; a day at Capharnaum       1:14-38
        b. Display of power, its double result: popular enthusiasm, hostility of the Pharisees       1:39 –3:35
        c. New tactics: public teaching in parables, private instruction of the Twelve       4:1 – 6:6

*Chapter VI*

# THE GOSPEL ACCORDING TO LUKE

✦✦✦✦✦✦✦✦✦✦✦✦✦✦✦✦✦✦✦✦✦✦✦✦✦✦

## AUTHOR

OUR ANCIENT sources attribute the third Gospel, and also the Acts of the Apostles, to Luke. On his early life we have no certain information. According to tradition he was a native of Antioch in Syria, of Greek, not Jewish parentage; in all likelihood his family occupied a good position, and he himself may well have been a Roman citizen. Moreover he seems to have practiced as a doctor in Antioch, and was certainly a man of high culture. The circumstances of his conversion are a matter of conjecture.

He enters Christian history as a companion of Paul; in fact, he belonged to the innermost circle of Paul's assistants, together with Timothy, Silas and Titus. Paul speaks of him as "the beloved physician" (Col. 4:14); in that capacity he must have been of great value to the Apostle, who was chronically ill and nervous. The story of his own association with Paul is given us by himself, in rather sketchy fashion, in his "second discourse", the Acts, notably in the three sections wherein the narrative is told in the first person plural (the celebrated "we-sections", as they are called: Act 16:10-17; 20:5-21:18; 27:1-28:16).

Luke first appears in the Apostle's company, as one who shared his counsels, during Paul's second missionary journey, about 50 A.D. With Paul he made the crossing from Asia Minor into Europe, one of the most decisive steps in the whole history of the Church. He assisted in the evangelizing of the city of Philippi, and apparently was left there when Paul went on to Athens and Corinth. At any rate, it was at Philippi that Paul met him again, some five or six years later; and together they sailed to Troas (20:6), and went on to Jerusalem, where Paul was arrested, and sent to prison at Caesarea for two years (56-58). It is supposed that during this period of separation from his master, Luke devoted himself to gathering his material for his Gospel from the many witnesses of the life of Christ who were still living in Jerusalem and Palestine. When Paul was sent from Caesarea to Rome to stand trial before Caesar, Luke accompanied him (27:1), and from the fact that the use of "we" is fairly continuous for the rest of the Acts, it seems that he was with Paul during the two years of the latter's first captivity in Rome (28:30). During this period he acted as Paul's "co-

[36]

worker" (Phm. 24; the letter to Philemon was written during this captivity). He also edited his Gospel, and somewhat later the Acts of the Apostles. One last mention of him is made in the New Testament, in Paul's Second Letter to Timothy, written during his second captivity in Rome and very shortly before his martyrdom in 67: "only Luke is with me" (4:11). Such is history's last glimpse of Luke: in faithful, tender service to the exhausted, lonely old man whom he loved so well.

Of his own death we know nothing certain, though an ancient tradition has it that he died at the age of 84, somewhere in Greece. His memory has always been dear to the heart of the Church, for no one can read his books without realizing that it was no accident that Paul termed him "the beloved physician". In that single, happy word we have his dominant trait: his devoted and affectionate nature that waked devotion and affection in those who knew him. He was in every sense a Christian gentleman, refined and scholarly in his tastes, broad in his sympathies, self-sacrificing and loyal in all his life.

## DATE OF COMPOSITION

Luke evidently conceived his Gospel and the Acts as forming one complete story in two parts; the continuity is clearly marked by the fact that the Ascension of our Lord constitutes both the end of the first part and the beginning of the second part. Moreover, the two parts must have been published in close succession, the Acts certainly in the year 63 (since it contains no mention of the outcome of Paul's trial) and the Gospel some little time before (as is clear from the prologue to the Acts, in which the Gospel is referred to as already extant). Hence we are safe in assigning the years 58-62 as the time during which the Gospel was written; doubtless the work had many interruptions. Finally, tradition asserts that the Acts were completed in Rome; and in Rome, too, should be placed the publication of the Gospel.

## AUDIENCE

That Luke has primarily in mind a Christian audience of pagan rather than Jewish origins is shown by the fact that he is studiously careful of pagan sensitiveness. For instance he omits the incident of the Canaanite woman (Mk. 7:24-30) wherein the Jews are preferred to pagans; and in one context he artfully substitutes the word "sinner" for "Gentile" (compare Mt. 5:47 with Lk. 6:33). Again, he introduces ideas and incidents that would be more pleasing to non-Jewish ears, for instance, the parable of the Good Samaritan (10:30-37). Finally, he emphasized the universal destiny of the Gospel (cf. 2:32; 21:24; 24:47 etc.).

His Gospel indicates too that he had in mind the pagan in so far as he was a product of the Greek rather than the Roman culture. This is natural enough in view of the fact that Luke himself was of Greek origin and a companion of Paul who preached mainly to a Greek audience. He dedicates his book to Theophilus (a Greek name) who evidently held a high position in the Graeco-Roman world since Luke addresses him as "most illustrious" (1:3). The dedication is made to honor Theophilus but doubtless also to secure for the book a wider circle of readers among the Christian converts from Greek paganism.

The tone and content of Luke's book is (as we shall illustrate later) especially adapted to the Greek cast of mind. In contrast to the Romans who were devoted to power, the Greeks were devoted to the development of human perfection in all its forms; in their picture of the ideal man they laid great stress on physical beauty and the intellectual and moral qualities which make for perfect goodness and happiness. Luke portrays Christ to them as the Man of whom their poets and philosophers had dreamed. He points out to them how far short of this ideal their own specimens of manhood had fallen by emphasizing Christ's moral purity, His sympathy with the poor and oppressed, His humility and self-denial, His all-embracing forgiveness and love. Luke further appeals to the Greek love for beauty by putting this picture of the divinely human life of Christ in a literary form of such simple beauty that Renan, the unbeliever, said of his Gospel: "It is the most beautiful book ever written".

## CHARACTERISTIC FEATURES

*Order*. Luke's Gospel appears to be modelled in its general framework on that of Mark. Luke, of course, prefixes his charming account of the Infancy; Mary was evidently the principal witness whom he interviewed on this subject. There follow then the incidents preparatory to the Public Life, namely, the Baptism and Temptation. The Public Life itself falls into three general parts: 1) the ministry in Galilee with its double result: popular enthusiasm and Pharisaic hatred; 2) the journey to Jerusalem; 3) the last days there, during which our Lord confounds all His adversaries. The turning point of the Public Life is clearly marked, namely, the Confession of Peter. Finally, there is the account of the Passion, Death and Resurrection.

But then, in addition to the story of Christ's infancy, there are two notable passages which are peculiar to Luke (6:20–8:3 and 9:51–18:14). These chapters are simply inserted in the framework of Mark's outline as followed by Luke; for that reason, they are called, respectively, the *lesser and greater* "*intercalation*" *or* "*insertion*". In these sections he collects a great many parables, instructions and deeds of Christ that are not found in the other evangelists, including with them other data already found in Matthew and Mark. In the "greater intercalation" (9:51-18:4), places and times are only vaguely noted; the general framework seems to be a journey to Jerusalem (9:51), or perhaps several journeys. It is not unlikely that Luke derived the material in these sections from written or oral sources in which times and places were not accurately noted; these would be among the "many narratives" and "eye-witnesses" which he mentions in his prologue. Consequently he is content with reporting his data just as he heard them, without attempting to introduce an order of his own.

Nevertheless, a second point must be borne in mind, namely, that Luke was not exclusively preoccupied with chronology in devising his "order" (1:3). Like the other evangelists, his order is one of exposition as well as of fact; he has certain ideas to put forward, through the medium of historical events. The first idea is the universal redeeming mission of Christ, to Gentile as well as Jew; and naturally Luke collects incidents, etc., that illustrate this idea. The second idea is that the history of our Lord's Life is the history of His rejection by the Jews, the failure of His mission to them, because of their stubborn clinging to their own ideas. For this reason, perhaps, he inserts the rejection at Nazareth at the beginning of the Public Life, whereas it was certainly later; it marks the beginning of the fulfillment of Simeon's prophecy, that the child would be "for the fall and for the rise of many in Israel" (2:34). From that moment our Lord's whole life appears as a "journey to Jerusalem" and to death. Hence Luke's narrative has a distinct onward sweep to it; it, too, marches toward Jerusalem, and toward our Lord's apparent defeat there, followed by His glorious victory. In this respect Luke's Gospel receives its completion by the Acts, his "second discourse," which begins in Jerusalem and follows the triumphant action of the Holy Spirit as it carries the Church outward from Jerusalem through Judea and Samaria, "even to the very ends of the earth" (Acts 1:8).

*Content.* Luke takes over rather completely the material of Mark, making slight changes and omissions. Moreover, about one fifth of his Gospel shows a clear dependence on Matthew, notably in regard to the words of Christ. Nevertheless fifty-three percent of his matter is proper to him alone (612 out of 1149 verses). It is, therefore, apparent that Luke has made a considerable contribution to our knowledge of Our Lord's life. His account of the Infancy is highly personal, notably in the prominence given to our Blessed Mother (in Matthew she stands somewhat behind Joseph). In addition, of the twenty miracles and twenty-three parables he records, six and eighteen respectively are told only by him. Again, he alone gives the history of the "Perean ministry" (in his "greater intercalation"), as well as certain individual incidents, for instance, the mockery of our Lord by Herod and his court during the Passion.

In his selection and use of the material of His Gospel, Luke is distinctly illumined by the spirit of his master, Paul. Luke did not, of course, owe his facts to Paul, but he did derive from Paul his profound intelligence of the facts. No one ever penetrated more deeply than Paul into the "idea" of Christianity as revealed in the mystery of Christ, namely, the tender love of God the Father for all men, His children, and His desire that all men should see the salvation that He gave them in the gift of His only Son. It is this Pauline insight into the meaning of Christ, adapted for special appeal to an audience imbued with the culture of Greece, which gives the third Gospel the following characteristics with regard to its content:—

*Gospel of Mercy.* First of all, Luke's master thought, as it was that of Paul, is the universal mercy of God; "all mankind shall see the salvation that is the work of God" (3:6). With this citation from Isaias he opens the history of the Public Life; and throughout the whole of it he shows the love of Christ surmounting all barriers of race and creed and caste, reaching out to sinners, Publicans, Samaritans, Gentiles, embracing all in its sweep. Luke alone gives us the incidents of the sinner in the city (7:36ff.), of Zaccheus (19:3ff.), of the Good Samaritan (10:25ff.), of the Pharisee and the Publican (18:9ff.), of the Prodigal Son (15:11ff.). Truly he merited the glorious title given him by Dante "Scriba mansuetudinis Christi" (historian of Christ's kindness.)

*Gospel of Sympathy for the Poor.* The second trait of Luke's narrative, betraying his own quality of heart, is his sympathy for the poor, that is, for the poor whose poverty has made them simple of heart, trustful of the Providence of God, detached from the things of this world. He is not the enemy of riches as such, but he brings into relief our Lord's denunciation of their abuse, of their tendency to close the heart against the appeals of charity. Luke alone tells the parable of the Foolish Rich Man (12:13ff.), of the Unjust Steward (16:1ff.), of Dives and Lazarus (16:19ff.). It is clear that our Lord's active sympathy for those who suffer patiently from this world's inequalities finds an echo in the heart of Luke.

*Gospel of Women.* The third subject on which he dwells with delight is family life, conjugal fidelity, filial and paternal devotion. His is the "Gospel of the Christian family" (Zachary and Elizabeth, Joseph and Mary, Bethany). In the same connection his Gospel has also been called the "Gospel of Women". Certainly women play a larger part in it than in the other Gospels, a fact which fits well with the Hellenic, not Jewish, culture of its author. Elizabeth, Anna, the widow of Naim, the sinner in the city, the "women who had been cured of evil spirits and infirmities; Mary who is called Magdalene, from whom seven devils had gone out, and Joanna the wife of Chuza, Herod's steward, and Susanna, and many others" (8:2-3), the only daughter of Jairus, the sisters Martha and Mary, the women of

Jerusalem on the way to Calvary, the Galilean women who stood by the Cross, the first messengers of the Resurrection; all these names are associated with Luke's Gospel. Nor is the role of women in the Acts less considerable. Luke's masterpiece, however, is his portrait of Mary, the Mother of Jesus, treasuring in her heart all the souvenirs of His infant and boyhood life.

*Gospel of Hymns and Joyousness.* It is his insight into the meaning of Christ that gives to the Gospel of Luke, as to the writings of Paul, their insistent note of joyousness. He sustains the note struck by the angels' song over Bethlehem: "I bring you good news of great joy which shall be to all the people, for there is born to you today in the city of David a Saviour, who is Christ the Lord" (2:10-11). Luke alone records the inspired hymns of joy and praise and thanksgiving to God contained in the Hail Mary, the Magnificat, the Benedictus, the Nunc Dimittis. The phrases "praise God" and "bless God" are characteristically Lucan, being found six times and three times respectively in him, not at all in Matthew or Mark. On this note his Gospel closes: "and they worshipped Him and returned to Jerusalem with great joy; and they were continually in the temple, praising and blessing God" (24:53).

*Gospel of Prayer.* From Paul, too, Luke may have derived his insight into the place in the Christian life of prayer, penitence, and the spirit of mortification in union with Christ crucified. He often represents Christ at prayer; for instance, in the narrative of the Baptism, he alone adds the detail: "and praying" (3:21), and he mentions our Lord's habit of retiring to solitary places to pray (5:16) (note the imperfect tense in the Greek, "He used to retire"). Of this habitual prayer of Christ, Luke gives six instances that are not found in the other Gospels. Likewise he alone reports several of Our Lord's parables on prayer: the Importunate Friend (11:1-8), the Judge and Widow (18:1-8), which is followed by the parable of the Pharisee and the Publican. Furthermore, Luke's Gospel abounds in examples of the fundamental Christian virtue of penitence, and it is insistent on the cost of following Christ (*cf.* 14:25-33; 15:1-9, etc.). Thus Luke achieves a balanced portrait of the Christian life, depicting both its joyousness and its sternness; the strong spirit of penitence for sin as well as the unbounded trust in God's mercy that must animate it.

## TEST QUESTIONS

1. Give a chronological outline of St. Luke's life and indicate the date when he wrote his Gospel.
2. Give reasons to indicate that Luke wrote his Gospel primarily for pagans of Greek culture.
3. Give a general outline of Luke's Gospel indicating how it follows the outline of Mark's Gospel.

4. What is meant by the lesser and greater "intercalations"? What chapters do they involve?
   How does the prologue to Luke's Gospel indicate the sources of these insertions?

5. Was Luke influenced by Paul in the same way as Mark was influenced by Peter in the writing of his Gospel? Explain.

6. Name and explain five characteristic elements of Luke's Gospel with regard to content.
   In each case, give a few examples (titles) of things that are narrated only in Luke.

## THE GOSPEL ACCORDING TO LUKE

| | | | |
|---|---|---|---|
| I. | 1:1-4: | Prologue to Theophilus | |
| II. | 1:5 – 2:52: | The Infancy and Hidden Life | |
| III. | 3:1 – 4:13: | Prelude to the Public Life | |
| | | a. Ministry of the Baptist | 3:1-20 |
| | | b. Baptism, genealogy, Temptation | 3:21 – 4:13 |
| IV. | 4:14 – 9:17: | The ministry of Jesus in Galilee | |
| | | a. Rejection at Nazareth; prophecy of faith among Gentiles | 4:14-30 |
| | | b. Display of power in word and deed throughout Galilee: popular enthusiasm and conflicts with Pharisees | 4:31 – 6:11 |
| | | c. Formation of His own party: the choice of the Twelve | 6:12-19 |
| *Lesser Intercalation:* | | Sermon on the Mount, display of love toward all classes, especially the poor and sinners | 6:20 – 8:3 |
| | | d. Withdrawal from the crowd (parables), private instruction of the Twelve by word, miracles, first mission, multiplication of loaves | 8:4 – 9:17 |
| Turning-Point: | | Confession of Peter, prediction of Passion, Transfiguration, etc. | 9:18 – 9:50 |
| V. | 9:51 – 19:27: | The march toward Jerusalem | |
| *Greater Intercalation:* | | Continued instruction of the Twelve on the costliness of following Him; on the universality of His redeeming love, on His rejection by the Jews | 9:51 – 18:14 |
| | | a. Other incidents and instructions | 18:15 – 19:27 |
| VI. | 19:28 – 21:38: | The Last Days in Jerusalem | |
| | | a. Triumphant entrance, Temple cleansed | 19:28-48 |
| | | b. Victorious debates | 20:1 – 21:4 |
| | | c. Prophecy of judgment on Jerusalem and on the world | 21:5-38 |
| VII. | 22:1 – 24:53: | The Passion and glory of Christ: mission of Apostles to all the world | |

*Chapter VII*

# THE GOSPEL ACCORDING TO JOHN

## AUTHOR

"JOHN THE APOSTLE, whom Jesus particularly loved, was the last of all to write a Gospel, doing so at the request of the bishops of Asia. . . ." So St. Jerome, in his "History of Illustrious Men", states the common tradition as to the authorship of the last version of the Gospel.

In the Synoptic narratives (though not in his own, by reason of his modesty) John plays an important role; in fact, next to Peter, with whom he is shown to be united in ties of affectionate friendship, he is the most prominent of the Apostles. He was the son of Zebedee, a fisherman on the Lake of Genesareth, a man of considerable substance, whose business was sufficiently extensive to demand that he employ hired help (Mk 1:20). His mother, Salome (Mk 15:41), was apparently the sister of Mary, the Mother of Jesus. Together with Mary Magdalen and Mary, the wife of Cleophas (whose sons were James the Lesser and Joseph), Salome was one of the three women who are represented as being closest to our Lord. During part of His Public Life these three were in His company, ministering to Him, both in Galilee and on His last journey to Jerusalem, and they, too, stood with him on Calvary (Mt. 27:56; Mk 15:41).

Consequently, John and his brother James the Greater, were the cousins of Jesus. John was the younger by a year or two. In fact, he seems definitely to have been the youngest of all the Apostles. He could hardly have been more than fourteen or fifteen when he was first called to follow Christ, that is, not much beyond the age of Jewish "manhood", the age when the Jewish youth was obliged to observe the full Mosaic Law. All the indications in the Gospel point to his extreme youth: neither he nor his brother was sufficiently mature to enable their father to dispense with hired help; their mother feels called upon to intercede for them with Jesus (Mt 20:20), and their own remark on this occasion is sufficiently childish (Mk 10:35); on other occasions they exhibit all the rashness of youth (Lk 9:49, 54); finally John is constantly represented as following the lead of Peter (Jn 20:2-10; Acts 3:1; 8:14).

John first appears as a disciple of John the Baptist, together with Peter

[43]

and Andrew, and probably also Philip and Nathaniel (later Bartholomew), and his own brother James. With Andrew he is the first of our Lord's disciples (Jn 1:35-40), and with him he returned to Galilee, where he lent assistance to his father. After the miraculous catch of fish (Lk 5:1-11), he and James, together with Peter and Andrew, received their definitive call, and joined themselves to our Lord's party (Mt 4:21 and Mk 1:19). Later he was given a place among the Twelve, as an Apostle. Moreover, with Peter and James, he formed one of the inner circle of three who witnessed the raising to life of the daughter of Jairus (Mk 5:37), the Transfiguration (Mk 9:1) and the Agony in the Garden (Mk 14:33). With Peter he is sent to prepare the Last Supper (Lk 22:8), and at it he had a place of honor on our Lord's right, so that leaning back he could repose upon His bosom (Jn 13:23). Finally, as a last mark of trust and affection, our Lord committed to him the care of His own Mother, on Calvary (Jn 19:26-27). Not without reason, then, does he call himself "the disciple whom Jesus loved" (Jn 13:23; 19:26; 21:7).

After the Ascension John worked in Palestine, in close association with Peter, up till the year of the Council of Jerusalem (about 49 A.D.). After that tradition is silent about his life, until the year 69, when he appears in Asia Minor, ruling the churches there. During the reign of Domitian (81-96) he was exiled to the island of Patmos where he wrote the Apocalypse. He died at Ephesus during the reign of Trajan (98-117) at an advanced age.

It is customary in Christian art to represent John as a youth of delicate beauty, slight and fair, with features suggesting only gentleness. In fact, at times a certain almost feminine quality is depicted in him. But the Gospel data do not substantiate this piece of idealization. We know the soubriquet given to him and his brother by our Lord himself: "Boanerges", meaning "sons of noise" or "sons of thunder". Apparently both of them were hot-tempered, impetuous, ardent, direct in speech and action, not overgiven to prudent reflection (*cf.* Lk 9:49, 54). But John's impetuosity was the product of a nature that was at once affectionate and wholly sincere. Though the appellation "the Apostle of love" has been much sentimentalized, nevertheless, understood in the strongest and noblest sense of the word, it describes him well. Jerome's story may well be true, that in his old age he was wont to preach nothing but "Children, love one another".

Less ordinarily emphasized are John's qualities of mind. All the evidence shows him to have been a man of particularly keen and direct intelligence, characterized by that type of genius that we call intuitive. The conventional symbol under which he is represented, the eagle, the bird of the piercing eye and the soaring flight, well conveys the quality of his mind. As his Gospel shows, no one penetrated more deeply than he into the meaning of Christ, and no one has elaborated more masterfully the profound significance of the "signs" that He wrought, and of the words that He spoke. John was truly a "seer"; and the one object upon which his vision was always bent was the transcendent figure of Christ, his Master and Lord.

Moreover, he was a man of very independent mind, as his Gospel shows. It differs profoundly from the synoptic records, in matter, order and style. It is a highly distinctive piece of work, the product of personal reflection. Yet, notwithstanding his clear-cut independence, John was characterized by a remarkable modesty; in his Gospel he studiously conceals both himself and his distinguished family. On one point only he speaks out boldly in his own regard, namely, on his qualifications as a "witness" and on the authority with which they invest him (1:14; 19:35; 1 Jn 1:1-4).

## TIME OF COMPOSITION

We are certain that John wrote his Gospel at Ephesus, the city that Paul had made the center of the Christian communities scattered throughout Asia Minor, and that John, who came to Asia Minor not long after the death of Paul in Rome, had made his headquarters, certainly after his return from Patmos and perhaps before his exile thither. The Gospel was written sometime between the years 90-100 A.D. For references are made to it by first century writers; and the work itself betrays the hand of an aged man, with its monotony of style, and its constant circulation about the one idea: Christ is the Son of God.

We know that John did not spontaneously undertake its composition, but as Jerome and others assert, was urged to it by the priests and faithful of the Asian churches. It is not improbable that portions of his oft-repeated accounts of our Lord's life and discourses had previously been committed to writing by a secretary or secretaries. And what the faithful desired was probably the completion of these fragmentary records and their ordering into a book. Moreover, from his first Letter, which serves as a sort of introduction to the Gospel, we know that in acceding to their requests, John was moved, among other reasons, by the desire to combat certain errors which threatened the faith of his children both in the Divinity and in the Humanity of Christ. But in the course of the book this apologetic scope became subordinated to an historical and doctrinal one.

## AUDIENCE

Though the style of the book betrays the fact that its author was a Jew, the book itself is clearly destined for Hellenic converts, to whom Jewish words, customs, etc., were not entirely familiar. And in spite of the differences that separate John from the Synoptists, he shared with them the same general purpose in writing, namely, to make known "the things about Jesus", that men might believe in Him. But it is clear that he supposes a class of readers already well initiated into the mysteries of the Christian religion (Baptism, the Eucharist, etc.: *cf.* chapters 3 and 6), as well as familiar with the history of Christ given by the Synoptists. He writes not as to children "ignorant of the truth" (1 Jn 2:21). His idea is to perfect their faith by leading them more deeply into the meaning and the mystery of Christ, and by the same token to strengthen their faith against the attacks of "antichrists" (1 Jn 2:18), who deny "that Jesus is the Christ (the Messias)" (*ibid.* v. 22), and who deny "the Father and the Son" (v. 23). Novelties were abroad even then, and John wished to recall his children firmly to "the old commandment which you had from the beginning (of your Christian life). The old commandment is the doctrine which you heard" (1 Jn 27). He feels that they were wavering, attracted to new ideas, because they had not properly understood the splendor of that doctrine, and had not deeply plumbed the unsearchable riches of Christ.

Hence Christ is the theme of the whole Gospel, what He is in Himself, and what is His meaning for mankind: "Many other signs, then, Jesus did in the presence of his disciples which are not written in this book. But these are written that you may believe that Jesus is the Christ, the Son of God; and that believing you may have life in His name" (Jn 21:30-31). This renewed, more intelligent faith in Christ, John knows, will bring to His children a joy that is complete (1 Jn 1:4).

## CHARACTERISTIC FEATURES

*Theology.* It has already been suggested in Chapter II, that John's Gospel is theology as well as history. The uniqueness of the book is the result of the purpose John pursues: a deeper intelligence of the mystery of Christ on the part of the Christians. To achieve his purpose, the author chooses a small number of particularly significant facts not found in the Synoptists, and devotes himself to revealing their profound meaning as "signs" (*cf.* 2:11, 23; 3:2; 4:48, 54, etc.). In general the "signs" are miracles (of which John narrates seven), through which glimpses are given into certain aspects of the Person of Christ. The meaning of these signs is declared by the discourses of Christ, of which John reports a great many. And both the facts and the discourses tend to illustrate the one great theme about which the whole Gospel revolves with a sort of majestic monotony; Christ, the Son of God, the Truth, the Light, and the Life of men.

Not all of the discourses of Christ in John's Gospel are introduced in order to interpret the previous narrative of a fact. Still, in many of them, this interpretative intention is very clear. Thus, for instance, there exists a close relation between the healing of the paralytic at the pool and Christ's exposition of His relations with the Father (5:1-47); between the multiplication of loaves and the instruction on the bread of life (6:1-59); between the healing of the man born blind (9:1-7) and Christ's presentation of Himself as "the light of the world" (8:12); between the resurrection of Lazarus (11:38-44) and Christ "the life of the world" (11:25).

Because of his theological preoccupations John, at times after reporting a discourse of Christ, drifts off into reflections of his own so that in places it is difficult to determine where the words of Christ end and his own begin. Similarly, after narrating an incident with astonishing concreteness and very effective pace, he embarks upon discourses and reflections quite abstract, and with a very definite sameness to them. This quality of monotony, both in ideas and even in language, is remarked by all students of John. His ideas are indeed very few, but they are all large ideas, and consequently have a certain inevitable vagueness. By constantly returning upon them, John wishes his readers to sink deeper into their inexhaustible meaning: Christ is Truth, Light, Life, God.

*History.* From all that has been said about the dominance of ideas in John's Gospel, it must not be concluded that he wrote simply a book of meditations on the mystery of Christ, or a sort of theological essay. On the contrary, in spite of its doctrinal purpose, John's work remains definitely a work of history. In fact, the achievement of its doctrinal purpose supposes the reality of the historical facts on which it is built. John vindicates his right to interpret the mystery of the "Word made flesh" precisely because he has been a witness of His life, in all its grandeur and in all its humanness. And the detailed and colorful character of many of his narratives clearly proves him to have been an eyewitness of them.

As a matter of fact, John completes in many valuable respects the history of Christ as given by the Synoptists. And apparently he does this of set purpose, lest the synoptic narratives create some false impressions.

The following are his major "historical corrections":

1. John's chronology aids us in determining the length of the Public Life. Had we only the synoptic accounts we might suppose that it lasted little more than a year, but John fixes its duration at a minimum of two years and a half. For he clearly mentions three Paschal feasts (2:13; 6:4; 13:1). In fact, some scholars would insert a fourth Pasch between 4:35 and 6:4, which would extend the Public Life to three years and a half.

2. John's account of the ministry of our Lord in Judea and Jerusalem clears up a difficulty that results from the Synoptic Gospels. In them Jesus arrives in Jerusalem for what seems to be the first time just five days before His Passion; and there He is greeted with wild enthusiasm by one party

(the common people), and with bitter hostility by another (the chief priests and perhaps a portion of the populace). John, however, explains this phenomenon by showing that Jesus had been in Jerusalem on the occasion of at least four great Jewish feasts and that His preaching and miracles had roused serious dissension among the people, and the implacable enmity of the priests. Moreover John relates the Raising of Lazarus which had roused popular enthusiasm to its highest pitch and at the same time goaded the enemies of Jesus to taking decisive steps towards His death. Consequently John affords the background, missing in the Synoptists, for the lament of Christ over Jerusalem: "Jerusalem, Jerusalem, . . . how often would I have gathered thy children together, as a hen gathers her young under her wings, but thou wouldst not!" (Mt 23:37-39).

3. John points more distinctly to the fact that the first multiplication of loaves constituted the crisis in the Galilean ministry of our Lord. The fact is suggested in the Synoptists; they depict a growing coldness on the part of the people from that time forth, and they mark the more complete withdrawal of Christ from the public eye and His wish to be exclusively with the Twelve. But they assign no clear reason for these unexpected effects of what was certainly one of the greatest of His miracles. John, however, supplies the reason: it was our Lord's refusal of the kingship they offered him. This defeated their hopes of a temporal kingdom for Israel, restored by Him. And their disappointment hardened to incredulity when, in the great discourse in the synagogue at Capharnaum, He refused them a second miracle of manna, and spoke to them of the true Bread, that comes down from heaven to give to the world a new life, but a spiritual one. This discourse, too, shows us that our Lord prepared the minds of His disciples for the institution of the Eucharist, which, in the Synoptists, has no preludes.

4. Again John supplies the background for the call of the four brothers from their fishing to the following of Christ. The Synoptists portray it as being exceedingly abrupt; John makes clear the fact that it had been prepared for by a preliminary call given on the banks of the Jordan, through the intervention of John the Baptist.

Finally, in addition to these major supplements given by John to the synoptic narratives, there are other points in which his information enables us to construct more accurately the life of Christ (*cf.* the detailed chronology in 1:19-2:12; the cleansing of the Temple at the beginning of the Public Life; the exact situation of the anointing at Bethany, and its effect on Judas; etc.).

*Order and Content.* As might be expected from all that has been said, the order and content of John's Gospel differ profoundly from that of the Synoptists. We shall here discuss mainly the outline of his Gospel and in doing so we shall necessarily indicate his characteristics with regard to content.

John planned his Gospel according to the development of ideas; he selected events and discourses to illustrate these ideas regardless of the time order in which they actually happened. There are *several* of these key ideas or themes which he simultaneously develops and illustrates. It is therefore impossible to outline the fourth Gospel according to any one of these single themes; no one of them, taken by itself as the linking thread of the whole, sufficiently indicates the rich content of the book. This point will best be clarified by showing what these themes are as stated in the prologue and then indicating how they are simultaneously developed throughout the remainder of the book.

*Dogmatic Prologue* (1:1-18).

A. *Christ is God.* (1:1-3, 14, 18.)

It is not with the time of Augustus or Herod that John begins; nor does he trace the origins of Christ only to Abraham or even to Adam; rather, he begins in the womb of eternity, when there was only God, "and the Word was with God and the Word was God". This theme is at once the prelude and the conclusion of John's Gospel; all of the incidents and discourses contained in the book are designed to illumine this central fact: Jesus is God Incarnate.

We have already indicated how the divinity of Christ is manifested in the seven miracles which John narrated and then expressed in the doctrinal discourses which accompany most of them. There are two other series of discourses, found only in John, which dwell with great emphasis on this point of Christ's oneness with the Father: the conflicts with the Pharisees (ch. 7, 8, 9, 10, 11) and the discourse to the Apostles at the Last Supper (ch. 13, 14, 15, 16, 17.). The Pharisees are the theologians of the nation and in his arguments with them Christ has an opportunity to dwell on points of abstract doctrine which were generally omitted from His sermons to the ordinary people. And in speaking to the Apostles, He is addressing intimate friends to whom He reveals all of His secrets without reserve.

B. *Christ is the Light of the World.* (1:4-5, 9-10).

The whole of John's Gospel may be looked upon as a drama, in some respects a tragedy, which traces the fortune of the Light that came into this world: its heavenly origin, its successive manifestations here on earth in the life of Christ, the varying reception it received from different classes (the men of good will, the indifferent, the hostile), then its apparent eclipse by the powers of darkness in the Passion, and finally its last irradiations upon earth in the Risen Life; the resulting idea being that the world judges itself by the judgment that it passes upon Christ the Light: "Now this is the judgment: The light has come into the world, yet men have loved the darkness rather than the light, for their works were evil. For everyone who does evil hates the light, and does not come to the light that his deeds may not be exposed. But he who does the truth comes to the light that his deeds may be made manifest, for they have been performed in God." (Jn. 3:18-21).

### C. *Christ the Life* (1:12-13, 16).

To those who have good will, Christ is not merely a Light who has come to show what He is and what they are by contrast. The Light draws them to Himself that He may give them a share in what He is: "that believing, you may have life in His name". (20:31) Thus John, while depicting the drama of Christ's conflict as the Light shining in darkness, at the same time tells another story of how Christ reveals Himself and His love most intimately to those who join the circle of His friends: this theme of grace and the divine life to be shared with His own, rises progressively to a climax of full revelation.

This theme is introduced in the very beginning of the Public Life: to Nicodemus it is represented as a "rebirth" (ch. 3), to the Woman of Samaria, as water springing up to eternal life and quenching thirst forever (ch. 4). From then on, while the conflict rages between the light and the darkness, He progressively gives a more intimate revelation of what this life is and where men are to find it; He is the Bread of Life and those who eat His flesh will never die (ch. 6); He is the Way, the Truth and the Life and he raises Lazarus from the dead to prove it; to His own he reveals the divine unity of the Father, Son and Holy Spirit and explains how men are to share in that unity through Him: "I am the vine, you are the branches"; this union of the Mystical Body in the new Life is the purpose of His death and the purpose of His apparitions after rising from the grave was to prove that what He died for was accomplished.

Despite this emphasis on our personal relationship to Christ as the Light and the Life, John is careful to avoid the type of individualism that would do away with the visible Church. He describes the whole work of the Saviour as tending to gather the children of God, who were dispersed, into one flock, under one shepherd (11:52, 10:16, 12:32). In the fourth gospel as in the Synoptics, the Twelve constitute a group apart whom Christ prepares especially to take His place. Finally in one of His last appearances on the shores of the lake of Tiberias, He gives reality to the promise made to Simon Peter when the latter had confessed Him at Caesarea Philippi, and bestows upon him the universal pastorate of the lambs and the sheep (21:15-18). Hence the Scotch exegete, E. F. Scott, remarks: "In every direction John enforces the spiritual concept of the Church, and at the same time he magnifies the outward institution". (The Fourth Gospel, Its Purpose and Theology, Edinburgh, 1906, p. 139).

*Historical Outline.* Despite the fact that the order of John's Gospel is dictated largely by its theological themes it does follow a general chronological outline. The narrative follows the succession of great Jewish feasts which seem to give it its chronological framework. The outline which follows is based on this pattern.

## TEST QUESTIONS

1. Outline briefly the life of St. John indicating the time and place of composition of his Gospel.
2. Explain in general how John's Gospel, in contrast to the other three Gospels, is a Theology.
3. Explain four ways in which John's Gospel corrects the history given in the synoptic Gospels.
4. State the three main themes of John's Gospel and show where they are contained in the prologue.
5. Trace in a general way the development of the two themes—Christ is Light of the World and Christ is the Life.
6. Name five feasts, giving year and month for each, which furnish a chronological framework for John's Gospel.

## THE GOSPEL ACCORDING TO JOHN

I.   1:1 – 1:18: Prologue: *the Eternal Word made flesh*

II. 1:19 – 12:50: Public Life: *the Word and the World:* "he came into His own, and His own received Him not".

    1. First disciples; wedding at Cana; Capharnaum 1:19 – 2:12

    2. FEAST: Pasch in Jerusalem: cleansing of the Temple; Nicodemus; work in Judea    2:13 – 3:36

    3. Return to Galilee: the Samaritan woman; cure of the royal official's son at Cana    4:1-54

    4. FEAST: unnamed feast in Jerusalem: cure of the paralytic on the sabbath; *discourse:* "My Father works until now and I work"    5:1-47

    5. FEAST: "Pasch was near," in Galilee: miracle of loaves; walking on the waters; *discourse:* the promise of the Eucharist    6:1-71

    6. FEAST: Tabernacles in Jerusalem:    7:1 – 10:21
       a. Division among the populace; *discourse:* mission by the Father, the living water; the schism    7:1-53

*Chapter VIII*

# CREDIBILITY OF THE GOSPELS

❯❯❯ ❯❯❯ ❯❯❯ ❯❯❯ ❯❯❯ ❯❯❯ ❯❯❯ ❯❯❯ ❯❯❯ ❯❯❯ ❯❯❯ ❯❯❯ ❮❮❮ ❮❮❮ ❮❮❮ ❮❮❮ ❮❮❮ ❮❮❮ ❮❮❮ ❮❮❮ ❮❮❮ ❮❮❮ ❮❮❮ ❮❮❮

HAVING UNDERSTOOD what kind of books the Gospels are, and grasped their unique purpose, we are now able to examine more critically their *human authority*. Credibility, when applied to a work of history, means that the document is reliable in regard to the events it treats. This involves three factors: authenticity (genuinity), integrity, and historicity.

To establish, therefore, the credibility of the Gospels, the first thing to be proved is their authenticity, *i.e.,* the fact that they were actually written by the men whose names they bear at the historical period in which they are said to have been written. The proof consists of two parts: 1) citation of the testimony of the ancient Fathers and ecclesiastical writers to the authorship and date (the external argument, the more scientific); 2) the examination of the books themselves, to collect whatever evidence of their authorship and date they contain (the internal argument, of itself not entirely conclusive).

The second thing to be proved is the integrity of the Gospels, *i.e.,* the fact that the copies of them that we have today reproduce without substantial alteration, by addition or subtraction, the original texts as written by their authors. This proof, too, consists of two parts: 1) the use of the science of textual criticism, which studies and judges the purity, value, etc., of manuscripts; 2) the examination of citations from the Gospels made by ancient writers, liturgical books, etc., to see if they agree with our modern text.

Given this proof of the authenticity and integrity of our texts, it is evident that we are actually reading what the four evangelists wrote. The question however arises: are we justified in giving human credence to what they wrote? May we accept on human authority, as historical fact, the deeds and claims of Christ as recorded by them? The question is answered by proving that these four men are reliable witnesses, whose testimony is acceptable because they knew the facts and reported them sincerely and truthfully. And with this, the proof of the historical value of the Gospels is complete. They can be used with full confidence as reliable historical documents, and from them evidence can be collected to show that Christ asserted Himself to be the true Son of God and founder of a Church, that He gave ample justification of His assertion, notably by working miracles, and that consequently all explanations of Him and of His life and work that deny His Divinity fail to fit the historical facts.

The main objective of this theology course is to study the contents of the Gospels; we already believe that what they say is true not only as human testimony but as the word of God. However, it seems reasonable at this point to enlighten and strengthen this faith of the student with some of the main reasons for the human credibility of the Gospels. We shall, therefore, present a brief outline of the evidence for their authenticity, integrity, and historicity. If the student at any time wishes to make a more complete, scientific study of this field, he may consult the manuals of apologetics which treat the subject in full.

## AUTHENTICITY OF THE GOSPELS

*Early Christian Writers.* An unbroken line of witnesses coming down from the second century testify that the Gospels were written by Matthew, Mark, Luke and John and these witnesses declare that they are handing on the tradition received from their predecessors. Some of these witnesses are Apostolic Fathers, *i.e.,* authors on theological subjects who either had direct intercourse with the Apostles or at least came indirectly under their immediate influence. To really appreciate the abundance of evidence from these witnesses for both the authenticity and integrity of the Gospels, one would have to read all the theological literature written by prominent Christians in the first three centuries. We shall merely list a few of the early authors or documents; the student should keep in mind the fact that we have no time for an exhaustive study of their testimony; the more important thing for the beginner, is to know who the witnesses are so that he is able to consult or refer others to their testimony if the occasion arises.

Testimony from the first century and early part of the second century is rather skimpy because there are so few manuscripts still extant from that period and because no one had as yet raised doubts which made it necessary to testify to the credibility of the Gospels. However, in order that the student may be introduced to names which are often quoted in manuals which deal with the authenticity and integrity of the Gospels, we list the following from the "Apostolic Fathers".

1. *The Didache* (Teaching of the Twelve Apostles) is perhaps the oldest of these "Apostolic" writings. Scholars assign it to a period between 70-100 A.D. It was rediscovered in 1875. The first part of this treatise is moral, the second is disciplinary and liturgical. It is a valuable witness to the teaching and practice of the early church. Aside from the fact that the whole of its doctrine is based on the Gospel (some of the Fathers of the Church

valued this treatise next to the Bible), it contains thirty allusions to or direct quotations from the first three gospels. (The Fourth Gospel had not, as yet, been written).

2. *St. Clement of Rome,* the third pope after Peter was a pupil of the Apostles; his name is included in the Canon of the Mass. About 96 A.D., as Pope, he addressed an Epistle to the Church of Corinth which was at one time read in the Churches of both East and West. This epistle is a valuable witness to the fact that Rome exercised authority from the beginning over the churches of the East but our interest at the moment lies in the fact that the epistle contains quotations from the gospels of Mark and Luke.

3. *St. Ignatius of Antioch,* in Syria (d. 107 A.D.). He too was a pupil of the Apostles who became Bishop of Antioch and was martyred in Rome; his name is also mentioned in the Canon. In several of his epistles which are still extant, he alludes to or cites passages from the Gospels of Luke and John.

4. *St. Barnabas,* also mentioned in the Mass, was a co-worker of the Apostles especially of St. Paul. There is an epistle still extant which is attributed to him but its authorship is uncertain. But whoever wrote it, it was composed about 130 A.D. and contains in its seventeen chapters quotations from the Gospels of St. Matthew and St. Mark.

5. *St. Polycarp* of Smyrna in Asia Minor (d. 155 A.D.), was a disciple of St. John the Apostle. He wrote a letter to the Christian community of Philippi, Macedonia, in which sentence after sentence is made up from the Gospel of St. Matthew.

6. *"The Shepherd" of Hermas* (Pastor Hermas), is a treatise written either in the second half of the first century or early in the second century. It is attributed to a man by the name of Hermas but it is uncertain to which of several men bearing the same name the authorship belongs. This book was highly regarded in the early Church; it was read publicly in the churches and regarded by many as a book of scripture. It chiefly relates visions and parables with the object of bringing the reader to penance and right living. It contains many quotations from the Gospels.

7. *Papias* (A.D. 70-165) was Bishop of Hieropolis in Phrygia. His testimony too is of special value because he was a disciple of St. John the Apostle. About 120 A.D., he wrote the "Oracles"—five books of explanation of the Gospels. Only a few fragments of these books are still extant but they were still in existence at the time of Eusebius (A.D. 260-340) who often quotes them. The following is an example of Papias' explicit testimony with regard to the first two Gospels:

"Mark having become the interpreter of Peter, wrote down accurately whatever he remembered. It was not, however, in exact order that he nar-

[55]

rated the sayings and deeds of Christ. For he neither heard the Lord nor accompanied Him. But afterwards, as I said, he accompanied Peter, who accommodated his instructions to the necessities (of his hearers), but with no intention of giving a regular narrative of the Lord's sayings. Wherefore Mark made no mistake in thus writing some things as he remembered them. For of one thing he took special care, not to omit anything he had heard, and not to put anything fictitious into the statements. Matthew put together the oracles (of the Lord) in the Hebrew language, and each one interpreted them as best he could". (Eusb. Hist. Eccl., III, 39).

*After the middle of the second century* the writings of Christians became more profuse and more of them have survived the ravages of time; besides, controversy made it more necessary to inquire into and safeguard the traditions concerning the scriptures. The following are some of the more notable witnesses of this later period.

8. *St. Justin, Martyr* (A.D. 105-167) was an outstanding Christian apologist of his time who taught and defended the faith in Asia Minor and Rome where he was finally martyred. He was a prolific writer but, of all his works, only three have survived—the two "Apologies" and the "Dialogue". These writings contain abundant quotations from the gospels (175 from Matthew alone) as well as such explicit testimony to their authenticity as:

"For the Apostles, in the memoirs composed by them, which are called Gospels, have thus delivered unto us what was enjoined upon them . . . For in the memoirs which I say were drawn up by His Apostles and those who followed them (it is recorded) . . ." (Apol. 1a, 66; Dial. 106).

9. *St. Irenaeus* (A.D. 140-202) Bishop of Lyons (France). He was born in Asia Minor where he was a disciple of St. John the Apostle; thus, Irenaeus was familiar with the traditions of the East. And, while Bishop of Lyons, he made a special study of the traditions of the West. Because of his holiness and learning and voluminous writings in defense of the faith, Irenaeus is listed among the Fathers of the Church. Most of his writings have perished, though numerous citations from them exist in later authors. But we still have two complete works in early translation from the original Greek; 1) "Adversus Haereses" (5 vol.), Latin Translation, which is largely a defense of the faith against Gnosticism in all its forms; 2) "Proof of Apostolic Preaching", Armenian and Latin Translations, which is largely a demonstration of the truth of the Gospels from Old Testament prophecies.

The following is a sample of his testimony to the authorship of all four Gospels:

"Matthew also issued a written Gospel among the Hebrews, in their own dialect, while Peter and Paul were preaching at Rome and laying the foundations of the Church. After their departure, Mark, the disciple and interpreter of Peter, also handed down to us in writing what had been preached by Peter. Luke also, the companion of Paul, recorded in a book the Gospel preached by him. Afterwards, John, the disciple of the Lord, who also had leaned upon His breast, did himself publish a Gospel during his residence at Ephesus in Asia". (Adv. Haer, III, 1, 1; Eusb. Hist. Eccl. V. 8).

10. *Clement of Alexandria* (A.D. 150-215) was the head of the Catechetical School of Alexandria and, as such, inherited a tradition that went back to the Apostles. He was born in Athens and was a great pioneer among the Greek theologians. His written works are too numerous to mention; perhaps the three most prominent ones are "Exhortation", "The Tutor" and "Miscellanies"—a trilogy of graduated initiation into Christian life based on explanations of the Gospels.

With regard to the origin of the Gospels, Clement says:

"When Peter had publicly preached the word of God in the city of Rome and, inspired by the Holy Spirit, had promulgated the Gospel, many who were present urged Mark to write down what Peter had preached, since Mark had already followed Peter for a long time and remembered his words. Mark, therefore, composed his Gospel and gave it to those who were asking him for it. . . . But last of all John, seeing that what pertained to the body of Christ had been handed down in the other Gospels, wrote a spiritual Gospel under the inspiration of the Holy Ghost at the request of his friends". (Euseb., Hist. Eccl. VI, 14).

11. *The Muratorian Fragment (Canon).* This is a fragment of an eighth century manuscript discovered by (and named after) Muratori in the eighteenth century. The original work, which has been lost, dates back to around 170 A.D. The author is unknown. It contains the oldest known list (canon) of the books of the New Testament.

The opening lines of this document have been lost; they undoubtedly referred to the first two Gospels. The document says:

"The third book of the Gospel (is) according to Luke. Luke, the physician, wrote it under his own name in orderly fashion after the ascension of Christ when Paul had taken him with him since he was eager for the journey. Yet Luke himself had not seen the Lord in the flesh; he commenced his account from the birth of John (the Baptist) according to the information he was able to gather. Of the fourth Gospel, John, (one of the Disciples) is the author".

12. *Tertullian of Carthage* (A.D. 160-240) was a forerunner of the great Latin theologians. He was a jurist, trained in Roman law, who became a priest at Carthage around 200 A.D. He was a savage defender of the faith but, about 212 A.D., he fell into the heresy of Montanism and later founded a sect of his own and wrote as strongly against the Church as he had previously written in her defense. He wrote many works on dogmatic subjects but his forte was Apologetics. In the field of Apologetics he wrote many works against particular heretics, but, of his general apologetic works the most notable are "Ad Nationes", "Apologeticus" and "Liber de Praescriptione Hereticorum". He was a master of pungent wit and the rapier-like

thrust and coined many immortal phrases such as "The seed of Christians is the blood of Martyrs".

A typical example of Tertullian's testimony is found in his writing against Marcion, an heretical Bishop who withdrew from the Church in 144 A.D. Marcion and his followers, forerunners of the Manichaeans, taught that matter is evil and hence were led to deny the Incarnation and Resurrection. In order to bolster this heresy, Marcion was logically forced to attack the Gospels; he edited his own edition of St. Luke's Gospel, corrupting the authentic text to suit his own doctrine and then insisted that his text of Luke was the only authentic one. In the following quotation Tertullian attacks Marcion on this point. The student should note from the quotation how vigilant were the defenders of the faith against any innovation in the gospel account; they used, as the norm of faith, the practice of the united churches with their faithfully guarded traditions dating back to the Apostles.

> "We affirm, first of all, that the source of proof which the Gospels furnish indicates the Apostles to be their authors. . . . I maintain that this Gospel of Luke existed from the very beginning of its publication in the Apostolic churches and in all those which were united to them through a common bond of faith, while that of Marcion was unknown to most of the congregations and if known to any was bitterly condemned. The same authority of the apostolic churches also supports the other Gospels which we possess through them and after them . . . namely, the Gospels of John and Matthew as well as the Gospel of Mark which is designated as that of Peter whose interpreter Mark was". (Adv. Marcionem IV, 5).

13. *Origen* (A.D. 185-254) succeeded Clement as head of the Catechetical School of Alexandria and was later ordained to the priesthood. He was considered the most learned man of his period. The total of his written works is estimated at 6,000; of his many exegetical works on the various books of the bible, his commentaries on the Gospels of St. Matthew and St. John are prominent in importance; seventeen books of these two commentaries have survived. Origen speaks with knowledge when he says:

> "The Church has four Gospels, heretics have many. . . . as I have received from tradition concerning the four Gospels which alone are admitted without controversy in the Universal Church of God which is under the heavens: first, namely, was written the Gospel according to Matthew, formerly a publican, then an Apostle of Jesus Christ, who issued it in Hebrew for the Jews converted to the faith; but the second is that according to Mark who composed it as Peter had explained it to him . . . ; and the third is that according to Luke, which is praised by Paul, and was written for the benefit of the Gentiles; and the last is that according to John". (In Mt. Tom. I; Euseb. Hist. Eccl. VI, 25).

14. *Eusebius* (A.D. 265-340) Bishop of Caesarea, is another amazingly learned and prodigious writer of these times. His many writings are in the fields of history, apologetics, exegesis, dogma and moral theology.

But posterity is grateful to him especially for his "Chronicle", an outline of history from creation down to 225 A.D., and his "Ecclesiastical History", a history of the Church down to his own time. It is from this latter work that the following quotation is taken:

"Of all the disciples of the Lord, Matthew and John alone have left us narratives in writing. When Matthew had first preached the faith to the Hebrews and was about to set out from there for other nations, he wrote his Gospel in his native language and by his book compensated for his absence. . . . They say that Mark, having gone to Egypt, preached there the Gospel which he himself had written. . . . Luke, a resident of Antioch and a physician by profession, lived for a long time as the close companion of Paul and was the eager associate of the other Apostles. He left us two divinely inspired books. The first of these is the Gospel which he tells us he composed according to the information he had received from the very preachers of the divine word who had seen Christ from the beginning and whom he says he had followed for a long time. The other book is called the Acts of the Apostles. . . . We shall mention the undisputed writings of the Apostle John. First of all, his Gospel must be received as authentic, since it is recognized as such in all the churches which are under heaven. The ancients rightly put it in the fourth place after the three others". (Hist. Eccl. II, 16; III, 4; III, 24).

*Testimony of Early Heretics.* From the very beginning of Christianity there were a number of heretical sects whose particular doctrines we have no time to describe in detail. (cf. Cath. Encyclopedia). They shared in common the errors of Gnosticism which claimed special divine enlightenment for an elite group of spiritual souls; the vast majority (the "unenlightened") were immersed in matter, which is evil, and therefore had no hope of salvation. Each of these Gnostic sects adapted Christianity to its own beliefs and developed its own particular brand of heresy. Each sect chose one of the Gospels containing the most texts which could be twisted in its favor and rejected the others. But in ignoring or rejecting the others they did not dare to doubt their authenticity, but claimed only that these Evangelists had misunderstood the true Gospel.

Thus, the Ebionites ("Poor Men") were largely Jewish Christians who denied the divinity of Christ and clung to the Mosaic Law as the means of salvation; they recognized only the Gospel of St. Matthew because, as we have seen, Matthew was at such pains to extol the benefits of the Law. We have already seen (pg. 58) how the Marcionites favored the Gospel of St. Luke. Cerinthus is another Gnostic heretic who was a contemporary of St. John; it is said that the Apostle wrote his Gospel against the Cerinthians. They denied the divinity of Christ and preferred only the Gospel of St. Mark. Valentinus was perhaps the most influential of these early heretics. Born in Egypt, he joined the Christian community in Rome where he began to preach his heresy. He was excommunicated and continued to preach heresy in Cyprus until he died in 160 A.D. The Valentinians preferred the spiritual Gospel of St. John because, among other errors, they taught that Christ had no real body and could not really suffer.

The testimony of such witnesses is of special value because, while it cost them great embarrassment, they felt the necessity of trying to adapt their peculiar doctrines to the Gospels. How great this embarrassment was, can be seen from the following passage of St. Irenaeus:

> "So firm is the ground on which these Gospels rest that the very heretics bear witness to them, and, starting from these (documents), each one of them endeavors to establish his own peculiar doctrine. For the Ebionites, who use Matthew's Gospel only, are refuted out of this very same, making false suppositions with regard to the Lord. But Marcion, mutilating that according to Luke, is proved to be a blasphemer of the only existing God, from those (passages) which he retains. Those again who separate Jesus from Christ, alleging that Christ remained impassable but that it was Jesus who suffered, preferring the Gospel by Mark, if they read it with a love of truth, may have their errors rectified. Those however, who follow Valentinus, making copious use of that according to John to illustrate their conjunctions, shall be proved to be totally in error by means of this very Gospel." (Adv. Haer. III, 11.7).

## INTEGRITY OF THE GOSPELS

After proving that the four Gospels are authentic, the next important step is to determine whether the texts we use today are the same as they were when originally written. We saw in Ch. I (pg. 6) that the earliest full manuscripts of the New Testament which we possess are copies made on vellum dating from the middle of the fourth century (350 A.D.). The earlier manuscripts from which these copies were made were written on papyrus, which is the main reason why they have not survived. Assuming that the original manuscripts written by the Evangelists survived until about 150 A.D., there is an interval of about two hundred years to be accounted for. Since the fourth century manuscripts agree substantially with our modern copies, our question is this: in the interval of two hundred years between the original writing of the Gospels and the vellum manuscripts which we now possess, was the original text altered either by fraud or error in any *substantial* way?

It is true that the manuscripts, translations and editions which we possess differ from one another in many minor ways, giving rise to what are called variant readings. But the evidence is abundantly clear that there has been no *substantial* change in the original text of the Gospels;—*i.e.*, there have been no changes, omissions or interpolations of such a kind as to give a meaning different from that intended by the Evangelists in matters necessary for determining the character and doctrine of Christ.

Our purpose here is not to make an exhaustive study of all the evidence for the integrity of the Gospels. We merely wish to state in outline the following four considerations from which objective certainty on this point can be derived.

1. *Early Christian Writers.* Many of the authors cited above in connection with the authenticity of the Gospels testify explicitly to the integrity of the Gospel texts and to the vigilance that was exercised by the Church to keep them integral. But aside from their testimony on this point, these authors so frequently quote the Scriptures in their writing that it would be possible to build up almost the entire text of the Gospel from these quotations and this reconstructed text would be substantially the same as the one we now possess. For example, Roensch, a German scripture scholar, has reproduced much of the New Testament from citations in the writings of Tertullian alone.

This argument must not be oversimplified; it involves a separate field of complicated, scientific research. We must remember that many original manuscripts of these early Christian writings have also been lost; as in the case of the Gospels, so in the case of these writings, we often have only copies of a later date. Hence, there is always the possibility that the copyists might have altered the scripture quotations in these writings to harmonize with the Scripture texts being used at the time the copy was made. But research often reveals that these quotations have not been tampered with. For example, scripture quotations in a particular manuscript may so differ in minor details from current scripture manuscripts as to make it clear that the copyist made no attempt to "harmonize", and yet so agree in substance as to certify that the scripture text which was current at the time of the original writing agreed substantially with the later ones. Or again, the context of an early Christian writing may make clear the precise wording of a quotation; *e.g.,* when a dispute involves argument from the precise wording of a text.

The point is that this argument involves the field of textual criticism. Many texts of the Fathers and early Christian authors have been critically edited. Much of this work is still going on. Enough has been done to provide overwhelming evidence for the integrity of the Gospels. For us, it is sufficient to accept the findings of eminent scientists in this field. But at the same time, we should realize that to see the internal force of this argument would involve intensive research into the manuscripts of the early Christian period.

2. *Heretics.* Another good source of evidence for the integrity of the Gospels is the writings of early heretics. Often, despite the fact that they were anxious to make the Scripture agree with their errors, they were forced

to accept the reading that was current in their day and that text, as they quote it, agrees with our modern text.

An outstanding example of such a case is that of Tatian (120-180 A.D.). He was converted by St. Justin, Martyr, and later adopted heretical views. After his defection from the Church, about 175 A.D., he published his *"Diatesseron"* (Harmony of the Gospels). He made this copy of the Gospels from texts that were very close to the originals and it agrees substantially with our text of the Gospels.

3. *Wide Diffusion of Copies.* Perhaps the most powerful argument for the integrity of the Gospels lies in the fact that so many copies were made before 150 A.D. and used in so many widely separated localities: in Africa, Egypt, Syria, Asia Minor, Greece, Italy, France and Spain. St. Justin, Martyr, writing about 140 A.D., tells us that it was the practice of his day to read from the Gospels at Sunday Mass: "And on the day which is called Sunday, there is an assembly in the same place of all who live in cities or in the country districts, and the records of the Apostles . . . are read as long as there is time." (Apology 67, 3).

It would have been impossible to alter these widely diffused texts either by fraud or error in any substantial way. Such alteration would have to have been done simultaneously in all these widely separated places without being noticed by the clergy or the people. We saw in the case of Tertullian (pg. 58) how vigilant were the ancient teachers and Bishops to preserve unadulterated the traditions of these early Christian churches; how anxious they were to preserve unity among them; how they compared the practice and teaching of one church with another to safeguard uniformity. The priests and faithful alike were vitally interested in preserving the word of God which they knew so well and regarded so highly. And the adversaries, like Marcion, would have been quick to pounce upon anything which would raise doubts about the uniformity of the Scripture texts used in these churches.

4. *Archeological Discoveries.* Up to modern times it was thought that the earlier papyrus manuscripts had perished completely. But archeologists have unearthed countless papyri in Egypt which have been preserved airtight through the centuries in the tombs of mummies and beneath the sand that covered the ruins of ancient cities. Many of these papyri manuscripts concern the Scriptures and give direct evidence of reading of the early texts.

The *"Chester Beatty Papyri,"* discovered by Chester Beatty in 1931, are the most important single collection of such early scripture manuscripts. This particular collection contains portions of eleven books of the Bible; eight of them are books of the Old Testament.

Of the three manuscripts of the New Testament, the most valuable are the following two: 1) Thirty pages of a book that was originally 110 pages long and contained the Four Gospels and the Acts of the Apostles (the thirty pages are not consecutive). They are written in a hand of the period between 200-250 A.D.; 2) The Epistles of St. Paul (86 pages out of 104), written about 200 A.D. These manuscripts agree essentially with our present text. They also testify to the early date of the original compositions—a point which many non-Catholics would not admit before these discoveries; the fact that these are copies which circulated in Egypt at this early date testifies to the existence of much earlier copies.

Another interesting example of such findings is a little scrap of papyrus identified and published by *Mr. C. H. Roberts in 1935*. In a pile of papyri containing business records, laundry bills, etc., Mr. Roberts found this piece (3½ by 3¼ inches) which contains texts of St. John's Gospel on each side (Ch. 18:31-33; 37-38). Experts agree that the writing dates back to 130-140 A.D. This little scrap of paper doesn't tell us much about the integrity of the Gospels, although the few texts it contains agree with our corresponding texts. But this finding is of great value in corroborating the date of the fourth Gospel. It means that there was a manuscript of John's Gospel circulating in Egypt in the first half of the second century; allowing a minimum of time for the copying and circulation of this work from its place of origin (Ephesus)—the date of the original composition is thrown back to our previous estimate (90-100 A.D.).

## HISTORICITY OF THE GOSPELS

It is clear from what has been said that our modern copies contain the Gospel story as written by Matthew, Mark, Luke and John. The final question, then, is: Do these narratives relate historical facts? We are concerned with the outstanding facts and sayings which form the main theme of the Gospels; i.e., the miracles of Christ in general, the substance of His sermons, His choosing the Apostles and founding of the Church, His passion, death and resurrection and ascension. Our certitude with regard to the substance of the Gospels is derived from the following considerations:

1. *The Evangelists knew the facts.* As we have seen, Matthew and John were eye-witnesses; Mark gave Peter's testimony; Luke was a companion of Paul and consulted eye-witnesses. In a manner that is strikingly simple and sincere, these Evangelists proceed to testify that what they write is true.

2. *Evangelists could not deceive.* How could these simple men have invented the perfect, divinely human character of Christ? Or how could they have invented a doctrine so sublime in its degree of practical and theo-

retical perfection as never before to be conceived by such philosophers as Socrates, Plato, Aristotle? The Gospels teach humility, poverty, mortification; a poor and humble Messias, a suffering and crucified Messias. Even if the Evangelists could have conceived it, how could they ever expect anyone, especially the Jews, to believe and accept it?

The events narrated were public; the narrative gives names of individuals, places, times that could easily be checked. Thousands of people who were thirty years old and saw the events were only sixty years old when the first three Gospels were written.

Indeed, the events were thoroughly checked; violently opposed to the whole Gospel story were the educated, wealthy, politically powerful classes among the Jews. They attacked the facts whenever they could; examples of this can be seen in the case of the man born blind (cf. Jn. c. 9) and the story of the resurrection; while they spread the rumor that the Body was stolen, they never could explain away the guards and when the Apostles maintained in the face of death that they ate and drank and conversed with the risen Christ, they could not refute them. In general, the Jews never attempted to deny or refute the facts which the Apostles were proclaiming; rather they attributed the miracles to Beelzebub and tried to prevent the Apostles from preaching the facts (cf. Acts 4:13-22).

The friends of Christ, as well as His enemies, had an interest in checking the Gospel stories. The Jews who believed did so at the cost of all their prejudiced hopes about the Messias and His kingdom; they were ostracized by family and friends, expelled from the synagogue, persecuted and often martyred. The Pagan converts, too, had an impelling motive for rejecting the shame of the Cross; they had to give up their immoral way of life and false gods with all the customs, feasts and ceremonies that attended the old worship; they, too, were isolated from their fellows, had their property confiscated, were imprisoned and martyred by the thousands. Neither of these classes of converts would have accepted the faith at such cost to themselves without being sure of the facts on which it was based. How, for instance, could we ever explain the general enthusiasm of the people of Palestine for Christ against their own leaders, if His miracles were not true?

The case of the Apocryphal Gospels shows that these early Christians did make a critical investigation of the credibility of the Gospels. These false gospels began to appear after the second century; the names of twenty of them are known; many have been lost but some are still extant. These forgeries were patterned on the true gospel stories and, because of their similarity to the true Gospels, one might have expected the early Christians to accept them. Indeed, some of these legends were accepted for a time in particular places, but, in general, they were rejected as unauthentic and only the four Gospels were declared to be trustworthy.

3. *Evangelists had no motive to deceive.* Certainly there was no hope of temporal reward; the Gospel story itself makes it clear that only the hatred of the Jews, persecution and death could result from preaching it. And as far as eternal reward is concerned, the Gospels themselves teach that eternal punishment is the reward for such blasphemies, sacrileges and fraud as they would contain if they were false. True, a man might suffer and die for false social or religious *principles* which he thinks are correct (*e.g.* Communism). But the Apostles gave their lives in testimony of *facts* which they knew for certain to be either true or false. Christianity is based on the fact that Christ rose from the dead; all worship of Christ in this life and all the hope of future reward is based on that fact. Why should the Apostles die if they knew this fact to be untrue? They could have lived in peace by denying it, or rather, by simply ceasing to preach it.

4. *Finally, the Gospel accounts themselves* evidence the fact that they are a sincere attempt to tell the truth. In a work of fiction, one would expect the Apostles to be glorified so that they would easily be accepted as the leaders of the new Kingdom. But the Gospels dwell on their humble origin, their undistinguished mode of life and their defects; *e.g.,* Matthew is a Publican, Peter's denial, Judas' betrayal, incredulity of Thomas and other Apostles, their flight from the crucifixion.

A comparison of the Gospel accounts shows that there was no collusion in their writing. They agree in substantials, and yet they vary so much in accidental details that they seem to contradict one another. For example, Matthew (9:18) says that Jairus' daughter was dead; Mark (5:21) says she was only at the point of death; the Gospels are full of such discrepancies in details which are sometimes very difficult to explain. The Evangelists are so free from any anxiety to make their Gospels harmonize with each other that they differ remarkably even in quoting directly the words of our Lord; *cf.* Mt. 6:9-13; Lk. 11:2-4 (Our Father); Mt. 15:26; Lk. 23:38 (Words on the Cross).

The Gospels omit many things that a fictitious account would have included and include others that a fictitious account would have omitted. Matthew wanted to prove that Christ was the Messias, yet in his narrative, Christ seldom uses this title of Himself. John wanted to prove that Christ was divine (20:31); and, where John himself is speaking, he clearly states Christ's divinity; but where he portrays Christ speaking, His divinity is stated only indirectly and in a way that needs explaining (*e.g.,* Jn. 10:24). Mark wanted to prove that Christ is both Messias and divine. Yet, he often narrates things which seem to contradict his thesis; *e.g.,* 10:18—Christ refuses to be called good; 13:32—Christ doesn't know the day of judgment; 15:34—Christ complains that the Father has deserted Him.

[65]

## CONCLUSION

The credibility of the Gospels is firmly established. They were written by Apostles or the disciples of Apostles; they have been preserved for us without serious change in their picture of Christ and His teachings; they claim to be history and the strongest proofs are at hand to assure us that the Evangelists knew the facts and recorded them honestly.

To reject such documents is to abandon all the principles of scientific historical study and to adopt in their place merely subjective prejudices. This becomes apparent from an investigation of the attempts made by the so-called "higher critics" to discredit the Gospels.

*Hostile Criticism of the Gospels.* Since the dawn of this so-called "age of science," the Gospels have been subjected to the most violent attacks. The fundamental prejudice underlying these attacks is the philosophy of Rationalism which rejects everything supernatural. Since the supernatural plays the chief part in the Gospels, the rationalists were compelled either to dismiss them entirely or to modify them in such a way as to exclude the supernatural.

These men reject the Gospels, not as the result of historical research into their validity but *beforehand,* because of their preconceived philosophical principle of Rationalism. Since the Gospels narrate miracles, they are condemned out of hand and the "critics" arbitrarily dream up various theories to explain them away. It is, then, to justify these preconceived theories, that the rationalists begin their historical research. The result of the research has been paradoxically, that the rationalists have added immeasurably to the evidence for the credibility of the Gospels. Some of them have seen and admitted the truth as a result of their research; others, when forced to abandon one theory, soon invent another and are consistent only in the ceaseless propagation of their dogma that the Gospels are unhistorical. Renan is one of these rationalists who unblushingly admits to this prejudiced approach: "That the Gospels are partly legend is evident, since they are full of miracles and the supernatural. Not because it has been proven to me that the Gospels are undeserving of an absolute faith in them but because they relate miracles, do I say: 'The Gospels are legends.' " (Quoted by Felder in Christ and the Critics, Vol. I, pg. 112, transl. by J. L. Stoddard, Burns, Oates and Washbourne, London, 1924).

G. Paulus (1761-1851) offered the *natural* explanation. He declared that the miracles were purely natural occurrences rendered marvelous by Oriental exaggeration. His attempts to explain the miracles in this fashion were so puerile that his theory was soon abandoned.

D. F. Strauss (1808-1874) fathered the *mythical* explanation. According to him the supernatural element in the Gospels is the outcome of myths which in the lapse of time clothed in flesh and blood the vague ideas that previously existed about the Messias. He acknowledged that his theory demanded a considerable interval between the time of Christ and the writing of the Gospels; consequently, to secure this proper interval, the Gospels must be dated from the close of the second century. The theory collapsed when even rationalistic critics surrendered this late date and approached nearer and nearer to the dates assigned by tradition for the writing of the Gospels.

Ferdinand C. Baur (1792-1860) advocated the *tendency theory*. In the early Church, he claimed, there were two opposite tendencies, one to St. Peter and the other to St. Paul; the Gospel of St. Matthew favored St. Peter while that according to St. Luke favored St. Paul, and later the other two Gospels tried to effect a reconciliation of these two opposing tendencies. Like the mythical explanation, this theory required a late date for the composition of the Gospels, and collapsed with the return of opinion to the traditional dates; besides, the Gospels show no essential differences to support the fancied tendencies.

The *evolutionary theory* was built up on the assumption that Christ, as exhibited in the Gospels, is not the real Christ as He was during His earthly career, but the ideal Christ produced by the enthusiasm of His disciples long after His death. As the actual events of His life slipped back farther and farther into the past, His disciples subjected Him to a process of idealization which ended in their acknowledging Him as the Son of God. The Gospels picture this ideal Christ or the "Christ of Faith," as distinguished from the "Christ of History," and consequently they can be accepted only as testifying to the current belief of Christians toward the end of the first century.

This theory ignores the obvious fact that the dogmas of the divinity of Christ and of His redeeming death were clearly and explicitly held long before the end of the first century; yet the Synoptists, who are supposed to be picturing the Christ of faith at the end of that century, bring out these dogmas only obscurely and, as it were, in an offhand manner or, according to many rationalistic critics, not at all. Such a process of idealization, moreover, by which a mere man, however wise and holy, was transformed into the Son of God, would have required far more time for its development than elapsed from the death of Christ to the writing of the Gospels. And, as we have seen, at the time the Evangelists were writing, many of the hearers of Christ were still living, so that it would have been impossible to foist upon the people an idealized Christ in place of the historical Christ. We have seen, too, how the Gospels give a faithful picture of the physical, political and religious life of the Jewish people at the beginning of the first century, as well as an unvarnished narrative of the false ideals and imperfections of the Apostles. Since in these matters there is fidelity to the facts without any attempt at idealization, the same fidelity should be accorded the narrative in all that concerns the character and deeds of Christ. Once more we can refer to the Apocrypha to see what the attempts at idealization really accomplished; their childish and ridiculous stories emphasize the simple honesty and divine sublimity of the Gospel narratives.

The utter lack of agreement among the rationalists themselves and the extremes to which they have gone rather than abandon the attack are perhaps the most obvious refutations of their arguments. Though they have succeeded in blinding many by their display of erudition, the position of the Gospels as truly reliable historical documents remains unshaken even when they are studied merely as human compositions.

But the Gospels are more than human writings; they are the word of God. It is this fact of their divine authorship which furnishes the subject matter of the following chapter.

## TEST QUESTIONS

1. Define—credibility, authenticity, integrity, historicity as applied to the Gospels.
2. Name fourteen early Christian writers or writings which testify to the authenticity of the Gospels.
   Identify these witnesses sufficiently to indicate the value of their testimony.
3. Outline four types of argument for proving the integrity of the Gospels.
4. Explain briefly four types of argument for the historicity of the Gospels.
5. Explain briefly four rationalistic theories attacking the credibility of the Gospels and indicate their weaknesses.
   Explain the basic attitude of the Rationalists which marks their approach as unscientific.

## Chapter IX

# INSPIRATION AND CANON
# OF THE BIBLE

⇶ ⇶ ⇶ ⇶ ⇶ ⇶ ⇶ ⇶ ⇶ ⇶ ⇶ ⇶ ⇶ ⇷ ⇷ ⇷ ⇷ ⇷ ⇷ ⇷ ⇷ ⇷ ⇷ ⇷ ⇷ ⇷

THE BIBLE is much more than a collection of historical documents. Each and every one of its books, though composed by men, was written through the inspiration of God. It is this divine inspiration that gives the Bible its unique character and sets it immeasurably above all merely human books; it is the "word of God."

St. Paul (2 Tim. 3:16) was the first to use the term "inspired" to describe this unique characteristic of the scriptures. From St. Paul, Christian writers, both Greek and Latin, took over the use of the term. Literally, the word means "breathed upon." Later on, we shall discuss the nature of this inspiration, but, for the present, it is sufficient to describe it as a positive action of some sort whereby God influenced the sacred writers to write all those things and only those things which He wished to be written in His name and given to His Church. It is because of this direct divine influence on the human authors that God is said to be the principal author of the books.

## FACT OF INSPIRATION

*The testimony of the Scriptures* to their own inspiration is incomplete; yet it is sufficiently abundant to indicate that the Christians of apostolic times accepted both the Old and New Testaments in general as the word of God.

With regard to the Old Testament, there are a few instances where individual writers testify that individual books or parts of books were written under God's direction (*cf.* Ex. 17:14; Is. 8:1; Wis. 7:15). But it is mainly the New Testament which testifies to the general inspiration of the Old. Christ, for example, refers to the words of Moses as the word of God (Mt. 22:31) and the words of David as inspired by the Holy Spirit (Mk. 12:36). Such phrases as "the Scripture says" or "it is written" occur 150 times in the New Testament; these together with such expressions as "search the Scriptures" (Jn. 5:39) or "the Scriptures cannot be broken" (Jn. 10:35) show that Christ and the Apostles attributed to the Old Testament

Scriptures an authority which belongs to God alone and imply that they are divinely inspired. And, finally, we have the explicit statement of St. Paul, which applies at least to the whole of the Old Testament, that: "Every Scripture is inspired of God" (2 Tim. 3:14-16).

The testimony is not so abundant with regard to the New Testament. Christ, of course, said nothing on the subject since the New Testament was not written during His earthly life. He did give the Apostles authority to teach infallibly, but this does not imply that their writings, even in things pertaining to faith or morals, would be inspired; still less does it mean that the writings of those who were not Apostles (Mk., Lk.) would be inspired.

St. Paul implies the general inspiration of the New Testament from the fact that he places it on the same level with the Old. He seems to link together quotations from the Old and New Testaments with the formula "the Scripture says" and to argue from them as of equal divine authority (1 Tim. 5:18): "For the Scripture says: thou shalt not muzzle the ox that treads out the grain and: the laborer is worthy of his wages" (cf. Deut. 25:4 and Luke 10:7). St. Peter classes the Epistles of St. Paul with the other scriptures; though we cannot tell how many of Paul's Epistles he refers to, still he here marks at least some of them as inspired: "And regard the long-suffering of our Lord as salvation. Just as our most dear brother Paul also, according to the wisdom given him, has written to you, as indeed he did in all his epistles, speaking in them of these things. In these epistles there are certain things difficult to understand, which the unlearned and the unstable distort, just as they do the rest of the scriptures also, to their own destruction" (2 Pet. 3:15, 16).

*Testimony of Church required.* While the Scriptures testify in a general way to their own inspiration, there is no definite statement in them as to which books are inspired or the extent to which particular books are inspired. For a complete proof of inspiration, therefore, the testimony of the Church is required. The Church, as we have seen, existed before the New Testament Scriptures and was given authority to teach the word of God until the end of time. By this authority, the Church determined the canon of the Old and New Testament and taught that they are the word of God. The necessity of turning to this teaching of the Church on this matter is thus expressed by Cardinal Wiseman: "As the inspiration of the sacred books is a divine operation not necessarily known even to the mind that is acted upon by the Holy Spirit, it necessarily follows that the testimony of God Himself is required to make men perfectly sure of its existence; but this divine testimony comes to their knowledge and is the absolute ground of their faith, only by the voice of that infallible and living Church which He has commanded us to hear." ("Doctrines and Practices of the Cath. Church" Lect. II).

There are, then, three steps which are presupposed in this argument for the inspiration of the scriptures 1] the credibility of the Gospels as historical documents; 2] the divinity of Christ established from the Gospels as historical documents; 3] the fact that the divine Christ conferred infallibility upon the Church. The first of these points has been established in the preceding chapter; the other two are presupposed for now but will be treated fully in our study of the life of Christ. At present, our interest lies in the fourth point, *i.e.,* what the Church teaches about the inspiration of the scriptures.

Adversaries of the Church are constantly asserting that this procedure is begging the question; we rely, they say, on the Gospels to establish the authority of the Church and then turn to the Church to establish the authority of the Gospels. A little reflection supplies the obvious answer to this objection; we rely on the authority of the Gospels *as historical documents* to establish the authority of the Church; and we turn to the Church to establish the Gospels, not as historical documents, but as *the inspired word of God.*

## Teaching of the Church

*First three centuries.* In the early period of Christianity the inspiration of the Scriptures was taken for granted; there were no official decisions or detailed explanations of the matter because no one questioned it. The early Fathers assert that the Scriptures were written by the Holy Spirit and they call them the "letters of God sent to men"; they explain that in composing them the human writers were the "instruments" of God. Thus, St. Justin Martyr speaks of the Holy Spirit playing upon the minds of the writers "as a musician plays upon the lyre" and Eusebius of Caesarea reports that "whoever does not regard the scriptures (of Old and New Testaments) as the word of God is to be looked upon as an unbeliever." It is only this assumption that the Scriptures are God's word which can explain why these early Fathers labored so diligently to find the exact sense of the text. The general attitude of early Christians is best summed up in the words of St. Augustine: "To the books of Scripture I have learned to pay such reverence and honor as most firmly to believe that none of their authors has committed any error in writing. If in these books I meet with anything which seems contrary to the truth, I will have no doubt that it is only the manuscript which is faulty, or the translator who has not hit the sense, or my own failure to understand." (Letter 82).

*Fourth Century Onwards.* At various times in these subsequent centuries, the inspiration of Scripture was either attacked by adversaries or misunderstood by Catholics themselves and these occasioned an official defense

and explanation of inspiration by various Popes and Councils of the Church.
The following documents give the canon of the Old and New Testaments and explain that they were written under the positive influence of God upon the writers in such a way that God is the principal author of the books:

Council of Rome 382, Denzinger 84.

Council of Hippo 393.

Council of Carthage I 397, Denzinger 92.

Council of Carthage II 419.

Council of Toledo 400.

Leo IX (letter) 1053, Denzinger 348-349.

Innocent III (letter) 1208.

Council of Lyons 1271, Denzinger 464, Ecumenical.

Council of Florence 1431, Denzinger 76, Ecumenical.

Council of Trent 1534-1549, Denzinger 783 ff., Ecumenical.

Council of Vatican 1869-1870, Denzinger 1787-99, Ecumenical.

Encyclical—Providentissimus Deus—Leo XIII—1893 Denz. 1941ff.

Encyclical—Spiritus Paraclitus—Benedict XV—1920 Denz. 2186ff.

Encyclical—Divino Afflante Spiritu—Pius XII—1943.

NOTE: All of the important decrees or definitions of Popes or Councils have been recorded in the Latin language in a book called "Enchiridion Symbolorum", edited by Henry Denzinger and John B. Umberg, Herder Co., Fribourg, Germany, 1937. These decrees are arranged in numbered paragraphs in chronological order. Hereafter, reference will be made to this book in the following manner: "Denz.", followed by the paragraph number.

The earlier of these documents are mainly concerned with the canon of the Scriptures because that was the first matter to come into dispute; the later documents treat of the nature of inspiration, each of them giving a fuller explanation of whatever points have been misunderstood or questioned since the previous explanation. Thus, in the course of centuries, the doctrine on inspiration has been developed to its present completeness. This does not mean that the Church in modern times teaches a new doctrine. The same doctrine has been taught from the beginning; substantially, it consists in the fact that God is the principal author of the inspired books. But controversy or misunderstanding has been the occasion for the Church to clarify and explain, explicitly and in detail, the implications of the doctrine that was taught by the Apostles.

Hence, while the traditional teaching of the Church may be traced back through the various Councils, such a process is not necessary for a full understanding of the teaching on inspiration. The more recent Councils and Encyclicals contain all that is found in the others plus a fuller explanation of modern questions. Accordingly, we shall turn only to these more recent documents for our explanation of the nature of inspiration.

## THE NATURE OF INSPIRATION

*God the Principal Author.* The Vatican Council says "These (books) the Church holds to be sacred and canonical, not because having been carefully composed by mere human industry they were afterwards approved by her authority, nor merely because they contain revelation without any admixture of error, but because having been written by the inspiration of the Holy Ghost, they have God for their author and have been delivered as such to the Church herself" (Denz. 1787).

It follows that each of the sacred books has two authors, God and the human writer. The relation between the two is that of principal cause and instrumental cause, God being the principal cause and man the instrumental. This may be illustrated, though very imperfectly, by the example of a man writing with a pen; the man is the principal cause of what is written, the pen is the instrumental cause; both work in harmony to form the letters and the words. But this illustration is imperfect, for in the production of an inspired book, the instrument used by God is a man, and that man acts with his human faculties of intelligence and free will.

It is, then, this positive influence of God upon the subordinate human writer that constitutes the essence of inspiration. Hence the council rejects the attempts of various theologians (Lessius, Bonfrerius, etc.) to minimize this direct, divine influence. Approval by the Church does not make the books inspired; if they were written without special divine influence on the authors, subsequent Church approval would not make God the author. Nor is inspiration the same thing as revelation; it prescinds from whether the things written down were divinely revealed to the writers or were learned from their own human experience; inspiration means that God directs the writing whether the things written are revealed or not. Finally, inspiration is not to be confused with the Church's authority to teach infallibly; infallibility might, in a particular case, involve direct influence from God or it might only mean negative preservation from error; inspiration demands a constant, positive influence on the writer, working on him "as the musician plays upon the strings of the lyre."

*The Divine Influence.* How, then, did God use man as His instrument in writing the sacred books? The explanation is given concisely by Pope Leo XIII in his encyclical *Providentissimus Deus:* "For, by supernatural power He (God) so moved and inspired them to write, He was so present to them, that the things which He ordered and those only, they first rightly understood, then willed faithfully to write down, and finally expressed in apt words and with infallible truth." (Denz. 1952).

In this explanation we may distinguish four elements:

a] The things written were those and those only, which God had ordered to be written; hence God determined the subject matter; b] The intellect of the human writer was illuminated by supernatural light so that he understood these things as matter to be written; c] His will was moved by the divine influence so that he resolved to write these things faithfully; d] In the act of writing he was assisted by God so that he selected words fitted to express these things with infallible truth.

*Action on Intellect.* The illumination of the intellect need not include revelation. The writer may already have all the needed knowledge or be able to acquire it by his own efforts. Inspiration then enables him to recognize this material as something to be written and, if need be, assists him in collecting it. But where supernatural mysteries or truths entirely unknown are to be handled, inspiration includes the revelation of these matters to the writer.

It is problematical whether the inspired authors were conscious of their own inspiration. They seem to have been conscious of some general divine assistance (*cf.* Acts 15:28; 1 Thess. 2:13; 2 Tim. 3:16); but there is no evidence that they were aware of the full extent of it. This divine influence is nothing more than a special actual grace which endured only while the books were being prepared and written; we are not directly conscious of the actual grace which accompanies all our supernatural acts; in the same way, the Evangelists may have known that God was helping them in their writing without being conscious of this divine influence in the concrete.

*Action on the Will.* The divine influence on the will is such that the writer wills to put down precisely those things which God wishes written; nothing will be written against God's will and nothing will be omitted that God wishes to have included. The writer is not deprived of his free will, but his will is so directed that it corresponds to the divine will. There is nothing to prevent this divine movement of the will from being preceded or accompanied by other influences urging the writer toward the same end; tradition says that St. Mark and St. John were asked by the disciples to write their respective Gospels; in these and similar instances, divine grace seconded that which was proposed by other motives.

*Selection of Words.* The actual composition of the book must also be controlled by God to secure not only inclusion of the matter God wishes included and the exclusion of all else but also the proper expression of the matter so that the expression itself, though perhaps not the best or the most literary, is always such as to convey the truth intended by God. At times this may amount to the conveying of the exact words if, as in the mysteries, the writer is unable to find the proper expression for himself. In general, however, inspiration simply insures such divine guidance in selecting the expressions as will prevent the choosing of erroneous or unsuitable forms.

The theory of "verbal inspiration" in the sense of mechanical dictation of the words to the writer has long since been abandoned. Such a theory is not necessary to explain that God is the author of the book; God is the principal author as long as He is solely responsible for the ideas in the book; the vocabulary which expresses these ideas admits of great variety. Nor will this dictation theory explain the differences of style and content between the various Gospels. St. Luke makes it clear that *he* determined to write his book and the contents of it were influenced by his "diligent investigation of all things"; if the Holy Spirit had suggested every word to him, then this fact-finding or word-finding process would not have been necessary.

God does not change the human nature of the inspired writers; each is intelligent and free with his own human limitations and characteristics of thought and expression. God elevates these concrete human natures to write under His direction without destroying their freedom or human qualities; He plays upon them "as the musician plays upon the lyre," but the music that results reflects the tonal qualities of each particular lyre.

## THE EXTENT OF INSPIRATION

Inspiration extends to everything written down originally by the human author. If, later on, others made mistakes in copying his book, these mistakes, of course, would not be his works and so would not be inspired.

Toward the close of the nineteenth century the attacks made by Rationalists upon the Bible induced some Catholic scholars to formulate theories restricting inspiration to certain parts of the Scriptures in order to meet more easily the objections brought forward especially from history and the natural sciences. In 1880, for example, Lenormant defended the theory that inspiration was restricted to matters of faith and morals; even in historical matters, said he, the sacred writers not only might make mistakes but in reality had often done so. His book was placed on the index. Even Cardinal Newman (1884) seemed to exclude the so-called "obiter dicta" (unimportant assertions) from inspiration.

The nineteenth-century controversy among Catholics as to the extent of inspiration was closed by Leo XIII; in Prov. Deus, Leo clarifies the teaching of the Trent and Vatican Councils when he says: "It is absolutely wrong and it is forbidden either to narrow inspiration to certain parts only of the Scripture, or to admit that the sacred writer has erred. . . . The system of those who limit divine inspiration to matters of faith and morals cannot be tolerated." (Denz. 1941).

## INERRANCY OF SCRIPTURE

Pope Leo draws the obvious conclusion which follows from the doctrine of inspiration: "It follows that those who maintain that an error is possible in any genuine passage of the sacred writings, either pervert the Catholic notion of inspiration or make God the author of such error." Hence, everything in the original books is infallibly true. Care must be taken, however, in determining just what the sacred writer says; the following points may be noted (*cf.* Encyclicals):

a] All direct assertions of Scripture are true;

b] When an inspired writer quotes the words of others with disapproval, their assertions are to be considered false (*e.g.,* in Psalm 13, we read: "The fool hath said in his heart, there is no God"; this assertion is evidently condemned by the Psalmist and so must be considered false);

c] When he explicitly quotes others with approval, their assertions are true insofar as and in the sense in which they are approved; if a lengthy quotation is given, it is true in its general tenor, though some of the minor points may be false since they need not come under the approbation given to the quotation as a whole;

d] When he explicitly quotes without approval or disapproval, then it is true merely that these assertions were made by the person or persons to whom he attributes them;

e] When he writes in a poetical manner, his work is to be judged by the rules of poetry where everything is not to be taken literally;

f] When he describes physical phenomena, he may be supposed to do so according to the way they strike the senses and not according to strictly scientific requirements; *e.g.,* the sun rises or sets or stands still in the sky.

g] When he narrates historical events, he must be supposed to give them substantially as they actually occurred.

*Copies and Translations.* Various transcriptions and translations of the Bible are said to be *equivalently* inspired in so far as they express exactly or equivalently the words of the original text. Since divine Providence has preserved the Scriptures in regard to their substance, our present-day text is substantially free from error. However, there are accidental errors which arose in the literary transmission of the text and with regard to them Pope Leo says: "It is true, no doubt, that copyists have made mistakes in the text of the Bible; this question, when it arises, should be carefully considered on its merits, and the fact not too easily admitted, but only in those passages where the proof is clear." (Provid. Deus).

*Sources of Error.* The early copies of the Scripture contain from two to four columns to a page. These columns are rudely divided; all the words are written in capital letters without accents, breathings, punctuation. It is easy to see how the eye of the copyist could wander from one line or column to another and how individual letters or whole words could be omitted or included in such wise as to corrupt the original text and give rise to variant readings in different copies.

*Correction of Error.* As early as the second and third centuries, Christian biblical scholars began to note the variations in the different copies and this corrective work has continued through the centuries. Providentially, these variations in the different copies are actually a help to discovering the true, original reading of the text. Experts in the field of textual criticism have divided the various manuscripts of the Bible into "families" and a comparison of one line of copies with another gives, in most cases, the true text. The following illustration may clarify this point:

A represents the author's original manuscript (which has been lost); B and C are copies which contain some errors (for the reasons explained above), but not the same in each. D and E will correct a few of those in B and add more of their own (but not the same in each). F and G will do likewise with regard to C.

By comparing the independent manuscripts D, E, F, and G, the true reading can often be found; all four will agree in most cases and where there are mistakes, those that occur in one will not be found in the other three. This illustration is an oversimplification of the matter for the sake of clarity; textual criticism with regard to the New Testament involves thousands of manuscripts of different periods and of varying relationships to one another (*cf.* Our Bible and the Ancient Manuscripts, Kenyon, pg. 22 ff.).

But the important point for us is that most modern critics (including non-Catholics) assert that we possess the text of the New Testament almost exactly as it left the hands of the inspired writers. The number of manuscripts of the New Testament (4,000) and of early translations from it and of quotations from it in the oldest writers of the Church is so large that it is practically certain that the true reading of every doubtful passage is preserved in some one or other of these ancient authorities.

This can be said of no other ancient book in the world. Scholars are satisfied that they possess substantially the true text of the principal Greek and Roman writers whose works have come down to us—of Sophocles, Thucydides, Aristotle and of Caesar, Horace, Ovid and Virgil. Yet our knowledge of these writings depends on a mere handful of manuscripts which were written as much as eleven centuries after the originals. The manuscripts of the New Testament are numbered by the thousands and some of them go back to within a century or century and a half of the original texts.

Dr. Hort, an eminent non-Catholic scripture scholar (Westcott and Hort), estimates the proportion of words in the New Testament about which there is some doubt at about one eighth of the whole; but by far the greater part of these consist merely of differences in word order and other unimportant variations and "the amount of what can in any sense be called substantial variation . . . can hardly form more than a thousandth part of the entire text." (The N.T. in the Original Greek, pg. 2). Each case of such doubtful or varying texts is cited in the footnotes of our present text.

Hence, as Sir Frederick Kenyon says: "The Christian can take the Bible in his hand and say without fear or hesitation that he holds in it the true word of God, handed down without essential loss from generation to generation throughout the centuries." (Our Bible and the Ancient Manuscripts, pg. 23).

## THE CANON OF SCRIPTURE

Our final question with regard to inspiration is to answer the question: Which books are inspired? The answer to this question can be known only through revelation as handed down in Apostolic tradition; the Apostles received the revelation and they and their successors handed it down to succeeding generations. Using this criterion of Apostolic tradition, the Church has decided which books are inspired and belong, therefore, to the canon of the Sacred Scriptures.

*Meaning of "Canon".* From about the fourth century, the term "Canon" has been used to signify the list or collection of the inspired books. Literally, the term "canon" means a "rule" or "measure". In the early Fathers, the doctrine handed down by the Apostles was called the "canon" (rule) of "faith". Soon the term was applied to the sacred books which contain the doctrine; hence, to call a book canonical is to declare that it belongs to the list of divinely inspired writings. By placing a book in the Canon, the Church does not make it an inspired book but simply gives official recognition to the fact that the author was inspired in writing that book.

*Protocanonical and Deuterocanonical Books.* Some of the sacred books were recognized as inspired from the beginning; these are called "protocanonical books", *i.e.*, books in the first canon. Others received this recognition only after a period of doubt concerning their inspiration; and so they are called "deuterocanonical books", *i.e.*, books in the second canon. This does not imply any higher or lower grade of divine authority; it simply calls attention to the historical fact that for a while some books were not recognized as canonical in some particular churches.

In the Old Testament the deuterocanonical parts are: Tobias, Judith, Wisdom, Ecclesiasticus, Baruch, the two books of the Machabees, and portions of Esther and Daniel found in the Greek text but not in the Hebrew (Esther 10:4-16, 24; Dan. 3:24-90; 13:1-14, 42). The chief cause for doubt concerning these books seems to have been that the early Christian writers used them either very seldom or not at all. They had been forced to act in this way because their controversies were with the Jews who rejected these books; but their attitude toward these books was later misunderstood and was taken to mean that they, too, rejected them.

The deuterocanonical books of the New Testament are: the Epistle to the Hebrews, the Epistle of St. James, the second Epistle of St. Peter, the second and third Epistles of St. John, the Epistle of St. Jude, and the Apocalypse. These books, because of their limited application in most instances, were not quoted as commonly as other books of the New Testament nor were they circulated as quickly and widely as the other books; consequently, they were slower to receive universal recognition; also, the appearance of numerous apocryphal works in the second century excited suspicion which extended in some cases to these lesser known genuine books.

*Canon Defined by the Church.* In 1546 the Council of Trent published with final authority the canon of the Church for both the Old and New Testaments (Denz. 783, 784). The list of books is the same as that of our Rheims-Douay version. This definition was occasioned by the doctrines of the Protestant Reformers who sought to exclude some of the sacred books. In 1870 the Vatican Council reaffirmed the canon of Trent (Denz. 1787).

The canon as defined by the Council of Trent was not something new; the same canon had been repeatedly recognized by the Church in official documents which go back as far as the fourth century. The most important of these pronouncements are: Council of Hippo 393, Council of Carthage 397 (Denz. 92), The letter of Pope Innocent I to Exsuperius, 405 (Denz. 96), the decree of Pope Gelasius, 495 (Denz. 162), the Council of Florence 1441 (Denz. 706).

And before the fourth century there is abundant evidence for the Apostolic tradition. As far as the Old Testament is concerned, the deuterocanonical books are contained in the Septuagint version of the Scriptures which is the text usually quoted by the Apostles and Evangelists. The canon of the New Testament can be constructed from the Muratorian Fragment (170 A.D.) and the writings of such authorities as Cyprian, Tertullian, Irenaeus and Clement of Alexandria. Not all of the deuterocanonical books are listed or quoted by these writers; different writers differ as to the number of books they use in their writings, but between them, as a group, they include all of the deuterocanonical books in their writings.

*Jewish Canon of the Old Testament.* For us, the only organization that has authority to fix the canon of Scripture is the Church. After Christ established the Church He handed over to Her the legacy of the Old Testament as well as the New. The Jewish authorities were no longer the divinely appointed custodians. Consequently, it matters little what the Jewish authorities say about the canon of the Old Testament. However, it helps in understanding the canon of the Church to understand how and why our canon differs from theirs.

Up to the first century before Christ all of the books listed by the Council of Trent were recognized as canonical by the Jews of Palestine as well as by the Greek-speaking Jews of the Dispersion. At this time, the Septuagint version, which contains all the deuterocanonical books, was recognized everywhere among the Jews. But during the first century before Christ and the first century after Christ, the Jews of Palestine eliminated the deuterocanonical books as not being in harmony with the Law of Moses and as of doubtful inspiration. The Jews of the Dispersion continued to recognize the deuterocanonical books as inspired.

Once Christianity had arisen and had accepted the complete canon, the unconverted Jews of Palestine manifested unrestrained hatred of the new religion and perhaps it was under the influence of this hatred that they excluded the deuterocanonical books from their canon. After this later fixing of the canon by the Pharisees of Palestine, the Septuagint version, which before had been held in esteem, was severely condemned and the day of its publication was declared a day of mourning.

*Protestant Canon.* Without an authoritative teaching body there can be no question of a canon in the strict sense of the term; the principle of private interpretation which lies at the heart of Protestantism does away with the recognition of an authoritative teaching body. But from the beginning of Protestantism, individuals or groups tried to set up a canon of the Bible. Luther rejected the deuterocanonical books of the Old Testament and other Protestant sects followed him in making the Protestant canon of the Old Testament identical with the present Jewish canon. As regards the New Testament, Luther rejected Hebrews, James, Jude and the Apocalypse for dogmatic reasons. Later on, these books were accepted by the Protestants and they conformed their canon of the New Testament to the Catholic canon.

But it must be remembered that many moderns who nominally belong to some Protestant denomination are Rationalists who deny altogether the divine inspiration of the Scriptures; to them, the Bible is only another human work. Hence, still less for them, can there be any question of a real canon; each critic rejects or accepts books and individual parts of books according to his own private judgment on their purely human value.

## CONCLUSION TO PART I

Thus far we have directed our efforts to an understanding of the Bible, and especially the New Testament, as a Book. Before constructing the Life of Christ from the Gospels, it is important that we have some appreciation of these books—of their value and characteristics as human documents and of their sacredness as the word of God. And now, before going on to the study of the Life of Christ, we still have an introductory or preparatory work to do. In the following chapters we shall briefly study the historical background of the Jewish nation as well as the beginning of Christ's public life. Such a study is obviously necessary to some degree if we are to understand the times in which Christ lived and of which He was a part.

## TEST QUESTIONS

1. Explain two arguments from the New Testament for the general inspiration of the Old Testament.
2. Explain how St. Paul implies the general inspiration of the New Testament.

   How does St. Peter indicate that Paul's Epistles are inspired?
3. Explain why the testimony of the Church is necessary and valid for the complete proof of the inspiration of Scripture.
4. Name three truths which are presupposed in using the testimony of the Church to prove the inspiration of Scripture.

   Explain why this process is not begging the question.
5. From what sources do we know the teaching of the Church on inspiration for the first three centuries?

   Explain why there are no formal definitions on the subject during this period.
6. Explain why, after the fourth century, the various councils and Popes began to define the canon and inspiration of Scripture.
7. Explain why the later pronouncements on inspiration contain a fuller explanation of inspiration than the earliest councils.

   Doesn't this fact show that the doctrine of the Church gradually developed into something new and different from what the Apostles taught?
8. Name two Councils and three Encyclicals which contain the fullest explanation of inspiration.
9. Explain inspiration in terms of principal and instrumental causality.
10. Explain why inspiration is not: )1 Church approval of certain books as God's word; 2) Revelation; 3) Infallibility.
11. Name and explain the four elements of inspiration as stated by Leo XIII in his encyclical.
12. Explain the extent of inspiration as stated by Pope Leo.

13. Explain the inerrancy of Scripture with reference to:—a) Quotations with approval, disapproval and with neither;
b) Physical phenomena, historical events.

14. Explain, in general, how errors arose in manuscript copies of the Scriptures and how these errors are detected and corrected to establish the original text.

15. Explain how our text of the New Testament is substantially free from any serious error.

16. Explain "Canon", "protocanonical" and "deuterocanonical" with regard to the Scriptures.

17. Explain, in general, how the Canon of Scripture has been established.

18. How does the Protestant Canon compare with the Catholic?

## SUGGESTIONS FOR READING ON PART I

1. LAUX, JOHN REV.—"Introduction to the Bible" (323 pgs.). Benziger, N. Y. 1932.
This is a very brief manual for beginners. It contains a brief outline of Ch. I, VIII, and IX of our text and then briefly treats each book of Old and New Testaments as regards Authorship, Purpose, Content.

2. STEINMULLER, JOHN E. REV.—"Companion to Scripture Studies" (3 vols., between four and five hundred pages in each vol.). Jos. Wagner Inc., N. Y. 1948
This is a good source book for College students who wish to go more deeply into any question treated in Part I of our text.

3. DOWD, WILLIAM A. REV.—"The Gospel Guide" (300 pgs.), privately printed at St. Mary of Lake Seminary, Mundelein, Ill.
This book treats all the topics of our foregoing chapters and then goes on to a brief Life of Christ constructed from the Gospels. In treating the "Introduction to the Gospels", Father Dowd is much more complete than Laux, much less than Steinmuller. A substantial portion of our Chapters VIII and IX is a synopsis (made with permission) of Father Dowd's chapters on these subjects.

4. HUBY, JOSEPH—"The Church and the Gospels" (230 pgs.), Henry Holt & Co. N. Y. 1931.
This book is a fuller treatment of our Chapters II to VII, inclusive. It treats mainly of the literary characteristics of the Four Gospels.

5. KENYON, FREDERICK (SIR), formerly curator of British Museum, "Our Bible and the Ancient Manuscripts" (256 pgs.), Eyre and Spottiswoode, London, 1948.
This is a very good history and description of the ancient manuscripts and gives a good idea of the method and value of "textual criticism."
Sir Kenyon is an Anglican and some of his side remarks are not in agreement with Catholic teaching. Permission should be obtained to read this book.

*PART TWO*

# BACKGROUND TO THE LIFE
# OF CHRIST

## Chapter X

# OUTLINE OF JEWISH HISTORY

C HRIST came into the world as the climax and fulfillment of a promise made to the human race at the Fall of Adam and repeated constantly to the Jews through two thousand years. To understand Christ or the Jews of His time it is necessary to glance briefly at the history of the Chosen People contained in the Old Testament. The student can and should fill in the outline by his personal readings from the Bible. The more he understands about the history, the law, the liturgy, the prophecies, which foretold and symbolized and prepared for the coming of the Redeemer, the more will he understand Christ and His Kingdom.

The first five books of the Old Testament are the oldest literature of the Israelites, written by Moses between 1460 and 1420 B.C. These five books are called the Pentateuch (Greek for "Five Books"). They relate the record of man's origin, his loss of union with God and the foundation of a divine plan for the reparation of that loss. The rest of the books of the Old Testament continue the story of God's plan for the redemption of the human race and culminate in the New Testament which describes the accomplishment of that plan in the coming of the Messias and the establishment of His Kingdom.

The dates given in the following historical sketch are approximate according to the most recent reckonings of scholars. No attempt will be made to enter into minute questions of chronology. It suffices for our purpose that these dates are approximately correct. We must merely keep in mind that variations will be found in different authors.

### HISTORY OF ADAM

No one knows the date of man's creation. Nor is there any detailed history of man recorded before two thousand B.C. The Book of Genesis gives no detailed history until the time of Abraham. But the book does record a few facts about the beginnings of the human race—facts essential to an understanding of God's redemptive plan.

Adam and Eve were created in a state of ineffable happiness and union with God to which their rational nature did not entitle them (Gen., ch.

[85]

1-2). This was the state of Original Justice which we study in detail in the second year of this course. Original Sin, whereby the human race lost the gifts of Original Justice, is described in the third chapter of Genesis. We also study the nature and effects of Original Sin in second year.

God immediately made it clear that the victory of Satan over the human race was not definitive or irrevocable. In the very sentence of condemnation pronounced against the first parents of mankind, God held out the promise of a restoration of what had been lost. Addressing the devil in serpent's form, God said: "I will put enmities between you and the woman, and between your seed and her seed; He shall crush your head and you shall lie in wait for his heel." (Gen. 3:15.)

Thus the redemptive plan of God was inaugurated at the time man fell from grace. The manner in which the restoration is to be brought about was not indicated at this time. Nor is anything suggested as to the time at which the restoration will take place. It is clear, however, that the plan did not begin to unfold at once. Mankind would have to sustain itself by the thought of that first promise until some future time at which God would bring about the restoration.

## ADAM TO ABRAHAM

Little is known of the human race between Adam and Abraham. It is not even clear how long man existed on earth before Abraham. The estimates of Scientists range up to a million years. The Book of Genesis is interested in tracing only one line of Adam's many descendants. It is the line through which the Promise of the Restoration is to be fulfilled.

Hence the Book of Genesis selects Seth, the Son of Adam, and lists his descendants down as far as Noah (ch. 5). After the deluge, Noah's oldest Son, Sem, is picked out and his descendants are listed down as far as Abraham, who was to be the remote ancestor and founder of the people of Israel (ch. 10-11).

The Jews are called "Semites" or "semitic" because they are descended from Sem. Other branches of Sem's descendants are also called semitic— Arabs, Babylonians, Assyrians, Aramaeans, Chanaanaeans, Phoenicians— all located in the districts now made up of Syria, Arabia, Palestine, Iraq, Iran, Armenia—known as the "Near-East" or "Middle-East."

In discussing ancient nations and peoples, Americans have to be careful not to think of them in the huge numbers to which the size of the United States and other "Great Powers" have accustomed them. In recent years Jewish authorities have computed the total number of Jews in the world at fifteen million. Since the frightful "purges" of our times, the number has been reduced to ten million. The numbers were obviously smaller in the early days. Even today the population of a nation like Austria is less than that of New York City.

## THE PATRIARCHS — ABRAHAM, ISAAC, JACOB

Now the history goes into great detail. With *Abraham* begins the long process of preparation which will culminate in the restoration to mankind of the privileges lost by Adam's sin. The probable date of Abraham's birth is 2200 B.C. His family, a branch of Sem's posterity, was settled in Ur of the Chaldees in the lower end of the Euphrates valley (Iraq).

God chooses Abraham to found a separate race which is to be especially favored (Gen. 2:1-3) and so the chosen family migrates to Chanaan (Palestine). After the migration, God makes a covenant with Abraham (Gen. 17:1-11). He and his posterity are to worship God in a special manner and God, for His part, promises to reward them with special blessings, temporal and spiritual. Abraham's name is changed from Abram (high father) to Abraham (father of the multitude). All who enter into this covenant are to bear the mark of circumcision.

The juridical effect of circumcision was to confer membership to the chosen people of God and so make its recipients sharers in the promises made to Abraham. Just as Baptism makes an individual a member of the Church of Christ, circumcision made a man a member of God's kingdom of the Old Testament. Females were affected through the males. The religious effect of circumcision was to restore the individual to God's friendship—the state of grace. Entering into a covenant with God supposes a state of friendship.

In later special revelations, God repeatedly makes similar promises to Abraham. Thus, for instance, when He tested Abraham's loyalty by commanding him to offer his beloved son, Isaac, in sacrifice. When Abraham was prepared to obey, God stopped him and said to him: "Since you have done this and have not withheld your only son, I will bless you, and will surely multiply your descendants as the stars of the heavens, and as the sands on the seashore. Your descendants shall possess the gates of their enemies. In your descendants all the nations of the earth shall be blessed, because you have obeyed me" (Gen. 22:16-18). It is clear, then, that universal salvation for all mankind is to come through this chosen people.

*Isaac* was born about 2100 B.C. and was chosen to succeed to the promises (Gen. 17:19-21). The promises are renewed to Isaac after Abraham's death (Gen. 26:1-5). Ismael, Isaac's brother, was not chosen (21:12) and consequently the sacred author dismisses him and his descendants in a short genealogy (25:122).

*Jacob* was born around 2000 B.C. Again, the promises are restricted to this one of Isaac's many sons (Gen. 28:13-14). Esau is rejected and so, after his family tree is described, he vanishes from the story (Gen. 36). The promises are renewed to Jacob (Gen. 22:16-18). His name is changed to "Israel," which means "to win God's blessing." That is why the Jews (descendants of Jacob, Israel) are called the Israelites and the nation is called Israel. It is well to note how God has changed the names of Abraham and Jacob to signify their position of leadership in His kingdom. Christ did the same thing when He changed Simon's name to Peter.

## PROMISES VAGUE

In these early revelations, God's promises are phrased in very general terms. It is clear that from this family is to come a new nation and through this nation some great blessing is to come upon mankind. These chosen souls may have tied up these promises of God with the earlier promise of a restoration to humanity of what Adam had lost. But it is not certain that they did. Looking back on these promises from the standpoint of the present, after they have been fulfilled in our Lord, it is easy to see what their full meaning was. But that full meaning may not have been evident at the time.

The main idea, however, stood out unmistakably; God was going to do something significant for all humanity through the Israelites. Attention is therefore concentrated on this family—Abraham, Isaac, Jacob, (Israel)—through which the restoration is to come.

## ENTRY INTO EGYPT 1900 B.C.

Abraham's descendants had been living in Chanaan for about three hundred years. They were herdsmen with large flocks and led an isolated life, frequently moving their camp from place to place. Jacob's descendants were just one of many tribes of Abraham, none of which had any art or literature or culture or any real national consciousness.

God's plan now was to separate the children of Israel from the other descendants of Abraham and Isaac and send them to school so that they could grow into the nation that He had promised. Egypt was the school chosen—the most cultured and one of the most powerful nations of antiquity.

One of Jacob's twelve sons, named Joseph, was sold by his brothers into slavery and was taken to Egypt (Gen. ch. 37). There he became a sort of Prime Minister (ch. 39-41). A famine broke out in Palestine and drove the family of Jacob to Egypt, where they were reunited to Joseph (ch. 43-46). The Egyptian king assigned them a section of the country in which they might live permanently (ch. 47). Thus Jacob and his family took up their residence in Egypt. The entire "family" numbered something between two and three thousand souls.

## TRIBE OF JUDA

Jacob's twelve sons were the founders of the twelve tribes of Israel. Just before his death, Jacob made it clear that God's promises did not extend to all of his children, but were restricted to his fourth son, Juda. (It is from the name "Juda" that the term "Jew" is derived.) And Jacob makes it clear for the first time that the promises refer principally to the coming of an individual King and Saviour, who will be descended from Juda.

In a prophecy which touches on the future of each of his sons, Jacob says of his fourth son:

> "Juda, your brothers shall praise you;
> Your hand shall be on the neck of your enemies;
> the sons of your father shall bow down to you.
> A lion's whelp is Juda;
> from the prey you have gone up, my son.
> He crouches and crouches as a lion;
> as a lioness, and who will disturb him?

> "The sceptre shall not depart from Juda,
> Nor the staff from between his feet,
> Until he comes to whom it belongs,
> To him shall be the obedience of nations.
> He tethers his ass to the vine;
> his ass's colt to the choicest vine.
> He washes his garment in wine,
> his robe in the blood of grapes.
> His eyes are darker than wine,
> his teeth whiter than milk." (Gen. 49:8-12)

A rich, powerful King is described in agricultural imagery to symbolize the spiritual beauty and blessings of Himself and His Kingdom. St. John, in view of this prophecy, calls Christ "the lion of the tribe of Juda." (Apoc. 5:5)

## LIBERATION FROM EGYPT

(Exodus, Leviticus, Numbers, Deuteronomy, Josue)

The Israelites lived in Egypt for three or four hundred years. They grew into a large people variously estimated at from six hundred thousand to two million souls. A subsequent Egyptian King feared them as a political threat and began to "purge" them. About 1500 B.C., God chose Moses and Aaron to free the Israelites from the Egyptians (Ex. 1-12). They were now a full-grown nation; they had experience of systematic government under the Egyptians; in addition to their knowledge of cattle raising, they had become skilled in irrigation and agriculture and in the arts and sciences of architecture and mechanics, which have made Egyptian construction and ornamentation a marvel even to modern times. They were now ready to have their own Law and their own Land.

Since it was God who delivered the Israelites from Egypt and gave them their Laws, they are in a special way His nation. Throughout their subsequent history He frequently reminds them of this. Thus, in the First Commandment—"I am the Lord, Thy God, who brought thee out of the land of Egypt, out of the house of bondage. . . ." (Ex. 20:2). Future generations would annually recall this liberation in celebrating the feast of the Pasch or Passover (Ex. 12:14, 42; 13:1-10); it was a symbol of the universal liberation from servitude to the devil, which we celebrate at Easter.

The Israelites crossed the Red Sea somewhere in the neighborhood of the Suez Canal and began their migration for forty years through the Arabian desert in the direction of Palestine. It was during this period of isolation that they were made especially conscious that they were God's people. At Mt. Sinai, God made the great Covenant with them. He gave them His law, made up of moral precepts, civic requirements for their life as a nation and ritualistic observances for their religious life (Ex. 20-23). The people in turn promised to "do all the words of the Lord which He had spoken" (Ex. 24:4).

This pact was solemnly sealed with a sacrifice. Moses sacrificed some animals to God as a sign that the people offered Him their lives. He carefully reserved some of the blood of the sacrificial victims in bowls. Then he read to the people the "Book of the Covenant" (Ex. 20:22-23:10). The people agreed to obey. Then Moses took the blood which had been consecrated to God and sprinkled the people with it (Ex. 24) as a sign that they, too, were consecrated to God, saying: "This is the blood of the Covenant which the Lord hath made with you concerning these words." This is a distant foreshadowing of the day when the Son of God would say, "This is My blood of the New Covenant," and would then seal the union by giving us His blood to drink.

The remaining books of the Pentateuch describe how God dwelt with the Israelites in the desert. He guided them as a cloud by day and as a pillar of fire by night; He was present in a special way in the Tabernacle He directed them to build; and all this was a symbol of the days when He would dwell with us in the flesh. He fed them with manna from heaven which was a symbol of the food He would give us of Himself as the Bread of Life (Jn. 6). Under His guidance the religious ritual, sacrifices and legislation were considerably developed (Leviticus, Deuteronomy, Numbers), and all these things would sustain the Jews through the centuries until the Light of the World would come and give the full revelation, a life-giving ritual and Himself as the Victim for sins to be offered in the One Sacrifice of the New Testament.

*Josue* succeeded to the leadership after Moses' death (Deut. 34). The Book of Josue records how, under his leadership, the Jews invaded and conquered Palestine (ch. 1-12) and divided up the territory among the twelve tribes of Israel (ch. 13-24). God has kept His promise; the Jews are now a distinct nation with their own Land and their own Law. It is a theocratic nation because God not only founded it but continues to appoint its rulers and guide its history.

The remaining books of the Old Testament, beginning with Judges, tell the subsequent history of the Jews. Their national life went through cycles of growth and decline. They were constantly failing in their part of the Covenant; their pagan, idolatrous neighbors influenced them to turn from the worship of the one true God and to fall from the high code of morality contained in their Law. When these things happened, God chastised them severely and always they recognized His heavy hand, repented of their fall and returned to Him. Their history is a whole series of little cycles, made up of such falls, punishments, repentance and restoration to God's favor.

God had two ways of bringing them to their senses when they sinned. The first was to give their enemies a free hand over them. The second was the series of Prophets whom God sent to rebuke them and stir them up to keep the Covenant and remember the promise of the great Prophet and Redeemer who was to come.

## THE PROPHETS OF ISRAEL

The Hebrew Prophets were men sent by God as His authentic and authoritative representatives to discharge some special mission among His chosen people. The prophet was an intermediary between God and His people. His office was not merely to foretell the future but to declare God's will whether it concerned the future or the present.

At times, the Prophets intervened to depose unworthy Kings and appoint new ones or give advice on policies which would affect the religious life of the people. They operated chiefly, however, in the strictly religious sphere. They worked constantly to keep Israel loyal to God and devoted to the practice of religion. They rebuked the people for their infidelities in scathing denunciations; they acted as religious teachers, explaining the Laws of God with authority from God.

Thus, through the instrumentality of the Prophets, God was able to keep in touch with His people and they in touch with Him. In this group of Prophets belong some of the great names of the Old Testament: Moses, Elias, Eliseus, Isaias, Jeremias, Daniel and others—men inspired by God to lead his people, direct them, declare His will to them, instruct them in the ways of God. The series of the great Prophets begins at the time of Moses (1500 B.C.) and runs for about a thousand years to Malachias (450 B.C.).

## MESSIANIC PROPHECIES

The Prophets did foretell the future although that wasn't their only function. Their main instrument in stirring up the hopes and expectations of the people was to tell them what the future Messias and His kingdom would be like. Thus they progressively describe His birth—that He would be of the tribe of Juda, a descendant of David, born of a virgin at Bethlehem. They describe His doctrine, the wondrous works of His life, His sufferings and death, His resurrection and his glorious triumph as King of God's universal kingdom.

These details about the Messias were given gradually through the centuries in a wealth of oriental imagery suited to the capacities of the people to whom they were addressed. The people were not able to interpret these prophecies as clearly as we do now, looking back after their fulfillment. As we shall see later, the people often took too literally the material images of wealth and power and glory in which the spiritual realities of the King and His Kingdom were described. But, at least, their hopes and expectations were aroused so that they looked forward to the happy time when the "Expected One" would arrive. And after Christ came, the Gospel writers were able to demonstrate to the Jewish people that all the prophecies were fulfilled in Him.

## JUDGES

Josue, great general that he was, maintained authority over the twelve tribes settled in the various districts of Chanaan. But after his death, the union of the tribes was greatly weakened. Great numbers of the Jews, tempted by the comforts of civilization that surrounded them and corrupted by intermarriage with the Chanaanites, fell away from the Law and into idolatry. As a result, even within individual tribes, government became weak and disorganized. Naturally, the union of the tribes with one another suffered even more.

From time to time individual tribal leaders were strong enough to exercise some authority over all the tribes. These leaders are called Judges and their stories are contained in the Book of Judges. But despite these periods of reform, God punished the Jews for their sins at the hands of their enemies— the Ammonites, the Medianites, the Philistines, and the Chanaanites. The Philistines (Phoenicians) were the strongest enemies of the Jews and often defeated them in battle. It was left to Samuel, the last of the Judges, to end the Philistine oppression (Kings Ch. 1-7).

## KINGS
### (1050-950 B.C. Four Books of Kings)

After some years, the people felt the need of a united kingdom and they asked the prophet Samuel to appoint a king. About the year 1050 Samuel, acting in God's name, designated the first king, Saul. He was the first of a series of three famous Kings (Saul, David, Solomon) who ruled Israel for about a hundred years. This century marked the highest point in the development of the nation. This was largely the achievement of King David (1000 B.C.). David, of the line of Juda, has always remained the great King of Israel.

David was also a poet. Under the inspiration of the Holy Spirit, he wrote more than half of the Book of Psalms. The remainder of the one hundred and fifty psalms are of later date. These songs of praise and love of God are full of prophecy about the Messias. They foretell that He is to be Prophet, Priest, King—God's own Son, who will become man, suffer, die and rise in triumph from the grave.

## COLLAPSE OF THE NATION 950-750 B.C.

About the year 950 the northern tribes rebelled against Solomon's son Roboam, and two independent kingdoms were set up—the Kingdom of Israel in the north, and the Kingdom of Juda in the south. The Kingdom of Juda was far inferior to the Kingdom of Israel in almost every respect. But it held Jerusalem, the religious center of the nation, and it was from this part of the divided kingdom that the Messias was to come, for it preserved the line of David and it was clear that the Messias would be of the line of David.

## FALL OF THE NORTHERN KINGDOM 721 B.C.

In the year 721 the Kingdom of Israel was conquered by the Assyrian Kings from the north. Samaria, the capital of the Northern Kingdom, fell to the invaders. The Israelites were deported from Samaria on a wholesale scale and absorbed into the vast Assyrian empire of their conquerors. These are the so-called Lost Tribes of Israel; and they never again regained their liberty, their land, or their national or tribal existence. They simply disappeared from history. The conquerors brought into Samaria foreign, pagan colonists (Babylonians, Assyrians, Arabs) who intermarried with the Israelites who were left and the Samaritans thus became a mixture of Jewish and Pagan blood, culture and religion.

## THE KINGDOM OF JUDA 750-168 B.C.

The Southern Kingdom endured for a century and a half after the fall of the Northern Kingdom. It was a precarious existence between two powerful enemies—Egypt on one side and Assyria on the other. It is a story of constant compromise, first with the Assyrians and then with the Egyptians. Corruption in morality and religion went with the compromise; an Assyrian altar was set up in the Temple in 732 B.C. and the Assyrian cults of Sun, Moon and Stars were introduced among the Jews.

The great prophet Isaias rose up to condemn this falling into idolatry. He was a member of the aristocracy of the Kingdom of Juda. He exercised his ministry for fifty years. Under his influence, the Jews often repented and reformed only to lapse again into infidelity. The Book of Isaias is full of prophecy concerning the Kingdom of Juda. Because of their sins, the Jews will suffer at the hands of Assyria (ch. 1-35); a century later, the Kingdom of Babylon will be God's scourge to drive them into exile (ch. 40-66). But God will eventually deliver them and from a remnant of the tribe will build up a kingdom from which the Messias will be born. All through the book, Isaias consoles and stirs up the hopes of the Jews with glorious pictures of this Messias and His Kingdom (ch. 7-12; 40-66).

## BABYLON

All that Isaias foretold came to pass. Babylon overthrew and absorbed the Assyrian Empire in 612 B.C. Juda allied itself with Egypt against the new enemy. In 586 B.C. Jerusalem was conquered by the Babylonian army. The city and the Temple were completely destroyed and all the soldiers, priests, scribes and upper classes to the number of 60,000-80,000, were carried off into captivity in Babylon. The poor classes remained behind to farm the land for the conquerors. This was the end of the sovereignty of the line of David and of national independence. From that time on, with the exception of a brief period under the Machabees, Juda was a subject nation.

Two great prophets sustained the Jews in these times of trial. Jeremias remained with the peasants who were left behind in Palestine and his lamentations tell of their hard lot and the tragedy of the Temple being destroyed. But he stirs up the hopes of the people with the prediction that after seventy years the exiles will return, the quarrel between Israel and Juda will be patched up and the Temple restored. But, greatest hope of all, he looks forward to the new age of the Messias when all men will be in the Kingdom of the chosen people and enjoy the fullness of God's truth and grace.

Ezechiel lived in the midst of the exiles in Babylon and kept them faithful to God and the Law during the period of exile. He, too, predicts the return from exile to a reunited kingdom. But it was especially his descriptions of the glorious age of the Messias which stirred the hearts of the Jews and made them willing to leave the rich money markets of the Babylonians and labor to rebuild from ruins the Kingdom of Juda.

## PERSIA

About seventy years after the destruction of the Kingdom of Juda, the Persian Empire conquered Babylon. The Persian King, Cyrus, gave the captive Jews permission to return to Palestine. These captives of the Southern Kingdom of Juda had had better fortune than their brethren of the North. They were allowed considerable freedom in Babylon and managed, especially under the influence of Ezechiel, to hold themselves together. Thus the Kingdom of Juda survived its exile more or less as a united people. In 537 B.C. about 50,000 Jews returned to Palestine, and they set up their nation pretty much as it had been before their conquest. They had rebuilt the Temple, a labor of five years, by 515 B.C. But they made no attempt to establish an independent political and civic unit. They remained as subjects of the Persian Empire, ruled by a civil governor appointed by the Persian King.

## MACEDONIA

About two hundred years later (332 B.C.), the Persian Empire was overthrown by Alexander the Great, and the little Kingdom of Juda became part of the Macedonian Empire. This Empire did not long survive the death of Alexander in 323 B.C. For twenty years his generals fought it out among themselves for mastery; individuals who had been appointed over various territories became, more or less, independent local rulers. Palestine was awarded to one of the generals, Seleucus, King of Syria to the north, but was actually taken over by another one of the generals, Ptolemy, King of Egypt to the south. For a hundred years it remained subject to Egypt, although the Syrian kings never conceded it to Egypt and several times tried to take it by force. Finally, in 198 B.C., the Syrian king, Antiochus III, defeated the Egyptians in a battle for Palestine and took over the country.

## SYRIA

The Syrian kings at once alienated the Jews by a number of blunders, and a strong anti-Syrian group began to develop among them. This group was encouraged by the fact that Syria was distracted by troubles with the rapidly growing power of Rome. In 168 B.C. Antiochus grievously offended the Jews by a number of measures which touched their religion and the climax was reached when a statue of the Greek god Zeus was set up in the Temple on the Altar of Holocausts and the Jews were ordered to sacrifice to it. The slumbering revolt broke out.

## INDEPENDENCE UNDER THE MACHABEES

The Jews rebelled under Matathias, who was succeeded by his son Judas Machabeus. Judas strengthened his hand by an alliance with Rome, and in a short time he and his two brothers, Jonathan and Simon, who succeeded him, liberated Palestine from Syrian rule. After four hundred years of subjection, the Jews were once more an independent nation.

Under the successors of the Machabees, the dominion of the Kingdom was extended north to take in parts of the area of the old northern Kingdom of David. But the various factions within the Kingdom were unceasingly in conflict with one another, and it was this that finally opened the way for a new conquest—this time by Rome.

## THE ROMAN CONQUEST

In the year 67 B.C., two brothers controlled the Kingdom, Hyrcanus as High Priest, Aristobulus as head of the army. Aristobulus forced his brother out and took over the whole nation. Hyrcanus allied himself with Arabs across the Jordan and marched on Judea. At this point the Roman army under Pompey was in Asia and Pompey took advantage of the situation. He stepped in at once, ordered the Arabs to withdraw and summoned the two brothers to appear before him at Damascus. Both gave themselves up, but the supporters of Aristobulus still held out in Jerusalem. So Pompey invaded Palestine and after a siege of three months took Jerusalem. This was the end of Jewish national independence so dearly bought a century before by the blood of the Machabees. Palestine was made a part of the Roman province of Syria, and Hyrcanus was made "Ethnarch", responsible to the Roman Governor of Syria.

The Romans, according to their custom with conquered peoples, allowed the Jews entire religious freedom and respected their national usages. A stranger nevertheless was on the sacred soil of Israel; tribute had to be paid to him; and the proud and intensely national Jew felt himself disgraced and humiliated. His deep-seated hostility toward the accursed pagan, wrought into his soul by former periods of captivity and oppression, flared up into a flame of new intensity. Revolts and riots were frequent, and their harsh suppression brought new causes of resentment.

## HEROD-ARCHELAUS

In the year 37 B.C., after about twenty-five years of Roman rule, a man named Herod, a Prince of Idumaea, a district outside of and to the south of the land of Israel, by skillful bribery got himself appointed by the Senate of Rome to be King of Palestine. In the Gospels there are two princes by the name of Herod—one who is noted at the time of our Lord's birth (Herod the Great) and another at the time of His Passion (son of Herod the Great).

In the Gospels, *Herod the Great* is known for his slaughter of the Holy Innocents. Yet that piece of barbarism could pass almost unnoticed among the rest of his crimes. He was an Idumaean by race—hence not a Jew. He was a physically magnificent man, gifted as an administrator and a soldier, but utterly irreligious and unscrupulous, ruthlessly cruel and ambitious. He obtained the position of King by bribery and force and maintained it by a regime of terror, espionage, and wanton butchery, winning the hatred of all classes of the Jews by his insufferable tyranny, his crushing taxations, his admiration for pagan culture and his slavish subservience to his Roman masters who had appointed him. For, of course, he was not an independent king, but rather what would be called today a "puppet" king. At the time of his death in the year four B.C., two years after our Lord's birth, his kingdom was divided into three parts, and each of his three sons received a part. None of them, however, was known as a "king".

*Archelaus* received a territory embracing three sections; Idumaea to the south, Judea, and Samaria. Archelaus was known as "Ethnarch" of this region, subject, of course, to Rome. The second son, *Herod Antipas,* received the territory embracing Galilee and Perea. This is the Herod who is mentioned in the Gospels as the murderer of St. John the Baptist, and as the one who was visiting Jerusalem at the time of our Lord's passion and mocked Him. The third son, *Philip,* received the territory embracing Iturea and Trachonitis, on the east side of the Jordan river and to the north. It was separated from Galilee by the Jordan river and from Perea by a boundary that was never clearly fixed. Philip does not figure anywhere in the Gospel stories.

Herod Antipas and Philip were known as "Tetrarchs". This term strictly speaking refers to one of four equal rulers who rules one quarter of a specified territory. But in the time of the Gospels it had come to be used as a general term designating any sort of a prince who was ruler of a district, and especially one who was a "puppet" ruler.

The first of the three sons, Archelaus, who inherited the territory of Judea, was truly an image of his father. When St. Joseph was bringing our Lord back from Egypt after the death of Herod the Great, he heard that Archelaus was ruling in Judea, and for that reason studiously avoided Judea and went to Galilee. The reputation of Archelaus was well known. His accession was greeted by a revolt in Jerusalem, which he suppressed after the manner of his father by killing three thousand Jews. Shortly thereafter there was a general insurrection, beginning in Jerusalem and spreading to all Galilee, where it was particularly ferocious, and the Roman army had to intervene.

At an hour's distance from Nazareth, where our Lord was living as a child of three or four years, the town of Seophoris was captured by the insurgents, then recaptured by the Romans, burnt to the ground and its inhabitants all sold into slavery. The insurrection was finally put down by Varus, the Roman Legate of the Province of Syria. As a punishment, and to discourage future rebels, he had two thousand Jews crucified. The incident left an indelible mark on Jewish memory; when our Lord bade His followers "take up the cross", the words must have flashed a vivid picture to their imaginations.

## ROMAN PROCURATORS OF JUDEA

At length the pitiless excesses of Archelaus exasperated the Jews into sending a delegation to Rome in the year 6 A.D., to petition the Emperor Augustus for his removal. The appeal was successful. Archelaus was deposed by the Emporer and banished to Gaul. His two brothers, Herod Antipas and Philip, were left undisturbed in their tetrarchies.

The territory of Archelaus, principally Judea and Samaria, was put under the control of the Imperial Legate of the Roman Province of Syria, located at Antioch, and was directly governed by a Roman "Procurator" or "lieutenant governor", who was subordinate to and responsible to the Legate of Syria.

The headquarters of the Procurator were established at Caesarea. From here he regularly went to Jerusalem to assert the Roman authority and especially to maintain order during the celebration of the great Jewish festivals, when anything might start a revolution. The fifth in a series of Procurators appointed to govern the territory of Judea under the directly Roman rule was Pontius Pilate, who was appointed in the year 26 A.D.

But the Roman administration did not bring Judea the peace it had desired. Generally speaking, there was justice at Rome; but Rome was far from Palestine, and the Procurators not seldom profited by the fact of the distance. Often they were hard, arrogant and avaricious men, who took little heed of Jewish sensitiveness. And at times they abused their power in brutal fashion. Probably Pilate was no worse than his four predecessors and he was very severely judged by Jewish writers. Thus Philo writes: "Pilate was by nature cruel, and in the hardness of his heart he stopped at nothing. During his governorship nothing was to be had in Judea except by bribery; everywhere pride and arrogance and insolence reigned; the land was given over to pillage, oppressed and outraged in every way; men were sent to death without preliminary trial; the implacable cruelty of the tyrant knew no bounds". Apart from his ignominious conduct during our Lord's trial, the Gospels casually refer to one other instance of his callous brutality, which was evidently well known, the massacre of some Galileans in the Temple at the time of offering Sacrifice (Luke 13:1).

## TEST QUESTIONS

1. How did God indicate to Adam that He would redeem the human race?

2. Explain the substance of God's covenant with Abraham. Explain two effects of circumcision.

3. Explain the circumstances under which Isaac and Jacob inherited the promises made to Abraham.

4. Explain how the Israelites happened to go to Egypt. What was God's purpose in this? How long did they stay?

5. Which of Jacob's sons inherited the Promises? What has this to do with the Messias?

6. Explain how the covenant with the Jews was made more explicit in the desert and how it was sealed.

7. Explain how the plan of a theocratic nation was fulfilled under Josue.

8. What were the main functions of the Prophets of Israel? Name five of the prominent ones. Why did they write and speak of the future Messias? What main details did the Prophets gradually reveal about the Messias in the course of the centuries?

9. How did the chosen people come to be ruled by Kings? When? What, in general, did David teach about the Messias?

10. Explain how the nation collapsed. How was it divided? How long did this division endure? Explain what happened to the larger portion.

11. Outline the history of the Kingdom of Juda from 750 to 37 B.C. Name three Prophets who were prominent in this period.

12. How did Herod the Great become ruler of Palestine? Who were his three sons and how was the kingdom divided among them?

13. How did Roman Procurators come to rule in Palestine? What provinces were subject to them?

## Chapter XI

# THE JEWISH WORLD AT THE TIME OF CHRIST

⇥⇥⇥⇥⇥⇥⇥⇥⇥⇥⇥⇥⇥⇤⇤⇤⇤⇤⇤⇤⇤⇤⇤⇤⇤⇤

THREE ASPECTS of the background of our Lord's life must be briefly sketched: 1] the political situation in Palestine; 2] the social situation, *i.e.* the various classes of people; 3] the religious situation, *i.e.,* the dominant religious ideas.

## 1. THE POLITICAL SITUATION

From what has been said in the previous chapter, we should understand the complex political setup in Palestine which St. Luke refers to at the beginning of our Lord's public life:

> ". . . in the fifteenth year of the reign of Tiberius Caesar; when Pontius Pilate was Governor of Judea; and Herod, Tetrarch of Galilee; and his brother Philip, Tetrarch of the district of Iturea and Trachonitis; and Lysanias, Tetrarch of Abilene; during the High-priesthood of Annas and Caiphas . . ." ch. 3:1.

Abilene may be disregarded. It was a pagan region and was part of Syria, rather than of Palestine proper.

Two other political units in Palestine should be mentioned. The first is the so-called "Decapolis". This is a Greek term, which means: "The Ten Cities". They were a league of Greek (not Jewish) towns, nine of them situated in Perea, on the east side of the Jordan river, and the tenth (Scythopolis) situated in Galilee. These were little communities of pagans, small pagan "islands" linked together for mutual support and protection against the Jews who lived all around them.

The second is *"Phoenicia"*. This was the district along the seacoast, northwest of the land of Israel, extending perhaps as far south as Mount Carmel. Although it had been made a part of the expanded Kingdom of Juda by the successors of "The Machabees", at the time of the Roman conquest Pompey had attached it directly to the Roman Province of Syria.

## ZEALOTS

We saw how the Jews continually chafed under Roman rule. Rebellion slumbered always and at times broke out. The party of the "Zealots",

[101]

formed among the Jews about the year 6 or 7 A.D. was a constant threat to Roman authority. The "Zealots" were fanatic nationalists; their party was professedly revolutionary, ready to use any means, even assassination, to rid the land of foreign oppression and even to punish those of the Jews who showed any tendencies towards "collaboration". Up till the year of the final great revolt in 66 A.D., they carried on a constant war, at times covertly, at times openly, against the pagan installed in Palestine. There was no peace in the land; it was in constant unrest.

From this brief sketch, at least an idea may be gathered of the general atmosphere of the age into which our Lord was born and in which He lived. It should show that He was not, as He has sometimes been falsely pictured, a white-robed dreamer, moving through scenes of bucolic peace, remote from all the harsh realities of the world. Son of God though He was, He was also son of Mary; He had the blood of His people in His veins. He was not isolated from their woes; He felt them as His own, though He saw more clearly their meaning. And His tender invitation; "Come to Me, all ye that labor and are heavily burdened, and I will give you rest", was spoken out of a heart that knew and felt the labors, the yoke, and the burdens that a century of oppression had piled on the back of the Jewish people.

## EFFECT ON JEWISH PEOPLE

1. *Zeal for Religion.* In general, the effect of political oppression, was to drive Israel back upon itself, to make it now conscious of itself as God's chosen people. In the face of the idolatrous pagan, the Jew affirmed his loyalty to the one true God of Israel; he intensified his zeal for the Law that God had given to Moses; and he cherished with new fervor the promises that God had made to His people throughout their history. Their longings for the Messias were raised to fever-pitch.

2. *Hatred of Idolators.* The Jewish reaction to the idolatrous pagan went too far. It led them to a fierce hatred of the idolators. This tendency to extremism is striking even in the Psalms. For the Hebrew it was not enough that his God should rule the heathen; He must break them with a rod of iron and smash them to pieces like so much crockery (Ps. 2:9; Ps. 108). Nor was it enough that his enemies and those of his God should be simply defeated, or even slain, but their bodies must be left unburied, the food of jackals (Ps. 62:10). And there are other examples of like ferocity (*cf.* Martindale, Towards Loving the Psalms, c. III Human Nature in the Psalms, pp. 20 ff.). The Jews separated themselves from the Gentiles absolutely; they were impure, and every contact with them was defiling. How ingrained was this state of mind may be seen even in the case of Peter in the Acts (*cf.* 10:28; 11:3); it required the persuasion of a divine vision before

Peter and the first Jewish Christians were convinced that pagans were to be admitted to the Church on an equal footing with the Jew. And all his life St. Paul had to battle against this division of Jew and Gentile (*cf.* Col. 2:11; Gal. 3:28).

3. *Pride of Race.* Similarly, the Jew's constant thought of God's alliance with Israel and His loving providence over the nation, led him to an over-weening pride of race that threatened to pervert his whole religion. And this pride of race was nourished by the very fact of Israel's humiliation under Roman and Herodian rule. Misfortune, when resented and rebelled against, always hardens the heart, makes it bitter, more prideful. So John the Baptist castigated this pride of race (Mt. 3:9-10). Our Lord Himself found in it one of His greatest obstacles; it closed the minds of His enemies against Him (read Jn. 8:31-33). And St. Paul, too, had to blast it out of his way (read Rom. 2:17-20).

4. *Formalism.* Jewish devotion and fidelity to the Law of Moses tended towards an adoration of the Law, a slavish devotion to its letter, a multipli-cation of precepts, a purely legal idea of sanctity. The result was formalism, which attacked the heart of religion, by making it simply an exterior thing, not an affair of the heart. And against this idea of religion and against those who taught it, the Pharisees, our Lord inveighed time and time again.

5. *Political Messias.* Finally, the fact that the Jews were politically oppressed contributed powerfully to the deformation of the idea of the Messias. Colored by hatred of the pagan ruler, whose yoke galled the proud Jewish neck, the Messianic hope got mingled with dreams of national inde-pendence and of revenge upon the intruder. Though it did not entirely lose its religious character, it acquired in the minds of the bulk of the people, a strong political tinge. But to that subject we shall return later.

## 2. THE SOCIAL SITUATION

Jewish society at the time that we are studying falls into two major divi-sions: the mass of the common people, and their leaders. In this latter class two parties are found, the Pharisees and the Sadducees. Though in opposition to each other, yet they made common cause against our Blessed Lord, each for its own special reasons. And together they engineered His rejection by the people, and accomplished His death. Hence it is important to know what brought them into opposition to Him.

## THE PHARISEES

About two hundred years before Christ (Machabees) two religious par-ties became prominent in Jerusalem. One, consisting mostly of the priestly aristrocracy, favored the introduction of Greek (hellenic) culture among the Jews. The other favored complete segregation from foreign alliances and customs and culture. About 130 B.C., these two parties became known, respectively, as Sadducees and Pharisees.

*Characteristics.* What distinguished the Pharisee was his devotion to the Law, to its exact knowledge and its exact observance; he was the representative of Judaism pure and simple; the man of the Law whose whole life was the Law. Pharisee means "the separated". In his fanatic zeal for the Law, the Pharisee considered all who did not observe the minutest customs of the Law, as legally unclean; the stigma was applied to liberal minded Jews as well as to the Gentiles. Hence, the Pharisees isolated themselves as completely as possible from the "unclean"; they regarded only the "legally clean" as their neighbors; this is the point of their asking our Lord to define "neighbor" (Lk. 10:29).

*Membership* to the party was preceded by a probation, and was granted if the candidate showed himself worthy by his knowledge and practice of the Law. During the reign of Herod it numbered about six thousand members, recruited from all classes, rich and poor, lay and priestly (though not many Priests were Pharisees).

*The Scribes* were the inner core of the pharisaic party. In the New Testament, they are also called the "lawyers", or the "doctors of the Law". Hence the expression "Scribes and Pharisees" does not indicate two separate and distinct groups, but rather means: "Scribes and other less important Pharisees".

*Their Power.* At the time of our Lord, the Scribes were the official defenders, interpreters and teachers of the Law. In a sense the Law belonged to them, since they transmitted it orally from memory; part of their training consisted in developing prodigious powers of memory, by a system of incessant repetition. Hence the religious authority and influence of these men were supreme; by their teaching in the synagogues they dominated and fashioned the Jewish soul; they were the masters of Israel, saluted by the title "Rabbi" (Master), and held in highest veneration, so that to have a son a Rabbi was the dream of every Jewish father. Their authority as spiritual directors derived not from any office or consecration (they were not priests) but solely from their knowledge; and they owed their knowledge to tradition, to the fact that they had been to school to a master, who had himself been taught by his master, and so on. Thus Paul, to impress a Jewish audience, speaks of himself as having been a "pupil of Gamaliel, and instructed according to the strict acceptation of the Law of our fathers" (Acts 22:3).

*The Good in Pharisaism.* In itself, a religious society, directed by theologians and jurists, and devoted to the practice of piety as prescribed by the Jewish Law, would seem to be a good thing. And as a matter of fact, it is only fair to recognize the good that the Pharisees did. For a century and a half before Christ they played a useful and at times glorious role in the history of their people.

In matters of doctrine they were the defenders of Jewish orthodoxy; by their uncompromising stand on the Law they kept Jewish religion pure and free from pagan infiltrations. They have been rightly called the "living flame of Judaism", and it is largely thanks to them that the Jewish nation survived the cataclysm of the destruction of Jerusalem. Moreover, although the Pharisees of our Lord's time were largely degenerate offspring of their illustrious ancestors, individuals among the group were good men whom our Lord welcomed as His friends and disciples, for instance, Nicodemus, Simon the Pharisee, and Joseph of Arimathea. The early Church won many converts from their ranks (Acts 15:5); the greatest of them being Saul of Tarsus. And our Lord Himself respected their knowledge, and enjoined obedience to their authority in matters relative to the Law: "The Scribes and Pharisees have sat on the chair of Moses. All things, therefore, that they command you, observe and do" (Mt. 23:2-3).

*Evil Effects of Pharisaism.* However, the point on which He joined issue with them and condemned them utterly was the religious ideal they set up, and the colossal pride that it engendered in them. He castigated their hypocritical formalism and their separatism, *i.e.* their avoidance and contempt of "common people" on the pretext of piety. It was this characteristic trait that got them the name "Pharisees", the while they preferred to call themselves "the Pious", or the "Companions". What then was this formalism and separatism, and how did it come about? To understand it, two things must be explained: 1] "the Law", and 2] the "tradition of the ancients". (*cf.* Mt. 15:2)

*The Law* (Torah) was that of Moses, the supreme legislator of the Jews, who flourished, as we have seen, about 1,500 years before Christ. It is contained in the "Pentateuch", the first five books of the Old Testament. Exodus, Leviticus and Numbers contain the body of Mosaic legislation, while Deuteronomy (The Second Law) repeats much of the legislation. This written Law contained three main types of legislation: the Moral Code; Civic Regulations; and the Ceremonial Law. The Ceremonial Law, besides regulating acts of worship such as sacrifices and the observance of the Sabbath, laid down the rules for legal defilement and purification. Since this last type of regulation is not self-explanatory, we must consider it more in detail.

*Legal Uncleanness and Purification.* These regulations are contained chiefly in Leviticus (cc. 11-15) and Numbers (c. 19). According to the Law, certain corporal functions and conditions defiled a man legally before God and excluded him temporarily from the *public* worship of God. To free oneself from this uncleanness, certain ritual cleansings were prescribed. There were various degrees of defilement and the corresponding "purifications" varied accordingly. Thus, the slightest defilement prevented a man from entering the court of the tabernacle or of the temple until the evening of that day; this defilement was removed by simply taking a bath and washing one's clothes. But defilement might also last seven or fourteen days or even longer. When it lasted at least seven days, a sacrifice had to be offered in addition to the washing.

Legal contamination is not sin. It was an uncleanness that was declared such by law; it was contracted independently of man's free will. It did not therefore put an end to man's *internal* union with God. It merely brought about a separation from the *external* worship of God in the theocratic community.

*The purpose.* God had many reasons for declaring such cases of legal contamination and laying down the conditions for purification. The particular reasons for a given case depend upon the nature of the case. But the general, basic reasons are twofold; physical hygiene and moral cleanness of heart. The Jews, a primitive people living a nomad life in tropical climate, had to be taught very strict rules of physical cleanliness if they were to survive as a nation. They also had to be lifted up above the mire of pagan immorality that surrounded them and made acutely sensitive to moral uncleanness; these legal impurities were a constant reminder of the effects of original sin and aroused a yearning in the Jews for the One who would redeem them from it all. God, as we have seen, was the Ruler of this theocratic community; He ran their department of public health as well as the religious element of their lives. And so He bound the two things together so that the one would motivate and advance the other; physical hygiene was made a part of religious practice.

*Particular Regulations.* These regulations concern the commonest things of ordinary life; food, sex, disease (leprosy) and death. An insight into the meaning and purpose of these legal prescriptions may best be obtained by perusing the regulations themselves.

Thus, in the case of *meats* (Lev. c. 11)—many of these meats are unsanitary in themselves; others, like pork, may be dangerous in a primitive, nomad society. Aside from reasons of health, the ban on certain meats would keep the Jews separated socially from the Gentiles; it would teach them obedience and temperance; and, by abstaining from animals that were physically unclean (*e.g.,* pigs), the Jews were taught to abstain from spiritual or moral filth. Legal contamination might also be contracted by touching certain types of animals (*e.g.,* flies and other disease-spreading insects). It is clear that "uncleanness" is not used in the sense of "sin"; v. 25 envisions that it might be necessary to contract contamination and v. 28 prescribes the washing after which this temporary defilement is nullified.

Cases regarding *sex* are treated in Leviticus ch. 12 and ch. 15. A woman is legally unclean after childbirth and barred from religious service for a time, after which prayers are said over her and a sacrifice offered and she is legally purified. Similarly legal uncleanness is contracted by the performance of the marital act, the issue of seed and blood, and menstruation; purification in these cases is obtained by washing. These things may be legitimate or necessary; but physical uncleanness and corruption is connected with them—even with the act of giving birth to a child. In his sex life, especially, man feels the inheritance of original sin. By making purification from this physical uncleanness a religious ceremony, the Jews were taught to think of the corruption of the soul which is the lot of human frailty and turn to God in humility to be cleansed from it.

*Disease,* of which Leprosy is an outstanding example (Lev. 13-14) and *death* (Num. ch. 19) are also the result of original sin. All the minute regulations concerning the defilement they involve were at once a precaution against the spreading of disease and at the same time a powerful reminder of the spiritual corruption which they symbolize.

*Tradition of the Ancients.* The teachers and legislators of the Jews commented on the meaning of the written Law and applied it to numberless situations of everyday life. Thus, through the centuries, there grew up a whole body of rules and regulations which was known as "the tradition of the ancients". It was handed down orally from teacher to pupil, each Scribe adding his own interpretations and applications; this tradition was not written down until the third century after Christ (Talmud). It contained much good solid doctrine which was common sense application of Mosaic Law to practical situations. The Jews maintained that this tradition started with Moses and contained prescriptions which were revealed to him and the succeeding prophets and handed on orally instead of being written down. Be that as it may, the fact is that the Scribes made their own contributions to this oral Law and claimed for their own merely human deductions the prerogative of divine authority. As we shall see immediately, these human regulations concerning piety often went to ridiculous extremes; but the Scribes imposed them on the people as the "Tradition of the Ancients" equally binding in conscience as the written Law which God revealed to Moses.

*Legal Formalism of the Pharisees.* In their zeal for "setting a hedge about the Law" (as they called it), the Scribes and Pharisees seized upon three points in particular: 1] the observance of the sabbath; 2] prescriptions concerning legal purity; 3] the payment of taxes. They multiplied the regulations endlessly and asserted that this "oral law" was of equal validity and obligation as the written Law of Moses; to violate it was a grave sin.

The purpose of the *sabbath regulations* (Exodus, Numbers) was to give the people a chance to worship God and think of the things of the soul and recreate themselves from the humdrum toil of daily life. Hence manual labor was forbidden; cooking, baking, plowing, sowing, reaping, carrying burdens, buying and selling. By a mad, fanatic, logical process which ignored the spirit and purpose of these regulations, the "lawyers" evolved such regulations as: walking on grass is a kind of threshing because the grass is bruised; catching a flea is hunting; wearing nailed shoes is carrying a burden; scattering corn on the ground to feed chickens is a kind of sowing; plucking a few grains of corn while passing though a field or eating an egg that was laid on the sabbath is reaping.

So too were the *legal contaminations and purifications* endlessly multiplied (*cf.* Mt. 7:3-5). The kinds of water that might be used in different cases was classified into at least six different types (rain water, flowing water, water in a cistern etc.) and there were solemn debates about when it was sufficient to wash the fingers or when it was necessary to wash the whole hand, the forearm etc. Many of the "traditions" were arrived at by enormously subtle hair-splitting that defeated the very object of the original law; Our Lord cites an example in Mark 7:9-13 (with relation to vows), and again in Mt. 23:16-22 (with relation to swearing). This inversion of values, "letting go the law of God to hold fast to the tradition of men", was of the essence of Pharisaism.

While this fantastic nonsense tickles our sense of humor, it is well to remember that it was evolved by men who were outstanding in intelligence and, very often, in sincerity. Nor is it something exclusively Jewish. There is a vicious tendency in fallen human nature which inclines all men to take the means of salvation and make of them the end; Puritanism and the "blue laws" and the hypocritical immorality that so often accompanies the severest, extremest views on "righteousness", are interesting parallels to the case of the Pharisees.

This legal formalism tended to make religion a purely external thing; what counted was the minute observance of an external rite or rule of conduct, and not the interior spirit. For real virtue, which is in the heart, it substituted external practices of legal piety. And for this purely external religion, this formalism, our Lord denounced the Pharisees (*cf.* Mt. 23:23-28). It led to the spirit of "covering up", the hypocrisy which He pitilessly exposed (*cf.* Lk. 12:1-3; Mk. 7:6-7). It effected a perversion of the whole "idea" of religion, that He stigmatized in startling, vivid terms (Mk. 7:17-23; Mt. 23:13-31).

*Separatism of the Pharisees.* Even more damnable in our Lord's eyes was the pride which this religious ideal wrought in the Pharisees. So many were the religious formalities that had to be observed, that ultimately it became impossible for ordinary people even to know them, much less to practice them. Hence sheer knowledge, especially of the oral law, was regarded by the Pharisees as sanctity, and ignorance of it shut one off from the favor of God: "this crowd which does not know the Law is accursed" (Jn. 7:49). To the Pharisee, ignorance was "sin" and the root of sin. For ordinary people, not knowing the Law, could not help but violate it; in fact, even if they did know it, its prescriptions were so minute and crippling in daily life that some of them had inevitably to be violated. Thus they incurred a legal impurity; they were defiled.

Consequently, since it was the first duty of the Pharisee to avoid all contact with that which was defiled, he had to "separate" himself from them. Thus were formed two sharply divided classes, the pious Pharisees, and the unclean, sinful multitude. The Pharisee had to live in proud isolation with his own companions, apart from the multitude, whom he despised as sinful and unclean. And he made this cleavage as complete as possible, lest he be contaminated: with the common people, the Pharisee could not marry, nor eat and drink, nor show any signs of charity, nor even do business (if it were avoidable). Moreover, the cleavage was on religious lines; for the "common person" might be a priest, or a person of social quality. That which made him "common" was his ignorance of the Law, which effectually disbarred him from sanctity.

This Pharisaic spirit of contemptuous separatism was held up to reprobation by our Lord in the parable of the Pharisee and the Publican, wherein it is perfectly portrayed (Lk. 18:9-14). And He had in mind to reverse the proud, disdainful judgment of the Pharisee on the "ignorant", when He blessed His Father for having willed to reveal the secret of the Kingdom to "little ones", hiding it from the "wise and prudent" (Mt. 11:25).

*Pharisees Oppose Christ.* There is scarcely a doubt that our Lord Himself was classed by the Pharisees (most of them at least) as a "common person", and despised accordingly. They were enraged that He should presume to teach, not having gone through their schools: "How does this man come by learning, since He has never studied? (Jn. 7:15). He disregarded their sacred traditions, in whose observance alone was sanctity; He violated the sabbath (Mk. 2:24; 3:26; Jn. 5:16; 9:16); He neglected ritual purifications (Mt. 15:1-2) and customary fasts (Mk. 2:18-19); worst of all, He went about making friends with sinners and publicans (Mk. 2:16); clearly then, He was defiled, His whole mode of action proved Him to be a "sinner" (Jn. 9:24).

But the reason for the Pharisees' opposition to Him was not simply His denial of their religious ideal of legal purity; rather it was the blow He struck at their influence with the people and thus at their personal pride. For it is a curious fact that their authority over the crowd was immense, in spite of the contempt they showered on it. To understand the fact, one must recall the deeply religious nature of the Jew, and the veneration for the Law that was ingrained in him. In these "men of the Law" he was taught to see sanctity; their rigid, narrow puritanism did not repel him as it does us. Hence the common people, though they were restive under the "heavy burdens" (Mt. 23:24) put upon them, reverenced the Pharisees in a completely loveless sort of way, and were obsequious in their outward signs of honor. Upon these the Pharisee insisted: "the first places at suppers and the front seats in the synagogues and greetings in the market place, and to be called by men, "Rabbi" (Mt. 23:6-7). Their pride was thus flattered; women especially were subservient to them: the charge of "devouring the houses of the widows" (Mk. 12:40) should doubtless be related to the fact, noted by Luke, that they were "fond of money" (16:14).

Consequently they were embittered and antagonized and wounded in their pride when our Lord challenged their authority over the crowd, both by His denunciation of them which worried even His disciples somewhat (cf. Mt. 15:12), and by the appeal of His gentleness and kindness, His genuinely tender sympathy with the poor and sick and sinful. His invitation: "Learn of Me, for I am meek and humble of heart" cut them cruelly by the contrast it pointed with themselves. They thrust at men an iron, impersonal Law; He offered men a personal love, and promised them what they had not found in the Law, "rest for your souls". No wonder that they said: "A new doctrine!" (Mk. 1:27).

It is understandable, then, that the Pharisees are found throughout the Gospels in irreconcilable opposition to our Blessed Lord. His most devastating charge was that recorded by St. John: "I know that you have not the love of God in you" (Jn. 5:42). He read their hearts; not true zeal for God but pride dictated their attitude. And He could not teach a proud man; for pride blinds a man to the fact that he is ignorant and needs to be taught. So He said to His disciples: "Let them alone; blind guides they are of blind men" (Mt. 15:14). But He Himself did not let them be; to the end He joined in personal conflict with them. But it is clear from the Gospel that the thing at stake was mastery over the people, who were swayed by their influence, and whom He wished to save from the disastrous "pit" (Mt. 15:14) into which their blind guides were leading them. He was Himself the master of their souls, Who would lead them into paths of light, if they would be humble enough to follow Him.

*Note.* The following texts, in which our Lord condemns the Pharisees, should be studied as a whole. In their uncompromising vehemence, they illustrate an important aspect of His character, and likewise serve to clarify somewhat the idea of "tolerance": Mt. 15:1-20 (Mk. 7:1-23); Mt. 16:6-12 (Mk. 8:13-21; Lk. 12:1); Mt. 23:1-36 (Mk. 12:38-40; Lk. 11:37-52;

Lk. 20:45-47); Lk. 16:14-15 and Lk. 18:19-14. Other texts will be seen later.

## THE SADDUCEES

These probably derived their name from "Saddoc" who was the high priest at the time of David and Solomon. At any rate, by 130 B.C. they were a party, opposed to the Pharisees, whose members came from the lay nobility and wealthy families as well as the priestly class. The party's most influential members were the High Priests, *i.e.*, the officials charged with the administration of the Temple, its services and finances, together with the representatives of the great aristocratic priestly families.

*Characteristics.* As far as religion was concerned, the Sadducees believed in God and held to the written Law of Moses but rejected the Pharisaic "tradition of the ancients". Their position was defended by their own set of scribes or "Rabbis".

But, though in their personal lives they professed devotion to the written Law, they were not generally devout or religious men. They lived for this world and were content with it, and were anxious to preserve the status quo, of which they were the chief beneficiaries. They bothered little with the coming of the Kingdom of God, and were not inspired with the Messianic hope. Their stake was in the here and now.

The Sadducees were the materialists and rationalists of their day. They undermined the meaning of the faith they professed by denying the immortality of the soul and the providence of God (Antiq. 13:5-10); the resurrection of the body and future reward or punishment (Mt. 22:23; Acts 4:1 ff.); the existence of Angels and Spirits (Acts 23:8).

*Their Power and Influence.* Through the priestly aristocracy, the Sadducees had control of the *Temple,* and profited much personally by the enormous revenues that poured into it from all Palestine and from the more than four million Jews of the "Diaspora", or "Dispersion", *i.e.*, the Jewish colonies scattered all over the Roman Empire. It is hardly doubtful that they derived a good income from the business done in the Temple precincts by the money changers and the sellers of animals for sacrifice (*cf.* Jn. 2:15).

*The Sanhedrin* was the chief instrument of power in the hands of the Sadducees. The Sanhedrin ("sitting-together") was the Grand Council, the supreme religious and judicial tribunal of the Jews. It was presided over by the high priest and composed of seventy-one members, distributed into three classes: the high priests, the "ancients" (laymen and priests of noble rank) and the scribes (*cf.* Mk. 15:1). Most, though not all, of the scribes, used by the Sanhedrin in the role of legal advisers, were Pharisees.

The jurisdiction of the Sanhedrin was extensive; they had their own police and could make arrests (Mt. 26:7; Acts 4:33; 5:17); they could inflict corporal punishment (Acts 5:40; 2 Cor. 11:24) and even the death penalty provided it was ratified by the Roman Procurator (Jn. 18:30). In Christ's time, their authority was restricted to Judea whereas previously there had been as many as seven such courts located in various parts of Palestine. But, indirectly, the Sanhedrin had authority, recognized by the Romans, over all the Jewish communities in the world; witness the deputation to John the Baptist in Transjordan (Jn. 1:19-28) and Saul's authority to arrest Jewish Christians in Damascus and bring them back to Jerusalem for trial (Acts 9:2; 22:5).

It is clear from the proportion of members that the Council was dominated by the Saducean element. Hence the Sadducees, by reason of their social rank and their influence in the Sanhedrin, played an important part in public affairs. Ambitious and anxious to preserve their authority and privileges, they were political opportunists, the liberals of the time, who made every effort to stand in well with the Romans.

Over the people and their religious and moral life, the Sadducees had little or no influence for obvious reasons. The priests did not teach, but occupied themselves solely with the liturgical services, sacrifices, etc., in the Temple. Besides, in their relations with the people they were rude and arrogant, tenacious of their privileged position, not a little avaricious, harsh and rigorous in their administration of justice (*cf.* Lk. 18:1-8).

*Sadducees Opposed to Christ.* It is easy to see why these men were instinctively hostile to Christ. As He challenged the religious ideal and the spiritual pride and hypocrisy of the Pharisees, so He appeared as a threat to the worldly privilege and the complacent materialism of the Sadducees. His violent assault on the Temple traffickers affronted them personally, and cut into their revenues. Against them, at least against their spirit, were launched His warnings against the "care of this world and the deceitfulness of riches" which are as thorns that choke the word of God (Mt. 13:22), and smother the higher aspirations of the human spirit that He saw dawning in the eyes of young men (Mk. 10:21-25). Moreover, their cherished doctrine, that this life is all, came under the axe of His censure: "You are therefore entirely wrong" (Mk. 12:27). Their cynicism concealed a profound ignorance both of the Scriptures and of the power of God: the real world of the spirit was unknown to them.

However, the decisive argument of the Sadducees against our Lord was that phrased by them at the fatal caucus meeting: "What are we doing? For this man is working many signs. If we let him alone as he is, all will believe in him, and the Romans will come and take away both our place and our nation" (Jn. 11:47-48). There is the typical Sadducee speaking; not a theologian or a jurist, debating a point of law or religious controversy (after the manner of the Pharisee), but a political realist, a man of affairs, interested in a practical course of action. To the Sadducees, generally, Jesus was primarily a political menace; and the proper solution was simply to do away with Him. It is sufficiently clear from St. John that the death of our Lord was planned and pushed through by the chief-priests, the Sadducees. It may at least be doubted whether the Pharisees as a group, if left to themselves, would have proceeded to such extreme measures. They might well have been satisfied with having Him put out of the way, as was John the Baptist. Similarly it was the Sadducees of the ruling priestly caste who took the lead in the first persecution of the Apostles (Acts 4:1).

## CONCLUSION

Here, then, we have two solid blocs of opposition arrayed against our Lord, the Pharisees and the Sadducees. And their common ground of opposition was pride: spiritual pride of intellect (the Scribes and Pharisees), worldly pride of place (the Sadducees). They were souls closed against Him. St. John puts them in a phrase: they "loved the darkness rather than the light; for their works were evil" (3:19). They could not see the light, nor see Christ as the Light, because they would not; they had no love for the light. They fled from it, lest it show them up for what they were. At that, so powerful was the "light shining in the darkness" (Jn. 1:5) that they could not shut it out of their souls completely; yet in cowardly fashion they shrank from the sacrifices to which it beckoned: "And yet even among the rulers many believed in Him; but because of the Pharisees they did not acknowledge it, lest they should be put out of the synagogue. For they loved the glory of men more than the glory of God" (Jn. 12:42-43).

## 3.  THE RELIGIOUS SITUATION

It is more difficult to describe the general religious state of the people as a whole, apart from the two factions that constituted the ruling class. The Gospels tell us that the Jewish nation, as a nation, rejected Christ as their Messias and their God. However, they also tell us that in His Public Life He did meet individuals, both men and women, with souls open to the light, who saw Him for what He was, and went over to Him.

Nathanael may stand as the type of them: "a true Israelite, in whom there is no guile", as our Lord called Him (Jn. 1:47). The Apostles were of the same stuff; straightforward, simple, hardworking men, in whom the ancient faith of Israel was strong. Even among the Scribes the type appeared, as in the one to whom our Lord said: "Thou are not far from the Kingdom of God" (Mk. 12:34). There were doubtless other families like that of

Bethany—Martha, Mary and Lazarus. And as a matter of fact, our Lord went through His life uncovering goodness in apparently unlikely places, among tax-collectors, beggars, robbers and prostitutes, as well as among priests and Scribes and Pharisees. In the parable of the Sower (Mt. 13:18-23) He Himself described the terrain on which He worked: mostly shallow, rocky, thorn-choked, but with patches of good soil here and there.

Moreover, there is one thing that can be said in general about the Jewish people as a whole: they were the "people of the Book". At the time of Christ they had as the source of all their religious and cultural life the forty-six little books of the "Old Testament", or the "Law and the Prophets", as they were called (Mt. 22:40). It was and is an incomparable literature comprising history, the Law, prophetic discourses, collections of proverbs, sacred poetry and hymnology. These books furnished the matter of formal education in the schools, and were familiar to all the people through the readings given from them in the synagogues, and the explanations added by the Scribes. So the ideas they contained were the common patrimony of the Jewish people.

Two of these ideas must be at least outlined, because of the light they throw on the course of our Lord's life; namely, the idea of God and of the Messianic hope.

## TEST QUESTIONS

1. Explain the governmental divisions of Palestine at the time of Christ.
2. Explain "Decapolis"; "Zealots".
3. Explain one good effect and four bad effects of the political situation on the people of Palestine.
4. Explain "Scribes and Pharisees" and the good and bad aspects of Pharisaism.
5. Explain what is meant by Legal Uncleanness and Purification in the Law of Moses. Where are these regulations found? What is their purpose?
6. Explain "Tradition of the Ancients".
7. Define "legal formalism" as applied to the Pharisees; give examples.
8. Explain the "Separatism" of the Pharisees.
9. Explain two general, basic reasons why the Pharisees were opposed to Christ.
10. Explain who the Sadducees were. What basic religious truths did they deny? Where was their power especially felt in public life and why?
11. Explain the "Sanhedrin"—its membership and jurisdiction.
12. Why were the Sadducees opposed to Christ?

## Chapter XII

# THE IDEA OF GOD AND THE MESSIANIC HOPE AT THE TIME OF CHRIST

## 1. THE IDEA OF GOD

JEWISH SOCIETY was very unlike our own in that there were no atheists or agnostics in it. On the contrary, the idea and the living reality of God permeated it completely. The unity of the people was based on the fundamental article of the national religion: there is one true God, Creator of the universe and its Sovereign Lord, merciful and just, who is the God of Israel by a special title, since He chose it out of all the nations of the earth, revealed to it His Name and His true cult, allied Himself with it, and wills to make it the herald of His Name to all the world.

### ONENESS OF GOD EMPHASIZED

God's revelation of Himself as the One Lord of all men and the Father of Israel was the providential preparation for the more complete revelation of His Unity. A firm faith in that was the necessary preparation for the further revelation made in Christ, that the One God is Three Persons, a Trinity in Unity.

So for nineteen hundred years, from Abraham to Christ, God kept the pure flame of monotheism burning in the midst of His chosen people. To speak humanly, but with all reverence, it was a difficult task for Him. Often the smothering pressure of their idolatrous pagan environment threatened to extinguish the flame. But always God kept it nourished by the burning words of the great prophets whom He raised up in times of danger. So God's Providence preserved the chosen race from apostasy, triumphing marvelously over the instability of the human instrument with which He had allied Himself for the working out of His plan.

*Prayers of Jews.* Twice a day, in the morning before he broke his fast, and again in the evening, the male Israelite was obliged to profess his faith in the one true God of Israel, and to pledge himself to His love and service above all else, by reciting the Shema (literally, "Hear!"), a prayer composed of three texts from the Scripture (Deut. 6:4-9; 11:13-21; Numbers 15:37-41). And in reciting its opening phrase: "Hear, O Israel, the Lord our God is ONE Lord", the Jews stressed forcibly the word "one". The rest of the prayer evoked in the Jewish soul the memory of the promises made to Abraham, Isaac and Jacob (Deut. 11:21) and the deliverance from Egypt and the covenant made with Moses on Mt. Sinai (Num. 15:39-41). It evoked too the thought of God's extraordinary providence over His people through their history. Hence that prayer was to the Jew what the sign of the Cross is to the Christian: the starting point of his religious life, the summary of his faith.

*Psalms.* It would be interesting to study the loftiness, the purity, the grandeur of the idea of God that is unrolled in the Old Testament, especially in the great prophets. However, let it be sufficient here to give one illustration of the power that the idea had, when grasped in all its majesty and tenderness. It summoned from the heart of the Psalmist what have been rightly called the most beautiful words of the Old Testament:

> "I am continually with Thee, Thou hast held me by my right hand; with Thy counsel wilt Thou guide me, and afterwards to glory take me. Whom have I in heaven but Thee? and besides Thee I have no other delight on earth.
>
> My flesh and my heart fail, but God is the strength of my heart and my portion forever.
>
> For behold, they that are far from Thee shall perish; Thou hast destroyed everyone who put idols in Thy place.
>
> But my good is to draw near unto God; I have made the Lord God my refuge, that I may tell of all Thy works" (Ps. 72:23-28).

In that prayer there comes to expression the ancient faith of Israel in all its purity, filled with awe and gladness at the thought of God. And the soul that prayed thus would be right on the threshold of Christian faith.

## CHRIST REVEALS TRINITY

The Blessed Trinity was not explicitly revealed in the Old Testament. There is an "economy" in God's teaching; not all at once does He give His secrets to man. Time is required; man, precisely because he is man, must be gradually educated.

"When the fullness of time came, God sent His Son . . ." (Gal. 4:4-5); Christ revealed for the first time that God is Father, Son and Holy Spirit. Moreover, Christ Himself, a Man, is the Son of God equal to the Father. It was an amazing revelation.

*Disbelief of Jews.* We can sympathize with the difficulty the Jews found in accepting the "new and amazing doctrine" (*cf.* Mk. 1:27); nevertheless it was not something unprepared for. He points out that He is somehow in their Sacred Books; that the whole of their history somehow leads to Him. And His miracles gave them overwhelming evidence that He is at least what they themselves so often called Him: a "great prophet from God". They should have believed Him.

But, as we shall see, He dashed their dreams of a political national, material Kingdom. So, they didn't want to believe Him. And to cover up this bad will, they turned to the Old Testament revelation and used it against Him. No longer are they little children yielding the right hand to their Father for guidance. They now become arbiters of who and what God is; they focus their minds on the Oneness of God that had been revealed to them and refuse to consider the new revelation of the Trinity. They accused the Father's Christ of blasphemy and eventually they put Him to death on the charge.

*Christ's answer* is an appeal to the Scriptures which they used to justify themselves: "You search the Scriptures", He said in one of His great debates in Jerusalem, "because in them you think to have life everlasting. And it is they that bear witness to Me; yet you are not willing to come to Me that you may have life . . . Do not think that I shall accuse you to the Father. There is one who accuses you, Moses, in whom you hope. For if you believed Moses you would believe me also, for he wrote of me. But if you do not believe his writings, how will you believe My words?" (Jn. 5:39-40, 45-47).

If they really understood and sincerely lived their own faith, their hearts would have been open to His newness. In the light of their own Sacred Books they should have been ready to see that He was their Messias, God Himself come to save them.

Why did they not see? The reasons are complex. But we have noted the most important one: narrow national ideas and fanatical national pride had succeeded in deforming the Messianic Hope in the minds of the majority. Christ did not at all fit with the idea of the Messias that they had made for themselves, nor did He preach the kind of "Reign of God" that they had deluded themselves into expecting. So they would have none of Him. To explain this, we must examine the Jewish Messianic hope as it existed at the time of our Lord.

## 2. THE MESSIANIC HOPE

By the Messianic hope of the Jews we mean the whole set of ideas and aspirations with regard to the coming of a new era in human history, planned and promised by God, and to be inaugurated at His good pleasure, during which He would newly assert and realize His dominion over men, through the instrumentality of His "anointed one", the Messias, who would be the visible head of the Kingdom of God.

The Messianic hope belonged to the very soul of Jewish religion. It was organically linked with their belief in one God, who had chosen Israel as His own people. And it was based upon the promises that God had given to His chosen people often in their history: promises made to Abraham of a "blessing" to come upon them and through them upon all the nations of the earth, promises of a "salvation", a rescue and a redemption to be accomplished by God through His Messias, promises, in a word, of a new Reign of God that would display His mercy and justice.

*Expectation.* It is clear from the Gospels that at the time of Christ the idea of the "Kingdom or Reign of God" was a terrifically exciting one, and that expectations of its proximate coming ran high. For instance, the Baptist created a country-wide commotion by his use of the phrase. Mark tells us that "all of the country of Judea went out to him, and all the inhabitants of Jerusalem" (1:5) when they heard his electrifying words: "the kingdom of heaven is at hand" (Mt. 3:2). And when our Lord Himself began His career by an identical proclamation (Mt. 4:17; Mk. 1:15), excitement rose to new heights.

Similarly, the idea of the "one who is to come", as the Messias was popularly called, had the minds of all in a state of straining anticipation. Many thought they had found him in John the Baptist (Lk. 3:15); in fact, even the officials of Jerusalem thought it necessary to "investigate" (Jn. 1:19 ff.). Again, after his first meeting with our Lord, Andrew flashed the glad news to his brother Simon: "We have found the Messias!" (Jn. 1:41). And to Philip also came the same thrilling thought (Jn. 1:45). Even the Samaritan woman is possessed of the idea (Jn. 4:25). And the general sense of expectancy transpires in the anxious question put to our Lord by the disciples of the Baptist: "Art Thou He who is to come, or shall we look for another?" (Mt. 11:3).

Consequently there is no doubt about the fact that (in addition to the political unrest) a religious ferment was in progress: the people were quite on edge for the coming of the Messias and the Kingdom of God. But the question is: just what were they expecting? What did they suppose the Kingdom of God would be like? How would it be inaugurated? And what picture of the Messias did they have in mind? Who would he be? What would he do? How would they recognize Him?

These are difficult historical questions, to which, however, our answers can be only brief, and adequate simply for our point, namely, an understanding of the reception accorded to our Lord. The fact is that there was a great variety of ideas concerning the Messias and the Kingdom of God. But they fall pretty well into two classes. Hence we shall consider: A) the ideas of the people (the multitude) formed and encouraged under the guidance of the scribes and Pharisees: and B) the Messianic ideas of these whom the New Testament calls the "just", the true Israelites, faithful to the highest spiritual traditions of their people.

## 2. A. THE POPULAR MESSIANIC HOPE

The Gospels, as well as other contemporary documents, make it clear that the popular Messianic hope was strongly political, narrowly national, and hopelessly material. In the mind of the average Jew, the Kingdom of God was to be emphatically a Kingdom for Israel. And two aspects of it in particular caught the popular imagination: first, with the coming of the Kingdom, the hated Roman yoke would be thrown off and world-power transferred into Jewish hands, and secondly, a "Golden Age" of material prosperity would dawn. In essential outline popular ideas ran as follows.

*National, Political Kingdom.* The just God, faithful to His ancient promises, will intervene to assure the triumph of His cause, which was Israel's cause. He will at last wreak vengeance on His enemies, who were their enemies, and whom He had permitted for a time to lord it over them, as a punishment for their infidelities. "The day of the Lord" will finally come: He will reign, in the reign of Israel.

"The day of the Lord" will be a day of judgment. Those who have oppressed His people will be called to account, and punished in their turn. The roles of oppressor and oppressed will be reversed. All the scattered people of Israel will be gathered together again in Palestine, to form a new nation. The kingdom of David will be restored with a new splendor, and its frontiers will be the ends of the earth. Jerusalem, rebuilt on a more lavish scale, will be the center of the world. There the Messias-King, a descendant of David, will be enthroned, and from it he will stretch forth his sceptre. From it, too, the worship of the one true God will be proclaimed and the observance of the Mosaic Law will be imposed. Thus Israel will have its revenge. The humiliation of the chosen people will be at an end. Kings will bend the knee before them, and pay tribute to them. And the proud pagan will be a footstool for their feet.

*Material Prosperity.* This revolutionary change in the order of the world will be ushered in by a catastrophe of some kind, a terrifying manifestation of God's power. Though Israel, too, will be purified by His justice, nevertheless, the vials of His wrath will be poured out fully only on the pagans. And thereafter will follow the Golden Age, wherein Israel will enjoy the fruits of God's victory.

There will be a new heaven and a new earth, flowing with all manner of sensuous delights. Sickness and distress will be banished, and wonderful physical beauty and vitality will be given to the children of Abraham. Fabulous riches will be the portion of every pious Jew. Wild beasts will come and serve them. And the earth itself will minister to their pleasure with fantastic fertility: no bunch of grapes will yield less than thirty casks of wine, barley will attain the height of palm trees and scatter meal already ground, and there will be no end of pigeons to roast. Life will be as some gigantic, unending feast, whose viands will never cloy. And to this feast no Gentile will be admitted. For them there will be no room in the Messianic Kingdom, and they will be allowed to come to Palestine only to bring gifts to the children of Israel, and to stare enviously at their grandeur and happiness.

*Coming of Messias.* To bring about Israel's triumph in an earthly paradise, the Messias will come as God's instrument. Two traits will characterize His coming; it will be sudden: no one shall know whence He comes, perhaps it will be out of the sea. And it will be spectacular; He will appear on the roof of the Temple, clad in dazzling light. By that light He will be recognized, as the coming of the Kingdom will also be discerned by celestial phenomena, awe-inspiring signs in the heavens, that He will work to announce its coming.

*Work of the Messias.* The Messias will be a prophet, in fact, The Prophet. But the *religious* significance and purpose of His work is dwarfed because of the Pharisees' unconscionable exaggeration of the Law. To them, the Law (including the "tradition of the ancients") was so perfect that nothing better could be given to man, even by God Himself. God had spoken to Moses; He would not speak again; He had nothing more to say. In the Law, religion had reached its highest, unimprovable form. Given, then, this absolute perfection of the Law, the religious mission of the Messias naturally had to be restricted to one purpose; at His coming He would encourage and bless and perpetuate obedience to the Law, by taking the full burden of it on Himself and observing its highest requirements, by instructing others in its observance, and notably by imposing the yoke of it upon the pagan. There would be no religious change, no new Reign of God upon the heart of man, no rescuing of man from sin or giving him the gift of sanctity; for the Jewish nation had already been rescued and redeemed by its acceptance of the Law, and sanctity was already within the grasp of all. Anyone could be the artisan of his own sanctity; the technique was at hand, namely, the perfect observance of the Law. The Messias, then, could be nothing more than the Pharisaic Scribe par excellence, and, in this sense, the Prophet of the Law.

Consequently, His real important task would not be religious but *political.* The primary advantage of His coming would be in the fact that He would free Israel from foreign political domination, in order that it might the more completely give itself to the observance of the Law. Primarily He will come as a Warrior-King, greater than Saul or David or the Machabees. And His triumph will be instant, miraculous, complete. He will destroy the pagan enemies of His people, or drive them from the land, simply with the breath of His mouth, by a single word of judgment spoken against them. He will proclaim the world-empire of Israel.

*The Person of the Messias.* This distorted idea of the work of the Messias had its counterpart in a stunted and arbitrary idea of His person. The Scribes decreed absolutely that He would be merely another great Rabbi, in fact the greatest of Rabbis, but with purely a human greatness, a man divinely gifted, but no more than a man. Similarly they made Him a great King, of the line of David, but no more divine than David was. All the strong tendencies of the Old Testament to invest the Messias with a dignity properly divine, all the strong suggestions that, even though a man, he would be somehow equal to God, were not only not understood (which might have been pardonable, since the prophecies were obscure, and needed the light of Christ's own coming to illuminate their profoundest meaning), but rigidly excluded and systematically gainsaid (which was not pardonable, since the Jews should at least have kept their minds open to receive fuller light on the full character of Him Who was to come).

And since the career of the Messias-King, as they conceived it, would be wholly one of glory and triumph, they looked to Him to end suffering, certainly not to submit Himself to it. Consequently, the idea of a Messias-Priest, and a "suffering Messias", who would offer His sufferings and make the sacrifice of His own life in atonement for the sins of His people—this idea was completely ignored by the scribes. Though the idea was to be found clearly enough in Scripture, chiefly in the prophecies of Isaias (*cf.* ch. 53), they never understood it, nor interpreted it to the people. Nor is this fact strange. In the political concept of the King and the material concept of the Kingdom that they had made for themselves, the idea of a "suffering Messias" would have made no sense. So it was simply left out.

These are the essential traits of the picture that rose to the minds of the Galilean and Judean multitudes, in greater or less detail, at the magic words, "Kingdom of God" and "Messias". Glimpses of them we shall find in the Gospels. Obviously, the popular Messianic hope was at bottom religious, since it rested on an ingrained sense of the justice of God and appealed to His ancient prophecies. But obviously, too, it had been corrupted by nationalistic pride, by worldly cupidity, by the carnal-mindedness that had always been a deforming influence on the God-given religion of this primitive Semitic people, highly imaginative and passionately emotional as they were.

## PROPHECY AND THE FALSE MESSIANIC HOPE

The idea of the Messianic kingdom as an earthly Paradise seems to have arisen from the habit (encouraged by the Scribes) of interpreting Scriptural prophecies in a slavishly literal and material sense, neglecting their inner, spiritual meaning. In many of the ancient prophecies, the joys of the Messianic Kingdom are indeed described in a luxuriant imagery; all the sheer details given above are to be found in them: the material delights, the fertility of the earth etc. One might read, for instance, the poems in the last chapters of Isaias (*cc.* 60-65). All these descriptions were taken literally by the Rabbis, whereas, as a matter of fact, they are to be understood metaphorically.

The aim of the prophets (of Isaias, for example, in the chapters cited) was to arouse in the people an ardent longing for the Messianic "deliverance". Moreover, they were speaking to simple-minded, primitive people, Orientals who delighted in hyperbole. And it is characteristic of simple people (even today) that, as St. Thomas Aquinas says, "they have scarcely an inkling of anything beyond what they can reach with the senses". Naturally, therefore, the prophets described the spiritual blessings of the Messianic Kingdom in material imagery. But the Rabbis stuck at the letter, and failed to reach the inner meaning. Similarly, in the prophetic descriptions of the glory of the Messias-King, His conquest of His enemies, His exaltation of Israel, His sway over the Gentiles, etc. (all of which had a spiritual meaning) they saw only the national, this-worldly, kingdom of their own narrow hopes.

One should read the Prophets to understand this point which is so necessary for an appreciation of Christ's, and later Paul's, conflict with the Jews. Even now, in the light of Christ's fulfillment, the language of the Prophets is not easy to interpret; aside from their use of sensible symbols to picture spiritual reality, they often use the same terms to mean different realities and pass from one meaning to another and back again at will; thus, for example, the word "Jerusalem" or "Israel" or "Sion" may at one time designate the earthly city or nation in Palestine, at another the Messianic Kingdom of the Church Militant, at another the Heavenly City or Church Triumphant, the dwelling place of the Blessed. Since we cannot now make a formal study of the Prophets, perhaps a few examples will help to show the student both the spiritual sense in which they should be interpreted and how easily they were misinterpreted by a proud and earthly minded people.

*Psalm 109* is a direct prophecy of the Messias which illustrates how He and His kingdom are depicted in *military terms*.

> 1. The Lord said to my Lord: "Sit at My right hand, until I make Thy enemies Thy footstool.

2. The Lord will extend the sceptre of Thy power from Sion: Rule in the midst of Thy enemies!

3. With Thee is sovereignty in the splendor of holiness on the day of Thy birth: before the morning star, like the dew, I have begotten Thee.

David, as our Lord points out (Mt. 22:43-45), calls the Messias his "Lord"; hence the Messias is superior to Israel's greatest king. Moreover, his enthronement at God's right hand suggests a divine dignity, equality with God. A complete victory over his foes is promised him by the power of God. These "foes" include the Jews themselves in so far as they are allied with the devil and do his work; but they interpreted it to mean the Gentiles.

4. The Lord has sworn and he will not repent: "Thou art a priest forever according to the order of Melchisedech".

The priesthood of the Messias is here asserted: like Melchisedech (Gen. 14:18), he is both Priest and King.

5. The Lord is at thy right hand; He will destroy kings in the day of His wrath.

6. He will judge nations, He will pile corpses high; He will crush heads all over the earth.

The total victory of the Messias on the day of God's judgment is described in typically drastic Oriental terms. These are poetic metaphors indicating the utter completeness of the Messias' victory over evil. The Jews were predisposed to interpret the metaphor literally and apply it to an earthly warfare and victory over the Gentiles.

7. From the torrent He will drink on the way, therefore He will lift up His head.

This final verse is best taken as spoken by God the Father about Christ, promising again (as in verse 1) the headlifting exhilaration of victory after the struggle with evil, in which His Messias has shared equally with the commonest soldier in the ranks. "From the torrent etc." is a metaphorical way of saying that the King himself shall share the heat of the battle, and have none but the common, chance refreshment that his soldiers have. Hence the verse hints mysteriously at the sufferings of the Messias.

*Chapter XI of Isaias* describes the Messias as the King of *Peace.* "The wolf shall dwell with the lamb, and the leopard shall lie down with the kid"; these and all the other images, describe how weak and strong, good and evil, men will be united in a kingdom of faith and justice and peace. But the Jews interpreted it literally to mean that Palestine was to be another garden of Eden where wild animals would be tame in the service of the Jews.

*In Chapter XXXV, Isaias* describes the rich spiritual fruits that will come with the Redeemer: "Then shall the eyes of the blind be opened, and the ears of the deaf shall be unstopped. Then shall the lame man leap as a heart, and the tongue of the dumb shall be free". These words bring to mind the miracles of Christ which were symbols of the new spiritual life that He was to give to men's souls.

[123]

"And that which was dry land, shall become a pool, and the thirsty land springs of water. In the dens where dragons dwelt before, shall rise up the verdure of the reed and bulrush" (35:7),

means something more than the absence of all physical evil in an era of material prosperity.

The Jews constantly mistook the heavenly "Sion" and "Jerusalem", with all the descriptions of bliss, as referring to the earthy city whose citizens they were by right of birth. They were the "redeemed" and the "glorified" because they were descended from Abraham and possessed the Law of Moses. Therefore, they appropriated to themselves and to their earthly city the Prophet's descriptions of the rewards of the just: "And the redeemed of the Lord shall return, and shall come into Sion with praise, and everlasting joy shall be upon their heads; they shall obtain joy and gladness, and sorrow and mourning shall flee away." (35:10).

*Chapter LXV* is perhaps the best example in Isaias of prophecy that these people, blinded by pride of race, perverted to the opposite of what it meant. Isaias is speaking of the vocation of the Gentiles to supplant the Jews in the Kingdom of God when he pictures God as saying:

"They have sought Me that before asked not for Me, they have found Me that sought Me not. I said: Behold Me, behold Me, to a nation that did not call upon My name" (v. 1-2).

The Jews applied these words to themselves because, despite repeated infidelities, they had always been the chosen people of God; they could not envision a future infidelity that would change their status; they had the blood of Abraham in their veins and that was enough, no matter what they did or did not do, to insure for them the promises made to Abraham.

Consequently, they applied to the Gentiles the condemnation that God meant for them:

"I have spread forth My hands all the day to an unbelieving people, who walk in a way that is not good after their own thoughts, a people that continually provoke Me after their own thoughts, a people that continually provoke Me to anger before My face . . ." (v. 2-3).

They are the ones who said to God: "Depart from me, come not near me, because thou art unclean" (v. 5), when they called Christ a sinner and invoked His blood upon their heads. They were exulting in their own condemnation when they gleefully applied to the Gentiles, the curse that was to come upon themselves: "These shall be smoke in my anger, a fire burning all the day" (v. 5).

Once the prideful mistake was made there was no limit to the misinterpretation. Thus, when the prophet describes the *Church Militant* he says:

"Behold My servants shall eat, and you shall be hungry, My servants shall drink and you shall be thirsty. Behold My servants shall rejoice and you shall be confounded; behold My servants shall praise for joyfulness of heart and you shall cry for sorrow of heart and you shall howl for grief of spirit" (v. 13-14).

The "servants" are those who believe in the King with a sincere heart; the "you" are they who, like the Jews as a race, "have forsaken the Lord" (v. 11); the "eating and drinking" or "hungering and thirsting" refer primarily to the flesh and blood of Christ and all the spiritual refreshment that He implies. What calamity resulted from the proud self-righteousness which led the Jews to mistake the identity of "You"!

Finally the Prophet passes on to a description of the *Church Triumphant* —the eternal glory of the heavenly Jerusalem.

> "For behold I create new heavens and a new earth; and the former things shall not be in remembrance, and they shall not come upon the heart. But you shall be glad and rejoice forever in these things which I create. For behold I create Jerusalem a rejoicing, and the people thereof joy. And I will rejoice in Jerusalem, and joy in My people, and the voice of weeping shall no more be heard in her, nor the voice of crying" (v. 17-19). "Rejoice with Jerusalem and be glad with her, all you that love her; rejoice for joy with her all you that mourn for her; that you may suck and be filled with the breasts of her glory." (66:10-11).

How easily such descriptions were read by earthly minds in an earthly sense!

*In Chapter LIII, Isaias* foretells the terrible price the Messias was to pay for this new life and strength and glorious victory of His Kingdom, the Church:

> "There is no beauty in Him, nor comeliness, and we have seen Him and there is no sightliness that we should be desirous of Him; despised and the most abject of men, a man of sorrows, and acquainted with infirmity; and His look is as it were hidden and despised, whereupon we esteemed Him not. Surely He hath borne our infirmities and carried our sorrows; and we have thought Him as it were a leper, and as one struck by God and afflicted. But He was wounded for our iniquities, He was bruised for our sins. The chastisement of our peace was upon Him, and by His bruises we are healed. All we like sheep have gone astray, and everyone hath turned aside into his own way; and the Lord hath laid on Him the iniquity of us all" (v. 2-6).

Once the dreams of material glory had been formed and confirmed, there was no room for such a picture of the Messias. It was an enigma that had to be ignored.

## 2. B. Messianic Ideas of the Just

It would seem that part of Luke's purpose in writing the history of the Divine Infancy was to indicate the character of the Messianic hope as it existed in the hearts of Israel's elite. We can gather it with sufficient clarity for our purposes from the three great "canticles of the Incarnation", taken together; a) the Magnificat of Mary; b) the Benedictus of Zachary; c) the Nunc dimittis of Simeon.

## THE MAGNIFICAT (Lk. 1:46-55).

46. *And Mary said,*

47.  *"My soul magnifies the Lord,*
      *and my spirit rejoices in God my Savior;*

48.  *Because He has regarded the lowliness of His handmaid;*
      *for, behold, henceforth all generations shall call Me blessed;*

49.  *Because He who is mighty has done great things for me,*
      *and holy is His name;*

50.  *And His mercy is from generation to generation*
      *on those who fear Him.*

51.  *He has shown might with His arm,*
      *He has scattered the proud in the conceit of their heart.*

52.  *He has put down the mighty from their thrones,*
      *and has exalted the lowly.*

53.  *He has filled the hungry with good things,*
      *and the rich He has sent away empty.*

54.  *He has given help to Israel, His servant,*
      *mindful of His mercy—*

55.  *Even as He spoke to our fathers—*
      *to Abraham and his posterity forever."*

Responding to Elizabeth's reverent blessing, our Blessed Mother utters her beautiful song of praise and thanksgiving to God for what He had done for her and through her for Israel and all the world. True, she does not name the "Kingdom of God" or the "Messias", but the idea she had of both breaks forth. The accent of the whole is that of joy; joy shall be the spirit of the Kingdom. For the work of God the Savior has begun. Faithful to His promises to Abraham, His design of mercy is now to be accomplished; He brings salvation to Israel. Not to all Israel, but to that Israel which is His "servant" (v. 54). Nor only to Israel, but to all those who will be His servants, who will believe and obey Him, as did Abraham (v. 50). His Kingdom, then, is not a national kingdom just for Israel. Nor is it to pass away: He has come "forever", His Kingdom is definitive (v. 55).

And how has this Reign of God been introduced? In all quietness. A Child has been conceived in His Mother's womb, and lies there hiddenly. From a Mother who is of no station in this world, the King comes. And the lowliness of the Mother stamps the character of His Kingship: He will not show Himself in the stiff dignity or glittering pomp of earthly royalty. Yet He is a King for all that, to whom the Lord God has given the throne of David, that He might reign over the house of Jacob forever, with no end of His reigning (Lk. 1:32-33). And so real is His Kingship that the splendor of it shall invest His lowly Mother in its shining, make her the Woman blessed among all women, her name on the tongue of every age (v. 48).

Thus the new era in history had already begun, by a hidden act of power on the part of God. His was the initiative: He wills to show Himself mighty, merciful, holy, loving. The era will be one of triumph over God's enemies, which are in the heart of man: pride, greed for power, self-satisfaction in the possession of the riches of earth. It will be a time, not of social revolution, but of interior, moral renovation; and its blessings are for the "lowly" and the "hungry", those who look to God for salvation and desire His justice (v. 50-53).

Thus Mary's idea of the Kingdom and the King shines through her rapturous song: it is a spiritual Kingdom, a universal Kingdom, a Reign of God over the heart of man, from which sin will be cast out, and to which a new Spirit will be given, the Spirit of God's own holiness. And the King is her Son, indeed, but more than that He is the Son, in whom God's promises to Israel were fulfilled, and in whom His Kingdom "came". Later, in the shadowy evening of His life, the Son would echo the theme of the song His Mother sang at its dawn, when He said to Pilate: "My Kingdom is not of this world" (Jn. 18:36).

## THE BENEDICTUS (Lk. 1:68-80).

68. *"Blessed be the Lord, the God of Israel,*
   *because He has visited and wrought redemption for His people,*

69. *And has raised up a horn of salvation for us,*
   *in the house of David His servant*

70. *As He promised through the mouth of His holy ones,*
   *the prophets from of old;*

71. *Salvation from our enemies,*
   *and from the hand of all who hate us,*

72. *To show mercy to our forefathers*
   *and to be mindful of His holy covenant,*

73. *Of the oath that He swore to Abraham our father,*
   *that He would grant us,*

74. *That, delivered from the hand of our enemies,*
   *we should serve Him without fear,*

75. *In holiness and justice before Him all our days.*

76. *And Thou, Child, shalt be called the prophet of the Most High,*
   *for Thou shalt go before the face of the Lord*
   *to prepare His ways,*

[127]

77. *To give His people knowledge of salvation*
    *through forgiveness of their sins,*

78. *Because of the loving kindness of our God,*
    *wherewith the Orient from on high has visited us,*

79. *To shine on those who sit in darkness and in the shadow of death,*
    *to guide our feet into the way of peace."*

Here is the second chant of praise and thanksgiving to God for the coming of His Kingdom and its King, the second expression of the idea of God's salvation. The accent is not the intensely personal one of the woman and the Mother; here a man speaks, first as a priest of Israel (68-75), telling of the mission of the Messias to Israel and the world, and then as a father (76-79), telling of the privilege of his own son, John.

Even more emphatically than in Mary's song, the canticle of Zachary shows the Kingdom of God as already come: the time of waiting is ended, God has fulfilled His promises, made through His holy prophets of old. He has visited, *i.e.,* shown favor and love to His people, and brought them redemption. And their mighty Savior ("horn of salvation") is of a kingly line, a son of David. He is a rescuing King, who will deliver Israel from her enemies. But the true goal of His Reign is clear; not simply to subdue the earthly enemies of Israel, but to subdue Israel itself to His spiritual power. His Kingdom is a kingdom of "holiness" and "justice", *i.e.,* He will give to men a new interior spirit, a new heart for the service of God, and bring them to the practice of all virtue, so that they may be in "peace", without fear, for their real enemies shall have been conquered, the enemies within them. Thus God shall reign over them definitively, "all their days".

Then Zachary turns to his own son, and to his role in the coming of the Kingdom. He shall be a prophet, one who teaches the truths of God. His task will be to prepare the way before the King, to be His herald. And this he will do by teaching the people what is the true character of the Reign of God and His Kingdom: it is a "salvation" not simply from earthly enemies, but from sin (v. 77). The coming Deliverance will be a forgiveness of sins, not national political success. God has not come on a mission of revenge, but of mercy: because of His "heart of mercy" He has made a dawn to arise. A time of light is at hand; the Redeemer is Himself, as it were, a new sun in the east, risen "to shine on those who sit in darkness and in the shadow of death", the thick shadow of sin that has fallen upon the traveller, so that he no longer knows the way, and not daring to move lest he lose himself, he "sits" to wait for the dawn. The light that has come will set mankind moving straight onwards again, guiding them into the path that leads to peace, the peace already described, which is to be found in the faithful, fearless, persevering service of God "in holiness and justice" (v. 78-79). So both parts of the canticle end on the same note: peace, the inward peace of the lightsome heart in which God is sovereign, and from which His dark enemies have been scattered in flight. Thus in the word "peace" are summed up all the Messianic gifts. With the message "Peace on earth" (Lk. 2:14) the angels of the Nativity announce to the shepherds the birth of the Savior-King.

Evidently, then, Zachary conceived the Reign of God in a religious sense, God's authority over the heart and will of man acknowledged and submitted to. And the Messianic "salvation" was to him essentially spiritual and not political, a rescue from sin, from the spiritual powers of darkness. And he sufficiently suggests its universal, not simply national, character.

It is to be noted that in both these canticles the idea of the Reign or Kingdom of God, as spiritual and universal, as bringing a deliverance from sin and an inward moral renovation, is abundantly clear. But both Mary and Zachary speak with more reserve of the King Himself. Nevertheless one thing stands out strongly from their words, namely, the fact that in the Child who has been given to Mary, God Himself has come to His people, as He had promised. The Divinity of the King cannot be gainsaid. They took literally the words of the angel: "He shall be called the Son of the Most High" (the Hebrew proper name for God).

However, another thing stands out: neither Mary nor Zachary at all describes the earthly career of the Messias. His work is indicated: to command obedience, to illumine, to "save". The general quality of His life is likewise indicated: King though He is, He will hardly appear as a King, for His royalty is spiritual, not of this world. Finally, the issue of His life is made clear—He will triumph over His enemies. But of further details there are none. However, Simeon will put forward one striking facet of His earthly life.

## THE NUNC DIMITTIS (Lk. 2:29-33).

29. *"Now Thou dost dismiss Thy servant, O Lord,*
    *according to Thy word, in peace;*
30. *Because my eyes have seen Thy salvation,*
31. *which Thou hast prepared before the face of all peoples:*
32. *A light of revelation to the Gentiles,*
    *and a glory for Thy people Israel."*
    *"And His father and mother were marvelling at the things spoken concerning Him. And Simeon blessed them, and said to Mary His mother, 'Behold, This Child is destined for the fall and for the rise of many in Israel, and for a sign that shall be contradicted. And thy own soul a sword shall pierce, that the thoughts of many hearts may be revealed.'"* (Lk. 2:33-35).

The third witness to the thoughts and aspirations of truly enlightened souls concerning the Messias and his Reign is a simple layman, Simeon, an old man, "just and devout, looking for the consolation of Israel" (Lk.

2:25), the Messianic deliverance. His canticle is again a burst of prophetic rapture over hope realized at last, but its tone differs from the ecstatic, feminine joyousness of the Magnificat and the wholly masculine tenderness of the Benedictus. There is a touch of intimate pathos about it: an old man salutes the dawn of a glorious day toward which his whole soul had been turned in longing, but through which he will not himself live. Beneath its gladness there is the peaceful melancholy of a farewell. With evident appropriateness it has always been sung at nightfall by the Church.

There are but two ideas in it: Simeon now can die in peace for his hope has been realized; God's salvation has come, as a Light streaming glory upon Israel, and piercing the veil of darkness over the pagan world.

Thus the Reign of God reveals itself to Simeon: not national nor earthly, but universal and spiritual, as light and truth are spiritual and of themselves expansive everywhere. The Messias is indeed the glory of Israel, but He is likewise a Light for all the world.

Thereafter, in Simeon's inspired words to Mary, comes a startling revelation of the true role of the Messias: Prophet and King, He is also Priest and Victim, who will bring salvation to the world by His own sufferings. "Behold this child is destined for the fall and for the rise of many in Israel": it is His destiny to occasion a division in Israel itself. Not all will see Him for what He truly is, and they will perish on that account, while those who do see Him truly will be saved. "And for a sign that shall be contradicted": controversy shall rage about Him, He shall be the target of the arrows of denial (such is the metaphor obscurely indicated). And what shall be the issue of the controversy? His death. The fate of the Son is suggested by the "sword" that will pierce the Mother's heart. And all this, the rejection of the Messias by His own people, and the salvation of only a part of them, has been permitted by God, "that the thoughts of many hearts may be revealed", *i.e.,* that it may be revealed who are the sincere and docile souls who see God's idea of His Kingdom and its King, and submit to His Reign, and who on the contrary are the proud and rebellious souls who cling to their own ideas and thus cut themselves off from salvation.

The brief analysis of the three Messianic canticles that herald the actual coming of the Reign of God and the Messias will serve to give a glimpse of one set of ideas concerning the nature of both. They were ideas doubtless shared by a small minority of the Jews.

Whence, then, did these "just" souls derive these ideas? The answer is: from their prayerful intelligence of the prophecies of the Old Testament. These were God's own ideas about the Kingdom to come, that He communicated to the Hebrew people through their great "seers". As a matter of fact, the description of the Messias that is to be found in the Old Testament prophecies is essentially the following:

## MESSIANIC PROPHECIES

### TRIPLE OFFICE

The Messias will be invested with a triple office, and He will bring to men a triple gift. First, He will be Prophet; and as such His gift will be a fuller knowledge of God, completing that given through Moses and the prophets; moreover, He will teach men the way to God, how God wills to be worshipped and served. Secondly, He will be King; and as such His gift will be an authoritative rule, to keep men from wandering into false paths; it will be a rule of love, like the care of a shepherd for his flock. Thirdly, he will be a Priest; and as such His gift will be the supreme gift of love, the sacrifice of Himself to death, that by His sacrifice He may win for men pardon of their sins and the favor of God. By the exercise of this triple office he will bring "salvation", a real salvation from man's real enemies, error and sin and the danger of losing oneself entirely, hence a salvation for the soul of man.

### UNIVERSAL KINGDOM

Moreover, this essentially spiritual salvation will not be exclusively national, but universal: the Prophet will be a light for all men, the King will extend His authority over all the nations of the earth, to form them into a unity; and the Priest will offer His sacrifice for the sins of every man who ever lived. God's Kingdom of souls will be open to every soul. The title of admission will be simply submission to the Prophet-King who rules it.

### JUDGE

Furthermore, the One anointed by God as the Prophet, King and Priest of humanity will also be its Judge. His Reign, in addition to being a manifestation of the mercy of God, will also be a time of judgment, a triumph of the justice of God: the Messias will mete out retribution to each according to his merits.

### DIVINE

Finally, the Messias will be a man indeed, a descendant of the royal line of David, born in the town of David (*cf.* Lk. 2:11), but not merely a man. Though His full Divinity, his equality with God Himself, is not clearly prophesied, nevertheless, it is very strongly suggested. For the Messias is represented as having pre-existed to His birth here on earth; He actually was, before He appeared as Messias. And He is described as One to whom divine honors are due, and who can claim divine prerogatives (that of being Judge of men, a prerogative that, according to Jewish belief, belonged only to the Creator of men, Who alone knows their hearts). Such in brief outline, is the authentic description of the Messias as contained in the prophecies of the Old Testament.

## CONCLUSION

We have been endeavoring to put ourselves into the total historical situation into which our Blessed Lord stepped, in order to grasp the point of view of His hearers, to share their ideas and hopes. It was absolutely necessary to do this, if we are at all to understand the plan of His life, His impact on the crowds, the economy of His teaching, the marvelous pedagogical skill He showed. Above all it was necessary if we are to gain some insight into the tragic conclusion of His life, the colossal misunderstanding that resulted in the crucifixion of God by the people He had come, in divinest love, to illuminate and to save.

We have sketched the men of His time, and the ideas they had. And from the sketch at least one major impression should emerge, namely, that our Lord was confronted with a simply stupendous task. He had one basic thing to say: "You believe in God, believe also in Me" (Jn. 14:1). But how would He win faith in Himself?

He was not the kind of Messias they were looking for; the Reign of God that He would inaugurate was not the one they expected. They had not been trained to want what He had to give them: a new idea of God, a new union with Him and with each other, in a spiritual and universal and visible Realm of God. Would they endure having their ideas contradicted and their hopes thwarted?

Powerful forces were arrayed against Him. He would have to reckon with the proud rulers of the people, jealous of their power and position, enslaved to the riches and flattery that flowed in their direction, men with souls that were narrow and hard and malicious and prejudiced, closed against the love of God, and cherishing little love for men. He would have to reckon, too, with the misguided populace, sheep betrayed by their shepherds, not heading in His direction but away from Him, their souls shriveled by poverty and injustice and contempt, so that they could dream only of earthly freedom and material joys, and cling obstinately to their dreams with all the power of ignorance.

How would He correct these warped ideas, straighten out these twisted hopes, set free these souls imprisoned in their own selfishness? How would He raise these earth-bound souls to the height of His own glorious designs? How would He persuade them that He Himself was their freedom and their riches and their joy? That in Him they would find the fuller life they craved? And that apart from Him there was nothing that really mattered?

He had, on His side, but three instruments of conquest. There was first, the light and the drawing power (we call it "grace") that His Father would send into their hearts. And in this was His major hope: "No one can come to Me (*i.e.* believe in Me) unless the Father, Who sent Me, draw him" (Jn. 6:44).

There was, secondly, the incomparable power of His own utterance, a gift of simple eloquence such as no other man has ever possessed: "Never has man spoken as this Man" (Jn. 7:46). And to strengthen even farther its appeal there was the radiant charm and the transparent holiness of His Person.

Finally, there was the tremendous power of His love for men, for the people who were in a special sense His own. So strongly did this current of love run in Him that it would break forth in miraculous expression: in food for their hunger, in healing for their diseases, even in new life for their dead. And at last this love would reach its sublimest expression in His own death, offered for the life of the world He loved. If that did not startle men into the vision of who He was, then their blindness had no cure.

Solely with these three powers God willed that His Son, made Man, should overcome the world. Equipped only with them, it might seem that He went into an unequal combat, just as it seems today that His Church, equipped only with spiritual powers, is unevenly matched with the world. But the issue of His struggle was not doubtful: Christ was born a King, and His unthwartable destiny was to reign. The apparent victory, it is true, rested with the world: it did crucify Him. But the real victory was His; out of the depths of defeat He wrested it.

It remains simply for us to follow the steps of His march to victory.

## TEST QUESTIONS

1. Why did God wait until the New Testament to explicitly reveal the Trinity? Why did the Jews find it especially difficult to believe the new revelation? How were they at fault in rejecting it?

2. Describe in some detail the kind of a) political kingdom, b) material kingdom, which the Jews expected of the Messias.

3. What did the Jews expect with regard to the manner of the Messias' coming.

4. Explain the reasoning which led the Jews to belittle the spiritual ministry of the coming Messias.

5. How did the Jews misread the prophecies to justify their false hopes? How were the Prophets justified in using language which could be so misunderstood?

6. Explain Psalm 109 and show how the popular Jewish interpretation differed from the true one.

7. Quote from Isaias ch. 35 to show how the Jews would justify their dream of a material kingdom. What is the correct meaning of the quotation?

8. Explain the true meaning of the following passages from Isaias ch. 65 and show how in each case the Jews perverted the meaning: a) v. 1-2; b) v. 2-5; c) v. 13-14.

9. Name a chapter of Isaias that describes in detail the sufferings of the future Christ. What was the common Jewish reaction to such prophecies?

10. Name three "canticles" of the New Testament which reveal the Messianic hope of the just. Summarize briefly the characteristics of the Messias and His Kingdom which these canticles reveal.

11. Outline the main characteristics of the Messias which can be found in the prophecies of the Old Testament.

## Chapter XIII

# THE CHRONOLOGY AND OUTLINE
# OF THE PUBLIC LIFE

⋙ ⋙ ⋙ ⋙ ⋙ ⋙ ⋙ ⋙ ⋙ ⋙ ⋙ ⋙ ⋙ ⋘ ⋘ ⋘ ⋘ ⋘ ⋘ ⋘ ⋘ ⋘ ⋘ ⋘ ⋘ ⋘ ⋘

A s a result of the work of the first semester it is supposed that the
student has acquired a general familiarity with the primary historical
sources of the life of Christ, the four Gospels. Moreover, the comparative
study of the outlines of the Gospels should have indicated to him the major
outlines of the life of Christ, since the three Synoptists are in general agreement as to the construction of the Galilean ministry, and John completes
their work by his report of the Judean ministry.

Hence it is possible now to undertake a more complete and organic
construction of the whole Public Ministry, and to pursue the study of it in
more exact, detailed and orderly fashion. The specific purpose and method
of this study will be stated below. For the moment, the important thing is
to fix firmly in mind the general chronology of the life of Christ, and to
sketch in skeleton fashion its outline. Thus, in this chapter we shall bring
together the scattered data already furnished by the study of the individual
Gospels.

## CHRONOLOGY

It has already been said that the Evangelists are less concerned with the
exact dating of events and with their chronological sequence than with the
substance of the Gospel, Christ, His doctrine and His work. Hence it is
not possible to establish with complete certainty the chronology of the life
of Christ. The system here adopted is supported by solid arguments, and
by a considerable weight of external authority, among both Protestant and
Catholic scholars. Hence it may be safely followed. The following major
dates serve as a framework:

Birth of Christ . . . . . . . . . . . . . . . . . . . . . . . . . . . . December 25, 6 B.C.
Baptism . . . . . . . . . . . . . . . . . . . . . . . . . . . . . . . . . January 6, 27 A.D.
First Pasch . . . . . . . . . . . . . . . . . . . . . . . . . . . . . . . April of 27 A.D.
Return to Galilee . . . . . . . . . . . . . . . . . . . . . . . . . . . May of 27 A.D.
Second Pasch . . . . . . . . . . . . . . . . . . . . . . . . . . . . . March of 28 A.D.
Tabernacles . . . . . . . . . . . . . . . . . . . . . . . . . . . . . . . October of 28 A.D.
Dedication . . . . . . . . . . . . . . . . . . . . . . . . . . . . . . . December of 28 A.D.
Passion and Death . . . . . . . . . . . . . . . . . . . . . . . . . . March 18, 29 A.D.

## CHRISTMAS

The first date may cause some surprise. However, it is certain that our Lord was not born in the year 1 of our present era. His birth was assigned to that year by an error. In 525 a Scythian monk, named Dionysius, and surnamed Exiguus, was charged by Pope John I to determine the year 1 of the era of the Incarnation, that that might be substituted for the era of Diocletian, or "the era of the martyrs", which was then in use in the Church. Dionysius placed the Nativity in the year 754 A.U.C. (anno Urbis conditae, *i.e.* from the founding of the city of Rome). But his calculations were somewhere mistaken. For, as a matter of actual fact, our Lord was born during the reign of Herod (Lk. 1:5), who died in the spring of the year 750 A.U.C. (or 4 B.C., as we reckon). Consequently our Lord was certainly born before that date. Moreover, another fact obliges us to put His birth still earlier, *sc.* the fact that He was born during the imperial census taken up while Quirinius was legate of the Roman province of Syria (Lk. 2:1-2). Since this census was probably begun in the year 8 B.C., it is reasonable to assign the year 7 or 6 as that of our Lord's birth.

For the day of the month we have no historical evidence. December 25 is traditional, and may stand. When the liturgical feast of Christmas was instituted at Rome in the first quarter of the third century, it was assigned to December 25, which was also the "natale Solis invicti", the major feast-day of the devotees of Mithras, the Sun-god. For Christians, Christ was the "Sun of Justice", whose rising on that day was the dawn of a new era in human history. In the East, however, the Nativity was long celebrated on January 6, together with the adoration of the Magi and the baptism of Christ; but in the fifth century the Roman date was accepted.

## GOOD FRIDAY

The date of our Lord's death is likewise uncertain. We know that He died under the governorship of Pontius Pilate (from 26 to 36 A.D.), that He died on a Friday, and at the time of the feast of the Passover (therefore at the full moon of the month of Nisan, *i.e.* March-April, in our reckoning). The Pasch fell on a Friday in the years 29, 30 and 33. Hence from these years a choice must be made, and it seems best to select 29. This date fits best with what Luke says about our Lord's age at the time He began His public life.

Consequently, if our Lord was born in 6 B.C. and died in 29 A.D., His death occurred at the age of thirty-three years and three months. Consequently, too, if His Baptism is put in January of 27 A.D., He was just past thirty-one when He began His public life (Lk. 3:23), and His public life embraced two years and three months. Another opinion would extend its duration to three years and three months, but with no convincing evidence.

## OUTLINE OF THE PUBLIC LIFE

It is useful first to give an outline of our Lord's life in terms of His journeyings, and their time-schedule. In this way, a survey of the geography of Palestine may be made.

## PERIOD I. PREPARATION

In the Fall of the year 26, John the Baptist began his ministry, which was to last less than a year, *sc.* until the following May, when he was arrested and thrown into prison.

*In January,* Jesus made His way from Nazareth to the lower reaches of the Jordan, perhaps some five miles north of the Dead Sea, where (as seems likely) John was baptizing. After His Baptism, He retired immediately into the desert, the wild country north and west of Jericho, where, on the hill of Quarantania, tradition situates the place of His first struggle with Satan.

Towards the *end of February,* He emerges from this retirement, goes back to the Jordan where He is introduced by John to His first disciples, and with them He returns to Galilee. At Cana, He is reunited to His Mother, and performs His first miracle, after which He proceeds to Capharnaum with His mother and disciples. He stays there but a few days and then goes up to Jerusalem for the (first) Pasch, in April.

## PERIOD II. CONSTRUCTION

1. *In Judea*—April, 27 A.D. to June, 27 A.D.

Our Lord's first public act in Judea, the cleansing of the Temple, evokes an initial outburst of hostility, as well as much interest. He lingers for a brief while in the city, and then retires to an unnamed place in Judea, not far from Jerusalem, perhaps at Bethel; there He carries on a quiet ministry for a month or perhaps two. At this time John the Baptist was arrested and imprisoned by Herod, apparently acting in conspiracy with the Pharisees, who were alarmed by John's popularity and angered by his outspokenness. The arrest of Jesus, too, seems to have been planned, since His popularity was bidding fair to surpass that of John. To foil the plot, Jesus leaves Judea at the end of May. He passes through Samaria, stops two days at Sichem, and again at Cana in Galilee, whence He goes on to His chosen headquarters at Capharnaum. The conclusion put to John's ministry is the signal for His own career to begin in earnest.

2. *In Galilee*—June, 27 A.D. to March, 28 A.D.

In June of the year 27, then, Jesus inaugurated His Galilean ministry,

[137]

and from then until the following March, Galilee was uninterruptedly the scene of His labors, whose focus was in the little triangle formed by the cities of Capharnaum, Corozain and Bethsaida. Here He chose His apostles, preached, wrought many miracles, waked high enthusiasm and bitter hostility, till finally all His hopes shattered on the twin rock of Pharisaic blindness and popular carnal-mindedness.

## PERIOD III. CRISES
### March to September, 28 A.D.

The crisis in Galilee is marked by the first multiplication of loaves and its allied event, the discourse in the synagogue at Capharnaum on the Bread of Life. The time was just before the Pasch of 28. The people turn away in disbelief when Christ announces that He is the spiritual Bread of Life Who has come down from Heaven. Christ, in turn, rejects their insistence on a material kingdom and, from this time on, He withdraws Himself from the crowds in Galilee.

In March of the year 28, Jesus goes up to Jerusalem for the (second) Pasch (understanding the "feast" of John 5:1 to be the Pasch). There His cure of the paralytic at the pool of Bethsaida precipitates a crisis in Judea, and makes it no longer safe for Him to labor there. Hereafter He is almost literally a homeless wanderer. Hereafter, too, practically His whole attention is centered on the instruction of the Twelve.

From Jerusalem, Jesus and His apostles now journey north into Phoenicia. It is not a missionary tour; rather, He is deliberately seeking obscurity in these pagan lands. He does not find it about Tyre; hence He moves north, passing through the territory east of Sidon, thence farther east to the sources of the Jordan, thence southward past Mount Hermon, and finally, by a lengthy detour through the region of the Ten Cities (Decapolis), He reaches the eastern shore of the Lake of Tiberias. Thence He crosses by boat to the western shore, to Magedan or Dalmanutha. But since even here His enemies pursue Him, He abruptly recrosses the Lake, landing near Bethsaida Julias on the eastern shore. Then the little party journeys northwards to the region of Caesarea Philippi. It was here that Peter made his great confession of Christ's Divinity and received, in turn, the promise that he would be the "rock" on which Christ would found His Church. This event, as has been pointed out before, forms the climactic point of Jesus' Public Ministry.

Six days later we find the party at Mount Thabor in Galilee, for the Transfiguration. Since Thabor is but two or three days' journey from Caesarea Philippi by direct route, it is to be supposed that they detoured west through Phoenicia and across the plain of Esdrelon. From Thabor, again by a circuitous route in order to avoid public notice, Jesus and His followers went to Capharnaum, for a short stay. In private, He continues the instruction of the Twelve.

The Summer of 28 was at an end, and the final departure from Galilee was at hand; Jesus was not to revisit it until after His resurrection. His adieu was solemn: a word of woe upon Corozain, Capharnaum and Bethsaida, the cities upon which He had showered His love, and whose hearts had been hardened against Him. From now on, His face is set toward Jerusalem and His death. The months that follow are rich in instructions and discourses, but the incidents are relatively few, and the journeyings are fairly definitely marked.

## PERIOD IV. CONFLICTS AND CONSOLIDATIONS
### October, 28 A.D. to March, 29 A.D.

Jesus arrives in Jerusalem for the Feast of Tabernacles, at the beginning of October. The clash with His enemies is violent; attempts are made to arrest Him, even to stone Him. Hence He retires to Perea, across the Jordan, where at a distance from the city, and among the friends of the Baptist and His own, He consolidates His work of the past two years.

However, He again goes up to the city for the Feast of Dedication, toward the middle of December. Another attempt is made to stone Him. He retires again to Perea. Thence after the lapse of some time, He is summoned by the news of Lazarus sickness, and goes to Bethany to perform the greatest of His miracles, which was also the motive of the definitive resolve of the Sanhedrin to put Him to death at all costs. Consequently, He retires now to Ephraim, a town north of Jerusalem, only about two hours from the borders of Samaria. There, in complete seclusion, He awaits the time for His final advance upon Jerusalem, at the Pasch. These final weeks are devoted to the Twelve.

## PERIOD V. CONSUMMATION
### March 12 to March 17, 29 A.D.

At the approach of the Pasch, Jesus leaves Ephraim for Jerusalem. Yet His way is not direct; it carries Him by Jericho, and brings Him to Bethany, six days before the Pasch. This journey was by no means secret; rather, it assumed the character of a triumphal procession. And the climax was reached when, after the sabbath-rest at Bethany, He entered Jerusalem as King, amid the frantic plaudits of the crowd, and to the sullen rage of His enemies. In the evening He returned to Bethany.

Monday and Tuesday saw His final victorious debates in the Temple; the nights were again spent in Bethany. And there, on Wednesday, He spent

His last day alone with the Twelve. On that day, too, Judas made his traitorous bargain with the priests.

On Thursday evening, after the Last Supper, Jesus gave His final lessons and words of love to the Eleven. That night, before the Sanhedrin, He gave His decisive witness to Himself, and made His final prophetic and kingly utterance. His prophetic mission was ended; thereafter He was simply Priest and Victim, whose work was to suffer and die.

The following is a brief synopsis of this outline of Christ's Public Life. Each period of it will be studied in detail in the following section of this book.

## OUTLINE OF THE PUBLIC LIFE

Period I. PREPARATION: from the appearance of the Baptist to Jesus' settlement of Capharnaum
*Scene:* Judea; journey to Galilee: Cana, Capharnaum
*Time:* January to March, 27 A.D.

Period II. CONSTRUCTION: from the first Pasch to the martyrdom of the Baptist
*Scene:* Judea; Galilee
*Time:* April, 27 A.D. to February, 28 A.D.
  Section A: *Judea* (April to the end of May). The Cleansing of the Temple, and its sequels
  Section B: *Galilee* (June, 27 to the end of February, 28)
    Phase 1. Proclamation of the Kingdom (from the call of the Four Brothers to the Sermon on the Mount)
    Phase 2: Hardening of Pharisaic opposition (to the preaching in parables)
    Phase 3: Supreme effort in Galilee (to the martyrdom of the Baptist)

Period III. CRISES: from the first multiplication of loaves to the farewell to Galilee
*Scene:* Galilee: Jerusalem; Phoenicia; Decapolis; Galilee; Caesarea Philippi; Galilee
*Time:* March to September, 28 A.D.
  Crisis 1: *Galilee:* multiplication of loaves, discourse in the synagogue at Capharnaum
  Crisis 2: *Jerusalem:* second Pasch, cure of the paralytic at the Sheep-pool
  Crisis 3: The *faith of the apostles:* Confession of Peter, first prediction of the Passion, Transfiguration, adieu to Galilee

Period IV. CONFLICTS AND CONSOLIDATIONS: from the feast of Tabernacles to the last journey to Jerusalem
*Scene:* Jerusalem; Perea; Bethany; Ephraim
*Time:* October, 28 A.D. to March, 29 A.D.

Period V. CONSUMMATION: from the anointing at Bethany to the trial before the Sanhedrin
*Scene:* Bethany; Jerusalem
*Time:* March 12 to March 17, 29 A.D.

## OBJECTIVE AND METHOD OF STUDY

The foregoing outline begins with the ministry of John the Baptist and ends with Judas' bargain just before the Last Supper. It omits the narrative of His Infancy and His Passion, Death and Risen Life. And the reason is that our particular study of His life is limited in scope.

As a matter of fact, our Lord had a triple office with regard to humanity: He was its Prophet, Priest and King (or Shepherd and Head). And in His life He did three things. As humanity's Prophet He revealed God to man with a new fullness. As humanity's King, Shepherd and Head, He founded the Church. As humanity's Priest, He offered the sacrifice of Himself on the Cross for man's redemption.

In this first year of the course in theology we shall concern ourselves with Christ as Prophet and King. In Sophomore year we shall study Christ's function as Priest while continuing, incidentally, to see the further revelation of His Prophetical and Kingly offices that is contained in the narrative of His life from the Last Supper to His Ascension into Heaven.

*Christ as Prophet.* Our attention will be chiefly focused on His revelation of two things (that are really one): 1) that He was Himself the Messias, long promised to the Jewish nation and to the world; 2) that He was Himself God, God's only begotten Son, come to earth to give to man new truth and hope and life. We shall indeed gather up many other elements of our Lord's doctrine as we go through His life; but without losing from view the central thing that He taught, namely, Himself, who He was.

Our Lord's essential message, his "gospel", was about Himself—the chief thing that He presented to men for acceptance was not an abstract doctrine, a system of truths *about* God, or a code of morality for men, but a concrete fact, the fact of His own Person, that He was Himself God-with-us-here-on-earth, God in the Person of His only Son made Man, the promised Messias. Here is the originality, the newness of our Lord as Prophet, and His essential distinction from the long line of Hebrew prophets who had preceded Him in history, from Jonah to John the Baptist. They were simply men, telling other men the truth about God. But Christ was Himself the Truth (Jn. 14:6). They told men what they themselves had been told; He spoke of what He saw: "No one has at any time seen God. The only-begotten Son, who is in the bosom of the Father, He has revealed Him" (Jn. 1:18).

Moreover, the peculiarity of our Lord's life, that sets it apart from any other life that was ever lived, even that of the holiest of men, lies in the fact that the whole of it constitutes for us a revelation of what God is. At the Last Supper, when the naive Philip put to Him the very human question: "Lord show us the Father and it is enough for us", our Lord answered: "Have I been so long a time with you, and you have not known Me? Philip, he who sees Me sees also the Father" (Jn. 14:8-10). He means to say: I have Myself through all My life been giving you the vision of God that you want. All My life, if you read it correctly, tells you that I am Someone divine, God's Son; and knowing Me to be Son, you know that God is Father. That is the whole meaning of My life, of all that I have said and done.

Consequently, in studying the Life of Christ, we are not merely looking for a series of abstract arguments for the fact that He is God; we shall be looking at His every thought and word and deed as a concrete manifestation in human terms of what God is in all His attributes.

The life of Christ, then, is to us primarily the revelation of what God is: it teaches us a "theology": God is Father and Son (and Holy Spirit, too, but that part of our Lord's revelation of God belongs to another place). This point can hardly be too much emphasized today, when the term "Christianity" is undergoing such curious transformations. True, it is not the object of this course to "refute" erroneous concepts of Christ, His mission and the religion He founded. We are not approaching Christ as a "problem" to be solved, nor are we "inquiring into His claims". On the contrary as Christians we adhere fully to the sheer objective fact of Him, the Son of God made man for love of us; He is already the object of our faith and hope and love; and our endeavor is simply to make our faith more intelligent and our adhesion more complete and vital.

*False Views of Christ.* Still, it may be useful to make ourselves conscious of the view of Christ and His life that is commonly taken in non-Catholic circles, in order that, quite incidentally, we may see how it stands the test of comparison with the original documents. The fact is that even in circles rather sympathetic to Him, Christ is regarded today simply as a peerless moralist, or a great "humanitarian", but not in any sense as a "theologian", *i.e.,* one who defined an idea of God. He is indeed acclaimed as the prophet of the "Fatherhood of God and the brotherhood of man", but in a very untheological sense, *i.e.,* as the prophet of a vague sort of benevolence that shines down from heaven, and should have some reflection in the dealings of man with man. He is termed, "the ideal embodiment of gentleness and tolerance" (so, for instance by Mr. Will Durant, in the "Sat. Eve. Post" for August 5, 1939, in an article entitled "The Crises in Christianity"). Amid the harshness and cruelty of modern paganism, men are glad to warm themselves at the glow of His humane wisdom and philanthropy, and to make Him the inspiration of a humanitarian program, whose watchword is "tolerance".

The only incidents of His life that are brought forward are those in which He is seen actively engaged in relieving human misery: feeding the hungry, healing the sick, consoling the bereaved, pleading the cause of the social outcast, the economically underprivileged. The only part of His teaching

[142]

that is emphasized is that in which He counsels kindliness, generosity, the forgiving spirit. And the phrase that is seized upon as summing up the significance of His life, and its meaning for future ages is that of Peter: "He went about doing good" (Acts 10:38), *i.e.,* as it is interpreted, being even-tempered, indulgent to human weakness, forebearing with human waywardness, ideally "tolerant",—in a word, the apostle of a sentimental kindness and decency to one's neighbor.

The portrait has indeed its foundation in fact, as has every caricature. But it is entirely inadequate, quite misleading, and, left uncorrected and uncompleted, it strips His life of its essential significance. An attentive study of *all* the details of our Lord's life will show us that. For it will make clear one thing: that everything our Lord said or did had one major purpose, namely, to furnish men (chiefly His chosen Twelve) with the materials for answering the one vital question: "Who do you say that *I am?*" (Mt. 16:15). Toward incomplete or false answers to that question He is, in the same context, completely "intolerant."

Moreover, our study will reveal how exact was His own summing up of the meaning of His whole life, and how properly He gave it an essentially "theological" significance, when at the Last Supper He addressed His Father in these words: "I have glorified Thee on earth; I have accomplished the work that Thou hast given Me to do . . . *I have manifested Thy Name* to the men whom Thou hast given Me out of the world" (Jn. 17:4, 6). To make known the "Name" of God, *i.e.,* what God is in Himself: that was His "work". And what was the "Name" of God that He made known? Certainly not the name of "Supreme Being", "Creator", "Lord of heaven and earth", etc.; for the Jews already had had God manifested to them under those names. Nor again the name of God as "Father" of men, in the sense of One who exercised over them a loving Providence; for again the Jews had long known God as "Father of Israel", and they had for centuries experienced His Providence in wonderful ways. Rather, the new "Name" of God revealed by our Lord was the name of "Father" in an altogether special and hitherto unheard of sense. He revealed that God is a Father who has an Eternal Son, equal to Himself in divinity, whom He had sent into the world to prove His love for it. In this properly theological sense Christ was the Prophet of the Fatherhood of God, in that He was the Prophet of His own Divine Sonship. Hence the primary point in His message to men is given us by Himself in other words that He spoke at the Last Supper—words that contain the theme of His last beautiful discourse to His Apostles, in which He formulated for them the significance of His whole life: "You believe in God, believe also in Me", *i.e.,* that I too am God, distinct from the Father, but divine as He is divine, His only begotten Son (Jn. 14:1). And as the grounds for that belief He offered the totality of His Life, all that He had said and done, together with His death and resurrection.

*Christ As King.* As we study the Life of Christ it will become increasingly clear that His main interest during His Public Life was centered on the Twelve Apostles, and that all else, His popular preaching, miracles, etc., though essential in His plan, were secondary. Our Lord's Public Life begins (after His Temptation) with a preliminary call issued to some of His future Apostles; its first few quiet months were largely devoted to giving them a chance to get acquainted with Him; its final year and three months were given over almost exclusively to them, with the exception of His relatively brief public appearances at the feasts in Jerusalem; and Wednesday and Thursday of Holy Week were theirs alone.

Later we shall have to study the methods He employed in their education, the stages through which He led them, etc. The point here is simply to note the fact of His dominant interest in them. The fact is supremely significant and important for the light that it throws on the essential meaning and general plan of His life. It shows us that His main work was not just to issue a message of salvation to individual men, as individuals; on the contrary, it was to lay the foundation of a visible society, a Church, the Kingdom of Heaven, by the choice and training of the men who were to be its hierarchs, its teachers, rulers and priests. As a matter of fact, the whole tenor of the Life of Christ demands that we see in Him not simply a Prophet, inaugurating some sort of a religious movement, or promulgating some sort of a new ethic; rather, to be true to history, we must see in Him essentially the King, the Founder of a Church. Only from this viewpoint does His life as a whole, with its intense, jealous devotion to the education of the Twelve, become at all intelligible. Consequently, the incident at Caesarea Philippi, and the words that He spoke to Peter on that occasion (*cf.* Mt. 16:13-19), cannot be regarded as forming a casual episode. On the contrary, that incident is rightly regarded by the Synoptists as climactic: it expresses the major significance of our Lord's Public Life since it translates into action His major preoccupation, the founding of His Church.

Hence, apart from our primary interest in the King Himself, we shall follow with a special interest each successive revelation of the nature of His Kingdom. For, it is only in proportion to our intelligent and loyal participation in the Kingdom that we can reap the full benefits of union with the King.

## TEST QUESTIONS

1. Give a chronological list of the major dates in Christ's Life beginning with His birth and baptism and following through the main feasts which occurred in His life up to His death.

2. Name the main stages of development in the Public Life of Christ and indicate the length of each period in terms of months.
3. *Period of Preparation.*
   a. Indicate the general time (year, months,) of this period.
   b. Draw a map of Palestine and indicate on it:
      1. The probable routes of our Lord's journeys—from Nazareth to the Jordan and back to Capharnaum.
      2. The main places that are involved in the story of this period.
4. *Period of Construction.*
   a. What was the time (year, months) of this period 1) in Judea; 2) in Galilee.
   b. Draw a map of Palestine indicating:
      1. Our Lord's journey back from Judea to Galilee and the places where He stopped.
      2. The towns which were the center of His ministry in Galilee.
5. *Period of Crises.*
   a. What occasioned the crisis 1) in Galilee; 2) in Judea; 3) in the Faith of the Apostles?
   b. Draw a map showing our Lord's journey from Jerusalem to Phoenicia to Caesarea to Thabor to Capharnaum.
   c. What was the main circumstance that determined the general outlines of this journey?
6. *Period of Conflicts and Consolidations.*
   a. Give the name and date of the two feasts during which our Lord appeared in Jerusalem during this period.
   b. Give the time (year, months) of this period.
   c. Where did our Lord spend most of this time?
7. *Period of Consummation.*
   Trace our Lord's activity through each day of this period.
8. What was Christ's triple office with regard to humanity? Which of these offices do we study this year? Why?

## SUGGESTED READINGS FOR PART II

*Old Testament History.*

Best to read the historical books of the Old Testament themselves. As a help in conjunction with this, the following brief works are recommended:

1. *The Kingdom of Promise* by Rev. Robert Dyson, S.J. and Rev. Alexander Jones, Burns, Oates and Washbourne, 1946, London (190 pgs.)
   It outlines the history but dwells on the theological implications. Several chapters are devoted at the end to showing how Christ fulfilled the Old Testament.
2. *Old Testament Stories* by Rev. Hubert Van Zeller, O.S.B., Newman Press, Westminster, Md., 1949 (214 pgs.)
   It condenses the story by selecting the outstanding events in chrono-

logical order and paraphrasing the scripture account of the important events.

3. *A Guide to Old Testament History* by Rev. Daniel W. Martin, C.M., Kenrick Seminary, St. Louis, Mo., 1951 (150 pgs.—each alternate page is blank to allow for notetaking).
These notes outline the history and give the scripture references for reading to fill in the outline.

*Political, Social and Religious background in Palestine.*

1. Articles in the Catholic Encyclopedia on the various Places of Palestine, or Organizations or Social and Religious customs, institutions, etc.

2. *Catholic Biblical Encyclopedia, New Testament,* Steinmuller and Sullivan, Joseph F. Wagner, Inc., N. Y., 1950.
This contains brief up-to-date articles on pertinent topics in so far as they are mentioned in the Gospels.

3. *Practical Handbook for Study of Bible and Bible Literature,* Dr. Michael Seisenberger, Joseph F. Wagner, N. Y., 1911.

4. *Outlines of Bible Knowledge,* Most Rev. S. G. Messmer, B. Herder, St. Louis, Mo., 1910.
Both of these books treat the desired topics under such headings as: Holy Places (Tabernacle, Temple, Synagogues); Holy Functions (Circumcision, Sacrifices, Legal Purifications); Holy Persons (Priests, Scribes, Sanhedrin) and Holy Times (Feasts).

5. *The Life of Christ,* Giuseppe Ricciotti, Bruce, Milwaukee, 1949, Pages 3 to 173, treat of the Political, Social and Religious background to the Life of Christ as well as the chronolgy of the Public Life.

*PART THREE*

# THE PUBLIC LIFE OF CHRIST

## Chapter XIV

# THE PUBLIC LIFE: PERIOD I. PREPARATION

❧❧❧❧❧❧❧❧❧❧❧❧❧❧❧❧❧❧❧❧❧❧❧❧❧❧❧❧❧❧

*Scene:* Judea; journey to Galilee; Cana: Capharnaum.
*Time:* January to March, 27 A.D.

|  | Mt | Mk | Lk | Jn |
|---|---|---|---|---|
| 1. Ministry of John the Baptist | 3: 1-12 | 1: 1-8 | 3: 1-18 | — |
| 2. Baptism of Christ | 3: 13-17 | 1: 9-11 | 3: 21-22 | — |
| 3. The desert struggle | 4: 1-11 | 1: 12-13 | 4: 1-13 | — |
| 4. Witness of John the Baptist | — | — | — | 1: 19-34 |
| 5. First disciples | — | — | — | 1: 35-51 |
| 6. First return to Galilee: |  |  |  |  |
| Marriage-feast at Cana | — | — | — | 2: 1-11 |
| Settlement at Capharnaum | — | — | — | 2: 12 |

THE GENERAL significance of this period is in the series of beginnings that it records. John the Baptist inaugurates the religious movement of which our Lord will take command, and to which He will give new meaning. Our Lord Himself inaugurates His work by an official act of consecration. Satan begins his assault upon the King who threatens his dominion of the world. Our Lord sets His hand to the foundation of the Kingdom, His Church, by the call of the men who will be its cornerstones. Our Lady begins her work as Mediatrix of all graces by impelling her Son to His first miracle. We shall briefly particularize the central significance of these events; their description, details, etc., can easily be gathered from the text of the Gospels.

## 1. THE MINISTRY OF JOHN THE BAPTIST

The purpose of John's mission in relation to that of Christ is given clearly by himself: "I am the voice of one crying in the wilderness: Make straight the way of the Lord!" (Jn. 1:23). John was the link between the Old Testament and the New, one greater than the ancient prophets (*cf.* Mt. 11:7-14), the Precursor of the Messias and the herald of the Reign of God.

[149]

He had three things to do: 1] fan to kindling-point the Messianic hope; 2] clarify the true meaning of the Reign of God; 3] point out the Messias to a chosen few.

The burden of his message was: "The kingdom of heaven is at hand!" And his dominant idea of the Kingdom was that of a judgment of God: a day of "wrath" is at hand, an "axe" is already descending, a "winnowing fan" is about to be wielded (Mt. 3:7, 10, 12).

But this judgment will not mean a divine revenge wrought only on the pagan, as so many Jews dreamed. The wrath of God will fall on those of the Jews, too, whose hearts are not right with God. Salvation will not come to them, as they thought, merely from the fact that they are of the race of Abraham (Mt. 3:9); the Messianic salvation is for all men (Lk. 3:6), but only if they are worthy of it.

In these menacingly forthright words, John struck at the prideful exclusiveness of the Pharisees and Sadducees, and their chauvinistic hope of a Kingdom for Israel. He struck, too, at carnal hopes for a time of material prosperity. That was not to be the Messianic gift. Rather it was to be a "Holy Spirit", that would be as fire to purify and enlighten hearts (Mt. 3:11; Mk. 1:8; Lk. 3:16).

Consequently in preparation for the coming of the Kingdom, John issued a call, not to arms nor to a feast, but to a "change of heart" ("metanoieite": Mt. 3:2). The Reign of God will be spiritual and universal; it aims at subduing the evil selfishness in the heart of man. So John outlines his program of preparation: a program of justice and charity, of gentleness and contentment with one's lot (Lk. 3:10-14). Moreover, he enjoined the acceptance of a purificatory rite, "a baptism of repentance for the forgiveness of sins" (Lk. 3:3). This rite signified two things: first, an interior change of heart, a turning from sin, and secondly, a turning toward the coming Kingdom, a desire for the Messianic gift of holiness. These two acts would prepare the way of the Lord into the soul, levelling the barriers of pride and self-sufficiency.

The startling power of John's words, enforced by his strikingly ascetic appearance, created a country-wide sensation (Mt. 3:5; Mt. 11:7-9), so much so that many began to think he was himself the Messias. John corrects them, bidding them look for "one mightier" (Lk. 3:16), of such towering holiness that John felt himself not worthy to do for him the humblest service. At this time John himself did not fully know who this Mightier One was (cf. Jn. 1:31, 33); the revelation came to him only at the baptism of Jesus. Thereafter he went on to fulfill the third part of his preparatory mission, of which we shall speak below.

Note, finally, how the reception accorded the Precursor preluded that to be accorded our Lord Himself: sinners believed, the Pharisees and Sadducees did not (*cf.* Mt. 21:32; Lk. 7:29-30). Proud and worldly, they felt no desire to confess their sins.

## 2. THE BAPTISM OF CHRIST

This is one of the most solemn and significant scenes in the Gospels: it is the authentic beginning of the Public Life of Christ (*cf.* Acts 1:22). The two parts of the scene (the baptism itself, and the subsequent theophany, the link between them being the prayer of Christ) dramatize the most intimate meaning of all that is to follow.

First, by coming to the Jordan, Christ recognizes the divine origin of the mission of John, His Precursor, and enables John to achieve its full, divinely-willed purpose. This is why He brushes aside John's protest (Mt. 3:14): He is not submitting simply to John, but to the will of His Father, according to which His own mission must establish continuity with that of John. God willed on this occasion to give John a fuller insight into the mystery of Jesus: that He was Son of God, and therefore, Messias, come to take away the sin of the world. Given this special illumination, John is accredited as the first official witness to Him: he can fulfull the final part of his mission, the manifestation of the Christ (Jn. 1:26-34). This was the way God willed things to be done (Mt. 3:15). Thus the spectacle was initially for John's benefit (it is uncertain whether it had other witnesses, or if it had, how much they understood).

In its more profound meaning, however, the Baptism was Christ's consecration of Himself to His Messianic work. As His first official act the Redeemer takes a place among the sinners whom He had come to redeem, as if He were one of them. The Church has always bowed in awe before this tremendous act of humility on the part of Him whose holiness was that of God Himself. However, though John's baptism could not have its first meaning in the case of our Lord, namely, a confession of sinfulness, nevertheless, it did have its second meaning, a self-consecration to the Kingdom of God. From this moment the private life of our Lord is at an end: He is given over entirely to the work of founding the Kingdom.

Luke alone mentions His prayer (3:21), doubtless a prayer of consecration similar to the one He later taught His Apostles: "Father, Who art in Heaven, hallowed be Thy Name, Thy Kingdom come, Thy Will be done, on earth as it is in heaven". In answer to the prayer, the heavens are opened: the Father manifests Himself and the Son: "Thou art (Mt. This is) my beloved Son" (in biblical usage, "beloved son" means "only son"). And a dove (a visible apparition) descends upon Him, symbolizing the Holy Spirit. This was the first historical revelation of the mystery of God, Father, Son and Holy Spirit.

[151]

By this extraordinary theophany, the divine seal of approbation is set upon the mission of Christ, and the nature of His work is authentically declared. He is the Son of God, made man; He is dedicated to the work of manifesting His Father's name (*cf.* Jn. 17:4, 6a); upon Him, in His humanity rests the fullness of the Holy Spirit; He will give this Holy Spirit to those who believe in Him, to be in them the principle of a new life, a new holiness, a new love of God and man, in a new Kingdom of God on earth.

The dove of the Baptism recalls the scene in Genesis (1:2) when the spirit of God hovered birdlike over the dark waters of the primeval chaos, to bring out of them order and life. At the Baptism a new creation took its rise out of the waters of the Jordan, a new life began for mankind. And the best commentary on the whole scene is the final commandment of Christ to His Apostles, when His own work on earth was complete: "Go, therefore, and make disciples of all nations, baptizing them in the name of the Father and of the Son and of the Holy Spirit" (Mt. 28:19).

## 3. THE DESERT STRUGGLE

The mystery of the struggle of our Lord with Satan is one of the most powerfully touching scenes in the Gospels, in that it brings Him so close to us: "For we have not a high priest who cannot have compassion on our infirmities, but one tried as we are in all things except sin" (Hebr. 4:15). It is also a decisive episode in His life; apart from some understanding of it, the mode of His teaching and action must remain for us an enigma. Really, in the desert He lived through the whole dramatic struggle of His Public Life, and accepted its final issue, the Cross.

The purpose of our Lord in obeying the impulse of the Spirit (Mt. 4:1) will be clear if one has in mind that He had assumed a perfect human nature, subject to all the laws of human nature insofar as obedience to them involved no sin. One of these laws is that man must pray to know God's will with regard to his particular work, and pray for strength to do it. Ordinary people should act thus; the saints have always acted thus: Moses, Elias, John the Baptist (Lk. 1:80), Paul, Augustine, Benedict, Ignatius of Loyola, all prepared themselves interiorly for their work by retiring into solitude, by prayer and penance.

Obviously, to our Lord the plan of God for His work of founding the Kingdom was clear, not only because He was Himself God, but also because of the perfect knowledge of all things relating to His work that was supernaturally infused into His human mind. But His need of prayer still remained real, as real as the human nature that was His. He willed to be like us in that need, to impress upon us our own need.

Moreover, God's will for man has a personal adversary, Satan (in Hebrew,

"insidious enemy", of both God and man, for man's good is identified with
God's will). Necessarily, then, our Lord willed to come into conflict with
Satan. And the purpose of the enemy is clear. He is "the god of this world"
(2 Cor. 4:4), "the prince of the world" (Jn. 12:31; 14:30). He sees One
arise who is mysteriously called "Son" by a voice from Heaven, and who
consecrates Himself to establishing the Reign of God over the world. Thus
he sees his own empire challenged. And consequently, he has two things
to do: first, he must find out if this Man be truly the Son of God, anointed
as humanity's true King, sent to free the world from sin. On this point he
has no certitude as yet, for it had not been given him. He knew our Lord's
sanctity, but he had no power to get inside of Him to find out what He
thought of Himself. Secondly, if this Man was truly the Messias-King,
Satan had somehow to thwart His mission in order to preserve his own
dominion. This he would do by somehow inducing the Messias to forsake
the divine idea of the Kingdom and take over worldly ideas. Consequently,
Satan tempted our Lord to disobedience of God's will for Him *as Messias*.
The struggle in the desert had a specifically Messianic significance; it is
with this alone that we are concerned, leaving aside other riches of meaning
in the mystery.

Satan's approach (whether it was in visible form, as the texts seem to
imply, or simply by interior suggestions which our Lord admitted to mind)
implied one essential thing: that if this Man were really the Son of God
and Messias He would have the power of doing miracles. Moreover, Satan
drew the material for the temptations from the current popular ideas of
the Kingdom and the King, namely, that it would be a time of temporal
prosperity, miraculously produced, that the King would establish it in some
magical way, revealing himself by a spectacular sign and compelling submission by a show of overwhelming power, and finally that he would be a
great political ruler, who would extend the sovereignty of Israel over all
nations, again by some magical means.

Hence Satan's major effort was to see if the Man before Him would
consent to realize these popular dreams by the use of miraculous powers.
If so, he would at once declare Himself as Messias, and be a traitor to the
divine idea of the Messias. For Satan was very sure that popular Messianic
ideas and hopes were not at all in line with God's designs. He had himself
helped powerfully to build up these illusions in Israel. He is "a liar and
the father of lies" (Jn. 8:44); illusions are the stuff he deals in; he is the
patron of the "crooked thoughts" that "separate from God" (Wisdom 1:3).

So the general bearing of the triple temptation is clear: Satan proposes
that Christ turn stones into bread (the magical material prosperity), that
He make a spectacular descent from the pinnacle of the Temple (the
magical Messianic "sign"), that He set Himself to win the kingdoms of the

world (national political dominion). In a word, he proposes that Christ become the illusory Messias of Jewish dreams, the *deus ex machina* they expected.

The attack was powerful. And the secret of its power was twofold: it lay in the tight hold that these hopes had on the popular mind, and in Christ's own tremendous love of His people. He foresaw then the tragedy of His whole life, a tragedy rather for His people than for Himself. Blinded by their own ideas, they would not rise to the height of His. And by adhering to His own idea of the Kingdom, a Reign of God over the soul of man, He would Himself be the occasion of the fall of many in Israel. And He loved them every one; His heart was torn by the tragic misunderstanding that would spell the doom of Jerusalem: the more decidedly He rejected the false notions of the Messias, and the more positively He applied to Himself the true, divine notion, the more clearly He would appear to Pharisees and people alike as a false Messias. At the end a pagan would unconsciously write the truth over His Cross: "This is Jesus, the King of the Jews" (Mt. 27:37), but His own deluded people would not see it. And in rejecting Him, they would condemn themselves.

Actually, it was straight into the perspectives of the Cross that He stared. So He wept in the desert stillness; He wept for them and for their children, not for Himself (Lk. 23:28). For by the power and wisdom of God the Cross would mean victory for Himself, but ruin for them. It would be the crowning scandal of His life: "to the Jews indeed a stumbling block and to the Gentiles foolishness" (1 Cor. 1:23). On the throne of David they would have worshipped Him, but not on the throne of the Cross.

Truly, Satan's attack was insolent and clever. Our Lord is absorbed in contemplating the splendor and sublimity of God's plan of the Kingdom: the Son of God Himself sent to earth to gather all men into a great spiritual and visible unity, a universal Church, by giving them His own Spirit of love and holiness. Satan suggests the narrow material, petty plan of men for themselves: bread and power and pride. And in the face of these suggestions (which were continual, not made just on one day, so Luke suggests) the seeming hopelessness of His task grew upon Him day by day; an immense discouragement rolled over Him, bringing with it a sense of utter forsakenness, as He felt the enormous gap that separated Him and His ideas from the people He had come to save. He would Himself be an enigma to them; the priceless spiritual gift He came to give, a share in God's own life, was a gift they did not understand and would not want. And what they could understand and did want, He could not give them, for He knew better than they that it was not anything real, satisfying, eternal.

Behind the figure of Satan He could see His own relatives saying scornfully: "If Thou dost these things (*i.e.*, miracles) manifest thyself to the world" (Jn. 7:4). He could hear the Pharisees demanding "a sign from heaven" (Mt. 12:38; 16:1 *cf.* Jn. 4:48). He could see the wild, deluded enthusiasm of the crowd, intent on making Him King, after He had given them bread to eat (Jn. 6:14-15; *cf.* 6:26). He could see Peter turning in horror and disbelief from the idea of His sufferings (Mt. 16:21-23). He could hear Pilate's sneer: "Thou art then a King?" (Jn. 18:37). He could hear all the words of incredulity with which men, Jew and Gentile alike, would answer His revelation of Himself and of God's plan. Above all, there rang in His ears even now the ultimate, unanswerable, cowardly challenge they would fling against Him: "If He is the King of Israel, let him come down now from the cross and we will believe him" (Mt. 27:42).

Such, perhaps, might be the best formula for His temptation: somehow to "come down". To fit Himself to popular ideas. To debase His miraculous power to the level of mere magic, and with it to capture the favor of the crowd. Not to demand belief in dogmas, in "hard sayings" (Jn. 6:61), in His own Divinity, in the necessity of suffering, etc., but to be the Great Humanitarian, the Warrior-King they wanted. To give them a kingdom of earth, and not the Kingdom of Heaven. And all this on the specious pretext of "saving" them: for if He does not do all this, He will "lose" them.

But against this betrayal of His Father, Himself and the men He loved, our Lord resolutely sets His human will. He affirms His submission to God's will in three texts from Scripture. The first (Mt. 4:4) is an act of *trust* in the power of God, who wills that men be brought to His Kingdom not by illusory hopes of "food that perishes" but by a sincere desire for the food "that endures unto life everlasting" (Jn. 6:27). The second is an act of *patience,* an alliance with the wisdom of God, who wills that men come freely to His Kingdom, drawn by love of His Son, not smitten into slavish obedience by awful "signs". The third, the decisive act that banished Satan, was a total act of *obedience,* a submission to the majesty and holiness of God: He will do His Father's work, according to His Father's will, and know no other rule of thought or action.

Vanquished, the Tempter left Him "for a while" (Lk. 4:13). He returned on the eve of the Passion, when there took place the struggle in the Garden, echo of the desert struggle. Satan returned in triumph, his prophecy fulfilled: Christ had pitched His demands impossibly high, men had not believed. And among the irons he drove into the soul of our Lord was that of a great fear, tremors of which had touched Him all His life: "If I had not come and spoken to them, they would have no sin. But now they have no excuse for their sin. He who hates Me, hates my Father also. If I had not done among them works such as no one else has done, they would have no sin. But now they have seen, and have hated both Me and My

Father" (Jn. 15:22-24). In His own Person He had given men a vision of His Father's love for them; they had answered with hatred. And they could not plead ignorance: He Himself had taken away that excuse. Though almost with His dying breath He will urge it in their behalf: "Father, forgive them, for they know not what they are doing" (Lk. 23:34).

In the light of this encounter with His Adversary we can understand two things: 1] the principles that governed our Lord's pedagogy, the economy of His message; 2] the principles that governed His working of miracles.

One thing was terribly clear: the people were not ready for His full message. Were He instantly to proclaim Himself the Messias, He would jeopardize His whole mission. They would read their own meaning into the assertion, and miss His whole point. More than that, there would be a political upheaval, and He Himself would be executed by the Romans in short order.

Hence His first pedagogical principle, that remained true even in the case of His Apostles, and at the end of His life: "Many things yet I have to say to you, but you cannot bear them now" (Jn. 16:12). Notably, at the outset they could not "bear" to be taught the mystery of His Person; their ideas about the Kingdom had first to be corrected before He could show Himself as King; their hearts had to be turned toward God their Father, before He could teach them that He was God's only Son. In a word, a moral preparation of heart had to precede His dogmatic instruction; for only the pure of heart can see God (Mt. 5:8).

From this flows His second pedagogical principle: "he that does the truth comes to the light" (Jn. 3:21). That is, he who puts into practice the moral instruction that our Lord first gives (it is summed up, as we shall see, in the Sermon on the Mount), will be prepared in heart and mind for the real Gospel, the dogma of Christ: His Divinity, His oneness with the Father. And having made that crucial act of faith, he will be ready for even fuller light, to take an even more difficult step: faith in the mystery of Christ's Passion and Death.

All through our Lord's teaching, these two principles will be seen operating. He does not let loose a blaze of light: it would only blind. Very quietly, gradually, discreetly He lets it shine forth, as His hearers are able to bear it. He does not force Himself upon anyone: He invites, but men must themselves "come". And always He stirs them to the necessary preliminaries of that coming: purity of heart, sincerity, good will, desire to be taught, love of the light. The prophecy of Isaias that Matthew applies to Him as Teacher, images perfectly the gentleness and respectfulness of His approach: "A bruised reed He will not break, and a smoking wick He will not quench" (Mt. 12:20), that is, He will not ruthlessly drive home

His lesson upon a soul somehow shocked by it, and when the light in a soul is weak and dim, He will not, as it were, douse it suddenly with oil. In a word, He will demand sincerity, but He will reverence "good faith".

Similarly, insight into the Messianic meaning of the desert struggle illumines for us the principles governing our Lord's use of His miraculous power.

He will, of course, work miracles, extraordinary, astonishing deeds, that present themselves as beyond the power of man or of nature to perform. They are called in the Synoptics, "acts of power" (dunameis; *e.g.* Lk. 19:37), and in John "signs" (*e.g.* Jn. 2:11). In fact, He will scatter them with a lavish hand: at least thirty-four distinct miracles are described, besides groups that are mentioned without further detail, and many that are left unrecorded (*cf.* Jn. 21:25).

He will offer them as grounds for belief that a divine power is in Him and that He is Himself God (*cf.* Jn. 10:37-38; Mt. 11:2-5; 9:6; etc.). As a matter of fact, He had to offer such grounds. To the Jews, only miracles (and the fulfillment of Old Testament prophecies) would prove that He was the Messias promised and sent by God (*cf.* Jn. 3:2). In this they reasoned rightly. If God sent Him, God had to "signify" the fact by signs, and these signs had to be recognizably divine. If men are to stake their immortal souls on belief in Christ, if they are to accept His teaching on His own authority, then God had to guarantee that they are not being deluded: God had to set His divine seal on this authority. And this divine seal could only be in the form of miracles, works that only God could do. True, the sublime and soul-satisfying doctrine of Christ strongly suggests its own divine origin; His personal holiness is the most powerful, persuasive reason for belief in Him; but the ultimate, decisive argument is His miracles: they *oblige* one to admit that He is from God and that He is Himself God.

Consequently, the working of miracles is an essential part of our Lord's mission. However, His repulse of the Tempter makes clear that He will use His miraculous power with certain limitations. Thus it explains three facts recorded in the Gospels:

First, it explains His refusal of the "sign" demanded by the Pharisees (*i.e.* some portent in the sky, or the envelopment of Himself in some dazzling light). He will do no miracle to sanction a false idea of the Kingdom or the Messias, such as they had. For a similar reason He scorns the display of power requested by His relatives (Jn. 7:4), and the "tricks" that Herod hoped to see done by Him (Lk. 23:8). He is not a magician, one who does astounding things simply to astound, and to show that He can do them.

Secondly, it explains His "inability" to work many miracles at Nazareth "because of their unbelief" (Mt. 13:58; *cf.* Mk. 6:5-6). His miracles do not come like bolts from the blue, to overwhelm resistance and compel assent even in the incredulous. They are not done merely to answer an insolent challenge "to be shown", nor a natural desire for a purely temporal favor, like health (*cf.* in Lk. 4:23, the skeptical and presumptuous challenge of the Nazarenes: "Do for us here the wonderful things you have done at Capharnaum!"). On the contrary, they suppose sincerity, good faith, and at least a will to believe in the spiritual reality of the Kingdom. Constantly, our Lord demanded these dispositions (*e.g.* the four miracles in Mt. 9:18-33).

Again the reason is that His miracles are not simply acts of absolute power. They have a spiritual significance. They are "signs" of His true character and true mission, the revelation of God's love (not simply His power) and the salvation of souls from sin (not simply the freeing of bodies from physical evils). Hence it would be useless to do them in the presence of bad will (*cf.* Lk. 16:19-31). They do not act like magic, independent of a man's attitude of soul. Their real meaning, the thing signified by the visible sign, namely, that Christ is God and Saviour, can be perceived only by men of good will, who sincerely seek the truth. The whole history of Christ (and of His Church) is witness to this fact (*cf.* Jn. 12:37).

John especially emphasizes the symbolic value of the miracles of Christ: Christ opens the eyes of the man born blind, a sign that He is the Light (Jn. 9:1-41); He raises Lazarus from the dead, a sign that He is the Life (Jn. 11:1-44). Yet Matthew, too, suggests that His healing of the body has a deeper meaning (Mt. 8:17). And our Lord Himself warns against being "scandalized" at the kind of signs He gives of His mission: deliberately He does wonderful works of love and mercy, and does not do the meaningless portents expected of Him (Mt. 12:38-42).

Finally, our Lord's encounter with Satan explains for us why He is so careful, especially at the outset, to keep His miracles quiet and to silence their recipients (Mk. 1:34, 44; 3:12; 7:36; 8:26). Altogether wrong conclusions would have been drawn from them; excited by His miraculous power, people would have imposed upon Him the concept of the wonder-working Messias that He rejected. Hence with His miracles as well as with His teaching He must take precautions and exercise reserve.

This, then, is the essential point we wish to draw from the incident of the desert struggle, namely, how it illumines the economy of our Lord's message. Wrong and dangerously explosive ideas of the Messias-King and of His Kingdom and of His powers were abroad; He must slowly and patiently correct them, and substitute His own. Fortified in spirit, He leaves His retreat, to live out now in fact the struggle with the prince of this world, through which He has already lived in anticipation. The issue will again be victory, but the road to it will be bitterly hard. Yet Origen's phrase describes Him: He goes "like an athlete gladly going out to the test". In accord with His plan, His destination is "Bethany beyond the Jordan" (Jn. 1:28), where the Baptist waits for Him.

## 4. THE WITNESS OF JOHN THE BAPTIST

The Fourth Gospel alone tells the story of the earliest beginnings of our Lord's public ministry, with a freshness and vividness that betray the indelible impression made on his youthful mind by his first encounter with his Master.

The initiative in this series of events is taken by the Baptist. On one day he gives formal notification to the delegation of Pharisees that the Messias is already in the land, not himself but Another, at Whose divine dignity he hints (Jn. 1:19-28). On the next day he points out Jesus to his own disciples as "the lamb of God", the Holy One who will take away the world's sin (29-34). On the third day he points Him out again to John and Andrew, with an implied command that they follow Him (35-42).

Thereupon the Baptist leaves the center of the stage, as it were, and moves to his exit. He has played his part: he has manifested the Redeemer in Israel (1:31). The time is come of which he will say: "He must increase, but I must decrease" (3:30). Again his dominant trait of character appears, his unselfishness: his life was wholly turned toward Christ. Part of his work had been the spiritual training of an elite, whom he taught to pray (*cf.* Lk. 11:1), and whom he exercised in austerity by "frequent fasts and prayers" (Lk. 5:33). Now he gives over to Christ the best of them. It is certain that some, and highly probable that all the Apostles, as well as many disciples of our Lord, had been to school to John. Certainly, all the Twelve knew him, for Peter lays such knowledge down as a qualification for the man who would take Judas' place (Acts 1:21-22). This is another indication of the close continuity between the work of Christ and that of His Precursor.

## 5. THE FIRST DISCIPLES

The mode of their enlistment is illuminating: our Lord takes possession of them by the sheer power of His personality: His human charm, His gentle authority, the startling power He has of reading hearts, the air of mysterious greatness that unmistakably surrounds Him. And their reaction to Him is one of expansive joyousness: having "found" Him, they must tell their friends of Him, and bring them to Him.

He accepts without demur their conclusion that He is the Messias. But He seems to have spoken to them largely in enigmatic hints. He asserts that Simon's name will be changed to Peter ("Rock"): to a Jew, this change of name would suggest some great role to be played in God's plans. He alludes to Jacob's vision of angels (Gen. 28:10-17), a hint that somehow they would see heaven brought to earth in Him, and that God would be with them. Here an important trait of His pedagogy begins to appear: He arouses questions before He gives answers, He wants them to be curious before He begins His lessons.

As yet their "call" is only preliminary; it will be followed by two more "calls" to a closer attachment to Him. But it is highly significant that at the very outset of His Public Life our Lord begins the foundation of His Church: He chooses the "Rock" of its unity, Peter, and its foundation stones, the Apostles.

## 6. THE MARRIAGE FEAST AT CANA

John clearly links the miracle at Cana with the call of the first disciples, and points to its immediate significance: Christ gives the first sign of His "glory", *i.e.,* His Divinity, visibly manifested in a deed of divine power (*cf.* Jn. 1:14). And His disciples believed in Him. Not that they yet believed in His Divinity; their faith was still very imperfect and unenlightened. The meaning is rather that they attached themselves more confidently to His Person (Greek: eis auton), as to One somehow sent and aided by God.

Nevertheless, the sign must have been somewhat disconcerting to them. Trained in the stern school of the Baptist, who never touched wine (Lk. 1:15), they come to a new and higher spiritual Master; and His first act is to bring them to the laughter and lightsomeness of a wedding, where He changes water into wine that no shadow may fall on its joy! It was their first introduction to the nature of His Kingdom: not a realm of desert-dwelling ascetics, or joyless observers of an impersonal Law, but a realm of human beings, whom He would sanctify in all their states, and whose every human joy, as well as sorrow, He would bless. The miracle is symbolic of the new order: pale water, wherewith the Jews did their legal purifications (Jn. 2:6), is the image of the old order, that sanctified externally; but ruddy wine, which gives strength and joy to the heart of man, is the image of the new, wherein the very soul of man is sanctified, that he may put a soul of sanctity into every detail of human life. Surely an echo of the Nativity-song of the angels is heard at Cana: "I bring you tidings of great joy" (Lk. 2:10).

Thus, our Lord's first sign is a sign of joy. Paradoxically, it is also a sign of sorrow. Like the multiplication of loaves, it is a symbol of the Eucharist, the pouring out of His Blood in sacrifice for the life of the world. Hence it reveals (to us, at least) Himself and His love for men: it is by His own sufferings that He will win for them the joy of feasting at the table of God.

Moreover, there is another significance to the miracle: it is a sign of the place and function of Mary in the plan of redemption: she is the all-powerful intercessor, the Mediatrix of all graces, through whom Christ and all His gifts are given to men.

Knowing not only His Divinity and power, but especially knowing that His public manifestation has already begun (the guests must have been full of talk, begun by His disciples, of Him as Messias), she requests His intervention in an embarrassing situation. His first answer is clearly a refusal, though a gentle and affectionate one. His "hour" is not yet come: His first public manifestation is planned for the Temple in Jerusalem at the Pasch, as was fitting. Yet the unspoken desire of her heart, born of her compassion for any distress, prevails: He does the miracle, for it is His Father's will that He refuse her nothing. She who had brought him forth into the world secretly, now brings Him forth publicly. The miracle is a sign of her power, as well as of His.

"After this He went down to Capharnaum, He and His mother and His brethren and His disciples" (Jn. 2:12). It is not certain whether this marks a definitive settlement at Capharnaum, or whether they went there to join the caravan for Jerusalem. At any rate, "they stayed there not many days".

## Chapter XV

# THE PUBLIC LIFE: PERIOD II. CONSTRUCTION
# A. IN JUDEA

➤➤➤➤➤➤➤➤➤➤➤➤➤➤◄◄◄◄◄◄◄◄◄◄◄◄◄◄◄

*Time:* April to the end of May, 27 A.D.

| | Mt | Mk | Lk | Jn |
|---|---|---|---|---|
| 7. Pasch 1: cleansing of Temple | — | — | — | 2: 13-25 |
| 8. Conversation with Nicodemus | — | — | — | 3: 1-21 |
| 9. Sojourn in Judea | — | — | — | 3: 22-36 |
| 10. Withdrawal from Judea | 14: 3-4 | 6: 17-18 | 3: 19-20 | 4: 1-3 |
| 11. Second return to Galilee: | | | | |
|     The Samaritan woman | — | — | — | 4: 4-45 |
|     The royal official's son | — | — | — | 4: 46-54 |

THE DOMINANT characteristic of this whole "Period of Construction" is the activity of Christ among the *crowds;* as the dominant character- istic of the ensuing periods will be His increasing *withdrawal* from the crowds and His more exclusive devotion to the education of the Twelve. However, both of these characteristics should be understood only in general: the Period of Construction is marked by many withdrawals from the crowd, and many indications that our Lord's major interest was the Twelve, just as the ensuing periods will see much public activity.

Again, generally speaking, this initial period is one of popular *enthusi- asm,* on the heels of which followed the increasing *hostility* of the religious leaders of the people. Finally, this initial period is *constructive,* inasmuch as our Lord gives a sufficiently full course of instruction in the true nature of the Kingdom (His primary point), and also gives sufficient evidence in which men of good will may begin to see the mystery of His Divinity.

The opening of this period in Jerusalem manifests our Lord's plan: the winning over of the religious center of Israel. He begins by cleansing the Temple, a bold and authoritative act, but one whose full significance is not immediately apparent. The result shows Him that further self-disclosure would be unwise, in view of the dispositions prevailing. So He retires, and takes up a ministry not greatly different from that of the Baptist. Soon, however, even this work becomes dangerous in Judea, and consequently He retires to Galilee. On the way through Samaria, where the reasons for

[162]

His economy in teaching do not obtain, He gives a clear declaration of Himself as Messias. Then, passing through Cana, He goes on to Capharnaum.

## 7. THE FIRST PASCH: THE CLEANSING OF THE TEMPLE

This is a very revealing incident. First of all, it shows our Lord's capacity for righteous wrath, and vividly manifests its irresistible power. There is no conclusive reason to suppose that His act was miraculous; He simply carried all before Him by the sheer authority that radiated from Him—His eyes, His gestures, His whole bearing.

Secondly, the event is singular in that our Lord took the initiative in it; it was seemingly long-planned. Ordinarily His actions do not seem to have been planned, but to have been dictated by circumstances, in which He recognized and followed the indications of Divine Providence.

The direct significance of the act was not Messianic. Still, on the face of it, it was the act of a "prophet" in the Hebrew sense, one sent from God on a religious mission, one whom we might call a "religious reformer". It was designed as a challenge. Like all His acts, it aimed at raising the question: Who is He? Why this assumption of authority?

The question was indeed asked, but not in a spirit of docility. He returns an enigmatic answer, and the hostile dispositions of the priests are shown in their contemptuous retort (Jn. 2:20). Characteristically, He goes no farther in the explanation of His meaning.

However, His fearless bearding of the haughty priests won Him the applause of the people, who had been ground by their avarice. He has won an audience for His teaching; He wins them further by the "signs" He did (Jn. 2:23). But right here one sees the character of the "crowd" as it is constantly depicted by John: impressionable, easily won by a show of power, but shallow, not intelligent or serious in their adhesion to Him. And His own constant future attitude toward them is revealed: "But Jesus did not trust Himself to them". He did not trust their loyalty, hence He did not entrust to them His real message, the mystery of His Person. And the reason is one that John frequently underscores: His penetrating knowledge of the heart of man. The whole incident is prophetic of the future: the hostility of the priests, already aroused, will be implacable; and the superficial enthusiasm of the crowd will be easily dissipated. Together they will bring about the realization of His mysterious sign: the temple of His Body will be destroyed, but He will raise it up again.

## 8. THE CONVERSATION WITH NICODEMUS

The incident is introduced by John to show the impact made by our Lord on another group, the Pharisees. John's theme develops: the Light

[163]

has flamed in the darkness; those whose works were evil (the priests) have already signified their love of darkness (*cf.* Jn. 3:19); others (the people) are wavering in a half-shadow; here is a soul that is moving toward the Light, though irresolutely.

Moreover, Nicodemus seems to be a delegate from a group of Pharisees; he speaks in the plural: "we know . . ." (Jn. 3:2). Certainly our Lord had as yet done nothing to arouse their hostility; for His cleansing of the Temple they would have had only approval. Initially, then, their attitude is one of curiosity, mingled with surprise: they want to know more about this young Rabbi from Galilee, and His ideas, chiefly about the Kingdom of God. Only later, when He challenges their own position, will their attitude pass through the stages of suspicion, open criticism, charges of diabolic help, to an alliance with the murderous conspiracy of the Sadducean priests.

Nicodemus begins respectfully: the topic is the Kingdom, and the relation to it of the new baptism foretold by the Baptist. He would discuss the matter as one Master with another. Characteristically, however, our Lord asserts His authority with gentle firmness. It is another trait of His pedagogy: those who come to Him must come as pupils, not as equals, and come to be taught, not to carry on academic arguments. Serenely, He lays down the law (3:3), nor is He troubled by Nicodemus' evident irritation at the fact that He should presume to demand, and not discuss (4-5). His whole tone is highly dogmatic, mingled with a gentle irony (*cf.* v. 10).

The theme of the discourse is theological: the Kingdom is entered by a new birth unto a new interior and spiritual life; the agent of this rebirth is the Holy Spirit, operating through the water of baptism; mystery though it is, the necessity and the reality of this rebirth are to be accepted on the authority of Christ, simply and unquestioningly; He is the qualified Master of heavenly mysteries, for He has come down from heaven and He *is* in heaven.

Thus far (to v. 15 incl.) our Lord speaks. What follows seems to be John's amplification of His meaning, a brief but sublime statement of the whole redemptive plan of God. God in love has sent His Son as the world's Saviour, bringing the gift of eternal life to whomsoever would believe in Him. But His very coming, as the saving Light, "divides" the world: those who love the Light of Truth receive the gift of Life, but those who hate the Light perish in the self-chosen darkness of error and sin.

So the interview turned out quite differently than Nicodemus had expected: instead of putting Christ to the question, he finds his own heart being searched. Still, there was sincerity in him, and our Lord saw it, and spoke to him far more freely than to others, though still with reserve. For instance, He merely hints at His own Divinity (Jn. 3:11-13). Nicodemus

stood the test well: his love of the truth finally brought him to the full
Light (Jn. 19:39).

These first days in Jerusalem clearly show the working of our Lord's
two pedagogical principles. He gives men only the truth they can bear. To
the priests He gives nothing, to the people, a little, to Nicodemus, more. And
men themselves decide the measure they are to receive by their willingness
to "do the truth" (Jn. 3:21).

## 9. THE SOJOURN IN JUDEA

In a city dominated by the Sanhedrin, whose animosity had been aroused
by His tentative opening stroke, our Lord could make little headway. Nor
does He wish to force the issue. So He retires with His disciples to an
unnamed place, probably near the northern border of Judea (Jn. 3:22).
There He takes up a ministry hardly different from that of the Baptist.
His aim is a fuller preparation of the people before further self-manifesta-
tions. Part of the ministry was a baptism, administered not by Himself
but by His disciples (Jn. 4:2). It was not what we know as the sacrament
of Christian baptism, but a rite like that of John's, but with a deeper
meaning.

The Baptist was still at work, at "Aennon near Salim" (Jn. 3:23). But
the drift of the people was to Christ, a fact that apparently waked jealousy
among some of the disciples of John, who has to rebuke them in calm and
honest terms that again reveal his greatness of soul (Jn. 3:25-30). His tribute to the superiority of Christ is further amplified by the Evangelist
(31-36).

## 10. WITHDRAWAL FROM JUDEA

Very shortly the tension of the situation was broken by two events. The
first was the arrest and imprisonment of the Baptist by Herod, spurred
by Herodias to angry revenge for John's bold denunciation of their adulter-
ous union which was incestuous, too, in the Hebrew sense, since she was
his sister-in-law (Mk. 1:14; 6:17-18). The second was the fact, suggested
by John (4:1), that our Lord Himself had now aroused the jealousy of the
Pharisees, doubtless by some criticism of them similar to that made by the
Baptist, as well as by His growing popularity.

In this fashion the alliance of our Lord with the Baptist is broken; apparently it was the signal for Him to enter actively on His own proper work.
But not in Judea, where the influence of the priests and Pharisees was too
strong. So He takes the road for Galilee through Samaria. It is about the

end of May; His stay in Judea has lasted about a month, but it is over four months since His Baptism. It is time for Him to display His power in word and work.

## 11. Second Return to Galilee

The enthralling incident of the Samaritan woman depicts with incomparable vividness the Savior and Master of souls at His work. The scene should be pictured, and the dialogue savored; a commentary would quite spoil it.

It is midday, and blazing hot; He has been on the road some six or seven hours. So He begins casually, asking for a drink. The woman, who had long since lost the habit of blushing, nevertheless, evinces surprise at His double breach of convention: the Jews had no dealings with Samaritans, nor Rabbis with women. He gives His customary enigmatic reply, to pique her curiosity. She is indeed intrigued; but politely skeptical, amused, smoothly ironical. But He cuts short her elegant persiflage and startles her into seriousness by a revelation of her secret: the restless desire for happiness that had thrown her into the arms of six men. To cover her confusion, and to find out more about this extraordinary Man, she puts forth a theological topic. She does not understand His answer, but it does not matter. His ascendancy is complete. To this sinful woman, sincere at heart, but deceived by her own desire for life, He reveals His own secret: He is the Messias, the world's hope of life and happiness. The approach of His disciples interrupts the conversation; excitedly the woman runs off to the city, to relate her experience. "A man who has told me all that I have ever done", is her summary of Him. But she had felt His very accusation as a pardon: she felt that He understood the why of it all, and willed to be Savior, rather than Judge.

Though no equally explicit statement of this Messianic office will come from Him until His trial before the Sanhedrin, two years later, its clarity need not surprise us here. Isolated from the Jews, the Samaritans did not share their false Messianic hopes; hence, He could be direct with them. The incident won Him many converts: and significantly they were won without any "signs", simply by seeing and hearing Him (Jn. 4:41-42).

Thus His first success was among the despised Samaritans. It puts Him in the mood of hope and exultation that can be felt through His words to the disciples (Jn. 4:32-38). In this mood He goes on to Galilee.

Of His entrance into Galilee, John relates two facts. The first is the cordiality of the welcome accorded Him; the Galileans had been vastly impressed by "all that He had done in Jerusalem during the feast" (Jn. 4:45). The other is the "second sign" (4:54) in Galilee, the cure of the son of an official in Herod's court, whom His advance fame had brought from Capharnaum to Cana. At first our Lord refuses his petition, but the father's anguished insistence prevails, and he is granted the favor. Our Lord acts in character: He will not leave unheard an appeal for help, be there ever so little real faith behind it. As a matter of fact, His reply to the official (4:48) is directed less at the man himself than at the Galileans in general. They are, He knows, avid for "signs and prodigies", eager to accept His favors; but they will be very slow to accept *Him,* reluctant to embrace His doctrine or to see into the real meaning of His Person.

Nevertheless, Galilee presents a more promising field. Notably, He will have more freedom of action. The species of religious terrorism exercised by the Sanhedrin in Judea did not extend so far north. At least men would not have to come to Him at night, like Nicodemus. It is true there were plenty of Pharisees; but their influence was not so paralyzing. And anyway, their opposition was not yet organized or bitter. So, during the next few months our Lord moves about and preaches with less hindrance than at any other time. Opposition does indeed develop shortly, but it is some time before He is compelled to break definitely with the Pharisees.

Moreover, the people themselves were more open to His message. The fertile soil of Galilee, rich in olive groves, orchards and wheat fields, and the waters of the Lake, swarming with fish, supported a population of sturdy farmers and fishermen, rustic in manner, but straightforward, independent and prosperous. They were despised by the Judeans for their lack of urban culture and their uncouth speech (*cf.* Mt. 26:73: Peter's experience). The proverb ran: "To make a fortune, go north; but for wisdom, south". And the Pharisees scouted the notion that a prophet could come from Galilee (Jn. 7:52). Nevertheless, the Galileans were faithful and religious in a narrow way, and above all, virile and courageous. In fact, they were justly reputed a turbulent people. Herod had trouble with Galilean brigands; and restlessness under Roman rule was more pronounced there than in Judea, where the pro-Roman Sanhedrin kept it under control. Hence our Lord had to be particularly prudent and careful not to inflame their political passions. But, generally speaking, He could talk more openly in Galilee than He could in Judea.

## Chapter XVI

# THE PUBLIC LIFE: PERIOD II. CONSTRUCTION
## B. IN GALILEE

➸➸➸➸➸➸➸➸➸➸➸➸➸➸➸➸➸➸➸➸➸➸➸➸➸➸➸➸➸➸➸

### PHASE 1. PROCLAMATION OF THE KINGDOM
*Time:* Late spring and summer, 27 A.D.

|  | Mt | Mk | Lk | Jn |
|---|---|---|---|---|
| 12. The Kingdom of God is here | 4: 12-17 | 1: 14-15 | 4: 14-15 | — |
| 13. The call of the four | 4: 18-22 | 1: 16-20 | 5: 1-11 | — |
| 14. Demoniac in the synagogue | — | 1: 21-28 | 4: 31-37 | — |
| 15: The mother-in-law of Peter | 8: 14-15 | 1: 29-31 | 4: 38-39 | — |
| 16. Miracles; enthusiasm; tour | { 4: 23-25<br>{ 8: 16-17 | 1: 32-39 | 4: 40-44 | — |
| 17. Cure of a leper | 8: 1-4 | 1: 40-45 | 5: 12-16 | — |
| 18. Cripple; Christ forgives sins | 9: 1-8 | 2: 1-12 | 5: 17-26 | — |
| 19. Call of Matthew; the banquet | 9: 9-17 | 2: 13-22 | 5: 27-39 | — |
| 20. Plucking corn on the Sabbath | 12: 1-8 | 2: 23-28 | 6: 1-5 | — |
| 21. Man with the withered hand | 12: 9-14 | 3: 1-6 | 6: 6-11 | — |
| 22. Widespread fame; crowds | 12:15-21 | 3: 7-12 | 6: 17-19 | — |
| 23. Choice of the Twelve | — | 3: 13-19 | 6: 12-16 | — |
| 24. Sermon on the Mount | cc. 5, 6, 7 | — | 6: 20-49 | — |

THE CONSTRUCTIVE period of our Lord's ministry in Galilee passes through three phases, which are organically connected.

The characteristics of the first phase may be thus briefly described. Our Lord emerges into full public view as a Teacher. The chief content of His teaching is the Kingdom of God; He begins to declare its true nature both in word and by His "acts of power". He issues a call for a moral reformation of life in preparation for entrance into the Kingdom, and lays down an extensive moral program. With regard to His own Person, He exercises a great reticence, shown in the title He adopts, "the Son of Man". Nevertheless, He begins very discreetly to put Himself forward as Son of God and Messias, chiefly by His evident authority, shown both in His manner of teaching and in His miracles. Similarly, He begins the actual foundation of the Kingdom by the choice of the future Apostolic College, the Twelve.

The effect He produces is twofold. Among the people great enthusiasm is awaked; but it has little depth and will have little permanence. They do not recognize Him (now or even later) as Messias; to them He is simply "a great prophet"; they seek His favors. On the other hand, the scribes and Pharisees are soon roused to suspicion chiefly by the freedom and largeness of view that characterize His teaching and manner of life, and also by His assumption of authority. Their opposition to Him begins gradually to grow.

## 12. "THE KINGDOM OF GOD IS HERE!"

The Synoptists unmistakably imply that at His first entrance into Galilee, our Lord for a brief while preached alone. His disciples went back to their trades. Moreover, it is also unmistakably implied that His first public appearances were greeted with acclaim. Yet we have seen that His "fame" (Lk. 4:14) did not come overnight; His way had been carefully prepared.

His initial message is simple: "The time is fulfilled, and the Kingdom of God is at hand; repent and believe in the Gospel" (Mk. 1:15). He takes one step in advance of the Baptist: He actually promulgates the Kingdom. He calls, as John did, for an interior conversion, a moral reformation. And He adds a call for faith in the Kingdom. The latter call is really a call for readiness to be instructed in the true meaning of the Kingdom, a readiness that will be the natural result of the "metanoia".

His method of reaching the people is equally simple: He goes to the synagogues on the sabbath-days. The method was entirely natural, and He will use it constantly during this whole period (cf. Mt. 4:23; Mk. 1:21; Lk. 4:15; Jn. 6:60). It was a sure way of reaching the entire public (cf. Jn. 18:20). St. Paul will later use it (cf. Acts 13:14 ff.). In the designs of God, the synagogue was to be the cradle of the Church.

The synagogue was at once a house of prayer, a meeting-place, a court and a school; but its prime destination was a place for the reading and explanation of "the Law and the Prophets". Anyone, on request or invitation of the authorities, might choose a text and develop it. In a typical scene in the synagogue at Nazareth (Lk. 4:16-21) our Lord does just this.

The evangelists record the "astonishment" of the people at His sermons, and the impression of "newness" they made, by reason of the "authority" with which they were delivered (Mk. 1:22; 6:2; Lk. 4:32). They were so "different" from the laborious and involved discourses of the Scribes. These men, not daring to make any straightforward assertions on their own account, were in the habit of sheltering themselves behind the name of some famous Rabbi; and often they lost themselves in a labyrinth of subtle questions of legal interpretation, that brought no spiritual nourishment to the souls of the people. Christ, on the contrary, spoke authoritatively; in simple words He set forth the meaning of the Scriptures; directly and without appeal to any authority other than His own, He stated moral principles and solved moral problems. The whole impression He made was that of a *Master*. And there was a serenity to His manner, and an ardor in His speech that won confidence and warmed the heart. The Sermon on the Mount is a type, in style and content, of His preaching during this phase of His ministry (*cf. infra.*).

## 13. THE CALL OF THE FOUR

It was not the plan of His Father that Christ should merely teach men some simple truths or trace for them a moral program. His Kingdom was to be a visible community, a Church, organized as a society, and having His authority. Its foundation was the work of our Lord's life. His general work of public preaching had a subordinate purpose: it was a means to the fuller education of the Apostles, and likewise a means of preparing souls for later entrance into the Church.

With the present incident we can see the major lines of His strategy developing. At the same time that His preaching entered into its first phase of victorious expansion, He recruits those who are to be the hierarchy of His Church, and begins their formal training. As time goes on and hostility develops, His work will become less extensive, but more intensive; He will turn increasingly from the crowds to the Twelve, till He is concentrated almost wholly on them. Even among the Twelve, He will distinguish three specially privileged ones, Peter, James and John. Finally, among these three one is singled out, Peter. Significantly, it is from Peter's boat that He teaches (Lk. 5:3). It may well have been in Peter's house that He dwelt at Capharnaum. Other indications of Peter's headship of the Twelve will appear later.

Luke apparently gives the full history of the call of the two sets of brothers; Matthew and Mark merely summarize it. Its meaning is clear: this is their summons to a definitive attachment to His Person. His own family life was ended; He was totally consecrated now to the work of the Gospel. They were called to a similar total consecration, to leave all things, in order to be completely His.

They had been well prepared for this, by the Baptist and by Himself. Moreover, their own trade had fitted them for their new work. For the fisherman's trade, even today, is a laborious and dangerous one, requiring courage, patience, tenacity, "toughness", willingness to undergo physical hardship. They were schooled in the art of working together (*cf.* Lk. 5:7-10); they were sincere, simple, docile.

At the moment they did not know what they were enlisting for. To them our Lord was simply "Rabbi", Master, though they glimpsed in Him a greatness they could not yet explain. In His Company they had already seen wonderful things; but what drew them was chiefly some secret power in His Person. This, more than the miracle, struck Peter to his knees (Lk. 5:8). It was definitely for Him personally that they gave up everything. He traced no blueprint of the future for them; characteristically, He simply drops a hint of a great work to be done; they would be "fishers of men". It sounded highly interesting. Little did they suspect that His call was the "terrible, sweet voice of death" sounding in their hearts. Ultimately, they would die for Him; but He does not tell them that now; they could not have "borne" it.

## 14. The Demoniac in the Synagogue. 15. Peter's Mother-in-law. 16. An Evening of Miracles

In these three scenes (with their epilogue, the retirement of our Lord to pray) we are given the history of a whole day at Capharnaum. It is apparently the first day of His full active work; and the impression it made on Peter is perceptible in the vividness and emotion of Mark's narrative. Moreover, the day was undoubtedly typical. It presents in miniature what our Lord's life was during this early expansive period: in the morning He teaches publicly, during the afternoon He instructs the disciples privately, in the evening He makes a lavish display of His power and love; tired, He rests briefly, then rises very early to pray, alone.

The general effect of the day is given in the excited words of "Simon and his companions": "Everybody is looking for You!" (Mk. 1:37). The people are "astounded" at His teaching (Mk. 1:22), "amazed" at His acts of power (v. 27). From all sides they flock to receive His favors (vv. 32-34). From now on, up till the critical events of the Second Pasch, He moves in the midst of crowds; Mark in particular notes the fact (cf. 1:45; 2:2; 2:13; 3:7-10; 3:20; 4:1; 5:21, 24, 31; 6:31, 33-34). Moreover, these graphic texts show how the enthusiasm of the crowd brings out its native rudeness: our Lord is pushed and jostled, not given time to eat, disturbed at His prayer, harried by importunate requests.

The marvelous gentleness and sympathy of His character is displayed in the fact that He does not once protest. But the rudeness itself suggests the superficial quality of the crowd's enthusiasm. Doubtless there were many who genuinely desired to be taught by Him; many, too, felt the mysterious attraction of His person, and sensed His love for them, and the compassion that was expressed in His works of healing. But, generally speaking, it was the "wonders" themselves that drew the crowd. And they failed to discern what was behind it all. They acclaimed the things He said and did, but they did not grasp what was signified by these authoritative words and wondrous works.

On His part, a great reserve is evident. He silences the devils He casts out (Mk. 1:34); He does not wish His miracles to be blazed abroad (Mk. 1:43); He refuses to stay long in one place (Mk. 1:38); He even attempts to avoid the crowds (Mk. 1:45). It is clear that He deliberately wishes to display His love for suffering humanity, and His power to heal it; but at the same time He endeavors to moderate the enthusiasm evoked. For He knew how unintelligent it was, and how dangerously likely to lead these impressionable people to false conclusions about Him.

Nothing reveals His own inward attitude more than His habit of seeking solitude, and using the dark quiet of the night for prayer (Mk. 1:35; Lk. 5:16). His public life of intense activity was sustained by a deep, interior life of prayer. It was not merely that He wished to point by example His injunction to us to pray always, to make prayer central in life. As a man, subject to human laws, He Himself needed strength of soul for His arduous work, and fittingly He sought it in prayer. Moreover, these long hours of prayer were infinitely delightful to Him. During them He was most Himself, the Son, turned wholly to His Father, whose will was His very meat and drink (Jn. 4:34), and in whose continual presence He lived.

The fact is that He must have felt very much "alone" among men. They were so distant from Him in spirit even when they "threw themselves upon Him" (Mk. 3:10) in the crowd. For they did not know who He was, or why He had come among them. Hence continually during His life, especially at moments of crisis, we see Him turning with love and gratitude and petition to the Father who "knew perfectly" His Son (Mt. 11:27), and was always "with" Him. "I am not alone, but with me is He who sent me, the Father" (Jn. 8:16). "He who sent me is with me; He has not left me alone, because I do always the things that are pleasing to Him" (Jn. 8:29). "You (i.e., the Apostles) will leave me alone. But I am not alone, because the Father is with Me" (Jn. 16:32). Around this thought His prayer constantly turned: the Father had sent Him, the Father was with Him, He and the Father "are one" (Jn. 10:30). This, His oneness with the Father, was the secret of His being, that He had come to reveal. It is also the key to an understanding of all the manly strength and beauty of His human life. Only when we see Him at prayer, the Son with the Father, can we understand why He was perfectly a Man.

It should be noted, too, that our Lord's "aloneness" with the Father is not to be understood in any merely individualistic sense, as if He were simply fleeing this world for the sake of His own personal comfort or escaping from men just in order to be alone and safe from their misunderstandings. On the contrary, when He was alone with the Father, He had the whole world in His heart, and all men before His eyes. He prayed as His Church today prays, for all men. Moreover, there was a hierarchy in His prayer, as in hers (*cf.* the first prayer, "Te igitur", in the Canon of the Mass). In a particular manner He prayed for Peter (*cf.* Lk. 22:31-32), who would be the Rock of His Church. Next He prayed for the men who were to be His Apostles (the pattern of His prayer for them, doubtless often made, is found in His Priestly Prayer at the Last Supper: Jn. 17:6-19). Then He prayed for all those who would be the future members of His Church; so for each one of us (*cf.* Jn. 17:20-26). Finally, His great soul reached out for the "other sheep" (Jn. 10:16), who were wandering far from Him, either then, while He still lived on earth, or in all the time to come. And for all without exception He had one desire, that the Father should give them the light to see the meaning of all that He, the Son, was doing and saying, that thus they might be "drawn" to Him (Jn. 6:44), and find the Truth and the Life in Him.

# 18. FORGIVENESS AND CURE OF A CRIPPLE. 19. MATTHEW'S BANQUET; THE QUESTION OF FASTING. 20. CORN PLUCKED ON THE SABBATH. 21. THE MAN WITH THE WITHERED HAND

Thus far our Lord's career in Galilee has been triumphant, at least, on the surface. The simple people have greeted His display of power with cries of wonder. But now the conflict begins to develop. For the first time the Pharisees appear on the scene. And in this series of five incidents, apparently linked, Mark and Luke record the causes of their opposition to our Lord, and its growth. From now on they will dog His footsteps, to spy on Him and combat Him at every turn.

However, the headquarters of opposition to Him was at Jerusalem. It was first set on foot there by the Sadducean priests. The leadership of it passed from them to the Judean Pharisees (*cf.* Jn. 4:1; Lk. 5:17: Pharisees from Judea follow Him to Galilee; Mk. 3:22: Judean Pharisees first formulate the damning charge of being the tool of Satan). The Pharisees of Galilee are enlisted, but seemingly those from Judea head and direct the attack (*cf.* Mk. 7:1; and Mt. 16:1). At the end the leadership will be reassumed by the Sadducean high-priests of Jerusalem.

He Himself had challenged the priests, but in the conflict with the Pharisees He was apparently not the aggressor. For instance, in the Sermon on the Mount, which typifies His preaching at this time, the Pharisees are not mentioned by name, though their religious ideas are hit (*cf.* Mt. 6:16-19). Moreover, He enjoins on the cured leper a strict observance of legal formalities, lest scandal be given (Mk. 1:44). Nevertheless, when a personal challenge is thrown down He picks it up instantly. But at first, He simply defends Himself and His own; only later will He take the offensive.

It is important to note the progressive development of the hatred and boldness of the Pharisees. In the first incident (n. 18) they dare not speak out their accusation of blasphemy; it is merely a thought in their minds; He Himself gives it words (Mk. 2:6-9). And in the face of popular acclaim of the miracle they maintain an angry and baffled silence. In the second incident (Levi's banquet), they are bold enough to put a question but not bold enough to put it directly to Him; they insidiously approach His disciples (Mk. 2:16). Their tactics begin to appear: they aim at undermining His influence with His followers.

In the third incident (the question of fasting, raised apparently by Levi's dinner, which may have taken place on a Monday or Thursday, fast-days for the Pharisees), they dare to question our Lord directly, but not by themselves. They come in the company of some puzzled or jealous disciples of the Baptist (compare Mt. 9:14 with Lk. 5:33 and Mk. 2:18). It is another piece of strategy: they strike at the authority of Christ by invoking against it the prestige of John, whose asceticism was known and admired. In the fourth incident (n. 20) they have so far overcome their awe of the Master as to interrogate Him directly and alone. But as yet their steadily growing fear and hatred of Him is under control; for the third time they merely ask "Why?".

Finally, in the fifth incident (n. 21) their full malice is revealed: they openly spy on Him, seeking a handle for action against Him (Lk. 6:7); their hearts are already quite hardened (Mk. 3:5). And when they are once again baffled, their "fury" (Lk. 6:11) is roused. They take decisive steps; they plot with the partisans of Herod, the same ones who had done away with the Baptist. Their idea was to "destroy" Him, that is, at least to put an end to His career by having Him clapped into prison with His known ally, John. Evidently, their enmity is already definitive and embittered. But it has not yet reached its final stage of open blasphemy; to that we shall come in the next period.

Already, however, the basic motive of their opposition is clear, namely, the growing authority of our Lord over the simple people, and His formation of a closely knit party of disciples, a school attached to Himself. Inevitably He was threatening their ascendancy over the people. And that was a blow at their pride. In all that follows, this, the real issue at stake, only grows clearer. He authoritatively declared Himself, and acted as Shepherd of the "great crowd" that He saw as "sheep without a shepherd" (Mk. 6:34). And the injured pride of the selfish shepherds, the Scribes and Pharisees, who had betrayed their charge, blinded their eyes to the proved truth of His claim. Ultimately, what they hated was His authority; it destroyed their own. And it is not strange that today's conflict between the Church and the world is drawn on the same lines. Ultimately, what men rebel against in her is not this or that doctrine or practice, but her authority to teach and rule. She is Mistress, as He was Master. And so, she, too, appears inevitably as a threat to human pride.

The actual indictment publicly put forth by the Pharisees against our Lord actually boils down to one count, namely, He was not a Pharisee. In particular, these five incidents and others (*cf.* Lk. 7:39; 13:14; Jn. 5:16; 9:14, 16) show that they resented the fact that He was the avowed friend of sinners, and that He was unconcerned about petty legal observances, notably with regard to the Sabbath. Moreover, these were not surface disagreements; actually, He challenged their whole manner of life and their whole concept of religion.

Their criticisms give Him the occasion to let fall indications of who He is and what He has "come" for. These indications are veiled and discreet, but sufficiently impressive to make men of good will think seriously. That is continually His plan of procedure: to tell men not only what they can "bear", but to stimulate them to come farther toward the light.

One of these indications, though it gives a glimpse into the real mystery of His Person, was undoubtedly too obscure to be grasped, namely, His use of the phrase, "I have *come*" (Mk. 2:17). He has used it before (Mk. 1:38: "for this is why I have come"; or as Lk. 4:43 has it, "for this is why I have been sent"). Here there is an allusion to His Divinity: He preexisted as God before He "came" as man. But this allusion was so mysterious that it was understandably missed.

But other indications should have been clearer. The first is His bold statement: "the Son of Man has power on earth to forgive sins" (Mk. 2:10), with its sequel: "I have come to call sinners, not the just" (Mk. 2:17). To us the meaning is luminous: He is the Messias whom God had promised to send to reconcile sinful men to Himself; more than that, He is Himself God who by His own authority remits the guilt of offenses against Himself. And this meaning is proved by the obvious miracle that He works precisely in order to prove it.

But the bystanders, astounded though they were, could not grasp this meaning. To them the mission of the Messias was not to be the forgiveness of sin. Still less were they prepared to believe that God Himself would appear on earth as Man. And the title our Lord gives Himself, "the Son of Man", left their minds a blank (to its meaning we shall return shortly). They saw the miracle, and in it the fact that this "man" had "power" (Mt. 9:8). That was all the impression He willed to make at the moment. If their good will held, the deeper meaning would gradually dawn on them.

The second glimpse given by our Lord into His mystery is His triple application to Himself of the name "bridegroom" (Mk. 2:19-20). It had already been applied to Him by the Baptist (Jn. 3:29). The people, especially the scribes, should not have been ignorant that the days of the Messias had been described in Scripture as a nuptial banquet, that would fulfill the prophecy of Osee: "I (God) will espouse thee forever" (Osee 2:19). The metaphor of God as the "Spouse" of the soul was common in the Old Testament (*e.g.*, Isaias 54:6: "Thy Creator is thy spouse . . . . The Lord hath called thee as a wife forsaken and grieved in spirit, even a wife of youth when she is cast off . . . ."). Hence our Lord's use of the figure should at least have led men of good will to inquire further into what He meant by it.

The third hint He gives of the source of His authority is in the forthright claim: "The Son of Man is Lord even of the sabbath" (Mk. 2:28). The Sabbath was of divine institution, they should have argued; hence if this "Son of Man" has authority over it, must not He be divine? Characteristically, our Lord Himself does not point the conclusion; He leaves it to suggest itself to men of good will. But in the same context (*cf.* Mt. 12:7) He clearly reveals the reason for the Pharisees' blindness: they do not understand the first principle of all religion, the love of God and man; their souls are petrified by a mechanical observance of petty ritual. They do not love the light, hence, they cannot come to it.

But our Lord's most important, though most obscure self-revelation at this juncture is contained in the title, "the Son of Man", which He here assumes for the first time in the Synoptics (we have already seen it in John 1:51 and 3:13). Henceforth He will use it as His official designation (it occurs at least 80 times in the Gospels). Its use was an essential part of the economy of His teaching, for the general reason that by it He discreetly raised just a corner of the veil on His true identity and Mission.

As Messias, He needed a name for Himself; but He dared not use the current ones, namely, Messias, King of Israel, Son of David, the Chosen One of God, the Holy One of God, the Prophet, etc. For all these had been invested by the Scribes and people with false connotations. Had He called Himself by them, the people would have thought Him the Messias of their national dreams, with disastrous results. We have heard Him silencing those who used them of Him (Mk. 1:24; Lk. 4:41; etc.).

So He found a true Messianic title, but not a dangerously provocative one, in "the Son of Man". In itself it is a Hebraism, which we would translate simply "man", or possibly "man born of woman", since in its Old Testament use it emphasizes the lowliness of man in contrast with the grandeur of God. In this sense Ezechiel uses it continually; so also in Psalm 8:4-5: "When I consider Thy heavens, the work of Thy fingers, the moon and the stars which Thou hast made, what is man that Thou art mindful of him, or the *son of man* that Thou visitest him?"

But the phrase acquired a Messianic meaning by its use in the famous prophecy of Daniel in which the victory of the Messias over the powers of earth is described: "I saw in a vision of the night, and behold there came with the clouds of heaven one like unto a *son of man,* and He came up to the Ancient of days (*i.e.,* a title of God, denoting His majesty), and was presented to Him. And there was given Him dominion and glory and a Kingdom, that all the peoples, nations and tongues should serve Him; His dominion is an everlasting dominion which will not pass away, and His Kingdom will not be destroyed" (Daniel 7:13-14).

The prophecy was recognized by the Jews as Messianic; our Lord Himself twice refers to it (Mk. 13:26; 14:62). Moreover, the use of the title "Son of Man" in a Messianic sense was not unknown. But it was by no means in popular use (*cf.* Jn. 12:34). And anyway, an enlightened faith would be required to see in the Man, Jesus of Nazareth, the mysterious Being, surrounded with a divine glory, of whom Daniel spoke. Hence our Lord is secure in using it. It accomplished His purpose: to put a problem to His hearers, to arrest their attention, without confirming them in their false ideas, and without forcing on them His own. He deliberately wished for a while to be an enigma, so He gives Himself this enigmatic name.

After His death it naturally drops out of use, and its place is taken by the Christian names, "Christ", "the Lord", "the Son of God", that clearly express the true character of the "Son of Man".

## 22. CONTINUED FAME; CROWDS

The public clash with the Pharisees in the synagogue leads to a change in our Lord's conduct. He is apprised of their plot and He leaves the city and goes to the lakeshore with His disciples (Mk. 3:7). He has no desire uselessly to provoke the violence of His enemies; so He gives up disputing with them in the synagogue. Matthew's citation from Isaias indicates the program He would follow: not loud arguments in public places, but a quiet nourishing of the few sparks of faith that He has aroused. He knew that controversy with the ill-disposed, though sometimes necessary, is seldom profitable to them, for it only hardens them in their views.

Nevertheless, the crowds flock to Him; they are as yet unshaken by the Pharisees' disapproval. Compassionate always, He "healed them all" (Mt. 12:15). But insistently He bade them to be quiet about His favors (Mt. 12:16); and "emphatically" He imposed silence on the demons who proclaimed Him "the Son of God" (Mk. 3:12). All this emotional uproar was no kind of atmosphere for the work He wished done, a work of quiet thinking in the heart.

## 23. THE CHOICE OF THE TWELVE

This incident, too, has an organic connection with the attitude of the Pharisees. As opposition to Him is organized, our Lord takes a decisive step in the organization of His own party.

All the details suggest the solemnity of the step. In the evening, our Lord goes alone up one of the hills behind the lake, perhaps having instructed His disciples to join Him in the morning. He spends the whole night in prayer, as always before a crisis. The plot of the Pharisees has presaged the future: His own death is decreed. He Himself has already prophesied it in His mysterious allusion to the time that is coming "when the Bridegroom shall be taken away" (Mk. 2:20). But His work must be eternal. He must now choose the men into whose hands He will give over His own authority to teach and rule and sanctify. They will be the builders of His Church. So for them and His Church He prays.

In the morning His disciples come (we do not know their number), and with them apparently the usual crowd. Our Lord always shunned the theatrical, but He must have so dramatized the scene as to underline the fact that He Himself was making a free choice of these twelve men from the larger ranks of His disciples. Mark insists: "He called to Him men of His own choosing, and they came to Him" (Mk. 3:13). There was no "volunteering"; He took the initiative. And frequently later He recalls to them the fact of their choice (cf. Jn. 6:71; 13:18; 15:16). He wishes them to think of it as a gift from Himself, that was entirely undeserved.

Only on one occasion does He give His reason for selecting them and not others. In His Priestly Prayer He says four times that they had been "given" to Him by His Father. Ultimately their choice is a mystery of God's own selective love, which has no reason save itself. The mystery deepens when one thinks of Judas. His choice was not a mistake, made in ignorance. Our Lord knew then that he would be a traitor. But at the moment he was worthy. His perseverance would be at his own free choice. And God so respects human freedom that He is willing to risk His own betrayal by it. Moreover, He has turned even Judas' treason to the good of the Church: by that example she is fortified against the scandal of evil priests. They stain themselves, not her.

The number Twelve is symbolic: there would be twelve foundation stones to the Church, as there were twelve Jewish patriarchs and twelve tribes of Israel. Hence the immediate concern of the eleven to fill the place of Judas (Acts 1:15-26: the mode of choice is interesting, they leave it to God "who knows the hearts of all men"; we see here the impression left on them by their own choice).

In listing their names, a hierarchy is observable that was not accidental.

The Twelve always fall into three groups of four each, and each group has its own head, thus: *Peter,* Andrew, James, John; *Philip,* Bartholomew (Nathaniel), Thomas, Matthew; *James the son of Alpheus,* Simon (the Zealous, or the Cananean), Jude (Thaddeus), Judas Iscariot (*cf.* Mt. 10:2-4; Mk. 3:16-19; Lk. 6:14-16; Acts 1:13). Peter always comes first, Judas last.

The purpose of their call is clearly marked: "He appointed twelve that they might be with Him, and that he might send them forth to preach. To them He gave power to cure sicknesses and to cast out devils" (Mk. 3:14-15). Their first duty is to be with Him, as witnesses to all He says and does. That will be the mode of their own formation; simply being with Him will gradually teach them who He is (their first lesson) and what is His work (their second lesson). Later their essential work will be to go into all the world as "witnesses" to Him (Acts 1:8; *cf.* 3:15). They will "invent" nothing, and "interpret" nothing; their single aim will be to tell what they "have seen and heard" (Acts 4:20; 1 Jn. 1:1-3).

So He takes them under His authority. He also purposes to let them share in it: during His life He will send them on two "missions", to preach and to heal. That will be part of their education. It will also be a prelude of their future definitive mission, when He shall hand over to them His full authority to teach and rule and sanctify (*cf.* Jn. 17:17; 20:21; Mt. 28:18-20). Thus the structural lines of His "Kingdom" are already clear. It will not be some sort of loose association of individuals, animated in general by the same religious spirit, but serving God simply as individuals, independently of one another. On the contrary, it will be a visible and hierarchical society, authoritatively taught and governed by men who are the direct delegates of Christ. Only they will wield His power, and hence to reach Him, men must come to them, and submit to them.

What kind of men were they? In the Acts (4:13) the Sanhedrin terms Peter and John uneducated and ordinary men. The meaning is that they were not educated as Rabbis. But, on the other hand, they and their companions should not be thought of as ignorant rustics from the lower classes of society. The fact is that they had the ordinary culture of their time; they could read and write, and they even knew some Greek. Moreover, they were not indigent, but solidly "middle-class", neither rich nor poor. Peter and his group had a successful fishing business. Philip and his group were probably professional men of some sort; certainly Matthew was such. Of the last group, we know nothing, save that Judas had a head for financial management.

What is clear is that our Lord chose men from the same social level, whom no great distinctions of fortune or education divided. For above all else, He wanted unity among them (*cf.* Jn. 17:11). Perhaps for this reason, too, His choice consecrated blood relationship, as well as friendships (*e.g.,*

Peter and John, Philip and Bartholomew). For the rest, He wanted real men, willing to learn, ready for sacrifice, accustomed to work, and to work "in harness". He Himself would bring out all their hidden potentialities, and patiently correct their wrong ideas and temperamental defects.

## 24. THE SERMON ON THE MOUNT

By His selection of the Twelve and their attachment to Himself as their Master, our Lord has taken a personal position with regard to the official teachers of Israel. He has drawn definitely apart from them, formed His own "school", and set Himself as its head. Now, as a complementary step, He must define His doctrinal position with respect to theirs.

The step is necessary. His teaching so far has aroused wonder because of its "newness". His mode of life has been strikingly different from that of the Scribes and Pharisees. Notably, He has taken a different attitude toward the Law. All these things have roused questions in the minds of His disciples, the public and His enemies. And so far His answers have been only fragmentary; He has simply declared Himself on particular points as occasion offered. It is time now for a fuller declaration of His principles. In particular, He has four questions to answer: 1) What is the relation between His doctrine and the ancient faith of Israel, as contained in "the Law and the Prophets"? 2) What is the source of His conflict with the Pharisees, and how does His spirit differ from theirs? 3) In the concrete, what does He demand of His followers? 4) The most important question: in virtue of what authority does He teach, recruit followers, make demands?

Significantly, to the last question Our Lord gives at the moment no answer in words: His whole life will be its answer. To the third question He returns a partial answer, all His audience could "bear" for the time being. But the Sermon on the Mount answers fully the first and second questions. It contains a statement, clear enough for men of good will, of the true spiritual nature of the new Reign of God, though it leaves other aspects of the Kingdom for later development.

Its general theme may be put thus: "the spirit and ideal of Christ as contrasted with the spirit and ideal of Jewish religion, especially as taught by the Pharisaic Scribes". In it our Lord lays down a program for a lofty moral perfection, motivated by a childlike love of God the Father, and affecting the inmost heart of man. This interior perfection is to be the ideal of the new Kingdom, supplanting the old ideal of legal righteousness, based on an exact observance of the Mosaic Law, and affecting chiefly man's external conduct.

It was His development of this theme that thrilled the hearts of the people. Whereas the Pharisees pointed to an impersonal Law, whose rigid prohibitions are not to be transgressed, He showed them God, as a Father, whose loving invitations to union with Himself are to be answered by a glad giving of oneself to Him, in full-hearted, energetic obedience to His every will. Thus He gave to religion a new life, a new purity, a new depth. He brought God so much nearer to them, and thus made His service at once more gladdening and more demanding. No wonder they were stirred as they had never been stirred before. As He spoke on in His quiet but compelling tones, in words so simple and suited to them, picturesque, pungent, at times even lit by a flash of humor, they felt their hearts opening and a great light beginning to dawn in their minds, the realization, never before experienced, that God is indeed One who has the name of Father, and that they were His children whom He intimately loved and desired to draw to Himself. Just why they felt this, they could not have explained; for they did not know that it was the Son speaking to them, and trying to show them with human words that which His whole soul gazed upon, the Face of His Father.

The two written versions of the Sermon, by Matthew and Luke, differ considerably. Luke has edited it in view of his Gentile audience; he contrasts the spirit of Christ with that of the world, not with that of the Old Law and the Pharisees, and he makes the whole Sermon a proclamation of the new law of charity. On the other hand, Matthew has introduced into it some words of Christ that were spoken on other occasions, and that are given by Luke in their proper setting. The original form of the discourse, much shortened, of course, even by Matthew, will be better seen if the following passages of Matthew are omitted (the student should bracket them in his text: 5:13-16; 5:25-26; 5:29-32; 6:7-15; 6:19-34; 7:7-11; 7:13-14).

The audience that our Lord had in view was primarily the Twelve, and then the larger group from which they had been chosen (cf. Lk. 6:20). But it is clear that "a great crowd of people" was also present. (Lk. 6:17-18).

For our purposes it will be sufficient to indicate: 1) the build and content of the Sermon (according to Matthew's full text, cc. 5-7), and 2) its situation and function in the unrolling of our Lord's message.

The discourse falls naturally into three parts: I. The Beatitudes (5:3-16). II. The main theme: the ideal of Christ, defined by contrast with the ideal of the Law and that of the Pharisees (5:17—7:12). III. A concluding warning and an exhortation to action.

I. The Beatitudes. In these vigorous sentences Our Lord gives His portrait of the soul that is ready for the Kingdom of Heaven. They are filled with allusions to the Old Testament, and are in fact a consecration of all that is best in Jewish religion. Indirectly He is saying: "If you live out what is deepest and most divine in your own faith, if you do the truth that you know, you will come to the Kingdom".

His Kingdom is for the "poor", *i.e.,* in the biblical sense, not necessarily the indigent, but the defenseless and oppressed who accept their lot without rebellion and turn in trust to God. It is for the "meek", those who humbly adore the will of God in all the details of life. It is for "those who mourn", who suffer interiorly from a sense of their own sinfulness, and exteriorly from the injustice of the world. It is for those "who hunger and thirst after justice", who aspire after an ideal of sanctity. It is for the "merciful", those who are generous in giving alms, in pardoning offenses, in showing to the unfortunate all marks of active sympathy. It is for the "pure in heart", whose souls are not shut off from God by the thick veil of sensual satisfactions, who are innocent, straightforward, sincere. It is for the "peacemakers", those who love unity among men, and give themselves actively to the divine work of creating it on earth. It is above all for those who "suffer persecutions" for the sake of Christ, those who are ready to give up things in order to have Him, who are willing to pay the cost of being "different" from other men by reason of their allegiance to Him. That is the critical test: entrance into the Kingdom means sacrifice.

The next words (vv. 13-16) are addressed to the disciples. The ideal just put forth is not to be an abstract theory. It is to be embodied in the life of the world. And that is their work. They are to be practical models of this ideal, and its artisans in the world of human society.

In Luke, the Beatitudes are given a different form. He omits all the biblical allusions, and points a vivid contrast between the spirit of Christ and that of the worldling. The latter seeks (and often finds) his happiness in the here-and-now, and in the joys it can give. The disciple of Christ looks beyond the horizon of this life to a "great reward", and in that perspective adjusts his standards of happiness. He will not risk losing his imperishable soul for that which perishes.

II. The "newness" of Christ. First of all, our Lord lays down His basic principle (5:17). He is a reformer, not a revolutionary, a builder not a wrecker: "I am not come to destroy, but to bring to perfection". His new way of life grows out of the old way, as the plant from its seed. The seed is the great commandment of love, that headed the Law (Deut. 6:5), but that the Jews had never fully understood. It will now be displayed in its perfection in the example of Christ Himself, and the perfection of it will be proposed to His followers as their ideal.

Our Lord selects five points to show how the Mosaic Law will be perfected in His new Kingdom (Mt. 5:20-48). It forbade murder and adultery; He forbids any motion of anger, any deliberate impure desire. It imposed obligations of veracity, of patience under injury, of active concern for one's neighbor. He heightens and broadens immeasurably the demands of those virtues and proposes an ideal of heroism in their practice: He enjoins a direct simplicity of speech that needs no oath to guarantee it, because it proceeds from an utterly truthful heart; a spirit of forgiveness that is willing to go to all lengths of sacrifice; a sincere love of all men, that excludes no one, not even an enemy, from its embrace.

In all five cases our Lord"s intention is clear: where the Law had merely punished the external act, He penetrates to the heart, checks its unruly impulses, and demands of it a limitless perfection. He would not have men take as their moral ideal simply the non-violation of certain prohibitions; He would have them turn their souls to God, their Father, and strive to be His children, like unto Him. He gives them a positive, divine ideal: "You therefore, are to be perfect, even as your heavenly Father is perfect" (Mt. 5:48). Thus He does not destroy the Law; all the "Thou shalt not's" of the Decalogue remain in full force. But they are brought to perfection; His disciples will go beyond them, in an effort to draw nearer and nearer to God and to make their human lives reflect more and more perfectly the holiness of God.

In the next section (6:1-18), our Lord contrasts His spirit with that of the "hypocrites", the Pharisees, in the three points in which Jewish piety chiefly showed itself: almsgiving, prayer, and fasting. The Pharisees did these things ostentatiously, in order to be seen by men, and gain a reputation for sanctity. Our Lord bids His followers do their good deeds, be they public or private, with complete and unselfconscious simplicity, as children striving to please a Father. He "sees in secret"; the heart of man is open to Him. And anything but complete honesty of heart is an insult to Him. Here our Lord lays bare the essential vice of Pharisaism, hypocrisy. He detested it. And He demanded of His followers above all else, an utter sincerity, a love of what is true, and real, and inward.

In the following section (Mt. 6:19-34), our Lord briefly develops the idea contained in v. 33: "Seek first the kingdom of God . . ." (Though probably these verses did not form part of the original Sermon; they are given by Luke in other contexts: *cf.* Lk. 12:33-34; 11:34-36; 16:13; 12:22-31: still, they fit well with the general argument of the Sermon). Nowadays we would call this idea the principle of the primacy of the spiritual: let man care first of all for his soul, for if he puts his soul wholly in the hands of God, he may implicitly trust that the wisdom and love of his Father will care adequately for the needs of his body.

Returning to the theme of the Sermon (7:1-6, 12) we find some pointed practical observations, which are then summed up in the "Golden Rule" (7:12). It is the law of charity of Deuteronomy: "Love thy neighbor as thyself". But it is given a wider range. "Neighbor" to the Jew meant another Jew (*cf.* Lk. 10:29-37); he did not feel obliged to love foreigners. But to our Lord, the law is universal: "neighbor" means simply "fellow-man".

What follows is the conclusion. First come three warnings: "Enter in at the narrow gate". "Beware of false teachers!" "It is what you do that counts, for it reveals what you are!" And the final word is in the form of a parable, whose meaning is luminous and weighty with warning: it is not enough to hear the truth, one must *do* it! The parable reveals the supreme principle that is behind the whole Sermon: he who acts according to the truth that he knows, will come to fuller insight into the truth.

In terms of this principle we must understand the relation of the Sermon on the Mount to the rest of our Lord's message. It was essentially an intro- duction to His "gospel"; it was a moral preparation for the lesson in theology He had come to give. He is telling them how to get their hearts ready for the light that He desires to give them, on what God is, and on what is His full plan for human life.

It is important to realize this point. Nowadays, especially among the ranks of purely "sentimental" Christians, the fashion is to see in the Sermon on the Mount the *whole* of Christ's message. Worse than that, it is often read as the charter of a vapid "tolerance", or a humanitarian program for making this world a less uncomfortable place to live in. The proponents of this view say: "Here is a perfectly lovely moral program, to which no one can reasonably object. Let us take it (of course, after carefully pulling all the teeth out of it, *e.g.*, Mt. 5:28-30). It will help much to "the good life". And let us not bother our heads with the awkward question as to who He was who gave us it". The view is about as sensible as saying: "Here is a perfectly lovely vestibule. Let us camp in it, and not be at all interested in opening the door to which it leads".

For a matter of fact, the moral grandeur of the Sermon on the Mount should not obscure from us the fact that it is essentially a vestibule, an introduction to the Person of Christ, God Incarnate. Only that fact makes it completely intelligible. It is not a summary of Christian doctrine: there is nothing in it about man's need of redemption or of grace, nothing about the Church and her power to teach and sanctify, nothing about the Holy Spirit and His work on earth, nothing about the sacraments, the com- munion of saints, etc.

Neither is it a summary of Christian morality. It does not accurately define all Christian duties; it does not distinguish precepts from counsels. It does not even state the Christian moral ideal in its highest form. The "Golden Rule" is only a preliminary formulation. The full Christian law of love will be promulgated only at the Last Supper, in the shadow of the Cross, after Christ, "Master and Lord", has washed the feet of His disciples, and before He goes to die for them. And it is not: "Love others as you love yourself", but: "A new commandment I give you, that you love one another; that *as I have loved you* you also love one another" (Jn. 13:34; *cf.* 15:12-13).

The fact is that the full Christian ethic is not promulgated until its dogmatic bases have been laid down, namely, the Divinity of Christ, and His redeeming death upon the Cross. Only when men have seen what He is, and what He did and suffered, will they understand what they are to be and do and suffer. Christian morality must be studied in the Letters of St. Paul, where the consequences of the Crucifixion are drawn with inexorable logic. For the basic principle of Christian morality is voluntary union with Christ Crucified. Its whole inspiration is "the Son of God, who loved me and gave himself up for me". And its program is this: "With Christ am I nailed to the Cross. It is now no longer I that live, but Christ lives in me (Gal. 2:20).

The sketch of the Christian moral ideal given in the Sermon on the Mount, and the practical suggestions it contains, were not designed by our Lord to be definitive and complete, but preliminary and initiatory to His great secret, the mystery of His own Person. In effect, He is saying to His disciples: "Live the life of a child of God, and your hearts will be ready to accept the fact, when I show it to you, that I am His Only-begotten Son, made Man to be your Redeemer". The whole Sermon is dominated by His two pedagogical principles: "I have yet many things to tell you, but you cannot bear them now", and "Do this truth, and you will come to the Light".

Still, the Sermon is more than a mere preparation for the revelation of Himself. In it He does actually reveal Himself, but most discreetly. In accordance with His plan, the main idea He puts forward is the idea of the Kingdom, its spiritual character, the fact that its coming will not mean a change in the world's political arrangements, but a change in the inmost heart of man. Nevertheless, He Himself appears in His words; He suggests who He is by the *authority* with which He speaks.

With perfect serenity He attributes to Himself an authority greater than that of Moses: "You have heard what was said to the ancients . . . But I say to you . . ." (Mt. 5:21, 27, 31, 33, 38, 43). To His hearers there was no higher religious authority than Moses, save God Himself. Moreover, our Lord does not speak as Moses himself spoke: "The Lord, God of your fathers . . . hath sent me to you" (Exodus 3:15; *et passim*). On the contrary, His formula has a simplicity that can only be divine: "*I* say to you . . ."

Equally significant is His other formula: "Blessed are you when men persecute you . . . for *My* sake" (Mt. 5:11; *cf.* Lk. 6:22: "for the sake of the Son of Man"). He has in mind what will happen to those who will believe in Him: they will be put out of the synagogue (*cf.* Jn. 9:22-34; 16:2). To the Jew no greater sacrifice was imaginable, save that of life itself. Yet our Lord serenely asserts His right to demand these supreme sacrifices. For Him, personally, they must be willing to do these things. And His own word of blessing will be their sole reward. Who, then, *is* this Man, who can so speak?

Again, He demands that they build on His words as on solid rock, though He gives no other guarantee that His words are true save the fact that He speaks them. And He asserts that anyone who hears His words and refuses to take them as the foundation of his whole life, is a "fool", and is headed for "ruin" (Mt. 7:24-27).

Moreover, He not only dares to put Himself at the beginning of life as its foundation, but He also firmly places Himself at its end, as the Judge of men. The ultimate test, that will decide man's eternal lot, is: What have you done for Me? And the sentence of condemnation, cutting man off forever from happiness, will be: *"I never knew you; depart from Me . . ."* (Mt. 7:23). He is Himself man's final beatitude.

Thus in the Sermon on the Mount our Lord reveals Himself. He puts Himself squarely there where only God Himself can stand, at the center of man's religious and moral life. By Him men are taught, pardoned, judged, condemned, saved, beatified. But as yet His assertions are discreet, unemphasized. He is still keeping His own Person in the background, shadowed. Later He will speak more clearly, notably of Himself as Judge (*cf.* Mt. 10:32 ff.; 25:31-46; Jn. 5:27). But already He has made one thing plain: somehow He is "all-important". To reach God, one must come to Him. But He—who is He?

That question still remains. But He has showed them the way to get the answer: let them be true children of the Father, penitent, confident in His Providence, prayerful, sincere, interior, faithful to the truth they have heard. If they have this childlike heart, they will be "teachable", and He will teach them more.

## Chapter XVII

# THE PUBLIC LIFE: PERIOD II. CONSTRUCTION
# B. IN GALILEE

## PHASE 2. HARDENING OF OPPOSITION
### *Time:* Summer and fall, 27 A.D.

|  | Mt | Mk | Lk | Jn |
|---|---|---|---|---|
| 25. Servant of the centurion | 8: 5-13 | — | 7: 1-10 | — |
| 26. Son of the widow of Naim | — | — | 7: 11-17 | — |
| 27. Embassy from the Baptist | 11:2-6 | — | 7: 18-23 | — |
| 28. Eulogy of the Baptist | 11:7-19 | — | 7: 24-35 | — |
| 29. The sinful woman | — | — | 7: 36-50 | — |
| 30. Women in Christ's entourage | — | — | 8: 1-3 | — |
| 31. Anxiety of His kinsfolk | 12: 46-47 | 3: 20-21 | 8: 19 | — |
| 32. Controversy with Pharisees: | | | | |
| Charge: agent of Beelzebub | — | — | — | — |
| Reply: sin against Spirit | 12:22-45 | 3: 22-30 | { 11: 14-26 <br> { 12: 10 | — <br> — |
| 33. His Mother and brethren | 12: 48-50 | 3: 31-35 | { 8: 20-21 <br> { 11: 27-28 | — <br> — |
| 34. Parables on the Kingdom | 13: 1-52 | 4: 1-34 | { 8: 4-18 <br> { 13: 18-21 | — <br> — |

THIS PHASE of our Lord's work in Galilee is continuous with the preceding one, and to a great extent its salient features are the same. He is intensely energetic; He teaches around Capharnaum, and makes a second tour of Galilee. The content of His teaching follows the lines of the Sermon on the Mount; it is a moral doctrine, an exhortation to those interior dispositions, canonized in the Beatitudes, which are indispensable for entrance into the Kingdom.

But the success of His teaching is poor. True, great crowds of people hear Him gladly and applaud, but they do not give Him what He wants, that sincere, interior change of heart. They build on the sand of an unthinking admiration for the wonderful things He continues to do, out of His endless compassion for their sufferings. To them He is primarily the great Thaumaturge, and then, too, a Prophet. However, as His power in word and deed makes a deeper impression, the thought does begin to suggest itself: may He not be Messias? Not that they begin to grasp His idea of the Messias' work; their own ideas still fill their minds. But at least the theory is broached; that is a development.

To it corresponds the most significant development of this phase, namely, the hostility of the Scribes and Pharisees. To check the enthusiasm of the people, and cancel their dawning theory, they circulate their own theory: He is the agent of the devil. In a violent altercation, our Lord refutes their blasphemy, and openly accuses them of pure, unredeemable malice. This incident marks His definitive rupture with them.

Then His own teaching moves into a new phase. Hitherto He has emphasized simply the spiritual character of the Kingdom; henceforth He begins to explain its more intimate nature, and correct popular ideas. But for reasons to be explained, He casts His teaching into the form of parables, a new departure. Moreover, His economy of light grows more marked: fuller explanations are given to His disciples than to the crowd.

## 25. THE SERVANT OF THE CENTURION. 26. THE SON OF THE WIDOW OF NAIM

Both of these incidents clearly belong to this part of the Galilean ministry, though their actual dates are not determinable.

The first is dear to the Church, which echoes daily in the Mass the words of the centurion (Mt. 8:8), words full of a humble, manly faith. Our Lord was "astonished" to hear them from this pagan soldier (ranking about as a sergeant with us), and they drew from Him the prophecy of the rejection of the Jews and the call of the pagans to His Kingdom (pictured under the customary image of a feast).

The second incident is one of the most touching in the whole Gospel (it is told only in the "Gospel of women"). And it illustrates in incomparable fashion both the human heart of Christ and His divine power. He does the miracle spontaneously, "touched with compassion" at the mother's tears. And He does it with a simple command. He is the Master of souls, and they obey His voice, and live or die at His will. Then, to add the final note of exquisite perfection to the scene, "He gave him to his mother", a charmingly simple gesture of courtesy. From the whole incident the Christ of Christian faith stands out: perfect God and perfect Man.

The impression produced was tremendous, in the literal sense. It was the most staggering prodigy that He had as yet done. Its witnesses were overcome with awe, that sentiment of religious terror that man experiences when he comes in contact with the divine. They felt God among them, and at once trembled and were joyous in praise. But they did not recognize

God *in* Him. God was *with* Him; He was "a great prophet": this they felt. But the real mystery was still shut off from them. Still, the event had a great effect: His fame spread throughout all Palestine.

## 27. THE EMBASSY FROM THE BAPTIST. 28. THE EULOGY OF THE BAPTIST

The incident is at first sight surprising: why should the Baptist send delegates to Christ to inquire if He were really "the One who is to come"? Had his faith begun to waver? That explanation is unbelievable, especially in view of the splendid eulogy of John that our Lord pronounces.

The fact is that the delegates were sent primarily for their own benefit. We have seen how some of John's disciples were jealous of Christ (Jn. 3:25-26), and some, too, were scandalized at His free way of life (Mt. 9:14). John himself had evidently been unable to correct their narrow, mistaken loyalty to him, or to make them share his own faith in Christ. So he sends them to our Lord, wishing Him to give some decisive clarification. The wish is gratified, to a degree. Characteristically, our Lord does not explicitly answer the direct question put to Him. He follows His own continual method: He lets them "see and hear" (Mt. 11:4) what He is doing. They should know the prophecies of Isaias about the miracles of mercy that the Messias would do. He is doing them. That is their answer. It is enough, but no more than enough. They had still to make the effort He always demanded, namely, to understand, and to trust. So He despatches them with a warning: "Blessed is he who is not scandalized in me" (Mt. 11:6). He means: let them not refuse to accept Him because He is not what they thought He should be, but let them try to understand Him as He is.

Was the lesson also for John? Possibly it was, in a sense. Not that John doubted now whether our Lord was really the Messias. But he could well have been surprised at the way He was going about His work. There is no reason to suppose that John was familiar with the whole plan of redemption and just how it would unroll. God tells His secrets to no man all at once. Actually, the splendid images John used in his preaching would seem to indicate his expectations that "the One who was to come" would somehow achieve a speedy and brilliant success: the Bridegroom would take unto Himself His bride, etc. In particular he looked for a great Judgment, a "sifting" of men (Mt. 3:12). He might well have been surprised at our Lord's delays, His desire gently to persuade and not to smite. So for him our Lord's words would have been an affectionate reassurance.

The whole incident has a permanent lesson. It shows how even good men could be puzzled by Christ, and prejudiced against Him. The prejudices of these men were honest, born of their incomplete grasp of God's plans, and the natural human impulse to impose their human ideas on God. And our Lord's whole method of teaching shows how He took all this into account. He never said He was "easy" to understand. He knew that the idea of God becoming man would be too colossal for human comprehension. Hence He did not flatly assert His own Divinity, and imperiously demand its instant acceptance. On the contrary, He asked only two things: first, that men should make a sincere effort to overcome their prejudices, to "open" their minds, and secondly, that they should honestly review the evidence for His claims. "Go tell John what you have seen and heard": that is His formula for arousing or strengthening faith in Him. By applying it, His Apostles converted the world: they simply told what they had seen and heard (Acts 4:20). The Church uses it today. And where prejudice, honest or malicious, does not obscure the truth, she is accepted, as He was. However, too many are like the perverse children our Lord describes; they cannot be pleased. Either she is too divine for them, or too human. He met the same objection.

## 29. THE SINFUL WOMAN

Luke reports three dinners that our Lord took with the Pharisees; they should really be studied together (cf. Lk. 11:37 ff. and 14:1 ff.). They indicate that even later our Lord never broke completely with individual Pharisees. However relentlessly He castigated their ideas and manner of life, He was always ready to go more than half-way with them personally. That is true "tolerance". However, in all three cases, as the sequel showed, He was not invited out of any desire to do Him honor, but rather to spy on Him, or perhaps pose as His "patron" before the people. In all three cases, too, the gentleness and strength of His character stands out strikingly. He is unfailingly courteous, in the face of manifest discourtesy. But He does not hesitate to speak very bluntly, and even scathingly. He is at once the model of the gentleman, and the gentleman of principle, perfectly mannered, but perfectly fearless.

The scene with the sinful woman (it is not implied that she was a courtesan, but definitely a woman of some notoriety) is highly dramatic, and very human. Its lesson is evident. This is His work, the forgiveness of sins. And here is the kind of soul to whom His forgiveness can be spoken. She had been guilty of "many sins"; He does not gloss over that fact. But she "loved much"; and her love, manifested effectively in an outward act of sincere penitence, is the motive of her forgiveness. Authoritatively, He grants it. The scene dramatizes the power of "perfect contrition" over the heart of God.

Was the sinful woman Mary Magdalen? Mary of Bethany, the sister of Martha? Both or neither? We do not know. Some see in the anointing of our Lord's feet by Mary of Bethany (Jn. 12:3 ff.) a souvenir of this scene that suggests the identity of the two women. But the text of Luke implies rather that the three women were distinct.

## 30. THE WOMEN IN CHRIST'S ENTOURAGE

In speaking of our Lord's tour of Galilee, Luke gives us a precious detail concerning the external conditions of our Lord's life. He and His Apostles were provided for by the devotion and generosity of a group of women, who prepared for His advent in different towns. The practice was common at the time. Our Lord condemned its abuse by the Pharisees, who "devoured the house of widows" (Lk. 20:47). But He accepted the service in His own case. Though He nourished others miraculously, He Himself lived simply and gratefully on alms, and taught His disciples to do likewise. Moreover, by His acceptance of this service He consecrated in advance the devotion of millions of women who would give their lives to His Church, to tend its sick and poor and train its children. Men would rule His Church, but women would minister to it. And this division He wished to be prefigured in His own life.

## 31. THE ANXIETY OF CHRIST'S KINSFOLK. 33. THE VISIT OF THE MOTHER AND RELATIVES OF CHRIST

The connection of these two episodes (interrupted in Mark by the altercation with the Pharisees) is somewhat obscure. The first step toward understanding them is to realize that this was a time of intense activity on the part of our Lord, and a time of popular turmoil. The second step is to translate Mk. 3:21 more exactly: "They said (impersonal meaning; 'It was being said'): He is beside Himself" (not "gone mad"; the word used means "to be carried out of oneself by some strong emotion"). The explanation is in the preceding verse: so occupied was our Lord with His work that He had not time even to eat. It is supposed that this was a regular occurrence. The report of this dynamic, exalted activity, and the concourse of people that stimulated it, was spread abroad. Perhaps there was some malice behind it, the effort of ill-disposed people to dismiss our Lord as a "fanatic", who was "going too far". At any rate, the report reached Nazareth, and alarmed "His own", *i.e.*, probably His relatives. And they "went out to lay hold of him" (Mk. 3:21).

Their motives are not stated. But we know the incredulity of many of

His relatives (*cf.* Jn. 7:3-5). Perhaps they feared that all this uproar would compromise them; perhaps it was a mistaken affection; it is not improbable that sinister rumors about the intention of the Pharisees were going about. At any rate, their idea is to put a stop to it, by obliging Him to "be sensible". To us there is something very painful about their sentiments, so narrow and blind.

At the time of their arrival at Peter's house in Capharnaum, our Lord is in the midst of a violent dispute with the Pharisees (to which we shall return). The crowd is so great that they cannot enter, so they send in a message to Him (Mk. 3:31). Here we learn that Mary has come with them, very naturally, when rumor had it that her Son was in danger. The meaning of her presence is clear: she feared a conflict if they attempted to impose their authority on Him, and she was there to insure peace. We can easily conjecture the difficult position she held among her own relatives, and how her gentle influence was needed to "manage" their stubborn incredulity. We know she was finally successful, and won them to Him (*cf.* Acts 1:14).

The reply of our Lord, given evidently in a mood of emotion, indicated by His "looking round" (Mk. 3:34), is illuminating. He does not deny His Mother; that is unthinkable. His words are for His disciples, to teach them that there is a spiritual relationship more noble and more intimate than family-ties. It exists between the members of His Church, who are united in their love of Him, and in their devotion to the will of His Father. Even Mary is the "Blessed" Mother primarily because she is united to Him spiritually, her soul perfectly one with His (*cf.* Lk. 11:27-28).

Moreover, He has another lesson. He will ask of others that they prize Him more than "father and mother and wife and children and brothers and sisters" (Lk. 14:26). He assures them that they will find in His companionship all the human tenderness that they desire. And He gives them the spur of His example: for His Father's work He gave up the companionship of the one person on earth who really understood Him.

## 32. The Altercation with the Pharisees: the Sin Against the Holy Spirit

It is possible that the Pharisees had a hand in circulating the rumor that our Lord was "beside Himself", an uncontrolled fanatic. But it is certain that they were about this time circulating a far more damaging accusation. Their cause was failing. Now the people were beginning to think: "Can this be the son of David?" (Mt. 12:33), *i.e.*, the Messias. Our Lord's deliverance of possessed persons was making an especial impression. The

Pharisees were forced to produce some "explanation" of this marvelous power, and they found it in the charge: "He is Himself possessed by a demon, and by the authority of Beelzebub, the prince of demons, He casts out demons".

This blasphemy followed logically from their opposition to Him. He had threatened their authority by His "new" teaching; unable to refute His teaching, they transferred their hatred to His Person. They attacked His sanctity, calling Him "a glutton, and a wine-bibber, and a friend of publicans and sinners" (Lk. 7:34). The calumnies had no effect on the people. His marvelous miracles of mercy enthralled them. Hence these had to be attacked. It was no good denying the facts; so they were "explained" by diabolic agency: He was the tool of Satan.

Apparently the "theory" was devised in Jerusalem; Mark puts it first on the lips of "the Scribes who had come down from Jerusalem" (Mk. 3:22; cf. Lk. 5:17). It was a damning charge, and the authority of the Scribes gave it great weight with the people. Hence our Lord takes energetic steps: Mark says explicitly that He "called them together" (3:23), i.e., to Peter's house.

In a vigorous argument He shows the absurdity of the calumny: Satan would not work against Satan. And He presses home His counter offensive by pitilessly exposing the malice of those who spread it. He had borne patiently their ridicule, their unjust criticisms, even their plots. But now they had gone too far. It was not simply against Him they had sinned; that sin could be forgiven. But they were sinning against the Holy Spirit, and that sin "will not be forgiven him, either in this world or in the next" (Mt. 12:32).

These are thundering words, spoken at what must have been a highly emotional scene. Their essential meaning is clear enough. Blasphemy against the Son of Man, i.e., the refusal to recognize Him as God, will be forgiven. The reason is His appearance as a simple Man, the concealment of His Divinity. These are circumstances that excuse or extenuate men's refusal of faith; they leave room for ignorance, error, self-deception. His Divinity is not *clear* to them.

But blasphemy against the Holy Spirit will not be forgiven. What is *this* sin? It is that of the Scribes and Pharisees: as religious men, learned in the Law, they knew clearly that His miracles could not be done save by the power of God; yet knowing this, and wishing to block His work, they deliberately attributed them to the power of Satan, the enemy of all that is holy. That was to blaspheme, not simply against the Son of Man, but against Divinity itself, against the Power of God, the "Holy Spirit" that was manifested in His miraculous works.

And that sin is "unforgiveable". Not that there is a limit to God's mercy, but that the sin of its nature precludes its own forgiveness. It is a sin against the light, a sin not of error, but of pure malice. Hence by it they deliberately shut themselves off from the light of grace that is necessary for repentance. They loved the darkness, and so they *could* not come to the light. Properly, it is the sin of Satan himself; and in the case of the Pharisees it was all the more grave in that they whispered their poisonous calumny into the ears of the innocent people, and thus blocked the expansion of the Kingdom of God, the work of Christ and His Holy Spirit.

This is an indictment of the utmost gravity, spoken by One who knew their hearts. And its gravity will be felt the more when one considers that He was also the Savior of men, who was to die that their sins might be forgiven.

Its very gravity was a grace for them. Yet He adds another light: "But if by the power of God I cast out demons, then truly the Kingdom of God has come among you" (Mt. 12:28). It is almost a direct statement that He is the Messias, the Strong One, who will win God's victory over Satan and sin. He has said nothing so clear to the crowd. It is another trait of His pedagogy, a prelude to His great "fighting discourses" in Jerusalem: it is in the face of blind and bitter opposition that He makes His clearest disclosures of Himself. For then the reason for His reserve, the desire not to extinguish the smoldering wick, did not hold.

This clash with the Pharisees is of great importance in our Lord's life. We see now the three classes with whom He is confronted. First, a solid bloc of opposition, the Scribes and Pharisees of all Palestine (*cf.* Lk. 5:17); though there were doubtless some exceptions. Their attitude was clear and fixed; they had a complete theory about His Person and His work. Generally, the enemies of Christ, even today, are more definite than His friends.

Secondly, a loyal group, who loved the light, and were attached to His Person, though still unenlightened about His real character. There were two circles in this group: one more intimate, the Twelve, and a wider circle of "disciples", who stood with Christ with varying degrees of intelligence and devotion. Hence this group shades off into the third group, the wavering ones. These were either confused about the issue, drawn between the conflicting authorities of Christ and of the Scribes, or unwilling to pay the cost of a decision on the issue. This was the largest group, the "sheep", distressed, and without a shepherd. They had neither sinned against the light, nor accepted it wholly; they were not ill-disposed, but puzzled, hesitant, imprisoned in the ideas that had been taught them, and slow to absorb new ones.

To meet this situation, our Lord's teaching passes into a new phase, both in content and in form. Its content grows deeper, but its form more obscure. He begins to explain more profoundly the nature of the Kingdom, but He does so in parables. He explains the parables to those in the inner circle, at their request. The parables are not explained to "those without", but serve as a means of stimulating their curiosity and prompting their questions.

## 34. PARABLES ON THE KINGDOM

*The Sower* (Mt. 13:3-9). Our Lord clearly rejects the idea of His audience that the Kingdom is to be an overwhelming political victory whereby the Jews will share in the Kingdom of the Messias just because they are Jews. Without arousing anger, He tells them that they will miss the Kingdom unless their hearts are right. They must co-operate with grace, put away their prejudices and sacrifice their earthly desires if they are to share the lot of the Messias. Even those who enter the Kingdom will yield fruit and share in the benefits only in proportion to this sacrifice of themselves (v. 8-9).

To us who have heard these parables from childhood together with the explanation of them (which Christ gave only to a chosen few), the lesson is obvious. But that it was not so to the Jews is clear from the complaint of the disciples (v. 10) and the detailed explanation that is given them (v. 18-23). In the parable itself there is no word of its spiritual meaning; it is simply a narration of what the people had seen every year at seed-planting time. From this example taken from their daily lives, the material minded among them, and they were the majority, would have at best a very vague idea that the word of God, like seed planted in a field, required good soil to grow. But they would not see in the story a burning condemnation of their own negligence in preparing their hearts, a prophecy that they were to miss the longed-for Kingdom through their own stubborn blindness.

Our Lord explains that this obscurity in His parables is the consequence and punishment of the blindness of the Jews (v. 11-16). To those who have co-operated with grace, more shall be given; but those who have "closed their eyes" will begin to lose even the little light that they have. The light will not be taken from them suddenly and completely. There is still time for them to co-operate. But now, to avoid arousing their bad will, they will be spoken to in a veiled manner and they must exert themselves all the more to find the truth. The fact that our Lord continues to speak to them, even in parables, is an act of great mercy on His part; if they inquire sincerely into the meaning of these parables, as the disciples did, they may still come to the light.

*The Weeds* (Mt. 13:24-30). Here again is a startling revelation in direct contradiction to what the Jews had expected. Membership in the Kingdom of the Messias is not to be a guarantee of salvation. Cooperation is required to the very end and many will be seduced by the devil who is portrayed as the personal enemy of the Kingdom. People, even today, are scandalized at this; they argue that if Christ's Church were genuinely from God there would be no evil in it. But it was revealed from the beginning that Christ's Kingdom, efficacious in itself for the salvation of men, depends on their co-operation for the degree of its success.

Christ's interpretation of the parable (v. 36-43) is remarkable for the direct clearness with which He shows His Messianic character and His divinity. He is the Sower and the Judge; it is He who presides over the harvesting when it comes, for the angels are His angels and they execute His commands. The doctrine of eternal punishment for the wicked and blessedness for the just is clear; we cannot make a choice, rejecting the imagery of the punishment of the lost, and preserving as a dogma, the description of the happiness of the elect.

*Growth* (Mk. 4:26-29). Here our Lord contrasts the laws of growth in His Kingdom to the expectation that it will be a sudden and miraculous affair. It is God who makes the seed grow. It will be a gradual, imperceptible growth, silent and continuous while we sleep and while we are engaged in the daily routines. It is an invitation to patience and calm confidence in the power of God to bring the seed to flower both in individual souls and in the world at large.

*Mustard Seed and Leaven* (Mt. 13:31-33). Both of these parables sketch the growth of the Kingdom from hidden, humble, small beginnings to powerful, glorious results. The images used by Christ were familiar to His hearers. The Jews had a proverbial expression "small as a mustard seed". And while the shrub that it ultimately became was certainly not a great tree, it was the greatest of the garden vegetables. The leaven, too, is small compared to the three measures of meal which it is to leaven. Thus did Christ reveal that His Kingdom was not to be characterized in its beginnings by some amazing decisive victory such as was anticipated in the popular belief of the time.

Nevertheless, despite its humble beginnings, there is to be power and glory in it. Like yeast, it will gain ground slowly and insensibly but it will come eventually to change the whole human race. The figure of the "birds of the air coming to dwell in its branches" was often used by the prophets. Ezechiel said of the Assyrian: "all the birds of the air made their nests in his boughs". Nabuchodonosor in a dream saw himself as a great tree, "under it dwelt cattle and beasts, and in the branches thereof the fowls of the air had their abode" (Daniel 4:9). By adopting the same image and applying it to the Kingdom of Heaven, Christ recalled to the imagination of His hearers all these great Empires of the past.

*Treasure—Pearl* (Mt. 13:44-46). Of such value is the Kingdom of Heaven that a man must buy it at the price of all that he has; and however dearly he pays, it will always be worth infinitely more. It points to the entire renunciation of self and of earthly possessions, required in the pursuit of the Kingdom. The Jews had persuaded themselves that it was to cost them nothing at all.

*The Net* (Mt. 13:47-50). This last parable strongly resembles that of the cockle, stressing the mixture of good and bad in the Kingdom. The Apostles appear in the light of fishermen who gather both good and bad into their net. It is not for them to effect the division between the two. This will be done at the end of the world when the angels will cast the wicked into hell, thus playing the same part as in the parable of the cockle. This parable must have been very striking to an audience among whom there were many fishermen.

*Chapter XVIII*

# THE PUBLIC LIFE:
# PERIOD II. CONSTRUCTION
## B. In Galilee—*Continued*

➤➤➤➤➤➤➤➤➤➤➤➤➤◀◀◀◀◀◀◀◀◀◀◀◀◀

## Phase 3. Supreme Effort in Galilee

*Time:* Fall, 27 A.D. to February, 28 A.D.

| | Mt | Mk | Lk | Jn |
|---|---|---|---|---|
| 35. Storm; demoniac of Gerasa | 8: 18, 23-34 | 4: 35-5: 20 | 8: 22-39 | — |
| 36. Daughter of Jairus; a woman | 9: 18-26 | 5: 21-43 | 8: 40-56 | — |
| 37. Two blind men; mute demoniac | 9: 27-34 | — | — | — |
| 38. Rejection at Nazareth | 13: 53-58 | 6: 1-5 | 4: 16-30 | — |
| 39. Another tour; miracles | 9: 35-38 | 6: 6 | — | — |
| 40. Mission of Twelve; advice | 10: 1-11: 1 | 6: 7-13 | 9: 1-6 | — |
| 41. Herod's anxiety | 14: 1-2 | 6: 14-16 | 9: 7-9 | — |
| 42. Martyrdom of the Baptist | 14: 5-12 | 6: 19-29 | — | — |
| 43. Return of the Twelve | — | 6: 30 | 9: 10a | — |

Our Lord's work with the general public reaches a climax of intensity during this last phase of the period of construction. Only six miracles are described in any detail, and two of these were worked apart for the instruction of the Apostles. But the Evangelists make clear that this five-month period was filled with sermons and miracles both on the part of our Lord during His third tour of the province and by the Apostles on their missionary tour.

A new stage of development is reached in the training of the Apostles who are sent out in pairs to do their own missionary work having the power to confirm their teaching, as our Lord did, with miracles.

The enthusiasm of the people reaches a new pitch of excitement and some are coming to the open acknowledgment that Christ is the Messias. But the Pharisees continue to attribute His wonderful works to the power of the devil and many of the people are influenced by the calumny. The rejection at Nazareth illustrates how those closest to Christ in His human origins are most inclined to follow the leaders of the nation in rejecting Him. It is a dark foreboding of the national rejection which will eventually come and the curse of God's rejection which will fall upon the Chosen People.

## 35. Storm; Demoniac of Gerasa

Our Lord leaves the people for a while that they might think over the parables and adjust their dispositions to the light they get from them. Meanwhile, He and His Apostles can get a much-needed rest in the relative peace and calm of gentile country. But even while resting He continues to work with them, deepening their faith in Him and preparing them for their future work in the Kingdom.

*Storm.* Christ's purpose in this miracle is not only to reveal His divinity to His disciples but to reveal to them a truth about the nature of His Kingdom. In the Sermon on the Mount, He urged them to confidence in God who cares much more for them than for the sparrows. Now He teaches them the lesson by practical experience. They will need that lesson. The day will come when He will no longer be visibly with them. There will be many storms. They must learn that He is not indifferent to their dangers and griefs even when He seems to be so. The same kind of faith is required of all those who will belong to His Kingdom.

The Lake of Galilee, especially in winter, was subject to sudden and violent storms. It is sunk in the earth like a deep basin and encircled by mountains on every side. The wind rushes through the gorges in the cliff on the east and lashes the sea into fury. This storm must have been especially violent to frighten the fishermen who were used to the lake. On this occasion the Apostles showed themselves weak but not wholly without faith. They believed in their Master and counted on His help; that is why they woke Him. But their faith is still very imperfect. It needs only the sleep of Jesus and His apparent indifference to extinguish it altogether. The storm is calmed with a word; the forces of nature obey instantly the command of their Master. The Apostles are filled with fear. Despite all the miracles they had seen, they are filled with new wonder at this one which touches them so personally and they exclaim: "Who, then, is this, that even the wind and the sea obey Him?" We must not look upon the faith of the Apostles as a static, lifeless thing. Like our own, it is a living faith which grows weak and fearful in the storm and awakens with new fervor at the manifestation of God's protective hand.

*The demoniac.* Gerasa was situated some forty miles southeast of the shore of the lake, but the whole country round about was called the land of the Gerasens. The miracle took place on the eastern shore of the lake. There were many caves hewn out of the rock. Such sepulchres would be convenient habitations for demoniacs and lepers.

Here again our Lord works a miracle for the special instruction of His disciples. They have seen Him command the forces of nature but He now shows them that His power extends far beyond, into the supernatural world over the evil spirits who were so much feared. The disciples had seen Him expel the devil before. But here is a special case revealing in a special way the power, fury and malice of the devil. In the parables, the devil was mentioned as the arch enemy of the Kingdom. Here he is found in person. His subjection to Christ is apparent: "I adjure Thee by God, do not torment me". Doubtless the devils are already in torment but it will not be until the last day that their punishment is complete. Meanwhile, their power and reality is manifest in the degraded condition of the man and his superhuman but blind strength. Again the blind, destructive fury is manifest in the self-destruction of the swine. Thus the disciples are given a vivid lesson in the reality and malice and power of the devil. They need that lesson. The devil is to be their enemy as he is the enemy of Christ; he is to sow the cockle while they are sowing the wheat. In our modern scientific world this belief in the devil as a personal enemy of every man's salvation is often looked upon as superstition. The fact is, as this and similar episodes in the Gospels make abundantly clear, you do not believe in Christ if you do not believe in the devil whom He revealed.

The man, freed of the devil's power, is a living picture of what Christ came to do for the members of His Kingdom. Under the devil's influence, the man was reduced to the level of a savage beast, the shame and terror of the country for miles around. Now he sits at the feet of Christ clothed and quiet, a decent member of society with the marks of human dignity once more upon him. The people, seeing this picture, are filled with fear at the supernatural power they see in Christ; they are frankly afraid of Him and implore Him to leave their coasts. The population of this country, still in large part pagan, was ill prepared for the Gospel message; the darkness shrinks from the Light. Christ, without noticeable resentment, complies immediately with their request and leaves the shores where He is not wanted.

It is notable that Christ, in refusing to take the man with Him, enjoins upon him the task of spreading the good news abroad. This is in sharp contrast to His oft-repeated command of silence about the miracles He worked in Galilee. It is due to two things: the fact that He has progressed now in His work to a new period when it is time to let the people know for better or worse who He is and, secondly, the fact that the people in this area did not share either the Jewish knowledge or misconceptions of the Messias. This man will prepare the ground for future planting. Later, the Apostles will be showing the heathen what God's grace can make of a man whom it has freed from the power of the devil and sin.

[200]

# 36. Woman with Hemorrhage, Daughter of Jairus
# 37. Two Blind Men; Mute Demoniac

*Hemorrhage.* Back in Galilee, our Lord is surrounded again by the pressing, importunate crowds eager for the miracles they know He can give. These miracles are given by the Evangelists as samples of the growing enthusiasm in this climax of our Lord's campaign in Galilee. The woman is suffering from a disease which was much feared among the Jews because it was practically impossible to cure and made one legally unclean. She could not make herself known without being driven away so she hoped to "steal" a miracle, so to speak. She touches His garment and the divine love goes out to her in healing power. "Who touched My cloak?", He asks, and, trembling with shame and emotion, the woman threw herself at His feet and confessed the whole thing. "Daughter, thy faith has saved thee. Go in peace, and be thou healed of thy affliction". Thus He rewards her humility and reveals to her that the cure was not due to magic, depending only on the physical contact with His garments, but rather to her faith by which she united herself to His Person.

*Daughter of Jairus.* When our Lord reached the house, the girl was already dead and the minstrels were wailing the songs of public mourners. Our Lord evidently wanted to lessen the excessive excitement that the miracle would cause; He says that the girl's death is only a sleep from which He will wake her. And for the same reason, He allows only a few privileged witnesses; Peter, James and John are now, for the first time, preferred to the other Apostles.

As at Naim, death is here conquered by a single word spoken with supreme authority, without a single prayer or prolonged effort as in the cases of raising from the dead performed by the prophets of old. It is enough for Jesus to command in His own name. Again, there is the human touch along with the divine. The girl is weak and hungry after the strain of her illness. Our Lord does not supply by miracle what could be done with human means. The parents and other witnesses are too stupefied by the miracle to notice the girl's need. Our Lord is mindful of it and tells them to give her something to eat.

*Blind men.* In the previous phase of our Lord's campaign in Galilee, we saw that the people were voicing the opinion that "A great prophet has risen among us" (Lk. 7:16). But now, for the first time, our Lord is addressed as the "Son of David" and a miracle is requested of Him in response to this clear Messianic title. Our Lord ignores both the title and the request and proceeds on His way. Direct public acknowledgment of the title would let loose too many popular prejudices and animosities. But His heart leaped for joy at the clear vision of the two blind men and, in the privacy of the house, He rewarded their faith and emphasized the fact that the physical cure was due to their co-operation with grace.

*Demoniac.* The main purpose of recording this miracle was to indicate the reactions to our Lord which prevailed during this period. The crowds are highly enthusiastic and the Pharisees are spreading the same old lies against the Holy Spirit: "By the prince of devils He casts out devils." These are not the reactions of a few people on this one occasion; these are convictions now being voiced over all the country by partisans of opposing factions.

## 38. Rejection at Nazareth
## 39. Another Tour; Miracles

*Nazareth.* There was much curiosity in Nazareth about our Lord. His numerous miracles were well known; so, too, His arguments with the Pharisees. The people of His home town felt that they, of all the people in Palestine, knew exactly who He was. It was because of this conviction of theirs and their consequent lack of faith that He was powerless to work miracles among them.

Our Lord owed it to His townsfolk that they should hear from His own lips who He really was. For their sake, He put it off as long as He could. He gave them a year or more to hear of the wonderful miracles He had worked in other places and think them over without the urgency of making an immediate decision. By this time, He had laid down some fundamental ideas about His Kingdom which they had a chance to compare at their leisure with the Prophets. And they would have heard about the band of men He had picked for His Apostles and their faith and enthusiasm for His cause. Now He ascends the speaker's platform to tell them with His own voice who He is and if the light is too strong for them it is because they have not prepared themselves.

The prophecy of Isaias which He read on this occasion was especially dear to our Lord. He had already used it in connection with Himself in His reply to St. John's messengers: "Go and relate to John what you have heard and seen; the blind see, the lame walk . . . the poor have the Gospel preached to them". (Mt. 11:15). He interprets it in the same way now, and with still more solemn emphasis: having rolled up the scroll and sat down, while all eyes were fixed on Him, our Lord began His discourse with the simple, astounding words: "This day is fulfilled this Scripture in your ears".

It was a moment of intense emotion. The Blessed Virgin was there in the synagogue which she had attended in silence and patience for so many years. At last had come the hour of the manifestation of the Son of God and a great joy must have been in her soul, mingled with a great anguish, when she thought what the attitude of her friends, neighbors and relatives was likely to be. Would they let themselves be touched or would they stiffen their necks and harden their hearts?

As our Lord developed His theme in words that have not been recorded for us, the impression, at first, was favorable: "And all gave testimony to Him". The testimony was not so much in words perhaps as in the way He held them in a spell; they were moved by the grace of His words, the authority with which He spoke, the power of the miracles which fulfilled the prophecy to the letter.

But then the spell is broken and they revert to their old prejudice. They dwell on the ordinary, humble, purely human life of Christ and His family as they had known them for thirty years. They could have argued from His humble beginnings and lack of human learning to the fact that only the supernatural would explain the marvelous doctrine He now taught, confounding the doctors of the Law with the wisdom of His teaching and the power of His miracles. St. Luke evidently gives us only the beginning of our Lord's sermon. Then, a discussion ensued which is amplified in the texts of Matthew and Mark. As always, they asked for signs and, again as always, Christ refused them, since they were not solicited by humble faith but demanded by an insolent curiosity. "And they took offense at Him" (Mt. 13:57). Then our Lord appeals to their very rejection of Him as proof that He is genuine. He goes back to their own history for what, He now reveals, was a symbol of the ultimate rejection of the Chosen People: Elias worked a miracle to help the Gentile widow of Sarepta survive the famine; again, it was a Syrian Gentile whom Eliseus cured of leprosy. So, too, will the Messias go to strangers if and when His own people reject Him.

Then the storm broke. At the mere suggestion that Gentiles might be preferred to the Jews, they rise in an excess of rage, drive Him forcibly from the town and seek to throw Him over the cliff. It is not clear whether He "passed through their midst" by a miraculous disappearance or, what seems more likely, by giving them that look of authority which made the crowd submissive in the cleansing of the Temple. The Cross was flaming in His heart when He walked away in defeat from His home town. And Mary was left behind to suffer in silence the ignominy of her Son. In the end, her love will triumph over the obstinacy of her relatives in the flesh (cf. Acts 1:14).

*Another tour.* This is the third missionary tour that is mentioned in this period of construction. The numerous sermons and miracles are mentioned collectively to remind us that those described in detail are mere samples of this intense period of activity. Our Lord is moved "with compassion for the crowds because they were bewildered and dejected, like sheep without a shepherd" (Mt. 9:36). He has an intense desire, out of love for them, to save them from the ignorance and prejudice and weakness in their souls to which their leaders are betraying them. They are dejected because they see the light dimly but shrink from the cost of surrendering to it. He spends Himself completely to help them make the decision. But He will not force them to it. They themselves must decide. If they refuse, they will miss Him altogether and the blessings He came to give them.

## 40. MISSION OF THE TWELVE; ADVICE

This marks a climax in our Lord's work of constructing His Kingdom. The Apostles are now to be sent out on their own for a trial mission. He has taken great pains to instruct them as to the meaning of His preaching. He has worked miracles for them personally to strengthen their faith in Himself. He has kept them with Him constantly that they might see how He reacted to the difficulties and dangers that confronted Him. Now it is time for them to go out on their own and get from personal experience some of the joys and hardships of their future work.

It was to be a new instruction for the people, too. They were to see what had never been heard of in Israel, that Christ had the power to delegate His power and authority. Many of the prophets had had the gift of working miracles but without any power to delegate to others. Christ manifests Himself as the supreme Master and Lord of these powers by investing them in His Apostles. It is a preview of what the future Kingdom is to be like.

*Instructions.* They are to travel by twos. Without experience and without the gift of the Holy Spirit which they would receive on Pentecost, they need the support of companionship. Their field of action is strictly defined. They are to stay within Israel. These instructions are not a permanent policy for the future; they are merely for the temporary mission which, like our Lord's own preaching, was directed only to the children of Israel.

The doctrine they are to preach is clear: the "Kingdom of Heaven is at hand". It is merely preparatory in character like that of John the Baptist. Not yet were the Apostles charged to make Christ known; as yet, they knew Him but poorly themselves. But by preaching the Kingdom of God they are to prepare souls to receive it. And at the same time they are to perform the miraculous works by which the advent of the Kingdom is to be marked.

They are instructed minutely as to what they are to wear. They are to take only what they need for immediate use. Nor are they to charge anything for their miracles. And they are to receive their lodging from those to whom they preach. Our Lord wants to teach His Apostles detach-

ment from worldly goods and motives. They must have confidence in God.
It is the great lesson that He will bring to their minds on the night before
He dies: "When I sent you forth without purse or wallet or sandals, did
you lack anything? And they said, "Nothing". (Lk. 22:35). Our Lord
wanted also to teach another lesson: that the "laborer deserves his living".
When the proper dispositions are present, that is, detachment on the part
of those who receive, and a spirit of faith in those who give, such an
exchange of service forges a new link drawing pastors and faithful closer
to each other.

## 41. HEROD'S ANXIETY; 42. MARTYRDOM OF THE BAPTIST; 43. RETURN OF THE TWELVE

*Martyrdom of the Baptist.* Meanwhile John is the victim of cruel revenge
on the part of Herodias (Mk. 6:17-29). The delicate little dancing girl,
delighted at receiving the saint's head on a dish, is another example of the
inhuman degradation to which the devils of Gerasa can lead a man. The
fact that the people do not rise in revolt against this murdering of their
Prophet indicates how completely their minds are taken up with the Christ.
And the hardened enmity of the Pharisees is evidenced by the fact that
they make no complaint; normally they would have been quick to resent
this barbarism of an Idumaean against one of their own; but John had
incurred their enmity by his condemnation of their pride and by his testimony to our Lord.

*Herod's anxiety.* A new wave of enthusiasm spreads through the country as the result of the mission of the Twelve. They "preached that men
should repent, and they cast out many devils, and anointed with oil many
sick people, and healed them" (Mk. 6:13). This use of soothing oil as a
symbol of the miraculous healing will later be raised to the dignity and
power of the Sacrament of Extreme Unction.

As a result of the mission, people are again speculating on the identity
of the One who sent the Twelve and gave them such power. Herod, naturally superstitious and suffering now from a guilty conscience, is convinced
that Christ is John the Baptist risen from the dead. The people in general
are making the usual compromise, confessing that Christ is a Prophet but
shying away from the conclusion that He is *The* Prophet.

*Return of the Twelve.* "And the Apostles came together to meet Jesus
and reported to Him all that they had done and taught" (Mk. 6:30). It
is a touching revelation of the familiar human intimacy between our Lord
and His Apostles. They insist on sharing their enthusiasm with Him; each
one has to tell how He worked this miracle or that, how he preached and

what was the effect in this place or that. And our Lord, burdened as He was with the news of John's death, listens to it all with interest offering comments and advice suited to the character and temperament of each one of the enthusiastic missionaries. They are all tired from their work and the people continue to press upon them "so that they had no leisure even to eat" (Mk. 6:31). It is to get a much-needed rest that He invites them "to a desert place" and they row over to the sparsely populated Gentile country on the other side of the lake.

But the people are watching His every movement now. They see the boats leaving from Capharnaum and so they hurry on foot around the end of the lake and, when the boats arrive, the shepherdless sheep are waiting by the thousands to be fed again.

## Chapter XIX

# THE PUBLIC LIFE: PERIOD III. CRISES

⇥⇥⇥⇥⇥⇥⇥⇥⇥⇥⇥⇥⇥⇥⇤⇤⇤⇤⇤⇤⇤⇤⇤⇤⇤⇤⇤⇤⇤

## CRISIS 1. GALILEE

*Time:* March, 28 A.D.

|  | Mt | Mk | Lk | Jn |
|---|---|---|---|---|
| 44. First miracle of loaves | 14: 13-21 | 6: 31-44 | 9: 10-17 | 6: 1-13 |
| 45. Refusal of the Kingship | — | — | — | 6: 14-15 |
| 46. Walking on the waters | 14: 22-33 | 6: 45-52 | — | 6: 16-21 |
| 47. Cures around Genesareth | 14: 34-36 | 6: 53-56 | — | — |
| 48. The Bread of Life | — | — | — | 6: 22-72 |

AFTER FIFTEEN months or more of tireless, unceasing work in Galilee, our Lord finally puts these people to the test. He prepares them by working the miracle of multiplying the loaves and they are highly enthusiastic. But their enthusiasm is for the earthly kingdom of their dreams and He refuses their attempt to force Him to establish such a kingdom. On the following day, in the Sermon on the Bread of Life, our Lord insists on faith in His heavenly origin and acceptance of the mystery of the Eucharist on the testimony of His word. The people turn away in disbelief and disappointment. In turn, Christ is forced to turn away from them. His miracles and preaching to the people will be greatly curtailed and He will spend the greater part of His time instructing the Apostles alone and apart.

## 44. FIRST MIRACLE OF LOAVES; 45. REFUSAL OF KINGSHIP. 46. WALKING ON THE WATERS; 47. CURES AROUND GENESARETH

*Loaves.* Instead of getting the rest He sought, our Lord spent the whole day curing the sick and instructing them out of a deep sympathy for their spiritual needs. Again, the human familiarity between Himself and the Apostles is manifest in the way they cut short His preaching with the explanation that it is getting late and the people must be dismissed if they are to find shelter and food.

Our Lord purposely emphasizes and calls attention to the fact that there is no food in the place. He first proposes to the Apostles that they might buy bread for the crowd but Philip sees an insurmountable difficulty in the amount that would be required and the cost, if such a supply could be bought. Then our Lord sends the Apostles searching through the crowd (Mk. 6:38). It must have taken a long time to inquire of ten thousand people and, as the question is passed around, all become conscious of the lack of bread. Finally, as a result of the search, they bring Him the five loaves and two fishes obtained from a young boy in the audience (Jn. 6:9). Again, considerable time was required for the Apostles to arrange the people in rows and expectation mounts regarding the intentions of our Lord.

Christ uses the same ritual He will later use at the Last Supper in giving thanks, blessing and breaking the loaves. He places the pieces in baskets and directs the Apostles to distribute them through the rows. Evidently as they hand out the pieces from the baskets, the supply remains unexhausted. And as they proceed from row to row, the marvel of it dawns upon the people; the exclamations of wonder increase with the handing out of each new piece until all are beside themselves with joyous excitement.

The time required for the feeding and the gathering up of fragments gave these people ample opportunity for thought and comment on the meaning of this great manifestation of love and power. Instinctively they would turn to their Scriptures for the meaning of the sign. Naturally the words of Ezechiel would come to mind: "For thus saith the Lord God: Behold I myself will seek my sheep, and will visit them . . . I will feed them in the most fruitful pastures, and their pastures shall be in the high mountains of Israel: there shall they rest on the green grass, and be fed in fat pastures upon the mountains of Israel. I will feed My sheep: and I will cause them to lie down, saith the Lord God". (34:11-15).

This, then, is the sign they have been looking for. Filled with the fresh, free bread, the shouting groups unite and with one accord sweep down to force Him to be the king of the kingdom of their dreams.

*Refusal.* Our Lord's first thought is of the danger to His Apostles. They are not immune from this spirit that possesses the crowd. They had basked in the sunlight of the miracle, passing out the bread, answering the questions and comments that were hurled at them, sharing in the general enthusiasm. They had not been touched by the real meaning of the miracle; "their hearts were blinded" (Mk. 6:52) by the distracting work involved and the dreams of earthly glory that arose when, for once, there was no bickering criticism or enmity, but only enthusiasm for the Master with whom they were identified. They must be gotten away from these attractive snares. Their reluctance to go is shown by the fact that He "made them" get into the boat and cross the sea to Bethsaida(Mk. 6:45). The sharp command extinguished the flame in their hearts; they are bewildered, disappointed, humiliated before the crowd as they set out over the dark waters.

Then our Lord dismissed the crowd. To dismiss a crowd of ten thousand highly excited people who are all intent on accomplishing by physical force a definite objective is indeed an amazing accomplishment. In itself it is a moral miracle manifesting the superhuman force and authority of His personality. The people too are baffled and angry at His coldness to their enthusiasm; their hearts are bitter at the way He raised their hopes only to dash them to the ground. There were many occasions when these people ran into this irresistible wall in Christ; they did not understand Him and they felt that He had no understanding of them. The resentment, caused by this aloofness of His, was buried deep in their minds; one day, it would spring to passionate life and enable them to cry: "Crucify Him!"

Meanwhile, Christ Himself, in anguish of soul, turns to His Father. The Father is the only one who understands Him. The urgency of it is expressed in the words: "He *fled* again to the mountain, Himself alone" (Jn. 6:15) and Mark adds that His purpose was "to pray" (Mk. 6:46). He is the good Shepherd working for the true good of His uncomprehending flock even when they think Him heedless of their welfare. All through the silent, lonely night He prays for these people and His Apostles while they murmur and grumble at His seeming indifference to their good intentions. His one continuous prayer for them is that the miracle of loaves will prepare them to believe in Him on the morrow when He reveals that He Himself is the Bread-come-down-from-heaven for the life of their souls.

*Apparition.* Meanwhile, the Apostles have been rowing against a strong wind. It is three o'clock in the morning and despite their "straining at the oars", they make little progress. They are exhausted in body and soul after the physical labor and emotional stress of the previous day. Now their hands are blistered and their hearts are as sore as their hands. They are ill prepared for the vision of the Master who is always thinking of them. They scream in terror until they hear the old familiar voice giving them the old familiar comfort: "Take courage, it is I, do not be afraid".

Peter is the first to rebound to the old enthusiasm (Mt. 14:28-31). As long as his mind and his eyes are focused on his Lord, he walks with all the supernatural buoyancy of Christ. But, human-nature-wise, he looks aside at the height of the waves and the force of the wind and, fearful, he begins to sink. The picture of Christ holding His vicar by the hand, supporting his human weakness with His own strength, is symbolic of the promise that is to be fulfilled. And when they got into the boat, the Apostles worshipped Him saying, "Truly Thou art the Son of God" (Mt. 14:33); it suggests what they had been saying before. Thus, by alternating periods of desolation and consolation, does He bring them to grow in faith. How tirelessly and painstakingly He has worked to prepare them for the test which the new dawn will bring!

*Genesareth.* They arrive on the northwest shore of the lake at the fertile plain of Galilee which is called Genesar (Genesareth). Tirelessly the work goes on; the sick are cured in droves; divine power flows out even through the tassels of Christ's cloak. Surely, they should be prepared for the revelation He is about to give.

## 48. THE BREAD OF LIFE

In this great discourse, our Lord reveals two main things: 1. That He is not merely human but from God and hence the source of man's salvation (Jn. 6:22-52); 2. That He will give His flesh and blood as spiritual food and drink to those who believe in Him and enter His Kingdom (Jn. 6:52-70).

1. *Heavenly origin.* Our Lord gives the clue to this part of the discourse when He upbraids the Jews for seeking Him only for the free, material bread they hope to get from Him (v. 26). The bread He hopes to give them is that which "endures unto life everlasting". That He has the power to give such bread arises from the fact that the Father has marked Him with the seal of His divinity; this is clear from the theophany at Christ's baptism and from the miraculous works which the Father has given Him to do. If they would have everlasting life they must believe in the Son and His relationship to the Father (v. 30).

The crowd demands a "sign" as the condition of belief. It is clear that this is not just a request for individual miracles like the ones He has been performing in such profusion all along. They want a permanent kingdom which corresponds to the material kingdom they have been expecting. Moses fed the people for forty years with the manna from heaven. Will He do the same? (v. 31). Our Lord replies that the manna which Moses gave, though it was from the sky, was not from heaven in the spiritual sense (v. 32). It was an earthly bread and the eating of it did not confer eternal life (v. 49). The true bread from heaven is that which comes down from God Himself and, because it does, gives to those who receive it the everlasting life that is proper to God alone (v. 33).

"They said therefore to Him: Lord, give us always this bread" (v. 34). Like the Samaritan woman ("Sir, give me this water that I may not thirst, or come here to draw"), they have no thought for anything but bodily refreshment. And just as the conversation with the Samaritan woman ended with the declaration, "I who speak with thee am He (the Christ)", so now He says to the Jews: "I am the bread of life" (v. 35) . . . "I have come down from heaven" (v. 38).

Unlike the Samaritan woman, the present audience is not docile. They begin to murmur and complain (v. 41). What shocked them was not the mystery of the Eucharist, which had not yet been clearly set forth, but the statement of the pre-existence of Jesus in heaven. Their difficulty is a repetition of what we saw at Nazareth. Instead of dwelling on His heavenly power manifested in His miracles and thus coming to believe in His heavenly origin, they concentrate on ("kept repeating") His earthly origin to the exclusion of all else. For the first time, John calls the audience "Jews", indicating that they are going over to the camp of Christ's enemies.

In answer to their complaints, our Lord merely restates His position (v. 45). In this repetition, He adds a new appeal by quoting Isaias, "And they shall be taught of God"; if God had promised to teach them directly, they should have expected the Messias to be from heaven.

And now our Lord reveals the ultimate reason why these Jews cannot believe or understand. Men cannot come to Christ, *i.e.*, they cannot believe His words, unless they are first "drawn" by the Father (v. 44). This drawing is what we call actual grace. It is an enlightenment of the understanding and a strengthening of the will which enables men to see that Christ is divine—"come down from heaven". Without this initial grace, it is impossible for them to believe in the divinity of Christ, and not believing in that, they are incapable of believing in the things of God which He came to reveal. This is the ultimate reason for the blindness of the Jews; because of their lack of co-operation, they have not been "drawn" by the Father and they cannot understand Christ.

Those who are drawn by the Father, though they do not see Him face to face, come in contact with Christ; from Him they receive everlasting life (sanctifying grace). Through this new life they now have the power to understand the things of God and do the works of God and grow in the Kingdom of God. When they die, this life within them will raise them up, even bodily, to the eternal life of God (v. 37-40, 46-47). Herein is the fullest revelation to date of the real nature of Christ's Kingdom.

2. *The Eucharist*. In this discourse, our Lord follows His old pedagogical principle. First, He gives the necessary step that all must take if they are to believe in the Eucharist; they must believe in Him as the Son of God who came down from heaven and took upon Himself human flesh. Only if they make that step will they be prepared to believe what He still has to say: that His divinity has sanctified His human flesh and those who eat His flesh and drink His blood will be lifted up to share in the power of His divinity. This crowd is not prepared (v. 41, 53), but they have had every opportunity. Now is the critical time for the further revelation—let each one react to it as he will according to his dispositions.

Our Lord introduces the new subject by shifting the emphasis to the fact that this bread come down from heaven is His flesh which He will give for the life of the world (v. 52). Then, in the face of their incredulity, He states emphatically the fact that His flesh is food indeed and His blood is drink indeed (v. 56). "As the living Father has sent me, and as I live because of the Father, so he who eats me, shall also live because of Me". (v. 58). He stooped down to our humanity by taking upon Himself human flesh and now, through communion with His body, He lifts us up to share in His divinity. St. Cyril of Alexandria explains this divinizing of His flesh: "The Savior's flesh becomes life-giving in virtue of being united to that which is life by nature—the Word of God. He touches the dead and, by His body, communicates life to bodies already infected with corruption. If, by the mere contact of His sacred flesh, that which is corrupt is quickened, how much more shall we be completely blessed and endowed with life when we actually eat it? For it will entirely transform those who receive it into its own proper quality, that is into life". Nor is this "eating" to be taken in a cannibalistic sense as though the flesh of Christ were lifeless meat. Mere lifeless flesh cannot give divine life (v. 64). It is the living, glorified body of Christ permeated with His divinity that will be given us to eat.

Despite the clear emphasis of our Lord that it is really His own flesh and blood that He will give us, the Protestant reformers abandoned the Catholic teaching of the Real Presence. Luther, Calvin and the others interpreted the Eucharist in a metaphorical sense. What we receive, they said, is actually nothing but blessed bread; but, receiving it as a religious ritual wherein we "remember" Christ by meditating upon Him and His passion with faith and repentance and love, we receive Christ in spirit into our hearts. This, in itself, is a good thing; it is what we would call "spiritual communion". But, in so far as it is a denial of our Lord's real presence in the Eucharist, it is a bad thing; it destroys the whole meaning of His promise as we shall see more clearly, perhaps, from what follows.

The revelation served only to scandalize the crowd, discourage His disciples and even prepare the treachery of Judas (v. 53, 61, 65). It is one of the most pathetic pages of the Gospel story. The people and their leaders have apparently already refused belief; St. John concerns himself only with the devastating effect of the revelation upon those who, up to now, have been in good faith; even the "disciples" find it a hard saying (v. 62). To save their tottering faith, He holds out to them the prophetic promise of His ascension into heaven (v. 63); His ascending into heaven will prove that He came down from heaven and that, in turn, gives reason for believing in His word. But, for the present at least, the shock is too great and "from this time many of His disciples turned back and no longer went about with Him" (v. 67).

Surely the "hardness" of the saying lay in its literal interpretation. If they were wrong in that, if He had meant a purely spiritual eating, consisting only in thinking about Him or meditating on His passion, a single word would have been enough to undeceive them and bring them back to Him. He owed it to them and to Himself to speak that word; it was not for this heart-breaking rupture that He had labored up to now. But He let them go. He is even willing, if need be, to let the Apostles go: "Jesus therefore, said to the Twelve: Do you also wish to go away?" (v. 68). He was not giving them leave to make a choice of alternatives to which He was equally indifferent; He was warning them. If they were not better than the Jews, they would be rejected like them and others would take their place.

The sadness in His heart is relieved somewhat by Peter's reply. They too found the mystery hard to accept. But their approach was the right one; they believed, not because they understood the mystery, but because of the word of Him who spoke to them. Yet, even this consolation was lessened by the knowledge that there was one, even of the Apostles, who did not believe (v. 72).

## CRISIS 2. JERUSALEM

### Time: March, 28 A.D.

| | Mt | Mk | Lk | Jn |
|---|---|---|---|---|
| 49. Cripple at the pool | — | — | — | 5: 1-16 |
| 50. On Judgment and Witness | — | — | — | 5: 17-47 |
| 51. Danger! Return to Galilee | — | — | — | 7: 1 |

Leaving the Galileans to their obstinate unbelief, our Lord goes down to Jerusalem, as was His custom, for the annual feast of the Pasch. There, in the capital city, His revelation of His divine origin provokes another crisis of bad faith.

## 49. CRIPPLE AT THE POOL; 50. ON JUDGMENT AND WITNESS; 51. DANGER! RETURN TO GALILEE

Our Lord cured the paralytic on the Sabbath day and told him to take up his pallet and walk (Jn. 5:8-9). It was a double violation of the Pharisaic traditions. Because of it, the Pharisees "kept persecuting" Jesus (v. 16). The phrase suggests that the discourses which follow were not all given on the same day; they are a summary of the type of argument and revelation which took place on different occasions during this festive period.

*Christ is divine.* In the discussion that ensues, our Lord does not follow the same line of argument which He usually used on such occasions in

[213]

Galilee. There, where the majority of His audience were simple, country people, He would answer such charges by showing that the Pharisees' absolute insistence on their human traditions was a violation of the spirit of the Mosaic Law. But, here in the Temple, He is talking to the Masters of Israel who spent their lives studying the Scriptures. Here He answers their complaints by revealing the deep mystery of His union with the Father, knowing that if they want, they can understand Him.

"My Father works even unto now, and I work" (v. 17). He places Himself on a level with the Father who works always, Sabbath or no, in preserving and governing the world. Jesus, like His Father, is above the Sabbath. The Jews see the point clearly: "This then is why the Jews were the more anxious to put Him to death because He not only broke the Sabbath, but also called God His own Father, making Himself equal to God" (v. 18). Our Lord does not correct their interpretation; He goes on to explain even more fully this equality between Himself and the Father.

In verse 17, our Lord was clearly speaking of Himself apart from His incarnation; He and the Father and the Holy Spirit (whom He does not mention here because it is not yet the time for it) possess the same divine nature in common and, therefore, all the actions of that nature belong to all three Persons. The Fathers of the Church interpret most of the following verses (19-21) in the same sense, *e.g.,* "Whatever He (the Father) does, this the Son does in like manner" (v. 20) may refer exclusively to the divine nature in Jesus. But then the declaration, "Neither does the Father judge any man, but all judgment He has given to the Son . . ." refers to Christ as man. And many commentators are of the opinion that all of these verses (19-30) refer to Christ in so far as He is God incarnate. In any case, Christ, even in His human nature, has all these prerogatives as Redeemer and Judge precisely because His human nature is substantially united with the divine nature. He can "do nothing of Himself" and "does not His own will but the will of Him who sent Him" precisely because the fullness of the divinity dwells within Him. He is the author of life inasmuch as He is God and He is judge inasmuch as He is man; but He is both the one and the other because the Incarnate Word unites the two natures in one and the same Person. It is on this basis that He claims, even as the Son of Man, equality with the Father: "that all men may honor the Son even as they honor the Father" (v. 23).

*Witnesses.* Our Lord anticipates the objections of the Pharisees and points to the witnesses who testify in His behalf. He does not rely on His own testimony, not because it isn't valuable in itself, but because legally no one was admitted as a witness in His own case (v. 31). Nor will He rest His case upon the testimony of John the Baptist as well He might (v. 33-35). But the great witness is the Father Himself (v. 36-38). The

Father's testimony consists in the miracles and other works which He has given the Son to do; these are the credentials signed by the hand of God which testify clearly to the divinity in Christ. Or if they prefer the written word of God, the Scriptures and specifically Moses, whom the Pharisees pretend to revere, speak clearly of Christ and testify that He is to be the Father's own Son (v. 38-47).

The response to this clear revelation of Himself is that the Jews are plotting His death (7:1). In consequence of this rejection, both in Galilee and Judea, our Lord will spend the next six or seven months almost exclusively with His Apostles. The people, in general, and especially their leaders, have failed in the test of faith. They are not prepared for any further revelation and our Lord restricts His miracles and sermons to the public to a very few occasions when He tries to prod them into re-examining the evidence and accepting Him for what He clearly is.

## CRISIS 3. THE FAITH OF THE APOSTLES

### Time: March to September, 28 A. D.

| | Mt | Mk | Lk | Jn |
|---|---|---|---|---|
| 52. Pharisaic traditions | 15: 1-20 | 7: 1-23 | — | — |
| 53. Phoenicia: Canaanite woman | 15: 21-28 | 7: 24-30 | — | — |
| 54. Decapolis: deaf mute | 15: 29-31 | 7: 31-37 | — | — |
| 55. Second miracle of loaves | 15: 32-39 | 8: 1-10 | — | — |
| 56. Leaven of the Pharisees | 16: 1-12 | 8: 11-21 | 12: 1 | — |
| 57. Blind man of Bethsaida | — | 8: 22-26 | — | — |
| 58. **The Confession of Peter** | 16: 13-20 | 8: 27-30 | 9: 18-20 | — |
| 59. First prediction of Passion | 16: 21-23 | 8: 31-33 | 9: 21-22 | — |
| 60. "Take up your cross" | 16: 24-28 | 8: 34-39 | 9: 23-27 | — |
| 61. The Transfiguration | 17: 1-8 | 9: 1-8 | 9: 28-36 | — |
| 62. The descent from Tabor | 17: 9-13 | 9: 9-13 | — | — |
| 63. Cure of the lunatic boy | 17: 14-20 | 9: 14-29 | ⎰ 9: 37-43 ⎱ 17: 5-6 | — |
| 64. Second prediction of Passion | 17: 21-22 | 9: 30-31 | 9: 44-45 | — |
| 65. Capharnaum: the didrachma | 17: 23-26 | — | — | — |
| 66. "Become like little child" | 18: 1-5 | 9: 32-36 | 9: 46-48 | — |
| 67. The stranger-exorcist | — | 9: 37-40 | 9: 49-50 | — |
| 68. Avoiding scandal | 18: 6-10 | 9: 41-47 | 17: 1-2 | — |
| 69. The lost sheep | 18: 11-14 | — | 15: 1-7 | — |
| 70. Fraternal correction | 18: 15-22 | — | 17: 3 4 | — |
| 71. The unmerciful servant | 18: 23-25 | — | — | — |
| 72. Adieu to Galilee: "Woe!" | 11: 20-24 | — | 10: 13-15 | — |

## 52. PHARISAIC TRADITIONS

Evidently it was to find occasion for carrying out their wicked plans against Him (Jn. 7:1) that some of the Pharisees of Jerusalem followed our Lord into Galilee (Mk. 7:1). At their instigation, a bitter dispute arises when the Apostles are caught neglecting the ritual of washing their hands before eating. Our Lord has no complaint against the tradition itself. The thing that angers Him is the hypocritical insistence on these human regulations under pain of sin while the real laws of God are neglected and thwarted: "For, letting go the commandment of God, you hold fast to the traditions of men, the washing of pots and cups, etc." (Mk. 7:8). Worse still, they managed, by their devilish sophistry, to "nullify the commandments of God" in order to keep their own traditions (Mk. 7:9). If in a moment of anger at his parents, a man said to them: "Any support thou mightest have had from me is consecrated to God", he was freed thereafter from any obligation towards them. This does not mean that the man's property had to be given to the Temple or to God. All it meant, according to the ruling of the Pharisees, was that everything belonging to him was to be considered by his parents as consecrated property which they were forbidden to touch. In this way, the man could harm his parents without suffering any loss to himself; the fourth commandment was nullified. This was not a rare instance of rabbinical sophistry; our Lord declares: "And many such like things you do" (Mk. 7:13). His adversaries are filled with rage, to the alarm of the Apostles: "Dost thou know that the Pharisees have taken offense at hearing this saying?" (Mt. 15:12).

*Revelation.* Our Lord uses the occasion to make a further revelation: even the sacred written Law of Moses regarding unclean foods is to be revoked. And He revokes it on His own authority as Master of the Law. The declaration was a solemn one, "Hear ye Me and understand" and it was made still more emphatic by the final exhortation which He usually employed on such occasions, "If any man has ears to hear let him hear" (Mk. 7:14-16).

The Law of Moses regarding clean and unclean foods was temporary; it served a pedagogic purpose. For one thing, it kept the Jews isolated from the paganism and idolatry of the Gentiles. But, though it was salutary for an infant people, it would have hindered the progress of the Gospel and the liberty of the Christians.

Our Lord is content for now to impress the principle on His hearers: "He declared all foods clean" (Mk. 7:20). Even that is more than the prejudice of the Apostles can stand; they think He is speaking in parables (Mk. 7:17). It would take a long process under the guidance of the Holy Spirit before they would understand the practical implications (*cf.* Acts 10—Peter's vision at Joppa). But for the present it is enough to sow the seed, to lay down the principle that material, external things are not important for their own sake; the spiritual things, the inner dispositions of the heart are the things that count. Ritual prescriptions are the protection of the spiritual life but can never be its substitute.

[216]

# 53. PHOENICIA; 54. DECAPOLIS; 55. LOAVES; 56. LEAVEN; 57. BETHSAIDA

*Phoenicia.* Threatened by the growing hostility of the Pharisees, our Lord leaves Galilee for a time to pursue in peace the work of training His Apostles. For the first time since the flight into Egypt in His infancy, He enters into pagan territory traveling north into Phoenicia, to the district of Tyre and Sidon (Mk. 7:24). He tries to keep His arrival secret but His fame has preceded Him and the Canaanite woman requests the cure of her daughter. Doubtless in addressing Him as the "Son of David", she was merely repeating what she had heard her Jewish neighbors say. The title prepared the way for our Lord's reply: the Son of David is come only to those of David's race. It was part of His plan to reserve His personal ministry to the Jews and if occasionally He allowed individual pagans to profit by it, that was in the nature of an exceptional departure from the rule. Our Lord knows that He will make an exception in this case but first He states the rule. In doing so He humbles and afflicts the woman in order to advance her virtue and teach the Apostles the efficacy of persevering prayer. She even accepts the epithet "dog" which the Jews commonly hurled at the Gentiles and, by her stubborn refusal to give up hope, she wrests, so to speak, her miracle from the Saviour.

*Decapolis.* Our Lord did not find the solitude He sought in Phoenicia and so He travels east from Sidon to the sources of the Jordan, thence southward past Mount Hermon, and along the eastern shore of the Lake of Galilee into the region of the Ten Cities (Decapolis).

It was in this region that our Lord cured the deaf mute (Mk. 7:31). He employs external ceremonies to make a greater impression on the rude pagan audience and gave thereby a figure of the sacraments which, later in His Church, would produce their effects by means of external signs. This particular ceremony has been incorporated by the Church into the ritual of Baptism which, in the supernatural order, opens our ears to divine truth and loosens our tongues to confess the faith.

*Loaves.* Our Lord travels north again to the eastern shore of the Lake of Tiberias. The crowds flock to Him from Galilee and He teaches them for three days before giving them, for the second time, this visible proof that He is the Bread of Life. Although this is substantially the same as the first miracle of loaves, and the same stereotyped form is used in the telling of it, there are many minor differences. Before, there were five loaves and two fishes and five thousand men; now, there are seven loaves, a few fishes and four thousand men; previously there were seven baskets of leftovers and now there are twelve. Later, our Lord speaks of both miracles and clearly distinguishes them (Mt. 16:1-10; Mk. 8:19-20). Truly, He is patient with this unbelieving crowd; He spares nothing that will help them to faith. But they themselves must make the step.

*Leaven.* Our Lord crossed immediately to the western shore of the lake to an unidentified place (or places) called Magedan or Dalmanutha. So obscure was this place in Galilee that it is impossible today to identify it. It was, in fact, chosen for its out-of-the-wayness. But even here, His enemies pursue Him. The second miracle of loaves caused great excitement among the people and the Pharisees are out to check it if they can. In the course of their disputing, they demand from Him a sign (Mk. 8:11). They are still insisting that He verify their preconceived notions of how the Messias should present Himself for their approval. "Sighing deeply in spirit" (Mk. 8:12), our Lord manifests the anguish and exasperation in His soul at this stubborn bad will. Again, He refuses what they ask and refers enigmatically to His resurrection in the sign of Jonas (Mt. 16:4); they remember it later as we shall see in the history of the passion. But now, He immediately leaves His native Galilee and crosses to the other side of the lake.

On the way over, our Lord takes the occasion of this latest attack to warn the Apostles of the doctrine of the Scribes and Pharisees; it affects the whole of life even as leaven affects the whole bread. The Apostles are literal minded. They have forgotten to bring bread with them. They think of it when He mentions leaven. They begin to argue and speculate about what they will do, how they will be able to procure enough to satisfy their needs. Our Lord's plaintive questions about their blindness of heart shows how heavily He is burdened with their slowness to learn (Mk. 7:17-18). It is not only the Pharisees who are blind. But His patience with them is without limit because they have good will. He recalls how plentifully He took care of them in the past and uses it as a reason why they should trust Him in the future. Then, at last, the light dawns on them that He had not been talking of material bread but of the doctrine of the Pharisees (Mt. 16:12).

*Bethsaida.* There are two Bethsaidas, one in Galilee, the other on the eastern shore of the lake, where our Lord now disembarks. The miracle here recorded is unique in the Gospels as an example of a progressive cure. In all other cases it was by a word or gesture that our Lord restored health to those who asked for it; but in the present case, the favor is conferred by degrees. Some authors think that the reason was the imperfect faith of the blind man or of his friends, and that our Lord was acting on the principle, "According to your faith be it done unto you". This seems probable. We are no longer on Jewish soil and it is possible that the faith of those who thus had recourse to Christ was very imperfect. It was not the blind man who made the request. It is quite possible that this poor man, knowing very little about our Lord, let his relatives and friends do what they liked with him and so came to Christ without any notable faith or hope in his heart. At any rate, Christ anoints him with saliva as He had previously done in the case of the deaf mute; only twice is it recorded in the Gospel that He used this method and both times it is on pagan soil.

It seems clear also that the man had not been blind from birth because he knows the difference between trees and men. If our Lord had cured him with a word, the miracle could easily have been attributed to a psychological cause induced by the excitement or by the man's own will. By working the miracle in progressive stages our Lord makes it clear that it is through His power, completely under His control, that the man receives his sight.

This miracle, the last recorded in the Gospel before St. Peter's confession, is a symbol of what was taking place in the Apostles' minds. Their eyes, too, are slowly and gradually being opened to the true significance of these mysteries which they had long witnessed without understanding. It is now the time for them to bear testimony to the light that is within them.

## 58. THE CONFESSION OF PETER

The little band, consisting of our Lord, His Apostles and perhaps some of the disciples, journeys northwards, past Paneas, a picturesque spot at the foothills of the range dominated by Mount Hermon, and so named from the sanctuary of the god Pan. There, He was in sight of the city of Caesarea Philippi, and in sight, consequently, of the famous cliff whereon was set, as on a gigantic pedestal, the temple of Augustus covered with gleaming marble. Perhaps the sight suggested to Him the metaphor; at any rate, He laid the foundations of His Church upon the "rock" of Peter as the reward of Peter's act of faith in His Divinity. This event forms the climactic point of Jesus' public ministry and inaugurates a new stage in His teaching.

St. Luke points out that our Lord was at prayer (9:18) before putting the decisive question to the Apostles. It is the same prelude that we saw to the choice of the Twelve before the Sermon on the Mount; it indicates the grave solemnity of the occasion. Then, as they walked, the conversation began. Jesus begins by inquiring about the general opinion of the people concerning Himself. The question was asked not so much to elicit information as to focus the minds of the Apostles on the all-important question and put them on guard for the personal response that would be demanded of them. The medley of replies reveals that the popular opinions have one thing in common: all agree that Christ is a supernatural personage, but beyond that all is uncertainty and confusion. Shrinking from the difficulties involved in admitting that He is the Christ and God's own Son, they seek a compromise in half-way solutions. Then comes the question: "But who do you say that I am?", and Peter, in the name of all, replies, "Thou art the Christ, the Son of the living God" (Mt. 16:16).

*Son of God.* The reason why Peter's answer deserved such praise from our Lord was because he professed that Christ was the natural, rather than merely an adopted Son of God. On other occasions, Christ had been called "Son of God"—*e.g.,* by Nicodemus and by the Apostles when He saved them from the storm; but the Jews ordinarily used the term in the sense of being favored by God in some special way by sharing in His authority or His power or His favors. But here, Peter is confessing that Christ is the Son of God by virtue of the eternal generation; He is the Son of the "living" God, having within Himself the life that is proper to God alone. Hence, it was not by any merely human means that Peter came to such faith; flesh and blood did not reveal it to him (Mt. 16:17); the Father had to "draw" him to this conclusion. Men might set up theories about the person of Jesus, but to attain certainty in this matter, the gift of faith is required. No one knows the Son but the Father and those to whom the Father deigns to reveal Him. As St. John Chrysostom says: "If he (Peter) had not recognized Him as born of the Father Himself, he would not have had a revelation; if he had thought that He was merely a son among other sons, his confession would not have merited such praise".

*Promises.* In response to this confession of faith, our Lord reveals for the first time that He is to found a Church (one), distinct from the Jewish synagogue, and that Peter and his successors are to be its supreme rulers. Peter is the rock from which the new society of believers will receive its unity and firmness just as a building rests on its foundation stone. The gates (or powers) of hell will never prevail against this Church, guided by the supreme ruler whom Christ has appointed for it. The gates of ancient cities were the principal places where courts were held and where the main defenses were located. The "gates of hell" means, therefore, the powers of opposition to Christ's Church—*i.e.,* heresy, schism, immorality and sin in general. Hence, our Lord here promises the indefectibility and perpetuity of His Church in its victorious opposition to these evil forces.

The fullness of Peter's authority is again symbolized by the "keys"; he has full power to open and shut the doors of the Kingdom as the one who rules it. In consequence, he has the power to "bind and loose" or to forbid and permit without limit. Whatever Peter or his successors determine in matters of faith or morals is sanctioned in heaven and binding on all Christians. Thus, the head of the Church has the supreme legislative, judicial and executive power in the Church. The collective power, given later to all the Apostles and to their successors, far from limiting Peter's privilege, is itself limited by it.

Later on, we shall have the occasion to examine these powers more in detail. But for the present, we should note the fact that Papal infallibility is implied in the doctrinal authority given to Peter. It is precisely because he is the rock or supreme teacher and ruler of the Church that the powers of hell will not prevail against Her. And this guarantee is given for all time (Mt. 28:20). Certainly, if Peter or his successors, as head of the Church, could teach heresy, the promise of Christ would be meaningless. The full implication of this promise with regard to Papal infallibility is expressed in the following definition of the Vatican Council: "We teach and define it to be a dogma divinely revealed that the Roman Pontiff, when he speaks *ex cathedra,* that is, when acting in his office of pastor and teacher of all Christians, by his supreme Apostolic authority, he defines a doctrine concerning faith or morals to be held by the whole Church, through the divine assistance promised him in Blessed Peter, he enjoys that infallibility with which the divine Redeemer willed his Church to be endowed in defining doctrine concerning faith and morals; and, therefore, such definitions of the said Roman Pontiff are irreformable of themselves, and not from the consent of the Church" (Denz. 1839).

Immediately after the institution of this office, Christ enjoined His Apostles to say nothing about His identity to anyone (Mt. 16:20). Many times already have we met these commands to secrecy and in this instance they are especially easy to understand. The reason why Jesus had come to a half-pagan country, far from Galilee and its lake, was because it was necessary for Him to flee from the snares of His enemies. It was at this precise period, when He had lost ground in Palestine, that He promised Peter that He would raise upon him a Kingdom that would know no end. This knowledge was meant only for those who had faith in the King; the others would be sure to misinterpret it, to their own harm and to the harm of the Kingdom.

## 59. First Prediction; 60. The Cross

As soon as this climax is reached in the faith of the Apostles, Christ begins to reveal more of the Kingdom and demand a growth of faith corresponding to the new revelation. This is characteristic of any relationship to Christ; it is never static; in this life, there is no sitting back and saying, "now I have all that there is to have". As soon as a soul has co-operated with the grace that it has, Christ is there anxious to give it more.

Up to now, our Lord has merely made obscure allusions to His passion. But now he speaks of it openly and often. The Apostles' faith is strong enough to bear the weight of these terrible predictions. It is a hard blow to their dreams when they are told that the King, the giver of eternal life, will be put to shameful death by the leaders of the nation in the capital city where they had expected His triumph. It will be a long, painful process before they face the reality of the cross. When the reality comes, they themselves will be crucified by their own pitiful shrinking from it. But afterwards, when He is risen again, the predictions of His suffering will help them to regain their equilibrium and come to an understanding of it all.

On the present occasion, Peter judges by the standards of human reason. Instead of adhering to his sublime confession of the divinity of Christ and finding out from Him what wisdom is, he takes the Master aside to correct His folly. Our Lord's reply expresses emotion and indignation of the deepest kind; He goes so far as to identify Peter with the Tempter himself. Indeed, Peter's words are a repetition of Satan's efforts during the forty days on the Mount; an attempt to get Christ to give up the Father's idea of the Kingdom and submit to the ideas of the world. The Apostle had spoken in the innocence of his heart, without reflection but with the vehemence of a short-sighted, purely natural affection. In his ill-considered words there lay hidden a poisoned dart, aimed directly at the very purpose of Christ's mission on earth—the redemption of the human race.

*The Cross.* Our Lord takes the occasion to explain that not He only but all His followers must carry the cross. He did not come to take suffering out of the world but to teach men to bear it, to give them the strength to bear it. By His death, He was to change the symbol of shame, slavery and degradation into a symbol of strength, glory and triumph. His followers would have to share the pain of it in submission to the Father's will and, by such faith, come to share in the glory of the resurrection.

In dwelling on the meaning of this self-denial, our Lord uses the word "life" in a twofold sense (Mt. 16:25). The one is the natural life of man, the other is the supernatural, eternal life. The two are in continual conflict; he who follows the dictates of worldly prudence, devoid of faith, in order to save or increase his natural life, loses both his natural and supernatural life in the end.

Our Lord is the motive for the sacrifice; it is He whom we must follow in carrying the cross, He whom we must confess, even to the point of death if necessary. And He is the final reward or condemnation: "For the Son of Man is to come with His angels in the glory of His Father, and then He will render to everyone according to his conduct". It may seem a long time to this day of reckoning, but He now gives a pledge of the future payment. Some who are standing there while He speaks will see the Son of Man coming in His Kingdom (Mt. 16:28). This is not the final coming mentioned in the previous sentence but, rather, the pledge of it. Mark separates this prophecy from the former by the phrase: "and He (also) said to

[222]

them . . ." (Mk. 8:39). Three of His Apostles will soon see Him transfigured in glory on Mount Thabor; all will see the Holy Spirit come upon the Apostles at Pentecost baptizing them with Christ's life and power; this will be the guarantee of eternal life to those who carry the cross.

## 61. THE TRANSFIGURATION

The Synoptists were not accustomed to date the facts that they record; but here they have taken care to mark the interval of time (six days) which separates the scene at Caesarea Philippi from the Transfiguration. The two events are closely related to each other. At Caesarea, Peter confessed to the divinity of Christ; on Mount Thabor, the Father Himself confirms the testimony of the Apostle. At Caesarea, Christ foretold to His Apostles His approaching death and the trial that they themselves would have to sustain; here, Almighty God wills to manifest His glory to restore their courage and to glorify in advance Him who is treading on to His death.

Thabor, where tradition places the scene, is a two-hour walk east of Nazareth in the northeastern corner of the plain of Esdraelon. It rises about 650 feet above the plain and surpasses all the surrounding hills in height and provides a view of all Galilee from sea to lake. Evidently the vision was at night as indicated by the fact that the Apostles were sleepy and that they descended from the mountain in the morning. Again, the three favored Apostles are chosen; Peter, prince of the Apostles; James, who is to be the first to be martyred; John, the beloved disciple.

Christ is transfigured while praying. Often when saints have been in ecstasy, their faces have appeared as if lighted up; but now a heavenly light transfigures Christ to an extent unapproached in the case of any saint. Our Lord's humanity whole and entire, body and soul, is substantially united to the divinity; He allows it now to be penetrated and imbued with the divine glory. From the discourse on the Bread of Life, we learn of the life-giving qualities of Christ's flesh, which was many times manifested even by miracles; the apparition on the Mount was only the sensible expression of the fact that Christ's body was wholly impregnated with divine power. Normally, Christ held this manifestation of divinity in restraint because it would have fed the popular idea of the Messias and destroyed His work. But now the Apostles are given a vision of His glory to help them through the hard days ahead.

The Law and the Prophets are represented by Moses, the greatest legislator, and Elias, the greatest prophet, of the Old Testament. Many a time the Apostles had heard their Master reproached with breaking the Law and overturning the traditions of Judaism. His calumniators were the revered masters of Israel, sitting in Moses' seat, whom the Apostles had been taught from childhood to revere. Their hearts were torn by the conflict between Christ and the leaders of the nation. But now, the apparition of Moses and Elias, in whom the whole of Judaism was enshrined, calmed all that, making them find in the Master, whom they were learning to adore, the realization of everything they had reverenced from childhood itself.

This appearance of Moses and Elias is a fresh revelation that all the Old Testament saints, patriarchs and prophets have not, through death, fallen into nothingness; they are alive in God. And it is also revealed that they played a decisive part in their peoples' history—prolonging even now in heaven the work of intercession and ministry which they had performed on earth. And so it is in the New Testament; those who have reached heaven are still active in promoting the Kingdom, and the Church has insisted, against much ridicule and opposition, on the invocation of the saints.

"And they spoke of His death which He was about to fulfill in Jerusalem" (Lk. 9:31). It was this conversation on the Passion that lent all its meaning to the Transfiguration. It was to remove from the Apostles' minds, the scandal of the cross. From the Transfiguration itself as well as from the conversation that followed, they should know that the Cross was not a defeat suffered by Jesus against His will but, in the designs of God, it was the culmination of His work. The manner and the place and the time were all settled in God's plans.

Peter is in a high state of consolation at the vision of the glorified Moses and Elias and of Christ transfigured. He instinctively wants to make it permanent—to forget all about the suffering in Jerusalem and rest in the glory of the present vision. His idea is to set up three tents made of branches of trees, such as travelers commonly used, and let the people come to the Mountain as to a shrine to worship Christ whose glory was so apparent.

A still more solemn testimony is given to Christ, the natural Son of God. Coming from the luminous cloud that overshadowed them, were heard the words: "This is my beloved Son; hear Him". Once again, as at the Baptism, the Father bestowed the seal of His sovereign testimony on His Son. And their hearts are striken with fear in the presence of His Majesty. Later on, the full fruit of the vision will blossom in the conviction of their own testimony: "For we were not following fictitious tales when we made known to you the power and coming of our Lord Jesus Christ, but we had been eye-witnesses of His grandeur. For He received from God the Father honor and glory, when from out the majestic glory a voice came down to Him, speaking thus: 'This is My beloved Son in whom I am well pleased'. And this voice we ourselves heard borne from heaven when we were with Him on the holy Mount". (2 Pet. 1:16-19).

## 62. THE DESCENT; 63. THE LUNATIC BOY; 64. SECOND PREDICTION; 65. THE DIDRACHMA

*The Descent.* The Apostles are commanded not to tell the vision, even to the other Apostles, until after our Lord has risen from the dead (Mt. 17:9). And Luke reports that they carried out the injunction (9:36). It would be too dangerous and harmful if the people, with their present dispositions, should hear of this sensational revelation. Evidently the sight of Elias in the vision sets the Apostles to wondering about the Pharisaic teaching that Elias would precede the coming of the Messias (*cf.* Malachias 4:5-6). This coming of Elias at the Transfiguration had been so short and hidden that they wonder if it would be sufficient to fulfill the prophecy. Our Lord, in His reply, seems to assert that Elias will come publicly before the second coming of Christ at the end of the world (Mt. 17:11). But already, the general expectation of Elias has been fulfilled in John the Baptist, who was another Elias in spirit and power (Mt. 17:12; *cf.* 11:14). And indeed, John was the forerunner of the Messias, not only in his preaching, but also in his suffering and death which was a foreshadowing of what the Jews would do to Christ (Mt. 17:12).

*The Lunatic Boy.* It may be that some traces of His glory were still manifest in the person of our Lord to account for the fact that His appearance at the foot of the mountain caused amazement and fear in the crowd (Mk. 9:14). The bickering contention and confusion at the foot of Thabor is in marked contrast to the peace and serenity and consolation which the three Apostles had experienced the night before. The other Apostles were disputing with the Pharisees (Mk. 9:13); evidently the Scribes, taking advantage of the Master's absence, had been challenging the authority and power of the Apostles to work miracles. And now, just when they wanted most of all to clinch the argument with a display of their power, the Apostles were unable to do what they had so often done before. Evidently they are overawed in the presence of the Scribes and their faith in their own miraculous power failed them in the face of the skeptical crowd. Later, when they inquire privately of the cause of their failure, our Lord tells them that, "this kind can be cast out in no way except by prayer and fasting" (Mk. 9:28). Their extraordinary power depended on their own confidence in God and our Lord now teaches them that prayer and fasting are among the most effective means of obtaining and maintaining this disposition. Their trouble had been that they were thinking too much of the Scribes and the difficulties involved and not enough of almighty God and the power He had conferred upon them.

Our Lord rebukes the crowd, especially the Scribes, for their incredulous attitude of mind (Mk. 9:18). Then He listens to the father's pathetic story.

From the detailed description of the boy's symptoms, it seems that he was suffering from epilepsy. In this case, the nervous disease was accompanied, or perhaps caused, by diabolical possession. Finally comes the petition which was feeble enough, in the faith and hope from which it sprang: "If *Thou canst* do anything, have compassion on us and help us" (Mk. 9:21). "If *thou canst believe,* all things are possible to him who believes" (9:22). It is the man's faith, not God's power, which is deficient, and the implied rebuke brings the man to tearful prayer that God might give him the gift of perfect faith: "I do believe; help my unbelief" (9:23). In response to such good will, our Lord grants the double boon—faith to the father and the cure to the son.

*Second Prediction.* Again, we are informed that such public miracles were only by exception in this phase of His public life. The general rule was that our Lord traveled in secret and spent the time instructing His disciples in private (Mk. 9:29). And the main theme of the instruction concerned His passion and death which is here repeated in stereotyped form (9:30-32). Still they are slow to co-operate with grace and face the unpleasant reality; they do not understand, and they are afraid to inquire about it, partly because they instinctively turn away from the bad news, and partly because of the severity of His previous rebuke to Peter. Failing to approach the Light on this subject, their minds remain troubled and confused and they are sad.

*The Didrachma.* But aside from the main point of instruction during this period, our Lord continues to enlighten and strengthen the Apostles on many other subjects. Here, St. Matthew gives but one example of how He emphasizes His own identity as the Son of God and Peter's favored position as His vicar. When approached by the collectors of the temple tax, Peter commits his Master (Mt. 17:23) to the payment of the didrachma (about 33 cents). Then our Lord privately instructs Peter, as well as the other Apostles, that he should not have been so sure that the tax was due in this case. The kings of this world do not tax their own sons but rather their subjects. And so is it with God's Son; the Son, with His Father, owns the Temple and is not liable to the tax. And then He goes to extraordinary lengths to show Peter that He is the Son and that Peter himself is identified with Him and shares His privileges as King. We have observed how our Lord never worked miracles to supply the material needs of the apostolic band; they lived on alms. And yet now He sends Peter to find the coin in the mouth of the fish. Therein He manifests His supreme power over the kingdom of nature and the miraculous coin, which was equal to two didrachmas, reveals to Peter the close bond that exists between himself and the King.

# 66. TO 71. DISCOURSE ON CHRISTIAN VIRTUES

This period of special instruction for the Apostles lasted for five or six months. And yet the events, as recorded in the Gospel narrative, would require little more than a week for their occurrence. They are merely samples of the many unrecorded deeds and sayings of Christ during this period. And now, too, we are given a series of verbal instructions on various virtues. They should be considered as typical samples rather than a complete account of all that our Lord taught during this period. For the most part, they are casual instructions arising from the concrete thoughts and words and deeds of the Apostles at the time, wherein our Lord takes the opportunity to point out, often by contrast with their own actions, the true spirit of the Kingdom which they are to have in their charge. In view of this connection with concrete circumstances, we must not expect of these discourses the same unity that would be found in a discourse on a single moral or dogmatic topic.

*Little children.* St. Mark (9:32) clarifies the actual circumstances which led to this part of the instruction. On the road to Capharnaum, instead of letting their thoughts dwell on the sufferings which Christ had just foretold, the Apostles were arguing about the division of prizes in the Kingdom. They know now that they have been chosen to hold a prominent place in it. But, evidently, jealousy has been aroused by the promises made to Peter and the preference shown to Peter, James and John on Thabor and, previously, at the raising of the daughter of Jairus. Now they are shamefaced at our Lord's question about their argument along the road. It is with great patience that He sits down to cure this deadly germ of worldly ambition in their hearts. Unless they kill it, they will have no place at all in His Kingdom (Mt. 18:3). The little child whom He tenderly enfolds in His arms (Mk. 9:35) is the model to be followed; the child is perfectly content with his littleness and his dependence upon others. So must they learn to accept the place God has given them in the Kingdom and do the work that has been appointed them in humility and simplicity, without any envy or jealousy against those who have been chosen for a greater part. It would take a long time and many such instructions to cure this human weakness of theirs (*cf.* Mt. 20:21-28; Lk. 22:24-30). In fact, the cure would be accomplished only after Pentecost when their hearts were full of the Holy Spirit of Love.

*Stranger Exorcist.* Evidently the foregoing instruction had caused doubts in the mind of John about the rectitude of his action in preventing the exorcist from acting in the name of Christ. He asks about it now. Our Lord makes clear that the Apostles are not to have a monopoly on the power of miracles. The fact that the man had the power shows that God approved of his faith in Christ and rewarded it. Therefore, he should have been encouraged.

*Avoiding Scandal.* Our Lord returns to His original theme of the child. He had said that it is necessary to become like a child in His Kingdom. And now He adds a stern warning to those who would seduce such humble, believing souls and lead them into sin. To receive such souls in Christ's name is to receive Christ; and so, to cause them spiritual harm is to harm the Body of Christ (Mt. 18:5-6). It is better to make any sacrifice rather than suffer the eternal punishment that awaits such sin (Mk. 9:42-49). The severe sacrifices one must make—*i.e.,* to cut off one's hand or pluck out the eye, in order to avoid sin, are not to be taken literally. A man "plucks out his eye", in the sense intended by Christ, when he denies his eyes those pleasures which lead to sin. In this sense, our Lord's words are not a matter of counsel but, rather, of strict precept.

*Lost Sheep.* The Apostles, then, are to hold dear these little ones of Christ. Each one of them is important enough in the eyes of the Father to have a guardian angel pleading his cause in heaven. Hence the Apostles, like the Father and the Son, must exercise zealous care and love over each of these precious souls as individuals (Mt. 18:10 ff.).

*Fraternal Correction.* The Apostles, acting as the shepherds of souls, will have to admonish and correct the faults of those in the Kingdom. Our Lord here applies the principles of zeal for souls and patient charity, from which such corrective action should proceed. First, private admonition should be tried before initiating any judicial action before witnesses. Only after these less drastic measures have failed, should the culprit be brought to the tribunal of the Church. But then, if he is still stubborn and refuses to listen to the authority of the Church, he is, for his own good and that of the Church, to be excommunicated: "let him be to thee as the heathen and the publican" (Mt. 18:17). Here, our Lord gives the power of "binding and loosing" to the Apostles as a group. It is understood, of course, that this collective power is limited by and subject to the supreme power of Peter who had previously been promised the "keys of the Kingdom" (Mt. 16:19).

*The Unmerciful Servant.* In the foregoing case, our Lord envisioned an offender who was stubborn in his refusal to repent. But now Peter has in mind the case of an offender who repents but keeps falling into new offenses. The question is, what limits, if any, should be put upon the number of times he is to be forgiven. The Rabbis taught that the same offense could be forgiven three times but that even God would not forgive more often. Peter sufficiently grasped Christ's spirit of charity to double the number. But Christ shows him that God's mercy is limitless to those who truly repent. The number "seventy times seven", indicates that there should be no limit to our willingness to forgive. If we always need the pardon of God, it is our duty, in turn, always to pardon our brothers.

The parable of the unmerciful servant reveals the principle that the only limit to God's forgiveness of us is the one we ourselves set, by refusing to forgive others (Mt. 18:23-35). It is the same principle which He taught and which we daily invoke upon ourselves in the Lord's prayer: "And forgive us our debts, as we also forgive our debtors" (Mt. 6:12).

## 72. Adieu to Galilee: "Woe"

We have seen, from the samples recorded in the Gospels, some of the intimate instructions and revelations with which Christ rewarded the faith which the Apostles placed in Him. In sharp and tragic contrast is the fearful condemnation, the awful curse, which Christ invoked upon His unbelieving countrymen before shaking the dust of Galilee from His feet. For fifteen or sixteen months now He had traversed Galilee in every direction sowing everywhere the good word of the Gospel and scattering His miracles in profusion. But still, they stubbornly stick to their carnal-minded aspirations and reject the "hard sayings" of His spiritual Gospel. Now comes the withering blast of divine anger: "Woe to thee Corozain! Woe to thee, Bethsaida! For if in Tyre and Sidon had been worked the miracles that have been worked in you, they would have repented long ago in sackcloth and ashes. But I tell you, it will be more tolerable for Tyre and Sidon on the day of judgment than for you. And thou, Capharnaum, shalt thou be exalted to heaven? Thou shalt be thrust down to hell! For if the miracles had been worked in Sodom that have been worked in thee, it would have remained to this day. But I tell you, it will be more tolerable for the land of Sodom on the day of judgment than for thee" (Mt. 11:21-24).

Even as earthly cities, these towns were most effectively withered by the curse; they have disappeared from the face of the earth, leaving no more trace than Sodom and Gemmorrah. Corozain has disappeared without a trace and Capharnaum is nothing but an area of excavations. The location of Bethsaida, once the home of Peter, James and Philip, is still a matter of dispute.

Christ is not to be tampered with. Faith in Him is not a matter of indifference, a condescension or favor which a man may bestow or not as he pleases. It is a matter of life and death. Christ is "the Corner Stone"; those who build on Him will endure forever. But the Stone will fall on those who reject it and "grind them to powder" (Mt. 21:44).

## Chapter XX

# PERIOD IV. CONFLICTS AND
# CONSOLIDATIONS

꙰꙰꙰꙰꙰꙰꙰꙰꙰꙰꙰꙰꙰꙰꙰꙰꙰꙰꙰꙰꙰꙰꙰꙰꙰꙰꙰꙰꙰

*Scene:* Jerusalem; Perea; Bethany; Ephraim

*Time:* October to March, 29 A.D.

|  | Mt | Mk | Lk | Jn |
|---|---|---|---|---|
| I. Jerusalem: Tabernacles | — | — | 9: 51 | 7: 2-13 |
| 73. Conspiracy of Pharisees | — | — | — | 7: 14-53 |
| 74. The adulteress | — | — | — | 8: 1-11 |
| 75. The Light of the World | — | — | — | 8: 12 |
| 76. Father's witness to the Son | — | — | — | 8: 13-20 |
| 77. Castigation of incredulity | — | — | — | 8: 21-30 |
| 78. Sonship of Abraham | — | — | — | 8: 31-59 |
| 79. Cure of the man born blind | — | — | — | 9: 1-41 |
| 80. The door. Good Shepherd | — | — | — | 10: 1-21 |
| II. Perean Ministry (infra) | — | — | — | 10: 40 |
| III. Jerusalem: Dedication | — | — | — | — |
| 81. "I and the Father are one" | — | — | — | 10: 22-39 |
| IV. Perean Ministry (infra) | — | — | — | 10: 40-42 |
| V. 82. Bethany: Lazarus | — | — | — | 11: 1-53 |
| VI. 83. Retirement to Ephraim | — | — | — | 11: 54-56 |
| VII. 84. Last journey to Jerusalem | | | | |
| via Jericho and Bethany | 20: 29 | 10: 46 | 18: 35 | 12: 1 |

FROM NOW on Jesus sets His face toward Jerusalem and His death. The months that follow are rich in instructions and discourses but the incidents are relatively few and the journeyings are fairly definitely marked. He arrives in Jerusalem for the feast of Tabernacles, at the beginning of October. The clash with His enemies is violent; attempts are made to arrest Him, even to stone Him. Hence He retires to Perea, across the Jordan, where at a distance from the city, and among the friends of the Baptist and His own, He is safe. With them, He consolidates the work of His Public Life by continuing to instruct them in the spirit of His Kingdom.

However, He again goes up to the city for the feast of Dedication, toward the middle of December. Another attempt is made to stone Him. He retires again to Perea. Thence after the lapse of some time He is summoned by the news of Lazarus' sickness, and goes to Bethany to perform the greatest of His miracles, which was also the motive of the definitive resolve of the Sanhedrin to put Him to death at all costs. Consequently, He retires to Ephraim, a town north of Jerusalem, only about two hours from the borders of Samaria. There, in complete seclusion, He awaits the time for His final advance upon Jerusalem, at the Pasch. These final weeks are devoted to the Twelve.

At the approach of the Pasch, Jesus leaves Ephraim for Jerusalem. Yet His way is not direct; it carries Him through Jericho and brings Him to Bethany, six days before the Pasch. This journey was by no means secret; rather, it assumed the character of a triumphal procession. And the climax was reached when, after the sabbath-rest at Bethany, He entered Jerusalem as King, amid the frantic plaudits of the crowd—to the sullen rage of His enemies.

## TABERNACLES

The feast of Tabernacles occurred either late in September or early in October, depending on the year. Its significance was twofold; a feast of thanksgiving for the safe gathering of the harvest of grain and fruit, and a commemoration of the forty years when God guided the nation through the desert to the Promised Land. It was considered the greatest and holiest of all feasts and was in a special manner a feast of joy, representing in type the glory of the Messianic days when the final deliverance would come and the Holy Spirit would be poured out like water upon the land. The name "Tabernacles" derived from the fact that during the seven days of the feast, the men lived in huts (tabernacles) made of leafy branches to commemorate the tents pitched in the wilderness of Sinai. These leafy tents were erected in the streets and squares, on the flat roofs of mansions, on the city walls and even in the court of the Gentiles. During the gay festival, Jerusalem looked like a forest.

Some of our Lord's relatives are anxious that He give up the hidden life He has been living for the past few months and go up publicly to the feast (Jn. 7:3-4). This urging does not spring from faith in Him (v. 5). They still cling to their hopes that the Messias will be a national liberator. Christ, with His power of speech and miracles, could fill the role. Now would be the opportune time, with Jews gathering from all over the world for the great feast. If the popular enthusiasm for the wonder-worker could be stirred up to accomplish the "coup d'état", they, His relatives, would share in the spoils.

Our Lord has no intention of joining one of the caravans from Caphar-naum and going down publicly to the feast. For several months, despite all His traveling through the tetrarchy of Philip and the Decapolis, He has been avoiding Jerusalem. On His last visit at the previous Pasch, the cure of the paralytic and the discourse in which He had declared Himself the Son of God equal to the Father, had aroused enemies in the city who were resolved to destroy Him. A public march on the city at this time would only play into their hands and the time appointed for His death was not yet come (v. 8). Hence, He deliberately allows the solemn inauguration of the feast to pass and then, quietly and privately, He slips into the city and appears in the Temple. His enemies, thus taken by surprise, are unable to arrest Him, once He is surrounded by the crowds and enjoys the protection of the Roman guards.

The crowds in the city and their leaders (the "Jews") had expected Him to come. They knew it was His custom to appear at the great feasts. During His long absence, the leaders have regained their ascendancy over the crowd. For fear of reprisals, the people dare not speak openly of Him; their comments are in "whispers" (7:12). His identity is the urgent topic in the city and, as usual, the people are divided between Him and their leaders. But now the hostile atmosphere is such that the best that Christ's friends can say of Him is that He is a "good man".

## 73. CONSPIRACY OF THE PHARISEES

When Christ appears, the force of His person and His eloquence is such as to give pause even to His most determined enemies. Even the leaders are forced to marvel (Jn. 7:15) and, unwittingly, they reopen the question of His identity. Our Lord takes the offensive and, after indicating to them the heavenly source of His teaching (7:16-19), He exposes their plot to kill Him and refutes their reason for it (7:19-24). Evidently many in the present audience are unfamiliar with the machinations in Jerusalem and they think Him insane (v. 20). But the natives of the city know of the plot and they marvel that the leaders are powerless to carry it out (v. 25).

Once more, now that His personal influence is felt, the question is not whether He is a good man but, rather, whether He is the Christ. Even those who stick to the old prejudice are not so sure (Jn. 7:26-27). And in the face of their incredulity, our Lord makes the solemn announcement ("cried out and said") that He is from the Father. The truth in His words wins many converts in the crowd (7:31).

Again, the Pharisees have lost the ascendancy, and they resort to the old plan of violence. Men are appointed to arrest Him (v. 32). They are convinced that He will not escape their hands. Where would He go? To the Gentiles (v. 35)? That would be a joke, indeed—that the Messias should go to the Gentiles!

## 74. The Adulteress

During His stay in Jerusalem at the time of the feast, our Lord withdrew every evening from the city lest the Pharisees catch Him alone and try to arrest Him. Then, in the morning, He would return to the Temple where, surrounded by the crowds, no one would dare to touch Him. It was on one of these mornings when He had returned to the city from the Mount of Olives that the Pharisees burst in on His instruction with the woman taken in adultery. Their plan was to trap Him into passing judgment on the case and then use it against Him. If He refused to condemn the woman to stoning, they could accuse Him of despising the Law of Moses. If He condemned her, He would appear before the crowd as violating His own gospel of mercy and would also be liable to the Romans who did not countenance such punishments which had long been out of use.

Our Lord stooped and wrote in the dust. There is no evidence that He was writing the secret sins of the accusers. His act of turning away and "doodling" in the sand was designed to indicate that He had no interest in the case. Judgment in such a case belonged to the Sanhedrin. But when the Pharisees insisted, He raised Himself erect and said to them: "Let him that is without sin among you be the first to cast a stone at her" (Jn 8:7). According to the Mosaic Law, the accuser had to cast the first stone after judgment had been passed. Jesus makes the accuser also the judge and, since in appealing to Him they were not interested in the due process of the Law, He makes the norm of judgment their own conscience with regard to their own lives. Now they are in the very spot they had planned for Him and perhaps it is from fear of what they know He *could* write in the sand that first the older ones falter and then they all slink away in turn (Jn. 8:9). Our Lord has no interest in the case in so far as it was a piece of legal sophistry. But the poor woman who had been used as bait is of concern to Him. Assured of her repentance, He wipes out the past and sends her into the bright future with the merciful injunction, "from now on sin no more" (Jn. 8:11).

## 75. Christ the Source of Life; Light of the World.
## 76. Father's Witness to the Son

On the last day of the feast of Tabernacles, our Lord made the solemn pronouncement that He, as Messias, was the fulfillment of this feast and all its ceremonies. There were two such formal revelations, one in the morning, the other in the evening.

*Source of Life.* Every morning during the week of ceremonies, the multitude made a procession to the Pool of Siloe, whence a priest drew water in a golden urn and, returning to the Temple, poured it out upon the altar amidst the sounding of trumpets and hymns of joy. The ceremony commemorated the miraculous water which gushed forth from the rock in the desert when struck by the rod of Moses; it also symbolized the happy Messianic times when the Holy Spirit would be poured out upon the people:

"You shall draw waters with joy out of the Saviour's fountains" (Is. 12:3).

It was while this ceremony was in progress or just completed that Jesus "stood and cried out saying: If anyone thirst, let him come to Me and drink. He who believes in Me, as the Scripture says: From within Him there shall flow rivers of living water" (Jn. 7:37-38).

The same revelation that was given to the Samaritan woman (Jn. 4:10) is now made publicly to all the people and, by it, Christ proclaims that He fulfills this Feast as previously He had declared Himself the fulfillment of the Temple and of the Sabbath.

Evidently our Lord developed this theme at some length dwelling, no doubt, on the many passages in the Prophets which speak of the waters of salvation pouring out from the Messias. Many of the people believe in Him as a result of this discourse, while others concentrate on what they consider the difficulties (Jn. 7:40-44). Even the attendants who had been commissioned to arrest Him are powerless under the spell of His eloquence:

"Never has man spoken as this man" (Jn. 7:46).

The Pharisees are in a rage, reviling the crowd for its ignorance, resisting the efforts of Nicodemus to introduce calm reason into their proceedings (Jn. 7:48-52).

*Light of the World.* A central feature of the nocturnal celebrations of the feast were the great illuminations. In the great Court of Women, to which all Jews of either sex had access, huge golden candelabra, seventy-five feet in height, were set up and surmounted by enormous lamps. The Levites chanted canticles accompanied by harps, lyres, cymbals and trumpets. The Rabbis who, according to the Talmud, describe these festivities, probably exaggerate when they say that by the light of these lamps the whole city was illumined as if by daylight and that the music could be heard as far away as Jericho. The significance of this illumination was twofold; it commemorated the guidance of Israel in the desert by the pillar of fire; and it typified the light which was to come in the person of the Messias:

"Arise, be enlightened O Jerusalem, for thy Light is Come". (Is. 60:1).

It was against this background that Jesus stood in the hall of the Treasury (Jn. 8:20), which was part of the Women's Court, and announced:

"I am the Light of the World" (Jn. 8:12).

Doubtless, in this case also He explained at length how He was the fulfillment of the prophecies in this regard.

[234]

*Father's witness.* The Pharisees know very well who He claims to be. They dare not let His claim go unchallenged. And so, they appeal to the legal requirements of at least two witnesses at a trial: "Thou bearest witness to thyself. Thy witness is not true". (Jn. 8:13). Jesus replies that He is not bound by the canons of human courts of law; He is the only one who knows His divine origin and His testimony to it is true even though it comes from Himself (8:14-15). But then, if they want two witnesses, they have them in Himself and His Father. The Father testifies to the Son in the works He has given Him to do. Both Father and Son are two distinct Persons (8:17-18) and yet, They are One and the same Being so that if anyone knows the Son, he thereby knows the Father (8:19). Once again, they try to seize Him but are powerless to do so (8:20).

## 77. CASTIGATION OF INCREDULITY;
## 78. SONSHIP OF ABRAHAM

Very likely, the long dialogue which follows (Jn. 8:21-59) took place on another occasion, after the feast of Tabernacles, when Jesus was teaching in the Temple. There is but one final way that these people might be saved. Of miracles, they have seen enough, and He has explained fully their significance with regard to His identity. There is nothing left to do now but take the offensive and attack these people, to expose their bad will and tell them clearly of the dire consequences to which it will lead. And so, He hurls Himself into open struggle with these Jews; letting loose the full power of His eloquence; He argues, explains, pleads, threatens, denounces. In the course of it all, He makes the clearest revelations of Himself.

Our Lord begins by alluding to His departure from this world; when He is gone they will seek Him in vain and will die in their sin (Jn. 8:21). When Jerusalem is destroyed, their national aspirations will collapse and, abandoned by God and men, they shall die in their unbelief:

"If you do not believe that I am He, you shall die in your sin" (Jn. 8:24).

"I am He" is the same expression with which He referred to Himself as the promised Saviour when speaking to the Apostles at the Last Supper (Jn. 13:19). And here, when the Jews pretend not to know what He means by it (8:25), He repeats the claim and appeals to His Oneness with the Father as the proof of it (8:28-30).

Despite the general hostility of the audience, there were many who, reflecting on His miracles, saw the truth in Christ's words and expressed their belief in Him (8:30). To strengthen and encourage them, Jesus promises that, as His disciples, they shall have the truth and the truth will make them free (8:31-32). But this implication that hitherto they have not been free, arouses the unbelieving ones among them and they cry out that they are the sons of Abraham: "How sayest Thou, You shall be free?" (Jn. 8:33). It is the old pride of race with the implication that carnal descent from Abraham assures them of all the prerogatives of the Chosen People; there is nothing further that even the Messias can give them by way of spiritual salvation.

Our Lord now sets Himself to the painful task of revealing to these unbelieving Jews who their real father is in the spiritual sense. There is but one way to judge; the works which a man does will alone reveal the state of his heart and his spiritual parentage. They are planning to murder Him (v. 38). Let them compare that work with His works and words; the comparison will reveal who is His Father and who is theirs; obviously, both cannot be the same (v. 38). And to their insistence that Abraham is their father, He invites a comparison with the works of Abraham. They seek to kill Him, in the face of all the signs that He is genuinely from God. Compare this work with all the works of Abraham, with Abraham's faith and reverence for God's word. Obviously, Abraham cannot be their father nor is Abraham's Father their Father (8:39-40).

At last the Jews perceive that Christ is talking of spiritual parentage and frantically they insist that their Father, as well as Abraham's, is God (8:41). "We have not been born of fornication"—*i.e.*, we are not attached to a different God than Abraham's God; the covenant was made between the Father and Abraham; no idolatry has intervened whereby we, the descendants of Abraham, have a different Father from the One who made the covenant.

Ah, but infidelity has intervened! Christ came with all the credentials as the Son of God and they refused to believe Him. How then can they be the sons of God? (8:42-43). But since their father is not God, he must be God's adversary, the devil. And two things prove this to be the case: (1) the devil was a murderer from the beginning (it was he who introduced death into the world; Wisd. 2:24; Rom. 5:12 ff.); (2) again, he is by nature a deceiver (*cf.* Gen. 3). These Jews resemble him in both features; their purpose is homicidal and they are unable to recognize the truth (Jn. 8:44-47). The stern, cold, damning logic of it is the final grace; it is the lash, wielded with purest love, to sting them to face the truth.

Stubborn pride bridles under the lash and they accuse the Holy One of being Himself possessed (8:48). Limitless love brushes the insult aside and offers eternal life; if they will believe in Him, they can avoid the death to which their sin is leading them. The truth will not only make them free of sin (v. 34), but of the death which is the result of sin (8:49-51). With deliberate captiousness they interpret Him in the carnal sense:

"Abraham is dead and the prophets . . . Art Thou greater than our father

Abraham who is dead? And the prophets are dead. Whom dost Thou make Thyself?" (Jn. 8:52-53).

The time for delicate maneuvering in such circumstances has long since passed; their will is as bad as it can be. Let the light blaze full in their faces. Perhaps the shock will move them.

> "Abraham your father rejoiced that he was to see My day. He saw it and was glad" (8:56).
>
> "The Jews therefore said to Him: Thou art not yet fifty years old, and hast Thou seen Abraham?" (8:57).
>
> "Jesus said to them, Amen, amen, I say to you, before Abraham came to be, I AM" (8:58).

The Jewish name for God, "Yahweh", is derived from the verb "to be". God is existence itself; He is not confined to the past or the future but embraces the whole of being in an eternal "now". And so when Moses said to God:

> "Lo I shall go to the children of Israel and say to them: The God of your fathers hath sent Me to you. If they should say to Me: What is His name? What shall I tell them?"
>
> "God said to Moses: I AM WHO AM. He said: Thus shalt thou say to the children of Israel: HE WHO IS, hath sent me to you" (Exodus 3:13-14).

Once again, not by messenger but in Person, HE WHO IS comes to the children of Israel. But this time, "they took up stones to cast at Him" (Jn. 8:59).

## 79. THE CURE OF THE MAN BORN BLIND

In speaking of the historicity of the gospel story (Ch. VIII), we made a special point of the fact that Christ's bitter enemies were sure to have investigated the facts and would have denied them if they could. Generally speaking, there is no record of such investigation in the Gospels, but it is an assumption warranted by the fact that they were so anxious to discredit the works of Christ. But, here, in his ninth chapter, St. John gives us a marvelously detailed example of how the Pharisees did make every effort to deny the fact of a miracle before resorting to the less convincing tactic of questioning its divine source. This is only one example, but in view of what we know of the Pharisees and their purpose, we should read it as an illustration of their general practice with regard to Christ's miracles.

The event is a public one in which Christ purposes to illustrate to all that He is the Light of the World (Jn. 9:4-5). The beggar is a public figure since he sat daily at the Temple reciting the pitiful story of his permanent affliction in order to elicit alms. Our Lord emphasizes the cure by the ritual He used and by sending the man to wash at the Pool of Siloe. After the cure, the man is questioned, first by the people (9:10-11) and then, officially, by the Pharisees (v. 15). Unable to deny the facts, some of the Pharisees yield to the evidence while others object that the cure was done on the Sabbath (v. 16). These latter again seek to undermine the fact of the miracle by calling the parents to testify. The parents, knowing that testimony displeasing to the authorities will lead to their excommunication from the synagogue, have every inducement to side with the Pharisees (9:22-23). Yet, they cannot deny that this is indeed their own son and that he was born blind and that he is now able to see (v. 18-20). But they refuse to be drawn into any conclusions about the source of the cure for fear of the harmful consequences to themselves. Again the beggar himself is called and testifies to the facts (v. 25) until, weary of reciting the details, with humorous irony, he asks:

"Why would you hear again? Would you also become His disciples?" (v. 26-27).

Thus, try as they might, the Pharisees are unable to deny that this man was born blind and that, after Christ had dealt with him, he was able to see for the first time in his life. In addition to these *historical* facts, the *philosophical* truth of the miracle is clear; the laws of nature could not account for this sudden removal of a life-long affliction. The *theological* truth, the fact that God is the source of the cure, is the only thing left to attack. Curiously, these learned theologians are most anxious to get the beggar himself to draw for them the conclusion that the miracle came from Beelzebub:

"Give glory to God! We ourselves know that this man is a sinner. . . . We know that God spoke to Moses; but as for this Man, we do not know where He is from" (9:24-30).

But they are powerless to impose such blindness on the man who has just received his sight. Unlearned as he is and in the face of all their power to do him harm, the beggar gives them a lesson in how to draw the theological conclusion from the historical and philosophical premises:

"Why herein is the marvel, that you do not know where He is from, and yet He opened my eyes. Now we know that God does not hear sinners (*i.e.,* does not sanction their sinful lives with the power to work miracles) . . . If this Man were not from God, He could do nothing" (9:30-34).

But darkness hates the light and the clearer the light, the more intense the hatred:

"And they turned Him out (of the synagogue)" (v. 34).

Christ is personally interested in this man who so fearlessly and at so much cost to himself, bore witness to the light that was in Him. It was to complete and bring to perfection this higher miracle of the man's spiritual vision, that Christ sought out the man and asked: "Dost thou believe in the Son of God?" The man answered and said: "Who is He, Lord, that I may believe in Him?" And Jesus, in response to his unquestioning good will, tells him simply and directly, as He told the woman of Samaria,

"Thou hast both seen Him, and He it is who speaks with thee" (9:35-37).

Our Lord then reveals the symbolic meaning of the man's physical cure. Christ came into this world to restore spiritual sight to all men, to illumine their minds with the gift of faith. But to receive this spiritual cure, men must co-operate with grace; the blind man had to go, of his own obedience to the Pool of Siloe and, again, to see Christ, he had to be willing to believe (v. 36 ff.). There are two kinds of spiritual blindness: that of the humble, docile souls who lament their ignorance and wish to be cured of it, and that of the proud who, relying on their own power to see, close their eyes to the light of truth. Therein lies the difference between Christ, the Light of the World, and the light of the sun; physical light dispels darkness by the fact of its presence, but the Light of Christ shines in the souls of men only in proportion to their willingness; if the darkness turns away from the Light, the darkness remains and increases:

"For judgment have I come into this world, that they who do not see may see, and they who see may become blind" (9:39).

If the Pharisees were only blind in the sense that the light of faith had not been offered them, they would have no sin. But, since the Light shines in their midst and they turn away, pridefully insisting on their own ability to see, their sin remains (9:40-41). The leaders of the nation are perishing from their worldly wisdom while the lowly outcasts, such as the beggar, are finding eternal life.

## 80. THE DOOR; GOOD SHEPHERD

We have seen how our Lord has taken great pains to reveal that He is the fulfillment of the history of the Jews, of their prophecies and of all the ceremonials of their feasts. He is the true manna, the bread come down from heaven; He is the rock from which the water flows that bubbles up into everlasting life; He is the Light that will enlighten all who come to Him. And now, again, He seizes upon the allegory, often used by the Prophets, of the Shepherd and the Sheep.

In Palestine, the sheep always remain outdoors. At night, they are protected by being penned up in an open enclosure. At one corner of the fold is a narrow gate through which the sheep enter and leave one by one so that they may be counted upon going and returning. Often several flocks will be together in the same enclosure and the shepherds take turns watching against wolves and robbers. In the morning, when one of the shepherds comes to take his flock, the man on guard lets him in and the sheep, recognizing his call, immediately separate themselves from the others and follow him in single file through the gate.

Our Lord first applies this familiar pastoral scene by comparing Himself to the gate of the sheep-fold:

"I am the door of the sheep" (Jn. 10:8).

Christ is the only way that leads to the Father; shepherds as well as sheep must enter through Him.

"All whoever have come are thieves and robbers; but the sheep have not heard them" (10:8).

There have been many false messiases (as there will be many more) and they have succeeded in enlisting some recruits and leading them to destruction. But, in general, the people did not recognize in them their true shepherd. The true shepherd enters by the door that is Christ.

Christ is not only the door to the sheep-fold; He Himself is the Good Shepherd and others are shepherds only in subordination to Him. Ezechiel prophesies the coming of this Shepherd:

"Woe to the shepherds of Israel, that fed themselves. . . . You ate the milk and clothed yourselves with the wool and you killed that which was fat, but My flock you did not feed . . . but you ruled over them with rigour and with a high hand. And my sheep were scattered because there was no shepherd and they became the prey of all the beasts of the field and were scattered".

"Behold I Myself come upon the shepherds; I will require My flock at their hand, and I will cause them to cease from feeding the flock any more, neither shall the shepherds feed themselves any more. . . . Behold I Myself will seek My sheep and will visit them . . . I will feed them in the most fruitful pastures . . . I will seek that which was lost . . . I will bind up that which was broken, and I will strengthen that which was weak. . . ." (Ezechiel ch. 34).

It was a day of reckoning for the shepherds of Israel and a day of joyful promise for the sheep, when Christ announced:

"I am the good shepherd" (Jn. 10:11).

He will bring other sheep from among the Gentiles and unite them with the sheep of Israel into one fold under one shepherd (v. 16). The price He will pay for their rescue is His own life (v. 15). He deliberately lays it down of His own free choice as the price which He and the Father have determined. And, to the eternal rejoicing of the sheep, He will take up His life again in His resurrection from the grave (v. 17-18).

## PEREAN MINISTRY

A period of four or five months elapsed between the feast of Tabernacles in October and the raising of Lazarus from the dead sometime in March. The only recorded visit of our Lord to Jerusalem during this period was at the feast of Dedication in December. Because of the intense animosity against Him in the city, He confined His ministry to the district along the Jordan in Perea (Jn. 10:40-42). There, He continued to instruct the Apostles and disciples and He preached with notable success to a popular audience that was, for the most part, favorably disposed.

In the nine chapters of his "greater intercalation" (9:51-18:14), St. Luke records many events and instructions which belong to this period of the Perean ministry. Some of these events also belong to other periods and we have seen them in parallel passages of the other gospels. St. Luke gives very little indication of the sequence of time in these narrations; we have listed them in a sequence of some probability in the Appendix to the outline of the Public Life. These chapters in Luke contain instructions in the true Christian spirit (often in contrast to that of the Pharisees) and include some of the most beautiful parables such as the Prodigal Son, Lazarus and the Rich Man, the Faithless Steward, the Pharisee and the Publican. But they add nothing new by way of revelation to the prophetic ministry of Christ and, since we are mainly interested in the general sweep of the Public Life, we shall not treat them in detail.

## 81. DEDICATION: "I AND THE FATHER ARE ONE"

Two months after the feast of Tabernacles, our Lord came down from Perea to Jerusalem for the feast of Dedication in December. This feast originated in the time of the Machabees (1 Mach. 4:36-59). In 168 B.C., Antiochus Epiphanes, the Syrian King who ruled over Palestine, introduced pagan worship into the Temple. This was the occasion for the revolt of the Jews under the Machabees and three years later, in 165 B.C., Judas Machabee purified the Temple of idolatrous worship and rededicated it to God. A joyous feast of eight days was inaugurated to commemorate the event. During these days, the houses in Jerusalem and other places were illuminated; hence, Josephus Flavius called the celebration the feast of "Lights".

Since it was the rainy season, our Lord was teaching in Solomon's Porch, a covered, colonnaded walk, longer than St. Peter's basilica in Rome, which ran along the eastern court of the Temple. The leaders of the people (the "Jews") broke in on His teaching and said to Him:

> "How long dost Thou keep us in suspense? If Thou art the Christ, tell us openly" (Jn. 10:24).

Again, it was a trap: they are looking for an open declaration which will furnish pretext for arresting Him or reporting Him for sedition to the Romans. In reply, our Lord goes much further than the name "Messias" with all its political connotations; He proclaims His relationship to the Father:

> "I and the Father are One" (10:30).

That is why no one can snatch His sheep away from Him; He is One in nature and power with the almighty Father. The Jews are aware of what He claims:

> "Not for a good work do we stone Thee, but for blasphemy and because Thou, being a man, makest Thyself God" (10:33).

In the face of imminent death, our Lord seeks to quiet their excitement by distracting their attention. He refers to the Judges of the Old Testament, who, even when they were unfaithful to their duties, were called "gods" because they had authority from God and represented Him (10:35). No one objected to the use of the name in their regard; the warrant for it lay in the fact that the Scripture called them "gods" and the Scripture must be true. So, in the case of Christ: they should not accuse Him of blasphemy because of a name which He applies to Himself; they should look to the evidence (His works) and see if the title is deserved. His works will prove to them that He is one Being with the Father (10:36-39). But the Pharisees are not interested in evidence; as soon as He comes again to the open declaration, they reveal the bad faith in which they asked for it, by attempting to seize Him (v. 39). It is hopeless to contend with such bad will and our Lord goes back to resume His work in Perea (v. 40-42).

## 82. BETHANY: LAZARUS

Our Lord was on terms of intimate friendship with the well-to-do family of Mary, Martha and Lazarus. During His visits to Jerusalem He often stayed with them at their home in Bethany, less than two miles from the city. When Lazarus became seriously ill, his sisters sent messengers to the other Bethany in Perea to tell the Lord: "Behold, he whom Thou lovest is sick". In the presence of the messengers, who certainly brought the words back to Bethany, our Lord replied:

> "This sickness is not unto death, but for the glory of the Lord, that through it the Son of God may be glorified" (Jn. 11:4).

To us, who know of the miracle, the meaning of the words is clear enough but what a trial of faith it must have been to Martha and Mary when the messengers returned alone with words so full of hope and Lazarus was already dead!

Indeed, the miracle is to be a solemn, public demonstration that our Lord spoke the truth in the Temple when He insisted that He is the Son of God. On the two previous occasions when our Lord raised the dead, He did it quickly and quietly and as secretly as possible to avoid the sensation it would cause. But now, in the case of His friend, He tarries for two days before going down; He wants the news of the death to spread and the fact of it to be well established and the multitude of mourners to be gathered at the home in order that all may see this overwhelming act of divine power. Shortly, the Jews are going to put Him to death; the reluctance of the Apostles to enter Judea shows how far advanced they are with their murderous plan (11:8-16). But before they do, they will have a demonstration of how completely the power over life and death is in His hands.

"Many of the Jews (the enemies of Christ) had come to Martha and Mary, to comfort them on account of their brother" (11:19).

Perhaps it was to avoid a clash between Christ and His enemies that Martha, on hearing that He was coming down the road, went off to meet Him without telling her sister. Her first words to Him reveal what the sisters had said to each other so many times as they helplessly watched the approach of death:

"Lord, if thou hadst been here, my brother would not have died" (v. 21).

They are the same words that come to Mary's lips when, later, she greets Him (v. 32). And now the sight of Him arouses new hope in Martha's breast:

"But even now I know that whatever Thou shalt ask of God, God will give to thee" (v. 22).

Perhaps it was a sudden flash of hope that He would do even that which He intended to do. If it was, it soon died; such a miracle is far from her mind when she objects to opening the tomb because of the advanced decay of the body (v. 39). Perhaps, rather, she who had often seen Jesus absorbed in prayer, merely meant to express the general petition that He would help the soul of Lazarus by His all-powerful prayer.

Our Lord's reply is also ambiguous: "Thy brother shall rise". Martha affirms the general Jewish faith in the final resurrection. And then, Jesus tells her that He Himself is the resurrection; it is not merely by intercession that He can help the dead; He Himself, in His own name, can recall from death whomever He pleases. Indeed, every believer in Him will live forever even though He die, for a time, according to the body.

"Dost thou believe this? And she said to Him: Yes, Lord, I believe that Thou art the Christ, the Son of God, who hast come into the world" (11:24-27).

Thus did He work to raise her soul to the heights of faith and His success was as sublime as with Peter at Philippi.

When Martha returned to the house, she informed Mary of the Master's arrival in a low voice so as not to be overheard by the Jews. But the Jews followed Mary out, thinking that she was going to the tomb. She and all who were with her were weeping with grief and

> "Jesus seeing her weeping and the Jews who had come with her weeping, He groaned in spirit and was troubled and (moving with them to the tomb) He wept" (v. 32-36).

He allows His heart to overflow with a wonderfully human compassion for them in their sorrow, for Lazarus, for all humankind who have been so profoundly stricken with the effects of original sin.

The tender humanity of Jesus is manifest to all: "See how He loved him!" And now He sets Himself to the work of revealing the divinity that lies hidden beneath. When they had taken the stone from the entrance to the tomb, He said,

> "Father, I give Thee thanks that Thou hast heard Me. Yet I know that Thou always hearest Me; but because of the people who stand around, I spoke, that they may believe that Thou hast sent Me".
>
> "When He had said this, He cried out with a loud voice: 'Lazarus come forth!' And at once he who had been dead came forth, bound feet and hands with bandages, and his face was tied up with a cloth. Jesus said to them: Unbind him and let him go" (Jn. 11:43-44).

This visible manifestation of Christ's power over life and death convinced many, perhaps the majority, of His enemies who saw it (11:45). The incredible thing is that some still remained hostile and went off to the city to inform those who were plotting against Him. The Pharisees and Priests unite in a council and pay tribute to the many "signs" He is working:

> "If we let Him alone as He is, all will believe in Him, and the Romans will come and take away both our place and our nation" (v. 48).

Caiphas breaks their indecision and gives a show of virtue to his evil designs:

> "You know nothing at all; nor do you reflect that it is expedient for us that one man die for the people, instead of the whole nation perishing" (v. 49-50). "So from that day forth their plan was to put Him to death" (v. 53).

Thus did the clearest revelation of the Light bring those who loved the darkness to their firmest resolution.

But God has the power to use evil for His own designs and, while leaving to men the fullness of their freedom, He gives their words and actions a meaning beyond their control.

> "This, however, He said not of Himself", says St. John, "but being high priest that year, he prophesied that Jesus was to die for the nation; and

not only for the nation, but that He might gather into one the children of God who were scattered abroad" (11:51-52).

The stage is set for God's plan of Redemption; unwittingly, the High Priest has officially designated the Victim to be offered in sacrifice for the people.

## 83. RETIREMENT TO EPHREM; 84. LAST JOURNEY
### TO JERUSALEM

The hour, too, will be of God's own choosing. Meanwhile, using only human means to save Himself, Jesus retires with His disciples to the town of Ephrem, twenty miles to the northeast of Jerusalem (v. 54). His stay there was brief, lasting not more than three or four weeks. Finally, seven or eight days before the Passion, Jesus began His advance toward Jerusalem going by way of Jericho (Mk. 10:46) and Bethany of Judea (Jn. 12:1). Some of the events recorded in Luke's greater intercalation belong to this period of our Lord's brief stay at Ephrem and final journey toward Jerusalem (cf. Lk. Ch. 17-19).

## Chapter XXI

# PERIOD V. CONSUMMATION

⫸⫸⫸⫸⫸⫸⫸⫸⫸⫸⫸⫸⫸⫷⫷⫷⫷⫷⫷⫷⫷⫷⫷⫷⫷⫷⫷

*Scene:* Bethany, Jerusalem

*Time:* March 12 to March 17, 29 A.D.

|  | Mt | Mk | Lk | Jn |
|---|---|---|---|---|
| 146. Saturday. Supper at Bethany | 26: 6-13 | 14: 3-9 | — | 12: 2-11 |
| 147. Sunday. Messianic entry | 21: 1-16 | 11: 1-10 | 19: 28-40 | 12: 12-19 |
| 148. Tears over Jerusalem | — | — | 19: 41-44 | — |
| 149. The Greeks. "Joannine Agony" | — | — | — | 12: 20-36 |
| 150. Return to Bethany | 21: 17 | 11: 11 | 21: 37-38 | — |

## 146. Saturday; Supper at Bethany

JUST SIX days before the Passover, our Lord arrived at Bethany (Jn. 12:1). It was probably on Friday evening as travel was impossible until after sunset on the Sabbath. The inhabitants gave a feast in His honor at the home of Simon the leper (Mt. 26:6) and Lazarus, the walking miracle, was seated at table, while his sisters were in attendance.

Mary's magnificently prodigal gesture of love, the pouring out of a whole vial of precious ointment, was a scandal to the onlookers including even some of the Apostles (Mt. 26:8). But Judas, for his own personal reasons, gives voice to the protest:

"Why was this ointment not sold for three hundred denarii and given to the poor?" (Jn. 12:5).

The motive for his irritation is mercilessly exposed by St. John:

"Now he said this, not that he cared for the poor, but because he was a thief, and holding the purse used to take what was put in it" (12:6).

It was indeed a lavish deed; three hundred denarii (each about seventeen cents) would represent almost a year's wages for an ordinary field laborer (Mt. 20:2). Philip had estimated that two hundred denarii would be enough to provide a bit of bread for more than five thousand people (Jn. 6:7). The onlookers felt, therefore, that there was justice in the rude criticism of the traitor.

Anyone less sure of his own dignity would have been embarrassed in

Christ's position. After preaching self-abnegation and love of the poor, how could our Lord justify such profligate "waste"? Unblushingly, He recognizes the fact that any creature, whatever its value, is well used in giving honor to His person:

"The poor you have always with you, but you do not always have Me" (Jn. 12:28).

Our Lord's words of reply (Mk. 14:6-9) are an exquisitely delicate expression of gratitude for Mary's generous love: "Amen, I say to you, wherever in the whole world this gospel is preached, this also that she has done shall be told in memory of her". But added to the joy which these words inspired was the pang of a numbing fear: "She has anointed My body in preparation for burial". With a woman's intuition, clarified by her deep love of Him, she may have felt the imminence of tragedy, and wished to be beforehand with her mark of honor and devotion. The memory of her deed will be a comfort to her in the dark hours ahead, when He is ringed by His foes, and she cannot reach Him with her love.

If we accept the identification of Mary Magdalen with Mary of Bethany (which is not certain, but has strong reasons for it), the incident has another touching aspect. That night in Bethany she began, in a sense, His burial by her anointing of His Head; on the following Sabbath she was the leader of the women who came early in the morning to complete His anointing.

## 147-150. SUNDAY

*Messianic Entry.* On the sabbath evening a great crowd of Jews came out to Bethany not only to see Jesus but also Lazarus, whose recent resurrection had caused such a stir. Lazarus, the living proof of Christ's power to give life, was the occasion of many conversions still, so much so that the chief priests were plotting his death as well as Christ's (Jn. 12:9-11).

Jesus had been avoiding the city for a long time, not out of fear of His enemies, but because His hour had not yet come. Now the hour is at hand and He advances deliberately upon Jerusalem for the feast of the Passover. It means His death, of course, and He knows it. But He will show His control of His own destiny; He will not die in a corner, the victim of stealthy cunning, and have His death hushed up as His enemies had planned. Rather, He will die in the full publicity of the Paschal feast, as the fulfillment of the feast, and have the news shouted through the streets of Jerusalem, thronged with pilgrims from all parts of the world.

On Sunday, the crowd that started out from Bethany was joined by a still larger crowd that had come out from the city to greet Him and form His cortege. The demonstration was planned, provoked and encouraged by our Lord. He was determined that He would make His entrance into His own city at this critical time in His rightful character as King. Now at last and for the first time, He will make public declaration of Himself as the Messias. Seated upon the colt of an ass, as the prophets had foretold, He accepts, without hindering them as before, the waving of palms, the casting of cloaks in His path and the acclaim of the crowd:

> "Hosanna! Blessed is he who comes in the name of the Lord, the King of Israel!" (Jn. 12:12-15).

His enemies are in consternation:

> "Some of the Pharisees said to Him: 'Master, rebuke Thy disciples'. He said to them: 'I tell you that if these keep silence, the stones will cry out'." (Lk. 19:39-40).

Even the Apostles, distracted by the tumult, did not advert until after the resurrection that God was using the crowd to fulfill some of the most manifest of the Messianic prophecies (Jn. 12:16).

*Tears over Jerusalem.* But at the very height of all this enthusiasm, Jesus bursts into tears at its hollowness. He knows that they are not acclaiming Him in His true character; their shouts are for the Messianic King of their deluded dreams. The tragic misunderstanding that runs through His whole life is here at its climax. Coming down the slope of the Mount of Olives, the city with its glorious Temple is open to His view. Knowing that He Himself is to occasion the ruin of all that He beholds, He prophesies the punishment that will fall upon the city within forty years of His speaking:

> "And when He drew near and saw the city, He wept over it saying: If thou hadst known, in this thy day, even thou, the things that are for thy peace! But now they are hidden from thy eyes. For days will come upon thee when thy enemies will throw up a rampart about thee, and surround thee and shut thee in on every side, and will dash thee to the ground and thy children within thee, and will not leave in thee one stone upon another, because thou hast not known the time of thy visitation" (Lk. 19:41-44).

Not only the towns of Galilee, but the capital city and the whole nation is under a heavy curse because of its obstinate blindness. It is not a gleeful curse of revenge, it is a just punishment, which brings salty tears of regret streaming from the eyes of the Saviour who made every attempt to avoid it.

*Joannine Agony".* John relates this incident that opens a window into Christ's inmost thoughts during these days. Perhaps it occurred on Sunday during His entrance into the city, or perhaps on Monday—the time is not certain. At any rate, John tells us that our Lord was sought out by "certain Greeks", pagans by birth, but sincerely religious men, who were drawn to the Jewish worship of the one true God. In itself the incident forms part of the story of triumph that filled these last few days. It was indeed a triumph that Gentiles should seek out a Jewish Master, and be desirous of learning from Him. And this modest triumph lifts our Lord's mind to the horizons of the future: He sees the triumph of His Church in the Gentile world, the host of pagans who will seek Him out and believe in Him. But then His mind returns to nearer horizons: His victory among the Gentiles will follow on His rejection by His own people. The hour of His death is close, so close that He regards it as already come. And He looks at it in its deepest meaning. It will not be an end for Him, but the beginning of His "glorification". It will be as the death of a seed that falls into the ground, not to perish utterly, but to be the principle of a new life, a rich harvest. His lifeblood, shed by His own unbelieving and deluded people, will be the means whereby millions of souls over all the earth will be quickened into a new life.

These are the thoughts behind His exultant words:

"The hour is come for the Son of Man to be glorified. Amen, amen, I say to you, unless the grain of wheat fall into the ground and die, it remains alone. But if it die, it brings forth much fruit" (Jn. 12:23-25).

In these words our Lord accepts once more the stern law of redemption that the Infinite Wisdom and Love of His Father has laid down. Then, as always, He imposes the same law on all who would be with Him:

"He who loves his life, loses it; and he who hates his life in this world, keeps it unto life everlasting. If anyone serve Me, let him follow Me; and where I am there also shall My servant be. If anyone serve Me, My Father will honor him" (Jn. 12:25-26).

Then the vision before our Lord changes. First He saw His death as the way to His own triumph and the triumph of those He loves. Now, however, the horror of the thing itself rises before Him: the treason of Judas, the struggle in the Garden, the flight of His Apostles, the ignominious trials and mockeries, and finally, Calvary and the Cross. And before this vision His soul recoils. There almost rises to His lips a plea for rescue if it be possible (as later in the Garden, when the prospect is closer, such a plea will actually be voiced). But then, resolutely He puts aside such a thought, and once again expresses His unchangeable will to be obedient to His Father's command:

"Now is My soul troubled. And what shall I say? Father, save Me from this hour? No, this is why I came to this hour. Father glorify Thy name!" (12:27).

Then, as twice before, a voice from heaven comes in answer to His strong act of self-consecration and loving obedience:

"There came therefore a voice from heaven; I have both glorified it, and I will glorify it again" (12:28).

[249]

The voice is for the crowd standing round, to give them warning. But they do not understand it; they think it a clap of thunder. But to our Lord it recalls again a vision of victory, and He resumes the thought of verses 23 and 24:

> "Now is the judgment of the world; now will the Prince of the world be cast out. And I, if I shall be lifted up from the earth, will draw all things to Myself" (12:31-32).

In these words, John adds, He was alluding to the kind of death He was to die, a lifting up on a Cross. This exaltation, despite its supreme ignominy, would exert upon the souls of all men, Jew and Greek, a unique and powerful fascination, and draw them to Himself.

All these words, as the context in John shows (12:34 ff.), were an enigma to those who heard them but they illuminate for us the meaning of the death of Christ. Again He reveals that His death is a supremely voluntary, free act of obedience to His Father, who has permitted that it should happen at the hands of evil men. He dies to glorify His Father's Name, to manifest the fact that He is the Lord and Master of human life, to whom man must be obedient even unto the death of a cross. Moreover, our Lord manifests the fact that His death is the point of departure for His own glorification here on earth, as the death of a seed is the condition for its fecundity. As His supreme act of obedience to His Father, it will merit His own Resurrection. And it will merit life for all those who believe in Him, provided they are willing to follow Him along the way of the Cross. The spectacle of His lifting up will draw to Him the hearts of men, in response to this piercingly dramatic manifestation of His love for them. And thus His death will be His victory over the world and its fascinations. And by it the prince of the world will have his mastery shattered, and be cast out by the power of Christ, the true King of souls.

*Return to Bethany.* The day was waning and it was time to think of retirement.

> "And He went into Jerusalem, into the temple. And when He had looked round upon all things, then, as it was already late, He went out to Bethany with the Twelve" (Mk. 11:11).

It was as though He wanted to look over the battlefield, planning His campaign of the next two days, before leaving to spend the night out of reach of His enemies.

## MONDAY

| | Mt | Mk | Lk | Jn |
|---|---|---|---|---|
| 151. Fig tree cursed | 21: 18-19 | 11: 12-14 | — | — |
| 152. Second cleansing of Temple | 21: 12-13 | 11: 15-18 | 19: 45-48 | — |
| 153. Return to Bethany | — | 11: 19 | — | — |

# 151. FIG TREE CURSED; 154. FIG TREE WITHERED

As our Lord was returning to Jerusalem with the Apostles, He gave them a vivid, symbolic illustration of the destruction of Jerusalem which He had described the day before and the rejection of Israel which He is again to prophesy in several of His parables on the coming Wednesday. A fig tree, in this climate, should be bearing unripe figs at the end of April. The small green figs appear before the leaves at the beginning of March and are fully ripe by the beginning of June. On this tree which they encounter along the way, there were no unripe figs but only the leaves. Jesus therefore curses the barren tree: "May no fruit ever come from thee henceforward forever!" Matthew, abridging the story, says that the fig tree withered up "immediately". But, while the curse was immediately effective and the tree died at once, Mark makes it clear (11:20) that the external effects in the withering of the leaves were not noticeable until the next day.

The whole thing is a parable in action corresponding to the spoken parable in Luke (13:6-9). The single fig tree standing alone signifies Israel whom God had planted and separated from the Gentiles. The appearance of leaves but no fruit symbolizes Israel's pretense to a righteousness which it should have possessed but did not. The Jews boasted of the Law, the Temple, the ceremonies and all their prerogatives as the chosen people, but these, instead of bearing fruit, produced only the external appearances of piety and love of God. True, it "was not the season for figs" (Mk. 11:13) in the sense of the ripened fruit that would come in the Kingdom of Christ, but still Christ had a right to expect of Israel at least the unripened fruit— the imperfect justice of the Old Law, even though it was not time for the full perfection of the New Law. Hence, this chosen Tree is cursed; never more will Israel, as God's chosen nation, have the opportunity to bear fruit (Mt. 21:19) or invite others to come and eat from its branches (Mk. 11:14). Israel was cursed and died spiritually at the time of Christ's crucifixion although, for a while, it still bore the appearance of spiritual life before it withered completely at the destruction of Jerusalem.

The immediate effect upon the Apostles is not so much the fearful truth of the allegory (which they, as Jews, would naturally be slow to see), but they marvel at the physical power of our Lord's words to deprive the fig tree of life. They are more interested in knowing *how* Christ worked the miracle than *why* He acted as He did. And, because they are to share in His power, He goes on to instruct them about the power of prayer with unwavering faith (Mt. 21:20-22; Mk. 11:20-26). But later, when they hear the Saviour castigating Israel and its leaders for not yielding the fruits of God's vineyard, this withering of the fig tree will give blistering reality to the punishments He threatens.

## 152. Second Cleansing of the Temple; 153. Return to Bethany; 155. Chief Priests' Challenge

On the first Paschal feast of His public life, our Lord drove out the buyers and sellers from the Temple (Jn. 2:13-17) and now, after a lapse of two years during which, with the connivance of the priests, the abuses returned, He does it again. It was fitting that He should thus publicly proclaim at the beginning and again at the end of His prophetic mission, authority over the house of His Father. It is a continuation of the Messianic revelations of Palm Sunday. And it is this final attack on the lucrative business of the High Priests' party in the Temple that, humanly speaking, sealed the fate of Jesus. Charges of hostility to the Temple played an important part in His trial (*cf.* Mt. 26:61; 27:40).

At this second cleansing, our Lord adds a profusion of miracles, curing the "blind and the lame" (Mt. 21:14) as Isaias had foretold of Him. And amidst the popular demonstrations of enthusiasm, even the little children, quoting from the hymns they had been taught to sing at the feasts of Tabernacles and Dedication, mimicked their elders by chanting in unison: "Hosanna to the Son of David". Again, the Pharisees are shocked and alarmed at the open acclaim:

"Dost Thou hear what these are saying? And Jesus said to them: Yes, have you never read: Out of the mouths of infants and sucklings thou hast perfected praise?" (Mt. 21:16).

Every jot and tittle of the Law is being fulfilled!

On that day, the Priests in charge of the Temple were struck dumb by our Lord's show of authority over the Temple and the popular enthusiasm that accompanied it. Meanwhile, He again spent the night at Bethany (Mk. 11:19). But on the next day, the Chief Priests and the Scribes and the Elders (apparently an official delegation from the Sanhedrin) challenge Him with the words:

"Who gave Thee this authority to do these things"? (Mk. 11:29).

The priests and elders were primarily interested in His infringement on their authority over the Temple. But doubtless the question also regarded the things that were most offensive to the Scribes and Pharisees—the whole Messianic entry into the city, with all the popular acclaim on the way, and in the Temple. The people certainly knew what authority He claimed; they were shouting it from the housetops. So did these leaders know. They were seeking to destroy Him (Lk. 19:48) by getting from His own lips an open declaration which they could use against Him.

But still it is not the time and our Lord, while "the people hung on His words" (Lk. 19:48), makes clear to all why He refuses the bait:

> "I also will ask you one question, and if you answer Me this, I in turn will tell you by what authority I do these things. Whence was the baptism of John? From heaven or from men?" (Mt. 21:24-25).

The members of the Sanhedrin must take sides. If they admit the divine mission of the Baptist, Jesus will be sure to say to them: "Why, then, did you not believe Him (when he testified to me)?" If they claim that the baptism of John was a purely human institution, the people, who regarded John as a prophet, will turn against them. They dared not give an answer.

> "Neither," said Jesus, "do I tell you by what authority I do these things" (Mt. 21:27).

Thus did Jesus confound His enemies while giving the people more motives to see in Himself the One whom the Father had sent.

## TUESDAY

| | Mt | Mk | Lk | Jn |
|---|---|---|---|---|
| 154. Tuesday. Fig tree withered | 21: 20-22 | 11: 20-26 | — | — |
| 155. Chief priests' challenge | 21: 23-27 | 11: 27-33 | 20: 1-8 | — |
| 156. The Two Sons | 21: 28-32 | — | — | — |
| 157. The Husbandmen and the Heir | 21: 33-46 | 12: 1-12 | 20: 9-19 | — |
| 158. The Marriage Feast | 22: 1-14 | — | 14: 16-24 | — |
| 159. Pharisees: tribute to Caesar | 22: 15-22 | 12: 13-17 | 20: 20-26 | — |
| 160. Sadducees: resurrection | 22: 23-33 | 12: 18-27 | 20: 27-40 | — |
| 161. Lawyer: great commandment | 22: 34-40 | 12: 28-34 | (10: 25-38) | — |
| 162. Counterattack: Son of David | 22: 41-46 | 12: 35-37 | 20: 41-44 | — |
| 163. Scribes and Pharisees: woe! | 23: 1-36 | 12: 38-40 | { 20: 45-47 (11: 37-54) | — |
| 164. Final lament over Jerusalem | 23: 37-39 | — | 13: 34-35 | — |
| 165. The widow's mite | — | 12: 41-44 | 21: 1-4 | — |
| 166. Ruin of Temple predicted | 24: 1-3 | 13: 1-4 | 21: 5-7 | — |
| 167. Eschatological discourse | 24: 4-51 | 13: 5-37 | 21: 8-36 | — |
| 168. The Ten Virgins | 25: 1-13 | — | — | — |
| 169. The Last Judgment | 25: 31-46 | — | — | — |

## 156-158. PARABLES OF REJECTION

On Tuesday morning, after our Lord had refused to answer the insolent and insincere demands for proof of His authority, He proceeded, by way of three parables, to tell these members of the Sanhedrin that they and their nation are to be rejected from the Kingdom because of their rejection of Him. A clever feature of these parables is that they tell a story in which some obvious injustice has been done and then, these "wise men" of the nation are called upon to pass judgment on the case. They cannot refuse in the face of all the people and indeed they willingly pronounce the verdict before its application to themselves is manifest. Then, our Lord draws the parallel with Jewish history and shows that they have passed judgment on themselves and the nation which follows their leadership. But there is more to it than the mere embarrassment of being bested in an argument; the punishment which they themselves have invoked will actually fall from God's hand upon the nation of Israel.

Thus, in response to the *Parable of the Two Sons,* the Jewish leaders readily agree that the son who first refused to work in the vineyard and then did go and work, was really the obedient one. The son who promptly agreed to work and then refused to do so was merely giving lip-service. Then, Christ explains the application: the Jews, as a nation, agreed to the Covenant:

> "All things that the Lord hath spoken we will do, we will be obedient" (Ex. 24:7).

But then, despite all their boasting of the Covenant and their insistence on the externals of the Law, these leaders and their followers did not keep the promise of really loving God and their fellow men. The climax of their disobedience and infidelity is now, in their rejection of Him, God's own Son. On the other hand, many who made no pretense of obedience to the Father, have come in the end to serve Him and accept His Son:

> "Amen I say to you, the publicans and the harlots are entering the Kingdom of God before you. For John came to you in the way of justice and you did not believe him. But the publicans and harlots believed him; whereas you, seeing it (their belief), did not even repent afterwards, that you might believe him" (Mt. 21:32).

*Vine-dressers.* The chief-priests and Pharisees pretended not to recognize themselves in the foregoing parable. "Hear another parable", says our Lord, and, in this one, the revelation of the nature of the punishment and the justice of it is much more explicit. It is not merely that the humble and despised souls among the Jews will come into the Kingdom while the proud and self-righteous will be rejected. The latter class, arrayed with most of the leaders, constitute the majority; they are the nation of the Chosen People and, as such, they shall be rejected. The Kingdom of God will be given to a new people; the Gentiles will be called to take the place of the Jews in the new and eternal covenant with God.

The pathos of God's special love for the Jews despite their constant rejection of it is strikingly suggested throughout this parable. God took great pains and special care in planting His vineyard—the nation of Israel. He put a special hedge around it in the prescriptions of the Law, to keep it apart from the rest of the sinful world. There was a watchtower constantly manned by a long succession of divinely appointed watchmen. And the vine-dressers (husbandmen) were entrusted with the care of this vineyard to nurture and gather its spiritual fruits in due season.

But when, at various times, God sent His servants, the Prophets, to receive His fruits from the vine-dressers, they
> "beat one, killed another and stoned another" (Mt. 21:35).

All the Prophets were more or less rejected by the people, and several of them were physically maltreated and a few of them, as Zacharias, the son of Joiada, and John the Baptist, were put to death.

Finally, the Owner of the vineyard
> "sent His own Son to them saying: They will respect My Son" (Mt. 21:37).

(Thus is Christ differentiated from all the previous prophets: they were but the "servants" of God; He is God's "only Son".) But in return for this divinest act of love,
> "they seized Him (the Son), cast Him out of the vineyard and killed Him" (Mt. 21:39).

Their purpose was to seize His inheritance (the vineyard) for themselves (v. 38). This final act of treachery hasn't happened yet but two days hence the Jews will reject the Son and hand Him over to the Gentiles (outside the vineyard) to be crucified.

While all the tragic implications to themselves are still veiled in the story of the parable, the members of the Sanhedrin find it easy to foretell what the owner of the vineyard will do:
> "He will utterly destroy those evil men, and will let out the vineyard to other vine-dressers who will render to Him the fruits in their seasons" (Mt. 21:41).

Indeed, that is what God will do: the spiritual inheritance will be taken from Israel and given to the Gentiles and the nation itself will be destroyed when its capital city is razed to the ground in 70 A.D.

Christ corroborates their verdict: their rejection of Him is the fulfillment of prophecy and proof that He is the Messias: "The stone which the builders rejected, has become the corner stone". This nation, because they rejected Him, will be "broken to pieces" and "ground to powder" (Mt. 21:45). And now, "when they knew that he was speaking about them" (Mt. 21:45), the chief priests were aghast and cried out "By no means!" (Lk. 20:16).
> "And though they sought to lay hands on Him, they feared the people, because they regarded Him as a prophet" (Mt. 21:46).

*The Marriage Feast.* While the iron is hot, our Lord strikes again in response to the anger and hatred which His preceding parable had evoked. The union of Christ with His Church is frequently compared to a marriage (*cf.* Mt. 9:15; Jn. 3:29; 2 Cor. 11:2; Apoc. 21:2, 9 ff. 22:17) and the

Kingdom of Heaven is compared to a banquet (*cf.* Mt. 8:11). The Jews were the first to be invited but when God repeatedly sent the final notice that the feast of His Son was ready, the Jews refused to come. It is emphasized that their pre-occupation with worldly hopes and ambitions is the fundamental reason for their failure to heed the call (Mt. 22:5-6). God, in turn, rejects them, and invites the Gentiles to take their place at the feast (Mt. 22:8-10). Not only did the Jews reject the summons but they treated God's messengers "shamefully and killed them" (Mt. 22:6). Evidently Christ is thinking here not only of the treatment given to some of the prophets like John the Baptist, but of His own death to be suffered at their hands. In this parable He is not one of the messengers but rather the Bridegroom; the historical reality surpasses the allegory and Jerusalem will be destroyed (Mt. 22:7) because it murdered the Son of God.

Our Lord extends this parable to teach an added lesson with regard to those who do answer the call and come to the feast. He develops the statement, made in the parable, that both "good and bad" (Mt. 22:10) will be in the Kingdom (*cf.* Mt. 13:36-43; 47-50). One of the guests, through his own acknowledged fault (Mt. 22:12), has insulted the King by appearing at the feast without the proper wedding garment. Putting aside the figurative language, this man has been given the gift of sanctifying grace to clothe his soul as a wedding garment. He still retains the gift of faith (or he would not be at the banquet at all) but he has failed to preserve the state of grace by charity and good works. Hence, he is cast out into

"exterior darkness where there is weeping and gnashing of teeth" (Mt. 22:13).

It is a fearful warning to the chosen souls that, if they do not co-operate with grace, they too will be rejected in the end.

"Many are called but few are chosen" (Mt. 22:14).

This verse refers to the first part of the parable rather than the last and the sense of it is this: although the Jews who were invited to the feast were many, yet comparatively few of them accepted the invitation and actually entered the Kingdom. Hence, this saying of Christ does not answer the question whether most or only a few of those who are baptized are actually saved. Such a question is completely outside the scope of this parable; it is a secret, like that of the time of Christ's second coming at the end of the world, which the Father keeps to Himself.

## 159-161. TRIPLE ATTACK

*Pharisees: Tribute to Caesar.* The leaders are more determined than ever that our Lord must die. The only question is, how can it be accomplished? The Pharisees hold a special council; they decide on a way to involve our

Lord politically and they carefully work out the plan (Mt. 22:15). Young disciples of theirs are to approach our Lord as though troubled in conscience at the payment of taxes to the Romans. They are to ask His advice:

"Is it lawful to give tribute to Caesar or not?" (22:17).

They hope for a negative answer. Then they can turn Him over to the Roman procurator as guilty of conspiracy.

The Herodians, supporters of Herod's dynasty, are interested in pleasing the Romans. For this reason they are opposed to Christ; they have reason to fear that anyone with Messianic claims would stir the people to revolt and they, with Herod, would suffer by the conflict. Hence, some of these men (whom the Pharisees hated as collaborationists) are craftily invited to join the delegation. They will have a keen sense for the slightest odor of revolution and if they, rather than the Pharisees, make the accusation to the Romans, there will be no suspicion that the Romans are being used as tools to settle a purely religious conflict.

But what if Christ surprises them and approves the tax? It would be a disappointment indeed but still much good would come of it from the Pharisees' point of view. The people hated the tax and clung to the hope that the Messias would free them entirely of Roman domination. Hence, even in this eventuality, Christ will lose His tremendous power over the people and forfeit, in their eyes, all Messianic claims.

The young Pharisees approach our Lord with insidious flattery, inviting Him, if there be any vanity in Him at all, to take a strong, bold stand against the tax:

"Master, we know that Thou art truthful, and that Thou teachest the way of God in truth and that Thou carest naught for any man; for Thou dost not regard the person of men" (Mt. 22:16).

The truth cuts through this hypocrisy and lays it bare: "Why do you test Me, you hypocrites?" And with that, He demands a coin that He might teach them the truth from an image. It was an axiom, admitted also in the Talmud, that if a people used the coinage of a certain king they also acknowledged his sovereignty. Hence, if the Jews accept the benefits of Roman rule—and they were many—then they also have the duty of contributing to the support of Roman government. They do nothing morally wrong in this, provided that at the same time they render to God whatever is due to Him:

"Render, therefore, to Caesar the things that are Caesar's, and to God the things that are God's" (Mt. 22:28).

By this answer, Christ neither approved nor disapproved of either the Roman Empire or of Jewish nationalism. His Kingdom is not of this world (Jn. 18:36).

In His reply, Christ laid down a general principle which is valid for all times. He recognizes the Church and State as distinct, each sovereign in its own sphere. Normally there should be no conflict between the temporal jurisdiction of the one and the spiritual jurisdiction of the other. A Christian has moral obligations to both authorities. As long as civil authority is not unjust and tyrannical and does not interfere in the legitimate sphere of religion, it must be accepted and obeyed as God's will (*cf.* Jn. 19:11; Rom. 13:1-7; 1 Pet. 2:13-17). But if any conflict arises between the authority of the State and the authority of God "we must obey God rather than men" (Acts 5:29).

Despite the failure of the Pharisees to trap our Lord into making a seditious statement, they did not hesitate, later, to accuse Him falsely before Pilate of "perverting our nation and forbidding the payment of taxes to Caesar" (Lk. 23:2).

*Sadducees: The Resurrection.* Apparently this attack had nothing to do with the previous trap set by the Pharisees which had failed so miserably. But "on that same day", the Sadducees decided to bring up a point of bitter contention between themselves and the Pharisees and see which side our Lord would take in the dispute. Prominent among the many supernatural things which the rationalistic Sadducees refused to believe, was the fact of the resurrection. On this occasion they make a joke of it by proposing an absurd case. According to the Law (Deut. 25:5 ff), long since fallen into desuetude, a man was bound to marry his brother's widow if she was childless, in order to perpetuate the name and lineage of the deceased. The Sadducees propose the extreme possibility of a childless woman who has thus, in turn, married seven brothers in succession. To whom will the woman belong on the day of resurrection? With that, they curiously watch to see how our Lord will extricate Himself from what they consider an impossible situation.

> "You know neither the Scriptures nor the power of God", said our Lord, "for at the resurrection they will neither marry nor be given in marriage, but will be as angels of God in heaven" (Mt. 22:30).

He opposes to their materialistic conceptions a simple statement, to be taken on His authority, of the spiritual nature of life in heaven. He compares it to the life of the angels, whose existence the Sadducees also denied. The Sadducees also rejected all the books of Scripture save the Pentateuch and claimed that, from these books of Moses, the resurrection could not be proved. Even the Pharisees were embarrassed at the difficulty of finding proofs from these particular books. Jesus surprises them all with the text He quotes (Ex. 3:6): "I am (not merely 'was') the God of Abraham . . . Isaac . . . Jacob". If God "is" the God of Abraham—Abraham must be alive (Mt. 22:32).

For once, the Pharisees were pleased with the wisdom that came from the lips of Christ and the "crowds marveled at His teaching" (22:33).

*Lawyer: Great Commandment.* Finally, the Scribes themselves decide to "test" Him by appointing one of their party to propose the question:

"Which is the great commandment in the Law?" (Mt. 22:32-35).

The Scribes engaged in endless disputes among themselves regarding the relative binding force of the more than 600 traditional ordinances connected with the Law of Moses. Some gave pre-eminence to the law of sacrifice, others to that of circumcision, or of the Sabbath, or of meats and washings, etc. If our Lord sided with one faction against the others—there were sure to be scholars in the audience who would oppose His position with arguments which, hitherto, had left the question a matter of contention.

Christ brushes aside these controversies concerning the ceremonial law and directs their attention to the moral law which was the purpose of the other precepts:

"Thou shalt love the Lord thy God with thy whole heart . . . and thy neighbor as thyself" (Mt. 22:37).

This is what was written, as a constant reminder, on the phylacteries which these Pharisees wore; they recited these words twice daily in the prayer called "Shema"; this is the beacon-light which gives meaning to all the other ordinances.

Evidently the Pharisees did not know until too late that the spokesman they chose from their number was a man of integrity and good will compared to the rest of them. He had been sincerely impressed with our Lord's confounding of the Sadducees (Mk. 12:28) and now, again, he sincerely praises the answer to his own question:

"Well answered Master, Thou hast said truly . . . that He (God) should be loved . . . with one's whole strength; and that to love one's neighbor as oneself is a greater thing than all the holocausts and sacrifices" (Mk. 12:32-33).

In contrast to His usual stern rebuke of Pharisaic hypocrisy, our Lord commends this man and encourages him:

"Thou are not far from the kingdom of God" (Mk. 12:34).

## 162. COUNTERATTACK: SON OF DAVID; 163. SCRIBES AND PHARISEES: WOE!; 164. FINAL LAMENT OVER JERUSALEM

*Son of David.* The result of our Lord's handling of the three "test" questions was that "no one after that ventured to ask Him questions" (Mk. 12:34).

Not that He inspired a silence of fear in those who sincerely sought the truth; "the mass of the common people liked to hear Him" (Mk. 12:37).

But the leaders who were plotting His death saw clearly that with each attempt to trap Him, their own hypocrisy or false teachings were exposed while Christ's influence with the people, and even with some of their own select group, was increased to an alarming extent.

But now Jesus Himself takes the offensive and puts a question to them. He has a higher purpose than merely to add to the confusion of His enemies. The "mass of the people" is standing about and His purpose is to enlighten them. Frequently and in various ways they had voiced, as an argument against His Messiaship, the complaint that: "we know where this Man is from, but when the Christ comes, no one will know where He is from" (Jn. 7:27).

Now, our Lord intends to show them that there is more to the question of the identity of the Messias than merely His human origin. Again, when the resurrection of Lazarus stirred enthusiasm to a fever pitch and the people did acclaim Him as "Son of David", they had a temporal king in mind, whose origin they supposed to be exclusively human. Christ would now show them that even David himself mysteriously implied that this his Son, was to have a far higher dignity than mere human descent from himself.

How is it that David, under God's inspiration, calls the Messias his Lord?

"If David, therefore, calls him 'Lord', how is he his son?" (Mt. 22:45).

The Pharisees, who all along had taught the people that David spoke here of the Messias, could not answer the question:

"And no one could answer Him a word" (Mt. 22:46).

The only answer was the one which they had refused to accept and because of which they plotted His death: in addition to His human descent from David, Christ had a heavenly origin in His eternal generation from the Father: "I have come down from heaven" (Jn. 2:38; cf. 6:41-42).

*Woe!* And now our Lord lets loose upon the Scribes and Pharisees the full severity of His condemnation. Their hypocrisy, their love of gain, their legal formalism, their pride and separatism and love of display fall under the axe that "is laid to the root of the tree". St. Matthew assembles all the charges leveled against them and makes of them a withering denunciation which is best appreciated, without comment, in the living fire of our Lord's own words (Mt. 23:1-36).

Christ ends the whole indictment in a plaintive cry of frustrated love addressed to the Jews who have followed these blind guides:

"Jerusalem, Jerusalem! thou who killest the prophets, and stonest those who are sent to thee; How often would I have gathered thy children together, as a hen gathers her young under her wings, but thou wouldst not! Behold, your house is left to you desolate. For I say to you, you shall not see Me henceforth until you shall say, "Blessed is he who comes in the name of the Lord!" (Mt. 23:37-39).

There is one consoling note to the dirge of desolation. At the end of the world, when the Son of Man comes for the second time, the nation of Israel, finally converted, will cry out: "Blessed is he who comes in the name of the Lord!" (cf. Rom. 11:25-29).

# 165. The Widow's Mite; 166. Ruin of Temple Predicted

Weary after the long, fatiguing day, our Lord retires with His disciples to the Women's Court of the Temple. Seated on the wide steps that led to the Court of Israel, they could watch the priests stationed at the thirteen trumpet-shaped alms boxes, collecting taxes and alms from the vast concourse of people who had gathered for the feast.

"Many rich people were putting in large sums" (Mk. 12:41).

Then the poor widow approached holding in her hand two mites which together were worth two-fifths of a cent. The priest, examining the coins to certify their genuineness, announces the amount of the offering in a loud voice as he throws it into the receptacle provided for it. The crowd glances in amusement at the woman who retreats in confusion.

The situation provided a lesson which our Lord did not want the Apostles to miss.

"Amen I say to you, this poor widow has put in more than all those who have been putting money into the treasury. For they all have been putting in out of their abundance; but she, out of her want, has put in all that she had" (Mk. 12:43-44).

Thus when His mind is filled with thoughts of His own death and the tragic end of the Old Covenant, He continues, from this little circumstance, to instruct the Apostles in the spirit of the new Kingdom that will rise from the seed of the old.

But the Apostles themselves, by an innocent remark, bring His mind back to the impending tragedy:

"As He was going out of the temple one of His disciples said to Him: Master, look, what wonderful stones and buildings!" (Mk. 13:1).

Indeed, they were one of the great wonders of the world! The Temple of Jerusalem, resting on its gigantic substructures, seemed built for all eternity.

"And Jesus answered and said to him: Dost thou see all these great buildings? There will not be left one stone upon another that will not be thrown down" (Mk. 13:2).

The prophecy has been fulfilled to the letter. Imposing ruins remain of the most famous temples of Egypt, Greece and Rome; but here, even the ruins have perished.

# 167. Eschatological Discourse

The little group sat on the Mount of Olives and watched the sun set over the Temple and the city. Their thoughts were of the dire predictions which had just been made. Four of the Apostles (Mk. 13:3) put the question which was in the minds of all:

"Tell us, when are these things to happen, and what will be the sign of Thy coming and of the end of the world?" (Mt. 24:3).

They take it for granted that the destruction of Jerusalem will be simultaneous with the end of the world.

In His reply, our Lord gives an answer to all three questions. Although His answer implies that there will be an indefinitely long period between the two catastrophic events (Lk. 21:24), He is not concerned with the question of dates (Mt. 24:36). He describes the destruction of Jerusalem as a miniature picture or type of the Last Day and many descriptive details which apply to the first calamity will also apply to the second. It is precisely because the first event is a type of the latter that Christ passes abruptly from a description of one to the other as though they were the same.

1. The Future of the Church (Mt. 24:4-14).

Both before the destruction of Jerusalem and again before the end of the world, there will be a period of extraordinarily calamitous famines, earthquakes, wars and persecutions of the Church. But the end of the world will not come until the Gospel is preached in the whole world, and it is not said that it will then come immediately.

2. The Destruction of Jerusalem (Mt. 24:15-22).

Two clear signs will precede the destruction of Jerusalem—the "abomination of the Temple" (Mt. 24:15) and the presence of hostile armies surrounding the city (Lk. 21:20). In 68 A.D. the fanatic Jewish revolutionaries, called the "Zealots", seized the Temple and with the aid of the Idumaeans, slaughtered many of the priests and nobles even within the Temple itself. And, even while this abomination was going on, the Roman armies were gathering outside the city to begin the final siege of 69-70 A.D.

3. End of the World and the Second Coming of Christ (Mt. 24:23-35).

Abruptly, without any words of transition, our Lord passes from the destruction of Jerusalem to the universal calamity which it symbolized. In this final period there will be a general upheaval of nature, a cooling of charity and an overflowing of vice and mass defections from the Church resulting from the prodigies and illusions of the false prophets and false Christs. Then, following upon these signs,

> "will appear the sign of the Son of Man in heaven; and then will all of the tribes of the earth mourn, and they will see the Son of Man coming upon the clouds of heaven with great power and majesty" (v. 30).

The preliminary signs of this Second Coming announce it as clearly as the other signs announced the catastrophe of Jerusalem and allowed the Christians to escape it.

> "When you see all these things, know that it is near, even at the door" (v. 33).

> "Amen I say to you, this generation will not pass away till all these things have been accomplished" (v. 34).

"This generation" refers, not to the Jews who were contemporaries of our Lord, but to the nation of Israel as such. Our Lord used the word in this sense when, earlier in the day, He said to the Pharisees: "that upon you (this generation) may come all the just blood that has been shed upon the earth, from the blood of Abel the Just unto the blood of Zachiarias, the son of Barachias, whom you (this generation) killed between the temple and the altar" (Mt. 23:35-36).

The men to whom Christ was speaking did not kill either Abel or Zacharias, but as members of the guilty race, they shared in the national crimes of their ancestors. So now, Christ means to say that the nation of Israel (this generation) will endure to see this end of the world and the triumphant coming of the Son of Man.

4. The Need of Watchfulness (Mt. 24:36-51).

> "But of that day and hour no one knows, not even the angels in heaven, nor the Son, but the Father only" (Mk. 13:32).

Our Lord certainly knows the date, not only as God, but even as man since He has, in His human intellect, the beatific vision and infused knowledge of all things. But, as the Prophet who was sent to reveal the things of God, He does not know it; it was not one of the things that He was sent to reveal.

> "Watch, therefore, for you do not know when the Master of the house is coming, in the evening, or at midnight, or at cock-crow, or early in the morning; lest coming suddenly He find you sleeping. And what I say to you, I say to all: 'Watch'" (Mk. 13:35-37).

In the parable of the *Ten Virgins*, our Lord dramatizes the same thought. The picture is drawn from the wedding customs of that time. On the day of the wedding, the bridesmaids assembled at the house of the bride. After sunset, the bridegroom, accompanied by his male friends, went to the bride's house where they were greeted by the bride and her bridesmaids, and then both parties returned together in a joyous procession, that was illumined by lamps or torches, to the wedding feast in the home of the bridegroom. In the parable, the five foolish virgins, through their own heedlessness, were excluded from the feast. So will it be with those in the Church of Christ who are caught unprepared when He comes to take His bride to the mansions of His Father.

## 169. THE LAST JUDGMENT

Our Lord concludes the whole discourse with a description of the general judgment which is to take place when
> "the Son of Man shall come in His majesty, and all the angels with Him, seated on the throne of His glory" (Mt. 25:31).

The picture of the sheep and goats is taken from the familiar pastoral scenes on the hill slopes of Palestine where these animals mingled together in the daylight hours of grazing and were separated at nightfall by their shepherds.

As the principle distinguishing the good from the bad, the Judge uses Charity—the supreme Law of which the other commandments are particular expressions. By attributing to works of mercy alone the efficacy of opening heaven to the elect (as their omission closes it to the damned), He would give us to understand that there exists a mysterious identity between Christ and the Christian, so that by coming to the aid of a member of Christ, we come to the aid of Christ Himself. Thus strikingly does He suggest the doctrine of the Mystical Body which St. Paul will later develop in all its implications.

Christ is the *motive* and the supreme *object* of all our lesser loves. Eternal union with Him in the kingdom of the Father is the *reward* for all who give this love (Mt. 25:34). Loss of Him is the supreme *punishment* for those who refuse (v. 41). Both the punishment and the reward are final and forever (v. 46).

In conclusion, Christ reminds the Apostles of the price He must pay for this eternal life which He will give to others:
> "You know that after two days the Passover will be here; and the Son of Man will be delivered up to be crucified" (Mt. 26:2).

### WEDNESDAY

|  | Mt | Mk | Lk | Jn |
|---|---|---|---|---|
| 170. Plot of the Jews | 26: 1-5 | 14: 1-2 | 22: 1-2 | — |
| 171. Judas' bargain | 26: 14-16 | 14: 10-11 | 22: 3-6 | — |
| 172. Epilogue of Public Life | — | — | — | 12: 37-50 |

# 170. PLOT OF THE JEWS; 171. JUDAS' BARGAIN

The bold appearance of our Lord in Jerusalem at the Paschal feast blocked the plan of His enemies to do away with Him more or less secretly. Hence they returned to a plan tried once before at the feast of Dedication (Jn. 10:24). On Tuesday in Holy Week, as we have seen, they attempted to spring the same trap:

> "So watching their opportunity, they sent forth spies, who should pretend to be just men, that they might entrap Him in His talk, and deliver Him up to the ruling power and to the authority of the procurator" (Lk. 20:20).

Given the growing veneration of the people for our Lord, as a "prophet", two points of tactics were forced on them: first to accomplish their designs with as little publicity as possible, and secondly, to throw the odium for His destruction on the Roman power. We saw how our Lord's irreproachable answer foiled them:

> "And they could not take hold of what He said before the people; and marveling at His answer, they kept silence" (Lk. 20:25-26).

But they are all the more incensed at His unparalleled castigation of themselves and the nation which was following their leadership. Hence we find them on Wednesday assembled in council, "in the court of the high priest who was called Caiphas" (Mt. 26:3).

It was not an official convocation of the Sanhedrin, but the secret meeting of a cabal of conspirators. But they are at their wits' end, fearful of precipitating a riot if they dare to act during the days of the feast (Mt. 26:5).

Then into the scene there steps an ally, as unexpected as he is welcome, Judas Iscariot.

> "What are you willing to give me and I will deliver Him to you?" (Mt. 26:15).

Doubtless, there was bargaining, and in the end "they counted him out thirty pieces of silver" (v. 16), thirty shekels, about twenty dollars in our currency, but in purchasing power worth much more. There followed a discussion of plans. Judas' role was clear: he was to watch "for an opportunity to betray Him without a disturbance" (Lk. 22;6). He was familiar with our Lord's habits and whereabouts, and with his aid the conspirators could get round their great obstacle, the danger of a riot.

Luke states boldly that "Satan entered into Judas" (Lk. 22:3), to take command of his soul and dictate its action. It is not too strong a phrase, for his deed was truly satanic. Yet the facts of the record tell us that Satan's mastery of the wretched man was not assumed in an instant. His nature was the same as ours, and to say that he was a demon incarnate, the personification of malice, does not explain him. For like us he was capable of both good and evil. Our Lord Himself chose him as one of the

Twelve, solely because He saw in him the stuff of an Apostle. And if he exists in our minds as the type of all that is base, we have to remember that he became what he was by his own fault.

Long before the Passion, he had begun, perhaps unconsciously, to slide down the fatal slope that would ultimately carry him into the abyss. His defection had begun interiorly around the previous Pasch (Jn. 6:71-72). Not long afterward comes the first hint from our Lord of an approaching "betrayal" (Mk. 9:30). Then, at the supper in Bethany, his hardened soul is revealed. The descent was rapid, but it was a real descent. At the time of his choice, Judas' heart was undoubtedly filled with lofty aspiration, and if at the end it was empty of all but hate, it was because he himself had opened the door, by failing to recognize and to remedy the flaws in his own character.

One of them we know with certainty, the others we can rather accurately conjecture. John says:

> "He was a thief, and holding the purse, used to take what was put in it" (12:6).

For what purpose? Perhaps he was laying by a hoard in view of a future desertion. Perhaps his avarice was stimulated by deeper defects, defeated ambition and small-souled jealousy. When he joined our Lord he undoubtedly shared the common ideas of the Jews about the Messias, that the coming of the Kingdom of God would bring great earthly position and prosperity to the Jews. As one of our Lord's chosen Twelve, he surely hoped (as did also his companions) for a favored place in the Kingdom, with much wealth and honor. Apparently our Lord's refusal of the kingship definitely shattered that illusion, and showed him the vanity of the ambition he had cherished "to no avail". Self interest had been his motive in following Christ, and when it was shattered he had nothing to fall back on. He had been shown the truth, but having no love for it, he began to drift farther and farther from it.

The disappointment of his selfish ambition began to breed embitterment, as it so often does. And hastening the process was the basest and most shameful of human vices, jealousy. He was a sort of stranger to his fellows, being the only Judean among them. Moreover, he seems to have been a more cultivated man. Yet from the beginning, Our Lord definitely put Peter at the head of the Twelve, and also took James and John, with Peter, into an intimacy from which the others were excluded. These clearly expressed preferences irritated the other nine, as their not infrequent disputes among themselves show. But Judas' irritation must have been extreme, given his narrow selfishness, his overweening ambition, and his greed. Naturally he was led to compensate himself by a misuse of the small office entrusted to him, the care of the common purse.

Every yielding to these faults strengthened their hold on him. He turned ever more completely against Christ, and by the same token submitted more completely to the mastery of Satan, the adversary of Christ. Yet he was apparently a man of great external control, very cool, and with a consummate ability for playing the hypocrite. We know that to the very last, the other eleven never suspected what was in his heart. His Master knew, of course, but His loyalty and His wish to save the man made Him keep silent. But very many of His talks must have been directed particularly at Judas. Remembering the presence of Judas, much of His teaching takes on a new point, as when He spoke against ambition and envy (Lk. 9:46-50), against the dangers of avarice (Lk. 12:13-21; 16:10-13), against the futility of hypocrisy (Lk. 12:1-3).

But all these warnings fell on deafened ears. And in the meantime the threat against Christ grew more menacing, and He Himself seemed to flee before it. Judas began to fear for his own safety, and to seek some way of escaping the coming catastrophe. More and more he became convinced that he had been duped, and his embitterment grew into hatred of the Man who had, he thought, so disappointed him. It is hard to escape the conclusion that he did hate our Lord. In betraying Him to the Jews, he knew that he was sealing his Master's doom. He knew their intentions. And one man does not betray another to certain death unless he hates him. Not even Judas' cowardice can explain his step. He is a striking illustration of "the mystery of iniquity", the mystery of man's hatred of God. But he serves to set in more brilliant contrast the mystery of God's love of man. Right up to the last moment our Lord will not cease to show this blinded and hardened traitor the marks of His respect and loyalty and even affection.

## 172. Epilogue of Public Life

The perfidy of Judas was but the personification in one individual of the infidelity of the Chosen People to their Covenant with God. Stubbornly, as a nation, they refused to accept Him who was the climax and fulfillment of the Covenant and, by betraying Him to the Gentiles to be crucified, they severed their national relationship with God. St. John sums up the tragic conclusion of our Lord's public work with this nation; it is as he had announced in the beginning:

"The light shone in the darkness and the darkness did not comprehend it" (Jn. 1:5).

The general blindness, it is true, admits of many exceptions even among the ruling classes (Jn. 12:42). Later on many of the Pharisees, at present paralyzed by human respect, will flock into the new-born Church. Nevertheless, the core of the most influential leaders and the mass of the common people remain incredulous: "though He had worked so many signs in their presence they did not believe in Him" (Jn. 12:37).

If they have not perceived these divine signs, it is because pride, self-interest, envy and ambition have closed their eyes or veiled the light. This blindness is their own work. It is true that the prophet has foretold their blinding (Jn. 12:38-40), but it does not happen because the prophet has foreseen it. On the contrary, the prophet has foreseen and foretold it because it has, this day, come to pass.

Our study of the Prophetic and Kingly mission of Christ ends here with the end of His public teaching. It is true that at the Last Supper and later during the forty days of His apparitions, He continues to reveal many things and give many powers to the Apostles. But from here on, the main emphasis is on the Priestly mission of Christ and so, we put off to Sophomore year the remaining events of His Passion and Resurrected life.

It remains for us now, in the fourth and final section of this book, to gather together in a doctrinal synthesis the individual dogmatic truths which concern 1] the Person of Christ and 2] the Church which He founded.

## SUGGESTIONS FOR READING

1. Prat, Ferdinand, S. J.—Jesus Christ, translated by John J. Heenan, S.J., Bruce, 1950 (2 Vols.).
2. Goodier, Alban, S.J., Archbishop—Public Life of Christ, Kennedy, N. Y., 1944 (2 Vols.).
3. Lebreton, Jules, S.J.,—The Life and Teaching of Jesus Christ our Lord, Burns, Oates and Washbourne Ltd., London, 1934.
4. Meschler, Maurice, S.J.,—The Life of Our Lord Jesus Christ in Meditations, translated by Sister Mary Margaret, O.S.B., B. Herder Co., 1950 (2 Vols.).

## A SYNOPSIS OF THE PUBLIC LIFE OF CHRIST

### PERIOD I. PREPARATION

*Scene:* Judea; to Galilee: Cana; Capharnaum
*Time:* January to March, 27 A.D.

|  | Mt | Mk | Lk | Jn |
|---|---|---|---|---|
| 1. Ministry of the Baptist | 3: 1-12 | 1: 1-8 | 3: 1-18 | — |
| 2. Baptism of Christ | 3: 13-17 | 1: 9-11 | 3: 21-22 | — |
| 3. The desert struggle | 4: 1-11 | 1: 12-13 | 4: 1-13 | — |
| 4. Witness of the Baptist | — | — | — | 1: 19-34 |
| 5. First disciples | — | — | — | 1: 35-51 |
| 6. First return to Galilee: |  |  |  |  |
|     Cana: marriage-feast | — | — | — | 2: 1-11 |
|     Capharnaum | — | — | — | 2: 12 |

## PERIOD II. CONSTRUCTION
### A. Judea
*Time:* April to the end of May, 27 A.D.

| | Mt | Mk | Lk | Jn |
|---|---|---|---|---|
| 7. Pasch 1; cleansing of Temple | — | — | — | 2: 13-25 |
| 8. Conversation with Nicodemus | — | — | — | 3: 1-21 |
| 9. Sojourn in Judea | — | — | — | 3: 22-36 |
| 10. Arrest of the Baptist | 14: 3-4 | 6: 17-18 | 3: 19-20 | 4: 1-3 |
| 11. Second return to Galilee: | | | | |
| The Samaritan woman | — | — | — | 4: 4-45 |
| The royal official's son | — | — | — | 4: 46-54 |

### B. Galilee
*Phase 1:* Proclamation of the Kingdom
*Time:* Late spring and summer, 27 A.D.

| | Mt | Mk | Lk | Jn |
|---|---|---|---|---|
| 12. The Kingdom of God is here | 4: 12-17 | 1: 14-15 | 4: 14-15 | — |
| 13. The call of the four | 4: 18-22 | 1: 16-20 | 5: 1-11 | — |
| 14. Demoniac in the synagogue | — | 1: 21-28 | 4: 31-37 | — |
| 15. Peter's mother-in-law | 8: 14-15 | 1: 29-31 | 4: 38-39 | — |
| 16. Miracles; enthusiasm; tour | { 4: 23-25 / 8: 16-17 | 1: 32-39 | 4: 40-44 | — |
| 17. Cure of a leper | 8: 1-4 | 1: 40-45 | 5: 12-16 | — |
| 18. Cripple: Christ forgives sins | 9: 1-8 | 2: 1-12 | 5: 17-26 | — |
| 19. Call of Matthew: banquet | 9: 9-17 | 2: 13-22 | 5: 27-39 | — |
| 20. Plucking corn on the Sabbath | 12: 1-8 | 2: 23-28 | 6: 1-5 | — |
| 21. Man with the withered hand | 12: 9-14 | 3: 1-6 | 6: 6-11 | — |
| 22. Widespread fame; crowds | 12: 15-21 | 3: 7-12 | 6: 17-19 | — |
| 23. Choice of the Twelve | — | 3: 13-19 | 6: 12-16 | — |
| 24. Sermon on the Mount | cc. 5, 6, 7 | — | 6: 20-49 | — |

## PERIOD II. CONSTRUCTION—*continued*
### B. Galilee—*continued*
*Phase 2:* Hardening of Opposition
*Time:* Summer and fall, 27 A.D.

| | Mt | Mk | Lk | Jn |
|---|---|---|---|---|
| 25. Servant of the centurion | 8: 5-13 | — | 7: 1-10 | — |
| 26. Son of the widow of Naim | — | — | 7: 11-17 | — |
| 27. Embassy from the Baptist | 11: 2-6 | — | 7: 18-23 | — |
| 28. Eulogy of the Baptist | 11: 7-19 | — | 7: 24-35 | — |
| 29. The sinful woman | — | — | 7: 36-50 | — |
| 30. Women in Christ's entourage | — | — | 8: 1-3 | — |
| 31. Anxiety of His kinsfolk | 12: 46-47 | 3: 20-21 | 8: 19 | — |
| 32. Controversy with Pharisees: | | | | |
| Charge: agent of Beelzebub | — | — | 11: 14-26 | — |
| Reply: sin against Spirit | 12: 22-45 | 3: 22-30 | 12: 10 | — |
| 33. His Mother and brethren | 12: 48-50 | 3: 31-35 | { 8: 20-21 / 11: 27-28 | — |
| 34. Parables on the Kingdom | 13: 1-52 | 4: 1-34 | { 8: 4-18 / 13: 18-21 | — |

### Phase 3: Supreme Effort in Galilee
### Time: Fall, 27 A.D. to February, 28 A.D.

| | | Mt | Mk | Lk | Jn |
|---|---|---|---|---|---|
| 35. | Storm; demoniac of Gerasa | 8: 18, 23-34 | 4: 35-5: 20 | 8: 22-39 | — |
| 36. | Daughter of Jairus; a woman | 9: 18-26 | 5: 21-43 | 8: 40-56 | — |
| 37. | Two blind men; mute demoniac | 9: 27-34 | — | — | — |
| 38. | Rejection at Nazareth | 13: 53-58 | 6: 1-5 | 4: 16-30 | — |
| 39. | Another tour; miracles | 9: 35-38 | 6: 6 | — | — |
| 40. | Mission of Twelve; advice | 10: 1-11: 1 | 6: 7-13 | 9: 1-6 | — |
| 41. | Herod's anxiety | 14: 1-2 | 6: 14-16 | 9: 7-9 | — |
| 42. | Martyrdom of the Baptist | 14: 5-12 | 6: 19-29 | — | — |
| 43. | Return of the Twelve | — | 6: 30 | 9: 10a | — |

## PERIOD III. CRISES
### Crisis 1. Galilee
### Time: March, 28 A.D.

| | | Mt | Mk | Lk | Jn |
|---|---|---|---|---|---|
| 44. | First miracle of loaves | 14: 13-21 | 6: 31-44 | 9: 10b-17 | 6: 1-13 |
| 45. | Refusal of the Kingship | — | — | — | 6: 14-15 |
| 46. | Walking on the waters | 14: 22-33 | 6: 45-52 | — | 6: 16-21 |
| 47. | Cures around Genesareth | 14: 34-36 | 6: 53-56 | — | — |
| 48. | The Bread of Life | — | — | — | 6: 22-72 |

### Crisis 2. Jerusalem
### Time: March, 28 A.D.

| | | Mt | Mk | Lk | Jn |
|---|---|---|---|---|---|
| 49. | Cripple at the pool | — | — | — | 5: 1-16 |
| 50. | On Judgment and Witness | — | — | — | 5: 17-47 |
| 51. | Danger! Return to Galilee | — | — | — | 7: 1 |

### Crisis 3. The Faith of the Apostles
### Time: March to September, 28 A.D.

| | | Mt | Mk | Lk | Jn |
|---|---|---|---|---|---|
| 52. | Pharisaic traditions | 15: 1-20 | 7: 1-23 | — | — |
| 53. | Phenicia: Canaanite woman | 15: 21-28 | 7: 24-30 | — | — |
| 54. | Decapolis: Deaf mute | 15: 29-31 | 7: 31-37 | — | — |
| 55. | Second miracle of loaves | 15: 32-39 | 8: 1-10 | — | — |
| 56. | Leaven of the Pharisees | 16: 1-12 | 8: 11-12 | 12: 1 | — |
| 57. | Blind man of Bethsaida | — | 8: 22-26 | — | — |
| 58. | THE CONFESSION OF PETER | 16: 13-20 | 8: 27-30 | 9: 18-20 | — |
| 59. | First Prediction of Passion | 16: 21-23 | 8: 31-33 | 9: 21-22 | — |
| 60. | "Take up your cross" | 16: 24-28 | 8: 34-39 | 9: 23-27 | — |
| 61. | The Transfiguration | 17: 1-8 | 9: 1-8 | 9: 28-36 | — |
| 62. | The descent from Thabor | 17: 9-13 | 9: 9-13 | — | — |
| 63. | Cure of the lunatic boy | 17: 14-20 | 9: 14-29 | { 9: 37-43 / 17: 5-6 | — |
| 64. | Second prediction of passion | 17: 21-22 | 9: 30-31 | 9: 44-45 | — |
| 65. | Capharnaum: the didrachma | 17: 23-26 | — | — | — |

| | | | | |
|---|---|---|---|---|
| 66. "Become like little children" | 18: 1-5 | 9: 32-36 | 9: 46-48 | — |
| 67. The stranger-exorcist | — | 9: 37-40 | 9: 49-50 | — |
| 68. Avoiding scandal | 18: 6-10 | 9: 41-47 | 17: 1-2 | — |
| 69. The lost sheep | 18: 11-14 | — | 15: 1-7 | — |
| 70. Fraternal correction; pardon | 18: 15-22 | — | 17: 3-4 | — |
| 71. The unmerciful servant | 18: 23-35 | — | — | — |
| 72. Adieu to Galilee: "Woe!" | 11: 20-24 | — | 10: 13-15 | — |

## SYNOPSIS OF THE PUBLIC LIFE

### PERIOD IV. CONFLICTS AND CONSOLIDATIONS
*Scene:* Jerusalem; Perea; Bethany; Ephraim
*Time:* October to March, 29 A.D.

| | Mt | Mk | Lk | Jn |
|---|---|---|---|---|
| I. Jerusalem: Tabernacles | — | — | 9: 51 | 7: 2-13 |
| 73. Conspiracy of Pharisees | — | — | — | 7: 14-53 |
| 74. The adulteress | — | — | — | 8: 1-11 |
| 75. The Light of the World | — | — | — | 8: 12 |
| 76. Father's witness to the Son | — | — | — | 8: 13-20 |
| 77. Castigation of incredulity | — | — | — | 8: 21-30 |
| 78. Sonship of Abraham | — | — | — | 8: 31-59 |
| 79. Cure of the man born blind | — | — | — | 9: 1-41 |
| 80. The door. Good Shepherd | — | — | — | 10: 1-21 |
| II. Perean Ministry (infra) | — | — | — | 10: 40 |
| III. Jerusalem: Dedication | — | — | — | — |
| 81. "I and the Father are one" | — | — | — | 10: 22-39 |
| IV. Perean Ministry (infra) | — | — | — | 10: 40-42 |
| V. 82. Bethany: Lazarus | — | — | — | 11: 1-53 |
| VI. 83. Retirement to Ephraim | — | — | — | 11: 54-56 |
| VII. 84. Last journey to Jerusalem via Jericho and Bethany | 20: 29 | 10: 46 | 18: 35 | 12: 1 |

## Appendix to Period IV

In this table are included a multitude of events, teachings, etc., related by Luke in his "greater intercalation"; many of them are proper to Luke. In general they belong to the last six months of our Lord's ministry, but it is almost impossible to determine the exact situation and sequence of most of them. Some occurred in Galilee, others on journeys to Jerusalem, still others in Perea. They are grouped here for convenience. Where parallels in Mt. and Mk. are included in parentheses, it means that they are to be found in their proper place in foregoing tables.

| | Mt | Mk | Lk | Jn |
|---|---|---|---|---|
| 85. Rejection by Samaritans | — | — | 9: 52-56 | — |
| 86. Half-hearted followers | 8: 19-22 | — | 9: 57-62 | — |
| 87. Mission of the Seventy-Two | — | — | 10: 1-12 | — |
| 88. Return of Seventy-Two | — | — | 10: 16-20 | — |
| 89. "I praise Thee, Father" | 11: 25-27 | — | 10: 21-22 | — |
| 90. "Come to me" | 11: 28-30 | — | — | — |
| 91. "Blessed are you who see" | (13: 16-17) | — | 10: 23-24 | — |
| 92. The Good Samaritan | — | — | 10: 25-37 | — |

| | | | | |
|---|---|---|---|---|
| 93. Mary and Martha | — | — | 10: 38-42 | — |
| 94. The "Our Father" | ( 6: 9-13) | — | 11: 1-4 | — |
| 95. The Importunate Friend | — | — | 11: 5-8 | — |
| 96. "Ask and you shall receive" | ( 7: 7-11) | — | 11: 9-13 | — |
| 97. Sign of Jonas | (12: 38-42) | ( 8: 11-12) | 11: 29-32 | — |
| 98. Christ, the Lighted Candle | ( 5: 15) | — | 11: 33 | — |
| 99. The Simple Eye | ( 6: 22-23) | — | 11: 34-36 | — |
| 100. Dinner with a Pharisee | — | — | 11: 37-38 | — |
| 101. Hypocrisy of Pharisees | (23: 4-6) | — | 11: 39-54 | — |
| 102. Fear God, not men | (12: 26-33) | — | 12: 2-9 | — |
| 103. The Holy Spirit, Counsellor | (10: 19-20) | 13: 11 | 12: 11-12 | — |
| 104. Folly of avarice | — | — | 12: 13-21 | — |
| 105. Confidence in God | ( 6: 25-34) | — | 12: 22-32 | — |
| 106. Treasure in heaven | ( 6: 19-21) | — | 12: 33-34 | — |
| 107. "Be you then ready" | (24: 42-44) | (13: 33-37) | 12: 35-40 | — |
| 108. Faithful and wicked servant | (24: 45-51) | — | 12: 41-48 | — |
| 109. Fire on earth. Sorrows | — | — | 12: 49-50 | — |
| 110. Not peace but a sword | (10: 34-36) | — | 12: 51-53 | — |
| 111. Signs of the Kingdom | (16: 2-3) | — | 12: 54-56 | — |
| 112. Therefore be reconciled | ( 5: 25-26) | — | 12: 57-59 | — |
| 113. Barren fig-tree. Penance | — | — | 13: 1-9 | — |
| 114. Cure of woman on Sabbath | — | — | 13: 10-17 | — |
| 115. The narrow gate | ( 7: 13-23) | — | 13: 22-30 | — |
| 116. Defiance of the "fox", Herod | — | — | 13: 31-33 | — |
| 117. The man with dropsy | — | — | 14: 1-6 | — |
| 118. The Great Feast | — | — | 14: 7-15 | — |
| 119. Christ, the highest love | (10: 37-38) | — | 14: 25-27 | — |
| 120. Cost of following Him | — | — | 14: 28-33 | — |
| 121. Salt grown tasteless | ( 5: 13) | 9: 48-49 | 14: 34-35 | — |
| 122. The Lost Sheep | (18: 12-14) | — | 15: 1-7 | — |
| 123. The Lost Coin | — | — | 15: 8-10 | — |
| 124. The Prodigal Son | — | — | 15: 11-32 | — |
| 125. The Unjust Steward | — | — | 16: 1-13 | — |
| 126. The Pharisees' avarice | — | — | 16: 14-15 | — |
| 127. Assault on the Kingdom | (11: 12-13) | — | 16: 16 | — |
| 128. Validity of the Law | ( 5: 18-19) | — | 16: 17 | — |
| 129. Divorce | ( 5: 32) | — | 16: 18 | — |
| 130. The Rich Man and Lazarus | — | — | 16: 19-31 | — |
| 131. "We are useless servants" | — | — | 17: 7-10 | — |
| 132. The ten lepers | — | — | 17: 11-19 | — |
| 133. The parousia | (24: 26-41) | (13: 1-37) | 17: 20-37 | — |
| 134. The Unjust Judge | — | — | 18: 1-8 | — |
| 135. The Pharisee and Publican | — | — | 18: 9-14 | — |
| 136. Divorce | 19: 1-12 | 10: 1-12 | — | — |
| 137. Christ and little children | 19: 13-15 | 10: 13-16 | 18: 15-17 | — |
| 138. The rich young man | 19: 16-30 | 10: 17-31 | 18: 18-30 | — |
| 139. Laborers in the vineyard | 20: 1-16 | — | — | — |
| 140. Third prediction of Passion | 20: 17-19 | 10: 32-34 | 18: 31-34 | — |
| 141. Request of James and John | 20: 20-24 | 10: 35-41 | — | — |
| 142. Exhortation to humility | 20: 25-28 | 10: 42-45 | — | — |
| 143. Blind men of Jericho | 20: 29-34 | 10: 46-52 | 18: 35-43 | — |
| 144. The publican Zacheus | — | — | 19: 1-10 | — |
| 145. Parable of the Talents | 25: 14-30 | — | 19: 11-27 | — |

# SYNOPSIS OF THE PUBLIC LIFE

## PERIOD V. CONSUMMATION
### *Scene:* Bethany, Jerusalem
### *Time:* March 12 to March 17, 29 A.D.

| | Mt | Mk | Lk | Jn |
|---|---|---|---|---|
| 146. **Saturday.** Supper at Bethany | 26: 6-13 | 14: 3-9 | — | 12: 2-11 |
| 147. **Sunday.** Messianic entry | 21: 1-16 | 11: 1-10 | 19: 28-40 | 12: 12-19 |
| 148. Tears over Jerusalem | — | — | 19: 41-44 | — |
| 149. The Greeks. "Joannine Agony" | — | — | — | 12: 20-36 |
| 150. Return to Bethany | 21: 17 | 11: 11 | 21: 37-38 | — |
| 151. **Monday.** Fig-tree cursed | 21: 18-19 | 11: 12-14 | — | — |
| 152. Second cleansing of Temple | 21: 12-13 | 11: 15-18 | 19: 45-48 | — |
| 153. Return to Bethany | — | 11: 19 | — | — |
| 154. **Tuesday.** Fig-tree withered | 21: 20-22 | 11: 20-26 | — | — |
| 155. Chief-priests' challenge | 21: 23-27 | 11: 27-33 | 20: 1-8 | — |
| 156. The Two Sons | 21: 28-32 | — | — | — |
| 157. Husbandmen and the Heir | 21: 33-46 | 12: 1-12 | 20: 9-19 | — |
| 158. The Marriage Feast | 22: 1-14 | — | 14: 16-24 | — |
| 159. Pharisees: Tribute to Caesar | 22: 15-22 | 12: 13-17 | 20: 20-26 | — |
| 160. Sadducees: resurrection | 22: 23-33 | 12: 18-27 | 20: 27-40 | — |
| 161. Lawyer: great commandment | 22: 30-40 | 12: 28-34 | (10: 25-38) | — |
| 162. Counterattack: Son of David | 22: 41-46 | 12: 35-37 | 20: 41-44 | — |
| 163. Scribes and Pharisees: woe! | 23: 1-36 | 12: 38-40 | { 20: 45-47 <br> { (11: 37-54) | — <br> — |
| 164. Final lament over Jerusalem | 23: 37-39 | — | 13: 34-35 | — |
| 165. The widow's mite | — | 12: 41-44 | 21: 1-4 | — |
| 166. Ruin of Temple predicted | 24: 1-3 | 13: 1-4 | 21: 5-7 | — |
| 167. Eschatological discourse | 24: 4-51 | 13: 5-37 | 21: 8-36 | — |
| 168. The Ten Virgins | 25: 1-13 | — | — | — |
| 169. The Last Judgment | 25: 31-46 | — | — | — |
| 170. **Wednesday.** Plot of the Jews | 26: 1-5 | 14: 1-2 | 22: 1-2 | — |
| 171. Judas' bargain | 26: 14-16 | 14: 10-11 | 22: 3-6 | — |
| 172. Epilogue of Public Life | — | — | — | 12: 37-50 |
| 173. **Thursday.** Preparation | 26: 17-19 | 14: 12-16 | 22: 7-13 | — |
| 174. Washing of the feet | — | — | — | 13: 1-11 |
| 175. "I have given you example" | — | — | 22: 24-30 | 13: 12-17 |
| 176. The great desire | — | — | 22: 14-18 | — |
| 177. The traitor unmasked | 26: 20-25 | 14: 17-21 | 22: 21-23 | 13: 18-29 |
| 178. Departure of Judas | — | — | — | 13: 30-32 |
| 179. The Sacrifice offered | 26: 26-29 | 14: 22-25 | 22: 19-20 | — |
| 180. Discourse after the Supper | — | — | — | 13: 33-17: 26 |
| 181. On the road to Gethsemane | 26: 30-35 | 14: 26-31 | 22: 31-39 | 18: 1 |
| 182. Gethsemane: the Agony | 26: 36-46 | 14: 32-42 | 22: 40-46 | — |
| 183. The arrest | 26: 47-56 | 14: 43-50 | 22: 47-53 | 18: 2-11 |
| 184. Episode of the young man | — | 14: 51-52 | — | — |
| 185. Before Annas | — | — | — | 18: 12-23 |
| 186. Before Caiphas | 26: 57 | 14: 53 | 22: 54 | 18: 24 |
| 187. Peter's triple denial | 26: 58, 69-75 | 14: 54, 66-72 | 22: 55-62 | 18: 25-27 |
| 188. "CHRIST, THE SON OF GOD" | 26: 59-68 | 14: 55-65 | 22: 63-71 | — |

# PART FOUR

# DOGMATIC SUMMARY

## Chapter XXII

# CHRISTOLOGY

➤➤➤➤➤➤➤➤➤➤➤➤➤➤⫷⫷⫷⫷⫷⫷⫷⫷⫷⫷⫷⫷⫷⫷

THE PURPOSE of this chapter is to sum up what we have seen on the subject of WHO CHRIST IS and then to look briefly, through the eyes of the Church, at the analysis of this truth which has resulted from the pondering of theologians for the past two thousand years. We shall begin with a summary of the facts, *i.e.,* that Christ is both God and Man. He is also the Messias, of course, but since this fact is included in the fact of His Divinity we shall not make a special point of it in this summary.

## DIVINITY OF CHRIST

Jesus Christ is the Word, the Son of God, the Second Person of the Blessed Trinity. He possesses the divine nature, whereby He is truly God. As Son, He proceeds from all eternity from the Father by way of spiritual generation, and in that generation He is given the same identical divine nature which is possessed by the Father. Thus He is equal to the Father in all things. There is no inequality, no inferiority, no dependence of One on the Other, no priority of One over the Other in time. They are One in all things except for the distinction of Persons: the Father is Father and not Son; the Son is Son and not Father. There is then in the Godhead one divine nature, possessed by three distinct Persons: the Father, the Son and the Holy Spirit.

Such, in very brief outline, is a statement of the Catholic doctrine concerning the divinity of Christ. The living voice of the Church is for us the supreme rule of faith, endowed with infallibility in matters of faith and morals. But one of the sources from which the Church derives her doctrine is the inspired word of Scripture. The following paragraphs contain a brief summary of the many scriptural arguments for the divinity of Christ which we have seen during our study of His Public Life.

1. *Christ's Statements.* Christ Himself often stated clearly that He is divine. It is true that these statements are usually indirect because of the hostility or weakness of His audience but their meaning is none the less clear. We must remember that Christ made these statements in the face of

the Pharisees' accusation that He was blaspheming in making Himself equal to God. And, though He denied the accusation of blasphemy, He did not deny their interpretation of what He said. (cf. Jn. 5:17-18; 8:57-58; 10:30-33; Mt. 22:44).

2. *Divine Attributes.* In addition to general assertions of His Oneness with the Father, Christ claimed to possess specific attributes which belong to God alone. Again, He made these claims in the face of the Pharisees' understanding that these attributes belong to God alone.

a] *Omnipotence*—Jn. 5:17; Mt. 28:18.

b] *Omniscience*—Mt. 25:31 ff. Only divine omniscience could enable Him as Judge to read the innermost thoughts of the millions of people who will have lived on earth.

c] *Eternity*—Jn. 8:58; 17:5.

d] *Forgiveness of Sins*—Mk. 2:1-12.

e] *Legislator Equal to Father*—Mt. cc. 5-7, Sermon on Mount. He revokes divorce (5:31-32), the law of talion (38-42), perfects the fifth and sixth commandments (21-30). He does this *on His own authority*— "I say to you".

f] *Center of our Religious Life*—We must *believe* in Him (Mt. 10:32), *hope* in Him (Mt. 11:28), *love* Him above all things (Mt. 10:37-39). He is the *motive* of our morality (Mt. 10:38-39), the *Judge*, the *punishment* or *reward* (Mt. 25:40, 45).

His flesh and blood are the source of everlasting life (Jn. 6:54-59).

3. *Miracles.* Christ performed an abundance of miracles in His own name and appealed to them as proof of His claim to be God (Jn. 5:36). He healed all manner of disease and infirmity *instantaneously,* He performed cosmic miracles (stilling of waves and storm), He drove out demons, He raised three people from the dead (Widow's Son, Daughter of Jairus, Lazarus) and finally, He rose from the dead Himself.

Christ's resurrection is the greatest proof of His divinity. He predicted it as the supreme "sign" (Mt. 12:39-40). He rose from the dead by His own power—the only instance in all history. The Apostles preached the resurrection as *the* proof that Christ was God. As St. Paul says,

"If Christ has not risen, vain then is our preaching, vain too is your faith . . . but as it is, Christ has risen from the dead . . ." (1 Cor. 15:14, 20).

4. *Prophecies.* Christ's prophecies prove the truth of His claim to be God. These predictions are detailed, not vague or ambiguous. The events predicted depended for their fulfillment on the *free actions* of countless men. One can predict with human knowledge an event due to necessary (non-free) agents, *e.g.*, the eclipse of the sun. But only God knows the future free actions of men. Thus, Christ foretold His passion, death and resurrection (Mt. 20:18-19), Peter's denial (Mt. 26:34), Judas' betrayal (Jn. 13:21-30), the destruction of Jerusalem and the Temple (Mt. 24:2 ff.).

5. *The Wisdom and Holiness* of Christ prove His claim. All critics acknowledge these attributes in Him. Yet if He were not God, as He claimed to be, then either He was a gross blasphemer and liar or else He was mentally unbalanced. Those who admit His wisdom and holiness and deny His divinity cannot answer this dilemma.

6. *The Faith of the Apostles.* Certainly the men of this select group were in a better position than anyone else to tell us what Christ claimed to be and whether or not He proved His claim. They clearly express their faith in His divinity which resulted from their close association with Him—

   a] John's prologue—"the Word was God . . . and the Word was made flesh and dwelt among us" (Jn. 1:1, 14).
   b] Peter's confession of faith (Mt. 16:16).
   c] Thomas: "My Lord and my God" (Jn. 20:28).

## THE HUMANITY OF CHRIST

As Man, Jesus possesses a human body which was conceived by the power of the Holy Spirit in the womb of the Blessed Virgin Mary. He possesses a human soul which was created and infused into the human body. Thus the Word, the Son, God from all eternity, without ceasing to be God, assumed a human nature at a definite point in human history. The divine and human natures were united in the person of the Word and will never be separated.

*Body of Christ.* Jesus was conceived and born like other men, grew to manhood, drank, ate, slept, grew fatigued from His journeys, suffered and died. Eighty times, in the Gospels, He calls Himself the "Son of Man". After His resurrection, He said to His disciples:

"Feel Me and see; for a spirit does not have flesh and bones, as you see I have" (Lk. 24:39).

*Soul of Christ.*

"My soul is sad, even unto death" (Mt. 26:38). "Father, into Thy hands I commend My spirit" (Lk. 23:46).

There is a *human* will in Christ:

"yet not My will but Thine be done" (Lk. 22:42).

There is a *human* intellect:

"And Jesus advanced in wisdom . . ." (Lk. 2:52)—

this refers to His human knowledge; His divine knowledge was infinite and admitted of no increase.

In general, for the fact that Christ was true Man, note John 1:14, "The Word was made *flesh*"—the use of "flesh" for "man" is quite common throughout the Bible.

# HERESIES

During the first four centuries of the Christian era, the heresies concerning the Person of Christ consisted in a denial of fact. Men denied either the true humanity or the true divinity of Christ and the denial sprung from pre-existing philosophies to which they tried to adapt the revelation of Christ's life. The following are two main heretical trends during this period.

*Docetists.* The Gnostics, and later the Manichaeans of the second and third centuries, taught that matter is evil. Logically, therefore, they were forced to deny that God could unite Himself with matter by becoming a man. Consequently, they explained Christ's life by saying that He had no real body but only the appearance of a body; hence their name, Docetists, (from dokein, to appear). The Docetists, then, denied that Christ really suffered or rose from the grave. To support their thesis, they corrupted the Gospel texts as far as possible; we saw an example of this in the case of Marcion whom Tertullian refuted and in the case of the Valentinians who were refuted by St. Irenaeus (*cf.* Ch. 8). St. John the Evangelist was aiming at such errors when he wrote:

> "I write of what was from the beginning, what we have heard, what we have seen with our eyes, what we have looked upon and our hands have handled: of the Word of Life" (1 Jn. 1).

*Adoptionists.* From the very beginning, there were those who for one reason or another denied the divinity of Christ. They taught that Christ was a mere man but that He was blessed by a special union with God. This union, they explained in various ways but they all held in common that Christ was no more than an adopted Son of God. Thus, the Ebionites and Cerinthians were Jewish Christians who, because of their Jewish prejudice against a plurality of Persons in God, taught that Christ was a mere man upon whom the spirit of God descended at His Baptism, making Him an adopted Son of God. St. John wrote his Gospel, in which he emphasized the divinity of Christ, to refute this heresy. At the end of the second century, the same type of heresy appeared in Rome and was refuted by Tertullian. Again, Paul of Samosata, as Bishop of Antioch, taught the same errors and was condemned by a synod of Antioch in 267.

*Trinitarian Heresies.* The early part of the fourth century was occupied with the great Trinitarian heresies. The question of how many Persons there are in God had to be settled as a logical prelude to the question of Christ's divinity. Arius, a priest of Alexandria, taught that the Word was not equal to the Father but merely a creature, much more perfect than other creatures, who was used by God in His subsequent works of creation. The Son was thus inferior to the Father and of a different substance. This was one of the most devastating heresies that ever afflicted the Church. It was condemned by the ecumenical Council of Nicaea in 325 (Denz. 54). It was this Council which gave us the Nicene Creed in which it is clearly stated that Christ is true God and true Man,

> "born of the substance of the Father . . . who, for our salvation, became Man and suffered and rose again on the third day".

The road was now clear for the great Christological controversies of the fourth and fifth centuries in which theologians were preoccupied with the mystery of how these two natures, human and divine, could be united in the one Christ.

*Schools of Alexandria and Antioch.* The big difficulty during this period was rooted in the fact that philosophers and theologians of the Eastern Church had no clear, distinct terminology to differentiate the concepts of *substance, nature* and *person*. These terms were used interchangeably where intellectual substances were concerned. Before the advent of Christ, there never had been a case where it was necessary to draw a sharp distinction between nature and person; hitherto, wherever there was a human nature existing, there too was a human person. But now, in the case of Christ, there were two complete natures, human and divine. How, then, could He be one being? Upon the oneness of Christ depends the whole doctrine of our redemption. It was this mystery of the unity in Christ despite His two natures, which the men of the period were laboring to explain.

Two opposing tendencies or schools of thought began to form at Alexandria and at Antioch. Neither of these schools wanted to deny either the humanity or the divinity of Christ. But, in the absence of any solution to the problem of the duality and the unity in Christ, each school began to emphasize one of these factors without satisfactorily explaining the other. Thus, the school of Antioch stressed the historical, scriptural data concerning the two natures in Christ. The school of Alexandria stressed the unity— the fact that Christ was one being. The exaggeration of these tendencies led respectively to the heresies of Nestorianism and Monophysism.

*Nestorianism.* Nestorius, Patriarch of Constantinople (427), publicly taught the heresy, inherited from Diodorus of Tarsus (378) and Theodore of Mopsuestia (392-428), which resulted from the stress, at Antioch, on the two natures in Christ. The distinction of these two natures was so emphasized that eventually it was taught that they were *separated*. Nestorius and his followers taught that God, the Word, is one Person, Christ, the Man, another. The union between the two natures in Christ was explained by the fact that the Word dwelt in Christ as in a temple (Adoptionism). Hence, according to Nestorius, Mary was the mother of Christ (a man) but not of God.

[280]

St. Cyril of Alexandria, the great protagonist of the unity in Christ, attacked this heresy of Nestorius. And, as a result, Nestorius was condemned and deposed from his See by the ecumenical council of Ephesus in 431 (Denz. 111).

*Monophysism* (one nature). In following the Alexandrine school which stressed the unity in Christ, Cyril made frequent use of the Greek word "phusis", nature. He insisted that, "the incarnate nature of the Word is one".

By that, he meant that Christ was one concrete individual, God and Man, and not two individuals as Nestorius contended. Cyril would have been more correct if he had said that Christ was one Person possessing two natures. But, as we have already observed, there was no unequivocal terminology in those days to indicate person and nature; "Phusis" was often used for either. Hence, Cyril continued to use ambiguous terminology but to explain it in a perfectly orthodox sense.

But it was only a question of time until the term "one nature in Christ" was interpreted in an heretical sense. Eutyches, a monk and disciple of Cyril (448), insisted that Christ had only one nature in the sense that the human and divine natures were fused together to form a third which was neither completely human nor completely divine. This was the heresy of Monophysism. The monophysites explained this fusion of the two natures in Christ by saying that Christ lacked a human intellectual soul; the Word took the place of the human soul in Christ. Hence, the completeness of Christ's humanity was sacrificed to save the unity. This heresy was condemned by a dogmatic letter of Pope Leo I (Denz. 143), and later by the ecumenical Council of Chalcedon in 451 (Denz. 148), and the second ecumenical Council of Constantinople in 553 (Denz. 213 ff).

The following quotation from the Council of Chalcedon will show how precisely and clearly the Church distinguished between "person" and "nature", insisting on the two natures in Christ united in the one divine Person of the Word.

> "In accordance with the teaching of the holy Fathers we all profess our faith in one and the same Son and Lord Jesus Christ, perfect in His divinity, perfect in His humanity, having a rational soul and a body, consubstantial with the Father according to the divinity, the same consubstantial with us according to His humanity, 'in all things like as we are except sin'; born before all ages of the Father according to the divinity, and the same in these last days born of Mary the Virgin Mother of God for us and for our salvation; one and the same Christ the Lord and only-begotten Son *in two natures* without confusion, change, division or separation, the difference of the natures being in no way suppressed by their union, but the proper manner of existence of each being safeguarded, while each nature is united with the other *in one person and hypostasis*".

# HYPOSTATIC UNION

The Council of Chalcedon made it clear that the two natures in Christ remain complete "without confusion, change, division or separation". Hence, the union of these two natures cannot be explained by a substantial change, as though Christ's human nature mixed with the divine nature to form a third; in that case, aside from the impossibility of it, Christ would be neither God nor Man. Nor is the union in Christ the same as the union between body and soul where two incomplete substances unite to form a complete human nature. Both the divine and human natures in Christ are complete so that Christ is fully God and at the same time a perfect Man.

But while these two natures in Christ remain distinct one from the other, they are united in a very intimate and mysterious union whereby Christ is only one being—one Person. The Council uses the word "hypostasis" to denote "person" and it clearly states that there is only one Person in Christ. That Person is the Word, the Son of God. The Second Person of the Blessed Trinity assumed human nature into His own personality; there is no human person in Christ. Since the union of the two natures in Christ consists in the fact that both natures are possessed by one and the same divine Person (hypostasis), the union in Christ is called "hypostatic".

In order to appreciate more clearly the mystery of the hypostatic union it is necessary to distinguish between "nature" and "person".

*Nature.* The essence of a thing is the sum total of all those notes by which a thing is what it is (*e.g.,* by which a dog is a dog and not a stone). The nature is that essence inasmuch as it is a principle of activity, a source from which the actions flow. Thus human nature (the body and soul united) is the principle, the source, from which flow human actions, such as, eating, sleeping, thinking, speaking, etc. The divine nature is that which makes God to be God and is the source of divine actions, such as creation, etc.

*Person.* A person is a *substance, i.e.,* a being existing in itself (not like *e.g.* color, which must exist in something else).

It is a *complete substance.* (The body is a substance, but it is incomplete in itself, it needs the soul.) A complete substance is not part of something else; it is separate and distinct from all other substances of the same kind.

It is an *individual* substance as opposed to the abstract notion of a substance (*e.g.,* this concrete man as opposed to the abstract notion of "man").

It is an *intellectual* (rational) substance. Only beings with intelligence are called persons; animals and the lower forms of creation are called individual beings but not persons.

It is *incommunicable,* existing in itself. The fact that a person is a complete substance excludes the possibility of its being a part of a whole. But a person is also incommunicable in the sense that it cannot be assumed into the unity of a higher personality so as to subsist by virtue of the latter's subsistence. The reason why we add this notion to the definition of "person" is because we know that our Lord's human nature, though it is a complete and most perfect individual nature, is, nevertheless, *not a person*. It is assumed into the Personality of the Second Person of the Trinity and is united hypostatically with this Divine Person. Hence, our Lord's human nature does not exist in itself.

*Relation between Person and Nature.* The person possesses the nature and is responsible for its actions. It is that ultimate reality in a rational being which is called the "I" (ego). Thus we say "I" eat, "I" read, "I" walk, "I" think, "I" decide. In a man, it is the person, the "I" which acts by means of the nature, *i.e.*, by means of the powers of body and soul.

Now in Jesus Christ there is only *one person,* and that is the person of the Word, the Son. This one Divine Person possesses both the divine nature and the human nature. Thus the actions of the divine nature, *e.g.*, creation, are attributed to the Second Person of the Trinity, and the actions of the human nature, *e.g.*, eating, sleeping, suffering, dying, etc., are attributed to that same divine Person since He possesses that human nature.

Hence it is proper to say that God was born, suffered, died. But these actions are not due to His divine nature; they are due to His human nature. Since, however, the Second Person possesses that human nature, the actions of it are rightly attributed to the Second Person. The divine nature could not suffer on the Cross, but the divine Person died through His human nature.

## CONSEQUENCES OF THE HYPOSTATIC UNION

1. *Divine Maternity.* Maternity, like other human relationships, is a relation between *persons.* Actually, only the human body is generated by the parents; the soul is created directly by God and infused into the body. Yet, a man does not say of his mother: "She is the mother of my body". Rather, he says: "She is *my* mother". In the case of Christ, only His human nature was generated from the virginal flesh of Mary. But when one asks whose Mother Mary is—the answer is: "God's mother", for there is only one Person in Christ possessing that human nature—the Divine Person of the Word. Therefore, Mary is truly the Mother of God. It is from this relationship to Him that all her other prerogatives, her supreme dignity among creatures, and her supreme power of intercession flow.

2. *Adorableness of Christ's Humanity.* Any act of praise, just as any censure or blame, is directed to a *person.* Thus in praising a musician, the reason for the praise may be his intellect or his sense of rhythm or the dexterity of his fingers, but the praise is directed to *him,* the person. So too, in praising the humanity of Christ or any part of it, the praise is directed to

the Person who possesses that humanity. That Person is God and therefore, the praise is supreme.

Adoration, in the strict sense, is the act of divine worship by which we acknowledge the infinite majesty and supreme dominion of God and our own dependence on Him and submission to Him. Hence, adoration belongs to God alone. Christ's humanity deserves this adoration because it was and always will be hypostatically united to the Second Person of the Blessed Trinity; it is God's body and soul. Thus, His Soul, His Precious Blood, His five wounds are adorable because they are inseparably united to the Word. Although the adoration is immediately directed to these separate parts or organs, the formal object or motive of such adoration is the Person of the Word.

What has been said thus far applies directly to the popular devotion to the Sacred Heart of Jesus. This devotion, which goes back to the eleventh century, received a great impetus from the revelations and promises made to St. Margaret Mary Alocoque in the seventeenth century at Paray-le-Monial, in France. The object of devotion to the Sacred Heart is the physical heart of the Word Incarnate considered as the symbol of His human love for God and for mankind. The Jansenists attacked this practice on the ground that to worship the human heart of Christ was to give divine honor to a creature. Pope Pius VI (1794) condemned the Jansenists and indicated the dogmatic truth which underlies the devotion when he said:

> "The faithful adore the Heart of Jesus considered as the heart of Jesus, that is, as the Heart of the Person of the Word to whom it is inseparably united, just as the body of Christ was adorable when for three days it lay dead in the tomb, unsevered and unseparated from the divinity".

Hence devotion to Christ is not devotion to a mere man, it is the worship of the Word Incarnate, and that worship embraces all that is in Him, all that is united with His Divine Person.

3. *Human Knowledge of Christ.* As God, Christ has infinite knowledge in the Divine Intellect which He possesses in common with the Father and the Holy Spirit. As Man, Christ is the most perfect of rational creatures because His human nature is united to the Divine Person. The infinite dignity of the Word demands that the human nature which He assumed should be the most perfect of its kind. Therefore Christ, in His human intellect, had perfect knowledge. We may distinguish in Him a threefold type of knowledge.

A. *Beatific Vision.* From the first moment of Its existence, the human soul of Christ enjoyed the beatific vision of God. He beheld the Godhead face to face. This fact has never been defined by a Pope or a Council of the Church but it is the common teaching of all theologians. Their reasons are rooted in the hypostatic union of Christ's human nature with the Divinity. Christ, as the most perfect of men, must have had, in His human intellect, a perfect consciousness of Himself. The "self" in Christ is the Divine Person. Therefore, Christ, in seeing Himself, saw God face to face. It was this beatitude which He came to give us. He Himself, therefore, must have possessed it in all its fullness. And in the beatific knowledge, He sees all creatures mirrored in the essence of God. He sees the whole created universe of which He is the appointed King.

It is not easy to reconcile this fact of the beatific vision in Christ's human soul with the facts of His passion. The difficulty is not so great with regard to His sensible, bodily sufferings. In itself, the beatific vision is a purely spiritual operation entirely independent of the body. When Christ rose from the grave, the supreme glory and joy in His soul overflowed into His senses. But, during His earthly life, these further sensible effects of the beatific vision were suspended. Therefore, He could suffer extreme torments in His senses and emotions while possessing supreme beatitude in His soul. Even in our human experience, we know of many heroes, such as martyrs, who suffered extreme physical pain while they mentally rejoiced in their suffering. St. Stephen, while suffering unto death in his body, was so enraptured at the vision of Christ that his face shone like an angel's.

But the difficulty is greatly increased when we consider the *mental* sufferings of Christ. We know that His vision of the malice and ingratitude of sin caused excruciating pain in His soul. How could this be, if His soul was in a state of perfect beatitude? We cannot solve this deep mystery. All we can do is look to the mysterious psychology of our own human nature for some inkling of the deeper mystery in Christ. The fact is that spiritual pain and joy are not incompatible. Suppose, for instance, a mother who has lost her home and all her belongings by fire; yet, she has saved her child from the flames at the cost, let us say, of much physical pain to herself and the child. There is much anguish in her mind over the evils involved; yet, who can measure her joy over the rescue? Such common and relatively puny experiences as this might help us to understand that the sins of mankind, which so grieved our Lord in His agony, could yet be a subject for intense rejoicing as He contemplated in the beatific vision the mercy of God for sinners and the infinite wisdom whereby He draws good even out of evil.

B. *Infused Knowledge.* It is also the common opinion of theologians that God, at the moment of creating the soul of Christ, infused into it a knowledge of all created things. Again, as God-Man, Christ had a formal claim to the most perfect knowledge of which His soul was capable. Adam had infused knowledge of the created world; and Christ, who came to restore what Adam lost, must have been equal to Adam in this realm of human perfection. He is our King whose humanity is forever wedded to the Godhead; it is fitting, then, that He should have in His human soul any and all of the ideas of creatures in themselves which His human subjects can acquire in the course of the centuries.

Such is probably the conclusion to be drawn from such passages of Scripture as Isaias 11:2:

> "And the spirit of the Lord shall rest upon Him: the spirit of wisdom and of understanding, the spirit of counsel and . . . of knowledge".

This seems to imply that Christ shall be constituted in the possession of all knowledge and that His knowledge shall be infused.

C. *Acquired Knowledge.* Besides the divine knowledge which Jesus enjoyed by virtue of the beatific vision and besides the angelic knowledge infused immediately into His human soul, He also possessed acquired knowledge, *i.e.,* that specifically human knowledge which is gained through sense perception and the natural use of reason. Although by virtue of the beatific vision and the infused knowledge of all things, Christ knew everything that experience could teach Him, still, He was, after a fashion, able to "learn", that is, to become acquainted with what He already knew from a different point of view, *i.e.,* that of human experience. It is this knowledge which St. Luke refers to when he says: ". . . and Jesus advanced in *wisdom"* (2:52).

Indeed, if our Lord did not have this experimental knowledge, all His human experience, recorded in the Gospels, would have been fictitious. Our Lord truly wondered at the faith of the humble and was shocked at the incredulity of the Pharisees. To understand this, we must again turn to our own human experience of different types of knowledge. You may know, for instance, by abstract knowledge, the day and the hour when your mother is going to die. But when the hour comes and the knowledge is gained from experience, it is still a surprise and a shock to the emotions. So was it with Christ. His personal experience of actual suffering was something totally different from the concept of His Passion previously existing in His human intellect.

4. *Holiness of Christ.* Holiness consists in union with God, the Supreme Good. In His divine nature, Christ is *identical* with God and is, therefore, All Holy. It is the *human* holiness of Christ which we must now discuss and we shall do so by considering—first, the negative aspects of His holiness, *i.e., freedom from sin,* and then its positive elements, *i.e., union with* God.

*Freedom from Original Sin and Concupiscence.* It is an article of our faith that Christ was free from any taint of original sin and from the concupiscence which we inherit from Adam (*cf.* Denz. 224, 711). Even as Man, Christ is the Natural Son of God. To assert that He was conceived in original sin would be equivalent to saying that God was tainted by sin.

"God alone is without sin",

says Tertullian,

"and the only man without sin is Christ, because Christ is God".

And if Christ was conceived without original sin, He must, for the same reason, have been exempt from concupiscence—*i.e.,* the rebellion of the senses which is one of the punishments of original sin.

It was to

"take away the sin of the world" (Jn. 1:29)

that Christ became man; it was impossible, therefore, that He Himself should be tainted by it. He came as

"a lamb without blemish and without spot" (1 Pet. 1:19), "tried as we are in all things except sin" (Hebr. 4:15).

*Freedom from Personal Sin.* The fact that Christ never committed the slightest personal sin is clearly defined by the Councils of Ephesus and Chalcedon (Denz. 122, 148). The Prophet Isaias says of the coming Messias:

"He hath done no iniquity, neither was there deceit in His mouth" (53:9).

St. Paul describes our Lord as

"holy, innocent, undefiled, set apart from sinners" (Hebr. 7:26).

We saw the innumerable manifestations of this supreme sanctity in all the details of our Lord's public life. He was unique among men when He dared to face His enemies and say:

"Which of you can convict Me of sin?" (Jn. 8:46).

*Impeccability.* Christ not only inherited no sin nor committed any sin but He was *incapable of sinning.* This fact has not been defined as an article of faith, though the Vatican Council intended to define it. But it is so clearly the teaching of the Church from the Fathers of the Church and early Councils down to our own day, that Catholics are not allowed to deny it.

The main reason which compels us to maintain the impeccability of Christ is based, again, on the hypostatic union of the two natures. Christ is God and God cannot sin. Fulgentius echoes countless expressions of the Fathers of the Church on this point when he says:

"The Godhead cannot be overcome and therefore also the humanity of Christ remained without sin, because it was assumed into the Godhead which of its very nature is incapable of sin".

It is difficult to reconcile this impeccability of Christ with the fact that

[287]

His will was free. Both of the facts, *i.e.*, the impeccability and freedom of Christ, are the clear teaching of the Church. But theologians differ widely in their opinions on how these facts are to be reconciled. One thing that must be kept in mind is the fact that freedom, of itself, does not mean liability to sin. God is supremely free and yet He cannot sin. The inclination to sin is a deordination of right reason rather than a perfection of the will. Christ, with all the perfection of His human knowledge and especially the beatific vision, saw and understood the infinite wisdom behind all things. And His will was perfect in its ability to adhere to what He saw. He adhered freely in perfect obedience to the Father's plan for His life and because of the perfection of His intellect and will He could not do otherwise. His free adherence was a positive act of His will and the freedom of it was not lessened, but rather made more perfect, by the fact that He saw clearly that it was the only thing to do.

*Substantial Holiness of Christ.* Human holiness is not the mere absence of sin; it is positive union with God. Now nothing could be more closely united with God than the human nature which He has made His own, which is joined with God substantially in the hypostatic union. This is the reason of the reverence which, apart from the consideration of any acts of virtue in Christ, we owe to His sacred humanity. This is the reason why, as we have seen, we give to that humanity a worship which belongs to God alone. In announcing the incarnation, the Angel Gabriel said: "the Holy One to be born shall be called the Son of God" (Lk. 1:35).

The Son to be born of Mary was the natural Son of God and it is because His human nature is hypostatically united to the divinity that He is called, without qualification, the "Holy One".

*Accidental Holiness.* Our sanctity consists in the state of sanctifying grace and the infused virtues and gifts of the Holy Spirit. We obtain these super-natural qualities of soul from Christ in the sacrament of Baptism. He is the natural Son of God and it is by being baptized into Him that we become the adopted sons of God. It follows then that Christ, the natural Son, by virtue of the hypostatic union, has the fullness of grace in His soul.

St. John expresses this truth thus:

> "And the Word was made flesh and dwelt among us . . . full of grace and of truth . . . and of His fullness we have all received, grace for grace". (Jn. 1:14-16).

Christ is here described as being "full" of that particular grace which we receive from Him, "grace for grace". Consequently, the soul of Christ must have been endowed with that same kind of grace which we receive and indeed He had such fullness of it that all who are redeemed by Him can participate in it without exhausting it.

# CHRIST THE KING

From all that has been said about the implications of the hypostatic union, we now can understand more fully the sense in which Christ as Man is King of all creation. He is not merely King in the sense that He was appointed by the Father—as though others from among men might have had the same dignity, had they been appointed in His stead. Nor is He King merely in the sense that He won the title by redeeming us from sin. But He is King in His own natural dignity and right. At the Incarnation, the humanity of Christ was assumed into a personal, substantial union with the infinite God and adorned by natural right with every possible natural and supernatural perfection. It is, therefore, His right to receive the homage of all creatures. As Cyril of Alexandria says,

"He has dominion over all creatures, a dominion not seized by violence nor usurped, but His by essence and by nature".

Or as St. Paul says:

"It has pleased God the Father that in Him (Christ) *all his fullness should dwell,* and that through Him he should reconcile to Himself all things, whether on the earth or in the heavens, making peace through the blood of the cross" (Col. 1:19-20).

## TEST QUESTIONS

1. On the Divinity of Christ.

   a. Cite and explain two passages from Scripture to show that Christ claimed to be equally divine with the Father.

   b. Name five divine attributes which Christ claimed for Himself and explain in a general way how He did this.

   c. How do the miracles of Christ substantiate His claim to divinity?

   d. Explain three instances where Christ predicted future events. How do these prophecies prove that He is divine?

   e. Cite a passage from Scripture where Christ appealed to His miracles and prophecies as proof that He spoke the truth.

   f. Name three examples to show that the Apostles believed that Christ was divine.

2. On the Humanity of Christ.

   a. Explain in a general way how you know that Christ was fully human.

   b. Prove specifically that He had a human intellect and a human will.

3. Explain briefly the following heresies with regard to Christ—Docetism, Adoptionism, Arianism, Nestorianism and Monophysism.

4. Explain in substance the definition of the Council of Chalcedon with regard to the duality and unity in Christ.

5. Define "nature" and "person" and explain the relationship between the two.

6. Explain fully the "hypostatic union".

7. Explain why Mary is truly the Mother of God.

8. Explain the sense in which we give supreme adoration to the humanity of Christ and, specifically, to the Sacred Heart.

9. Explain why we say that Christ had the beatific vision and infused knowledge of created things in His human soul.

10. Explain the sense in which Christ could "grow in wisdom".

11. Explain why the Church teaches that Christ was free from original sin, concupiscence, personal sin, and the possibility of sinning.

12. Prove and explain that Christ was 1] substantially holy; 2] full of sanctifying grace.

13. Explain how Christ, as Man, is by nature King of all creation.

## Chapter XXIII

# THE CHURCH

➤➤➤➤➤➤➤➤➤➤➤➤➤➤◄◄◄◄◄◄◄◄◄◄◄◄◄◄

IT REMAINS for us now to summarize very briefly the general outlines of the kingdom which Christ came to establish. At the outset of His Public Life and continuously thereafter, our Lord, as Messias, announced that the "Kingdom of God" (or "Heaven") was at hand. This "Kingdom" is another expression for "Church"; Christ Himself used the words interchangeably in the same sentence when He made Peter the rock of His Church and gave him the keys to the kingdom (Mt. 16:18-19).

Our present purpose, then, is to draw together the main details which our Lord revealed about this kingdom; to see its purpose, its nature, its main powers and characteristic features. Next year, when we complete the Life of Christ, we shall be able to add more details to this sketch of the *juridical* nature of the Church. And finally, the entire third year of this course will be devoted to the complete picture of the Church as a *living organism*—the Mystical Body of Christ.

## VISIBLE SOCIETY

*Adversaries.* The notion of the Church as a fully constituted society is a stumbling block to most non-Catholics in the world today. The liberal Protestant theologians, following the leadership of Dr. Adolph von Harnack, deny that Christ founded a Church at all. The so-called orthodox Protestants admit that Christ founded a Church but they deny that it is a society because, as they assert, it is invisible. To them, membership in Christ's Church consists in some invisible, personal quality of the heart such as internal faith (Luther) or being predestined to eternal salvation (Calvin). Hence, according to this view, the Church of Christ does not consist of a group of individuals who are visibly united together in a common worship. It consists of people who, independently of whether or not they belong to any church-going group, have certain qualities of soul hidden from the eyes of other men and usually from their own. The main reason why Protestantism has made religion such an individualistic, private affair is that it denies to the Church one of the main elements of a society—*i.e.,* authority. In most Protestant churches there is no governing body which can, with any *claim* of authority from Christ, lay down just what is to be believed or how men must worship or even how they must live if they are to remain in the society and achieve its goal.

Analogous to these traditional Protestant views is the modern antithesis between "the religion of authority" and the "religion of the spirit". The modern tendency is to overemphasize Christ's insistence on the dispositions of the heart to the point where it is denied that He founded a kingdom which is visible in this world. The extreme expressions of this view are to be found in such religions as that of Jehovah's Witnesses whose Watch Tower is erected against all "organized" religion. Especially in America, where "democracy" is the measure of all that is good (Blanshard), the tendency is to deny that Christ founded a kingdom with divinely appointed rulers to whom all men are obliged to submit if they are to reach eternal salvation.

*Church of Christ a true Society.* The fourth session of the Vatican Council (1870), refuting the errors of Protestant Reformers, defined that the Church is a fully constituted society with visible members united under visible and divinely appointed rulers in the bond of one faith and one charity. The Council then proceeded to describe in detail the characteristics of this Church as a supernatural society and especially to explain the nature and extent of the power exercised by its rulers (*cf.* Denz. 1821-1842). Before we go into the details of this teaching, it seems best to define the word "society" and then to explain under separate headings how all the elements of this definition are verified in the Church of Christ.

A society may be defined as 1] a permanent association of persons who 2] are united together and strive by their mutual co-operation 3] for the attainment of a common purpose 4] under the direction of a common authority. This definition is verified in the natural societies of family and state and in such voluntary societies as political parties, business organizations, etc. It remains for us now to show how the four elements of this definition are verified in the supernatural society of the Church.

## 1. Membership in the Church

Christ clearly revealed that His kingdom was to have all the elements of a true society and, in doing so, He revealed many of its specific characteristics. The kingdom is not confined to Jews alone but is open to all men of all ages until the end of time. It is to be a *universal* kingdom. This fact which He often expressed in His Public Life is best summed up in His final commission to the Apostles:

> "All power in heaven and on earth has been given to Me. Go, therefore, and make disciples of all nations, baptizing them in the name of the

Father, and of the Son, and of the Holy Spirit, teaching them to observe all that I have commanded you; and behold, I am with you all days, even unto the consummation of the world" (Mt. 28:18-20).

St. Mark, in his parallel passage, brings out the fact that this commission to preach is an authoritative one so that there is an obligation imposed upon mankind to hear the message and submit to it:

"Go into the whole world and preach the gospel to every creature. He who believes and is baptized shall be saved, but he who does not believe shall be condemned" (Mk. 16:15-16).

Entrance, therefore, into this Kingdom is to be through *faith* and *baptism:*

"He who believes and is baptized shall be saved".

The visible ritual of Baptism and the external profession of faith which is a part of it, make a man a member of the visible community of believers. Thereby, the person who is baptized submits to the common faith and worship and government of the Church. And now that He is a member of the Church, his salvation will depend on how he fulfills the duties that go with this new citizenship in the Kingdom of God.

*Sinners not Excluded.* While the members of the Church must strive, as the Church directs them, for the sanctification of themselves and others, we must not think that failure in every case excludes them from membership in the Church. It is true that, having lost the state of grace, they are no longer full and living members. But they retain the baptismal character and may still have supernatural faith; they are still incorporated into Christ, although imperfectly, and may still be revivified by the state of grace.

Our Lord made it clear that both good and bad would be members of His kingdom (*cf.* Parable of the Weeds, Mt. 13:24-30, and Parable of Net, Mt. 13:47-50). It is true that success in attaining the goal of the kingdom will depend upon the co-operation and internal dispositions of the members (*cf.* Parable of the Sower, Mt. 13:18-23). Even in the case of the just, the degree of success will vary according to the degree of co-operation with grace, some bearing fruit and yielding

In one case a hundredfold, in another sixtyfold, and in another thirtyfold" (Mt. 13:23).

But even those who bear no fruit at all will not necessarily be separated from the kingdom until, in the next life, they face the Judge Himself.

Nevertheless, it is possible for a man to be cut off from membership in the Church either by ecclesiastical penalty or by the nature of the sin which he commits. As Pius XII says in his Encyclical on the Mystical Body of Christ:

"Only those are to be accounted really members of the Church who have been regenerated in the waters of Baptism and profess the true faith, and have not cut themselves off from the structure of the Body by their own unhappy act or been severed therefrom, for very grave crimes, by the legitimate authority".

We shall later discuss this power of the Church to excommunicate; it is sufficient to observe for the present that even such a juridical penalty does not wholly and irrevocably separate a man from the Church. He may still come back, by the proper reformation of his life, to enjoy the rights and privileges of those in communion with the faithful. Later, too, when we study the Act of Faith, we shall look more closely at certain sins (apostasy, heresy, schism) which, by their very nature, cut a man off from membership in the Church.

*One Church.* It is clear also, from the texts that have been cited, that it is one and the same Church to which all men are to belong. The Apostles were commissioned to teach the one set of truths, one form of worship, one way of Christian life—"all that I have commanded you"—and it is this which all men are to accept under penalty of being "condemned". Hence, our Lord always spoke of His Church in the singular number—the one Kingdom of God or Kingdom of Heaven or the one Sheepfold.

"And other sheep I have that are not of this fold. Them also I must bring, and they shall hear My voice, and there shall be *one fold and one Shepherd*" (Jn. 10:16).

## 2. THE COMMON GOAL OR PURPOSE OF THE KINGDOM

This Church of Christ is a *spiritual* kingdom. The common religious goal is the attainment of eternal life. In this world, that "eternal life" consists negatively, in the forgiveness of sins (Mt. 26:28) and positively, in the gift of a new life of sanctifying grace (*cf.* Jn. 3:5; 3:16; ch. 6). In the next world it consists in the eternal happiness of heaven (*cf.* Mt. 6:19-20; Jn. 3:16).

Hence the Church is not to be the temporal, political kingdom which the Jews expected. It is to be *in* this world as is clear from all that has been said. But it is not to be *of* the world either in regard to its ultimate goal or the means of attaining that goal. This is what Christ meant when He said:

"My Kingdom is not of this world" (Jn. 18:36).

## 3. THE COMMON BOND

We have seen that the members, in striving for the common purpose of the kingdom, are to be united by one faith, one baptism and obedience to one authority. This means that they are to share in a uniform religious activity consisting of belief in definite doctrines (Mt. 28:20), obedience to certain precepts (Mt. 5:17 ff.), communion of prayer, sacrifice and other religious exercises (*cf*. Mt. 6:9 ff.; 18:19-20; Lk. 22:19; Acts 2:42-46). It remains, as the work of this entire four-year course in Theology, to examine in specific detail the nature and scope and function of this spiritual life in the members of the Church.

## 4. COMMON AUTHORITY

Our Lord, as we have seen, was Prophet, King and Priest and, corresponding to this triple office, He gave to the Apostles the power to teach, rule and sanctify the members of His Church. Their very name, "Apostles", means that they were *sent* to perform these offices in His name. Christ made it clear in conferring these powers upon the Apostles that they were to be handed down to their successors (the Popes and Bishops) and that, through them, the Church would be safeguarded against the power of the devil down to the end of time.

The power to *sanctify* is the power of Holy Orders by virtue of which the Apostles and their successors can offer sacrifice, forgive sins and confer divine life on the members of the Church by such priestly ministrations as the conferring of the Sacraments. We shall wait until Sophomore and Junior years to study in detail this power of *Orders* in the Church.

It remains for us now to discuss the *teaching* (doctrinal) and *ruling* (jurisdictional) power which Christ established in His Church. We shall first discuss these powers as they are found in the whole teaching and ruling body of the Church as such, *i.e.*, in the Apostles or Popes and Bishops taken together as a body. And finally, we shall discuss the nature of these powers as they are found in Peter or the Popes considered apart from the other Apostles or Bishops.

### A. DOCTRINAL AUTHORITY.

*Infallible.* We have seen how the Apostles and their successors were commissioned as a group to teach with authority in Christ's name and with the solemn promise that He would be with them in the performance of this office until the end of time (*cf.* Mt. 28:18-20). The purpose of His "being with them" is obviously to guarantee that they would teach *all that He commanded them* without error or omission until the end of time.

This implies that the Church enjoys the charism of infallibility. This infallibility, as we shall see later, is both *active* in the sense that it pertains to the teaching body of the Church in its office of teaching and *passive* in the sense that the body of the faithful are protected against accepting, as a body, any belief contrary to what Christ commissioned the Apostles to teach. But for the present, we are interested only in active infallibility as it is found in the teaching body of the Church (the Pope and Bishops united together).

Certainly the powers of hell would prevail against the Church of Christ if that Church could teach error or falsehood as the true doctrine of Christ. The devil was a "liar from the beginning" and it is mainly by obscuring and distorting the truth that he leads men to destruction. It was precisely to give men a safe harbor against such perils that Christ founded His Church and promised to be with it and protect it. If, then, the official teaching body of the Church could lead the Church astray, Christ's promise would itself be false and a supreme triumph of the deceitful powers of hell.

*Councils.* In Junior Year, when we study the concrete life of the Church, we shall see how conscious the Apostles were that they, united as a group, enjoyed this charism in teaching the word of God. "The Holy Spirit and we have decided" were the words in which St. Peter, speaking in the name of all, announced the decisions of the Council of Jerusalem (Acts 15:28). It is, then, in connection with this first Council of the Church, that we shall discuss the authority of councils in general and the infallibility which is attached to the definitions of ecumenical (general) Councils of the Church.

## B. JURISDICTIONAL AUTHORITY.

The Apostles and their successors were given the power to rule over the Church in the name of Christ. This jurisdictional power includes the power 1) to legislate, 2) to sit in judgment and 3) to impose penalties, in matters which pertain to eternal salvation.

*They have legislative power, i.e.,* the power to make laws and the power to apply those laws to individuals in the form of a command. It was to the Apostles as a group that our Lord said:

"Whatever you bind on earth shall be bound also in heaven . . ." (Mt. 18:18).

The fundamental laws governing the actions of Christians were laid down by Christ. But the Church has been promised the assistance of the Holy Spirit in adapting, interpreting and developing these laws for the faithful in the particular circumstances of practical life. Thus, the Council of Jerusalem laid down rules with regard to the observance of the Mosaic Law (Acts 15:28-29). And St. Paul made regulations concerning marriage which have received the name "Pauline privilege" (1 Cor. 7:12 ff.). The Code of Canon Law exemplifies how the Church has carried on this practice through the centuries.

*They have judicial power, i.e.,* the authority to pass judgment on those who violate the laws of God or the precepts of the Church. Our Lord

Himself indicated that the Church was to exercise such judicial power when necessary and pass even the extreme sentence of excommunication when the circumstances demanded (Mt. 18:15 ff.).

*They have coercive power, i.e.,* the authority to punish those who have been found guilty of violating the law. The power to excommunicate is an example of this coercive power; St. Paul imposed such a penalty in the case of the incestuous Corinthian (1 Cor. 5:3-5). Such penalties imposed by the Church normally consist in depriving a person of some spiritual benefit (*e.g.,* the sacraments) or imposing some act of penance (fasting). (*Cf.* the Code of Canon Law—canons 2214-2219.)

*Hierarchy.* The whole constitution of the Church is, therefore, hierarchic rather than democratic. This means that the governmental authority of the Church was given immediately by Christ to the Apostles and their successors. It was not given to the members of the Church as a group and conferred by them, in turn, on individuals. The pastors in the Church derive their office, not from the people but from God.

## PRIMACY OF THE POPE

We have already seen how the supreme power of jurisdiction in the Church was promised to St. Peter (Mt. 16:18-19). In a series of three metaphors, whose meaning has already been explained (*cf.* ch. XIX, No. 58), Peter was established as the rock or foundation of the Church (*i.e.,* the supreme ruler); the "keys" of the kingdom were given to him as a sign of his absolute authority over Christ's house; and finally, he was given the absolute power to "bind or loose" the members of the kingdom in Christ's name and with Christ's full sanction.

This supreme legislative, judicial and executive power, so clearly described in the promise, was conferred on Peter after the resurrection when our Lord gave him the mandate: "Feed My lambs . . . feed My lambs . . . feed My sheep" (Jn. 21:15-17). Christ Himself is the "good Shepherd" (Jn. 10:11) who offered His life that there might be "one fold and one shepherd" (Jn. 10:16) and He handed over the sheepfold to Peter's care before He Himself ascended to the Father. Christ still remains the "chief Shepherd" (1 Petr. 5:4) but Peter is His visible representative, His Vicar, and the other Apostles are shepherds under the leadership of, and subject to, the authority of Peter. Peter's supreme authority, like the Church which is founded upon it, is to last to the end of time and is handed down in succession to the Popes.

*Vatican Council.* The Vatican Council defined the supremacy of Peter and his successors in the following terms:

"We, therefore, teach and declare that, according to the testimony of the Gospel, the primacy of jurisdiction over the universal Church of God was immediately and directly promised and given to Blessed Peter the Apostle by Christ the Lord. . . . At open variance with this clear doctrine of Holy Scripture, as it has been ever understood by the Catholic Church, are the perverse opinions of those who, while they distort the form of government established by Christ the Lord in His Church, deny that Peter in his single person, preferably to all the other Apostles, whether taken separately or together, was endowed by Christ with a true and proper primacy of jurisdiction; or of those who assert that the same primacy was not bestowed immediately and directly upon Blessed Peter himself, but upon the Church, and through the Church on Peter as her Minister.

"If anyone, therefore, shall say that Blessed Peter the Apostle was not appointed the Prince of all the Apostles and the visible head of the whole Church militant; or that he directly and immediately received from the same our Lord Jesus Christ a primacy of honor only, and not of true and proper jurisdiction; let him be anathema". (Denz. 1822-1823).

Likewise, the Council concludes its teaching on the perpetuity of this supreme office with the following pronouncement:

"If, then, any one shall say that it is not by the institution of Christ the Lord, or by divine right, that Blessed Peter should have a perpetual line of successors in the Primacy over the Universal Church; or that the Roman Pontiff is not the successor of Blessed Peter in this Primacy; let him be anathema" (Denz. 1825).

## PAPAL INFALLIBILITY

We have already seen how immunity from error was promised to the teaching body of Christ's Church by virtue of the promise that the "gates of hell will not prevail against it".

Now this promise was made to the Church precisely in so far as it has Peter and his successors as its rock foundation. It follows, therefore, that Peter, acting as the divinely appointed shepherd of the flock, will be protected from error when he feeds the flock with the truth of Christ. The infallibility that was promised to the teaching body of the Church as such (the Pope and Bishops united together), far from limiting the supreme doctrinal authority of the Pope, is, in turn, limited by it. We shall discuss this matter later when we treat of the Councils of the Church.

Hence, from the very beginning, the Church accepted the Pope as the supreme and infallible teacher in matters of faith and morals. It would require a careful study of the whole history of the Church to see how this important matter of faith was preserved through the centuries in the face of rebellion against it by individuals and, eventually, by whole nations. But, for the present, we are interested only in the nature and extent of papal infallibility. This is most clearly defined by the Vatican Council in response to the denial of it which came to its climax in the Protestant Reformation.

> *Vatican Council:* "We teach and define it to be a dogma divinely revealed that the Roman Pontiff, when he speaks *ex cathedra,* that is, when acting in his office of pastor and teacher of all Christians, by his supreme apostolic authority, he defines a doctrine concerning faith or morals to be held by the whole Church, through the divine assistance promised him in Blessed Peter, he enjoys that infallibility with which the divine Redeemer willed His Church to be endowed in defining doctrine concerning faith and morals; and therefore such definitions of the said Roman Pontiff are irreformable of themselves, and not from the consent of the Church" (Denz. 1839).

*Ex Cathedra.* Much of the modern hostility to the doctrine of Papal infallibility arises from ignorance of the scope and limitations of it which are clearly indicated in the above definition. An *ex cathedra* definition is one in which the Pope speaks solemnly as the head of the universal Church and makes an irrevocable decision on matters of faith or morals with the clear intention of binding all the faithful to accept it as a matter that must be believed as belonging to the deposit of faith.

The Pope is not speaking infallibly when he speaks merely as Bishop of Rome. And even when he speaks as Pope, he may be giving instruction to only a section of the universal Church; or again, he may address the whole Church but without the intention of defining anything as of faith. All of the "ordinary" teachings of the Pope demand a respectful, internal assent on the part of the faithful; but they are not necessarily "irreformable" and do not necessarily have the sanction of infallibility behind them.

## SUPREME JURISDICTION

We have seen how the power of jurisdiction includes within itself legislative, judicial and coercive authority. The fullness of this jurisdictional power in the Church is vested in the person of the Pope. The Pope is subject to no one but God while all the members of the Church, including the Bishops, are subject to him. It was to Peter, apart from the other Apostles, that Christ gave, without restriction or limitation, the keys to His Kingdom and the power to bind and loose in His name (Mt. 16:19). This supremacy of papal jurisdiction is most clearly defined by the Vatican Council.

> *Vatican Council:* "Hence we teach and declare that by the appointment of our Lord the Roman Church possesses a superiority of ordinary power over all other Churches, and that this power of jurisdiction of the Roman Pontiff, which is truly episcopal, is immediate; to which all, of whatever rite and dignity, both pastors and faithful, both individually and collectively, are bound, by their duty of hierarchical subordination and true obedience, to submit, not only in matters which belong to faith and morals, but

also in those that appertain to the discipline and government of the Church throughout the world, so that the Church of Christ may be one flock under one supreme pastor through the preservation of unity both of communion and of profession of the same faith with the Roman Pontiff. This is the teaching of Catholic truth, from which no one can deviate without loss of faith and of salvation.

"If then any one shall say that the Roman Pontiff has the office merely of inspection or direction, but not full and supreme power of jurisdiction over the Universal Church, not only in things pertaining to faith and morals, but also in those which relate to the discipline and government of the Church, spread throughout the world; or that he possess merely the principal part, and not all the fullness of this supreme power; or that this power which he enjoys is not ordinary and immediate, both over each and all the Churches and over each and all the Pastors and the faithful; let him be anathema" (Denz. 1827 and 1831).

*Monarchy.* It follows, then, that, while others (the Bishops) in the Church have jurisdictional power which they receive from God, the Church partakes of the nature of a monarchy in the sense that the fullness of authority was given solely to Peter, Prince of the Apostles, and to his successors, the Bishops of Rome. The Pope, the Vicar of Christ, is a King participating fully in the ruling power of the King of Kings.

*Modern Difficulties.* Unfortunately, such absolute authority is looked upon, especially in America, as despotism of the worst kind. "Democracy" (a much misunderstood term) has come to be considered the supreme and only good where governments are concerned. And so, many have come to look upon the "authoritarianism" of the Church as a clear sign that it is not from God.

But God, however fully the ideals of democracy are found in His sharing of the One Divine Nature among Three Persons, is and cannot help but be our supreme Lord and Master. Christ came to us as our absolute King. And whatever one may think of despotism being an inherent evil in human monarchies or dictatorships, the infinite wisdom and holiness and justice of God preclude these evils from His rule. Christ established His Kingdom in order to shower upon us the unspeakable benefits of His infinite love. But we would take the infinity out of that love if we stripped Him of His divine attributes and made Him one of ourselves in the democratic sense.

What men fail to see, and it is impossible to see it without the gift of faith, is the fact that Christ communicated to the Church a share in His own divine attributes—the absolute, indefectible power to teach and rule and sanctify in His own spirit of truth and love. Submission to this power is not a loss of freedom; it is a coming to the source, the fountain of truth and life and incomprehensible love. The Church as our Mother and the Pope as our Father share in the attributes of Christ that they may fulfill in our regard their divinely appointed tasks. The Holy Spirit of God is labor-ing constantly in both the Church as a whole and the Pope as an individual to make their absolute authority the reign of tender love that conforms to the reign of Christ the King.

## Four Marks of the Church

We have seen that the Church which Christ established is a visible society. Like any other society, it has its own nature and purpose and recognizable properties. And just as all men of good will who came in contact with Christ were able to recognize Him for what He was, so it must be possible for them to recognize His Church as His institution. In this connection, the Vatican Council says:

> "That we may be able to satisfy the obligation of embracing the true faith and of constantly persevering in it, God has instituted the Church through His only begotten Son, and has bestowed on it manifest notes of that institution, that it may be recognized by all men as the guardian and teacher of the revealed word; for to the Catholic Church alone belong all those many and admirable tokens which have been divinely established for the evident credibility of the Christian Faith. Nay more, the Church by itself, with its marvelous extension, its eminent holiness, and its inexhaustible fruitfulness in every good thing, with its Catholic unity and its invincible stability, is a great and perpetual motive of credibility, and an irrefutable witness of its own divine mission.
>
> And thus, like a standard set up unto the nations (Isaias 11:12), it both invites to itself those who do not yet believe, and assures its children that the faith which they possess rests on the most firm foundation. And its testimony is efficaciously supported by a power from on high" (Denz. 1793-1794).

In treating the *four* marks of the Church, we do not mean to say that these are the only characteristics or properties given to the Church by Her divine Founder. Some of the characteristics of the Church are not exter-nally perceptible (*e.g.,* infallibility), while, of those which are in some manner visible, the "four marks" are the main ones and the others are reducible to them.

## 1. Apostolicity

We have already seen that Christ gave to the Apostles and their succes-sors the power to *teach* and *rule* and *sanctify* the members of His Church. It follows, then, that the Church of Christ existing in the world today must have that same triple power, handed down in an unbroken line of succes-sion from the Apostles. We have seen, also, how the Primacy of Peter is the crown of the Apostolate; the Bishops, in exercising their threefold power,

[301]

are subject to the supreme authority of the Pope. Hence that Church, and that Church only, which has a visible head who can trace his succession to the first primate, namely, to Peter, is in fact and by right Apostolic *in the fullest sense*.

*Verified in the Church.* It is clear to all the world that the Catholic Church claims to have in all its fullness this property of Apostolicity. And the Church has all the appearances of possessing what it claims. Since no other Church in the world even makes the claim to Peter's Primacy, and since the Church of Christ must endure, with Peter at its head, until the end of time, the mere fact of the claim and the external appearances which corroborate it, are proof enough of the genuinity of the Church. Those who desire *intrinsic* evidence that the Apostolic succession in the Church is genuine must study the history of the Church and trace back the succession of the present Pontiff along an uninterrupted line of 262 Popes to Peter, the "First" of the Apostles.

*Application to Other Churches.* It is beyond the scope of our present study to discuss in detail the varying degrees in which other churches lack (or have) this note of Apostolicity. It will suffice to indicate briefly the main points to be considered in this regard.

*Orders.* Most other churches in the world today make no claim to possessing the power of Holy Orders, *i.e.*, the power to sanctify to which Christ ordained the Apostles. They have abandoned the notion of priesthood and sacrifice and, in that respect, do not even claim to be the Church of the Apostles. The Anglican Church makes claim to this power of Holy Orders but its claim is rejected by the Church of Rome (*cf.*, the decree of Leo XIII, *Apostolicae Curae*, 1896); historical research into the validity of Anglican Orders would be necessary if one wanted to satisfy his mind on this point independently of the decision of the Pope. The schismatic Churches (*e.g.*, Russian Orthodox) claim and have the power of Holy Orders. Hence, the lack of Apostolocity in these Churches consists in their break from the succession of Peter's Primacy.

*Jurisdiction.* Most other Churches reject also the succession of the power of jurisdiction; they make no claim to possessing the power to rule which Christ the King conferred upon His Apostles. Here again, the schismatic churches claim and have the episcopal powers. But, rejecting the Primacy of Peter, they, too, lack an essential feature of the Apostolicity of Jurisdiction.

*Doctrine.* Again, most other Churches do not even claim to have the doctrinal authority which Christ gave to the Apostles. True, much of their doctrine is the same as that which the Apostles taught; in that sense, it could be called Apostolic. But, aside from the fact that they do not teach the *whole* of the doctrine ("All that I have commanded you"), they lack the apostolic note of teaching *with authority*. It is a cardinal principle of Protestantism that each one may interpret the Scripture for himself. That is a far cry from the injunction:

> "He who hears you, hears me; and he who rejects you, rejects me; and he who rejects me, rejects Him who sent me" (Lk. 10:16).

*Origin.* In general, therefore, it should be understood that the note of Apostolicity is lacking to non-Catholic Churches in varying degrees. But none of them possesses this note in the full sense of being the "one fold" under one shepherd. They all admit to having "broken off" from the Church of Rome. Whatever elements they took with them from the true Church and preserved after the break was made, the *break itself* makes it manifest that they lost some of the characteristics of the true Church of Christ. The following table will indicate the origin of these Churches; the dates of their founding and the names of their founders are an indication that they do not go back, *as these specific Churches,* to the Church that was founded on Peter, the Rock.

(This list is taken from *Upon This Rock,* by Rev. A. F. Alexander, p. 135, Catholic Book Store, Cleveland, Ohio 1950.)

| Name | Founder | Date | Place |
|---|---|---|---|
| Orthodox churches | Michael Caerularius | 1054 | Constantinople |
| Lutheranism | Martin Luther | 1520 | Germany |
| Anglicanism | King Henry VIII | 1534 | England |
| Mennonite sects | Menno Simons | 1550 | Switzerland |
| Presbyterianism | Calvin and Knox | 1560 | Switz. & Scotland |
| Congregationalism | Robert Brown | 1582 | Holland |
| Baptist sects | John Smyth | 1606 | Amsterdam, Holland |
| Society of Friends | George Fox | 1624 | England |
| Methodism | John Wesley | 1744 | England |
| Unitarianism | Theophilos Lindsay | 1774 | England |
| Mormonism | Joseph Smith | 1830 | Fayette, N. Y., U.S.A. |
| Adventist sects | William Miller | 1840 | Boston, Mass., U. S. A. |
| Salvation Army | William Booth | 1865 | London, England |
| Christian Scientists | Mary Baker Eddy | 1879 | Boston, Mass., U.S.A. |

## 2. UNITY

A superficial reading of the Gospels reveals that the Church of Christ must be one in teaching and faith, in government and obedience, in worship and the means of salvation. The student should be able to give abundant evidence that this triple unity is found in the Catholic Church. Our Lord referred to this oneness in doctrine and worship in such singular terms as *the* Gospel or *this* Gospel and, before the summary of it was ever written, He commissioned the Apostles to preach the whole of it—"all that I have commanded you." This "all" is not restricted to what is explicitly recorded in the written Gospels; it embraces everything which our Lord revealed to the Apostles.

*Orders and Jurisdiction.* In our treatment of the Apostolicity of the Church, we have seen that the great majority of non-Catholic churches do not even claim, much less have, the unity that comes from the power of Holy Orders and the power of Jurisdiction which Christ established in His Church. It is for this reason that these churches must ever lack unity of faith and worship which receives its stability from unity of government. Even the schismatic churches, which have the power of Orders and the Episcopal power to rule, deny the supremacy of Peter and the Roman Pontiffs and are, therefore, not united under one visible head.

*Doctrine.* As far as doctrine is concerned, Protestantism is often looked upon as one Church. But, although it is common to all Protestants that they profess devotion to the same Christ and agree in a general way on some of His fundamental teachings, this apparent unity manifests itself as purely nominal when we consider the numberless sects into which Protestantism is divided. This division among them is not merely a fact; it is something which they profess as a *principle* in their rejection of the jurisdictional power of the Bishops and its full primacy in the Popes. The principle of "private interpretation of the Scriptures" precludes by its very nature a unity of doctrine or belief. As Dr. Harnack says in his book, *What is Christianity?*:

> "When we are reproached with our divisions and told that Protestantism has as many doctrines as heads, we reply, 'So it has, but we do not wish it otherwise; on the contrary, we want still more freedom, still greater individuality in utterance and in doctrine" (translated by G. P. Saunders, Putnam, N. Y., 1901, p. 269).

Protestantism is not only divided into sects, but, within any given sect, it is equally impossible to find uniformity either in teaching or belief. The daily newspapers reveal how widely the individual members of a given Church will disagree on such an important matter as who Christ is, to say nothing of the details of what He came to reveal. The teachings of the "Red Dean of Canterbury" evidence the fact of such division even in the relatively conservative, "traditional" Church of England. The telling force of this individual example lies in the fact that the Dean is not in revolt against the authority of His Church or teaching without its sanction; rather, the Church of England denies any supreme ecclesiastical authority which can control the opinions or teachings of the Dean in matters of faith and admits that he, no matter what his beliefs, has as much power to teach as any Bishop in his Church. The principle and source of unity thus denied, unity of faith cannot be maintained.

## 3. SANCTITY

The infinitely holy Christ obviously founded a Church which is holy in *purpose,* in *doctrine,* in *worship* and the means that are used for the sanctification of its members. The Holy Spirit, who is the living source of holiness, was promised to the Church of Christ forever:

"And I will ask the Father and he will give you another Advocate to dwell with you forever, the Spirit of truth whom the world cannot receive, because it neither sees him nor knows him. But you shall know him, because he will dwell with you, and be in you" (Jn. 14:16-17).

Through Her preaching of the Word of God, through the Holy Sacrifice of the Mass and the Seven Sacraments, the Church maintains and nourishes this life of the Holy Spirit in Her members.

*Christ's Prayer*. In His all-powerful prayer to the Father on the eve of His efficacious death, our Lord revealed the sanctity which He conferred upon His Church as Her permanent gift until the end of time:

"Father, the hour has come! Glorify Thy Son, that Thy Son may glorify Thee, even as Thou has given Him power over all flesh, in order that to all Thou has given Him He may give everlasting life. Now this is everlasting life, that they may know Thee, the only true God, and Him whom Thou hast sent, Jesus Christ . . .

I have manifested Thy name to the men whom Thou hast given Me out of the world. They were Thine, and Thou hast given them to me, and they have kept Thy word. Now they have learnt that whatever Thou hast given Me is from Thee; because the words that Thou hast given Me I have given to them. And they have received them, and have known of a truth that I came forth from Thee, and they have believed that Thou didst send Me.

"I pray for them; not for the world do I pray, but for those whom Thou has given Me, because they are Thine; and all things that are Mine are Thine, and Thine are Mine; and I am glorified in them. And I am no longer in the world, but these are in the world, and I am coming to Thee. Holy Father, keep in Thy name those whom Thou hast given Me, that they may be one even as We are. . . . I do not pray that Thou take them out of the world, but that Thou keep them from evil. They are not of the world, even as I am not of the world. *Sanctify* them in the truth. Thy word is truth. Even as Thou hast sent Me into the world, so I also have sent them into the world. And for them I sanctify Myself, that they also may be sanctified in truth.

"Yet not for these only do I pray, but for those also who through their word are to believe in Me, that all may be one, even as Thou, Father, in Me and I in Thee; that they also may be one in Us, that the world may believe that Thou hast sent Me. And the glory that Thou hast given Me, I have given to them, that they may be one, even as We are one: I in them and Thou in Me; that they may be perfected in unity, and that the world may know that Thou hast sent Me, and that Thou hast loved them even as Thou hast loved Me". (Jn. 17:1-23).

*Sanctity of Members*. We have already seen that the Church, like Her Founder, is here to embrace sinners; and despite Her constant sanctifying work in the power of the Holy Spirit, sinners will still be found in the "net" when the Judge comes to separate the good from the bad. But Christ's infinite wisdom in establishing the means of sanctification, His pledge of the abiding presence of the Holy Spirit in the Church, and His efficacious prayer for the accomplishment of this goal, is a guarantee that the Church will have conspicuous success in the work of sanctifying Her members. This is to be a mark of the Church as an organization and not necessarily an endowment of every one of its members.

The success of this work is observable in the Church, as our Lord foretold, in varying degrees. A notable part of the members manifest "ordinary" holiness and yield at least "thirtyfold fruit" in their faith and obedience to the Church, their participation in the Mass and the Sacraments and their striving to observe the Ten Commandments. The Religious Orders of men and women as well as great numbers of lay individuals in their conspicuous works of prayer, penance and charity are a striking example of those who are striving to yield sixtyfold in the observance of the counsels; the general success of this striving is manifest in the extraordinary holiness of their lives. As far as the "hundredfold" fruit is concerned, there is the long line of Martyrs, Confessors, Virgins and other canonized saints who testify in numerous ways that their heroic sanctity was due to the means supplied to them in the doctrine, the government, the sacrifice and sacraments of the Holy Catholic Church of Rome.

*Application to Other Churches.* The touchstone of "holiness" is an obvious and easy rule for eliminating, as the true "Church of Christ," any religion which manifestly violates the natural law in matters of doctrine or worship or rules of personal conduct. It is easily applied to those oriental "religions" which introduce obscenities into their very ritual of worship. It might also be applied to a few American religions or evangelical movements which glorify passion and emotion and aim at the dethronement of reason in their religious "revivals."

But Protestantism as a whole, thanks be to God, has preserved some of the teaching of the Catholic Church with regard to faith and much of it concerning morals. No one can doubt that the people who adhere to the various sects achieve in great numbers varying degrees of holiness from their personal faith in Christ. But this holiness is a personal, individualistic affair and is not attributable to any particular church in so far as it is an organization which differs specifically from the Catholic Church. Nor is this holiness conspicuous or extraordinary in the degree of its perfection or the number of people in whom it is found. There is, in these churches, no observable or widespread practice of the counsels pertaining to poverty, celibacy or obedience as has been traditional since the days of the Apostles. Neither is there any profusion in them of the charismatic gifts of heroic sanctity.

## 4. CATHOLICITY

The word "catholic" means "universal." It is clear from Christ's mandate to the Apostles that the Church was to reach all mankind throughout the world; He Himself promised to be with it until the end of time and help it in the accomplishment of this mission. The Church, then, is to be universal in *time* and *place*.

In Junior Year, we shall study this outward movement of the Church and see the marvelous rapidity with which it came to embrace the whole world in a short time; it is revealed in the Acts of the Apostles that this was due to the compelling influence of the Holy Spirit overcoming the natural repugnance of the Apostles. So widespread was the growth of the Church by 107 A.D. that St. Ignatius of Antioch attached to it the name "Catholic" and it has been known as the Catholic Church ever since.

It is merely a matter of consulting statistics to see how, in our own day, the Church deserves the name "Catholic" because of the number of places in which it is established and the number of people of all nations who live under Her government in the bond of one faith and one charity. The Church is constantly laboring and the faithful are constantly contributing to the support of this divinely appointed work of establishing the Universal Kingdom.

*Other Churches* are not universal in time since the date of their founding does not go back to Christ. Nor are they universal in place. It is constantly represented that the Protestant Church is spread throughout the world. But there is no such thing as *the* Protestant Church. Protestantism is an extrinsic union of an indefinite number of individual sects whose only claim to oneness is their common protest to the Catholic Church; there is no internal bond uniting them together in the one faith, one government, one worship of a single Church.

These individual churches are not established throughout the world and they embrace in their membership a relatively small number of people. The Anglican Church, for example, is a national Church of England; the Lutheran Church is largely confined to people of Germanic origin and the Orthodox Church is peculiar to the Slavic nations. Despite the laudable attempts being made by Protestant leaders of our times to unite all the Protestant Churches into one, their effort is doomed to failure by the principle of individualism which is at the core of Protestantism.

*Conclusion.* From all that has been said about the Four Marks of the Church, it is clear that an individual Church, not established by Christ, may possess some of these marks in some degree. The reason for this consists in the fact that, in breaking off from the Church which Christ founded, these Churches retained some of the doctrine and worship of the original, genuine Church. It is equally clear from all that has been said, that the four prominent characteristics which were to mark the true Church of Christ are to be found together in all their fullness only in the One, Holy, Apostolic, Catholic Church of Rome.

## EPILOGUE

In this First Year of our Theology course we have seen how Christ, as Prophet, revealed Himself as King and established His Kingdom. It remains, as the work of the succeeding years, to see how Christ, by His priestly Sacrifice, draws men together into the unity of one Body and gives the fullness of His life to that Body as a Whole and to the individual cells which constitute its members.

## TEST QUESTIONS

1. Show how all four elements in the definition of "society" are verified in the Church.
2. Show that the jurisdictional power of the Church includes legislative, judicial and coercive authority.
3. Explain the word "hierarchy" as applied to the Church.
4. Prove that the Pope is infallible and explain what it means to speak "ex cathedra".
5. Show that our Lord promised Peter supreme jurisdictional authority in the Church and that this applies to his successors in office.
6. Answer the objection that the Church is authoritarian and a dictatorship.
7. Explain how each of the Four Marks is verified in the Church and the sense in which other churches lack these marks.

## SUGGESTIONS FOR READING

The student is again reminded that our intention is not to give a bibliography on Christology or the Church. These few suggestions are given in order that the student may know where to turn for more detailed treatment of this part of the textbook. Further references may be obtained from the teacher or the Library.

1. *The Teaching of the Catholic Church*, edited by Rev. George D. Smith, Macmillan Co., N. Y., 1949 (2 vols.).

   These two volumes contain a good treatment in essay form of all the dogmas of the Church. Individual dogmatic tracts are written up by various prominent Catholic theologians.

*Christology—Cf.* Vol. I (pp. 360-466) by Rev. G. D. Smith; also Ch. XII and XIII by Archbishop Goodier, S. J.

*The Church—Cf.* Vol. II (pp. 691-730), Ch. XX by Dom Aelred Graham, O. S. B.

2. *Christology,* by Rev. Joseph Pohle, adapted and edited by Arthur Preuss, B. Herder, St. Louis, Mo. (1 vol.).

   This is a full treatment of the subject according to traditional scholastic, "thesis" method.

3. *Fundamental Theology,* by Rev. John Brunsman, S. V. D., freely adapted and edited by Arthur Preuss, B. Herder, St. Louis, Mo. (3 vols.).

   Volume III treats, according to scholastic method, The Church of Christ—Establishment, Nature, Properties and Notes.

4. *The Catholic Encyclopedia* contains very fine articles on every individual point of doctrine.

5. *Mary in the Documents of the Church,* Paul F. Palmer, S.J., the Newman Press, Westminster, Md., 129 pp., 1952.

This valuable little book traces the main doctrines concerning Mary back to the Fathers and early Councils of the Church and shows that our beliefs concerning Her were shared by the early Christians. The student will find it profitable to look at Christology through the theology of Christ's Mother.

# INDEX

Abraham, 86-87
  chosen to found a favorite race, 87
  God's covenant with, 87
  not the father of unbelieving Jews, 236
Acquired knowledge of Christ, 286
Actual Grace, 211
Adam, history of, 85-86
Adam to Abraham, history of human race from, 86-87
Adoptionists deny Divinity of Christ, 279
Adorableness of Christ's Humanity, 283-284
Adoration, meaning of, 284
Adulteress, 233
Advice to Apostles on being sent to preach, 204-205
Alexandria, school of, 280
Alexandrine Manuscript of the Bible, 6
Alms, Christ lived on, 191
Aloneness of Christ with the Father, 172
Altercation with Pharisees, 192-194
Ancient Books, 3-4
Ancients, tradition of, imposed on the Jews by Scribes, 107
Andrew and John, first of Christ's disciples, 44
Antioch, school of, 280
Anxiety of Christ's kinsfolk, 191-192
*Apocalypse,* 3
Apocryphal Gospels
  contrasted with Gospels, 68
  rejected by early Christians, 64
Apostles
  as "ministers of the word," 10
  choice of, 178-180
  commanded not to tell of Transfiguration, 225
  concentration of Christ's attention upon, 170
  faith of, 199, 215-229
  familiarity with Christ, 207
  first duty to be with Christ as witnesses, 179
  foundation stones of Christ's church, 160
  given lesson in reality, malice, and power of the devil, 200
  hierarchy among, 178-179
  literal-mindedness of, 218
  made jealous by promises to Peter, 227
  meaning of the name, 295
  miracles worked for instruction of, 199
  mission of, 204-205
  new stage in training of, 198
  not to have monopoly over miracles, 227
  Pentecostal gift of eloquence to, 10
  power of "binding and loosing" given to, 228
  prepared by Christ as a group apart, 50
  purpose of their call, 179
  reliable witnesses to historical value of the Gospels, 53
  return from mission, 205-206

  the kind of men they were, 179
  witnesses to Christ, 11
Apparition upon the waters, 209
Approbation of Christ's mission in the theophany at His baptism, 152
Apostolicity of the Church, 301-303
Apostolic Catechesis, 11-12
Apostolic Fathers, witnesses to authenticity of Gospels, 54-59
Apostolic succession, 302
Aramaic, a language of the Bible, 3
Archeological discoveries and integrity of Gospels, 62
Argument for inspiration of Scripture does not beg the question, 71
Arius, author of Trinitarian heresy, 279
Arrest of the Baptist, 165
Assyrians conquer Kingdom of Israel, 94
Authenticity of the Gospels, 53
  evidence for, 54-60
"Authoritarianism" of the Church, 300
Authority greater than that of Moses claimed by Christ, 185
Authority of Christ hated and feared by Pharisees, 174-175
Authority of the Church, 294-300
  a threat to human pride, 174-175
Authority of Peter, 220
Authors of the Bible, 73

Babylon conquers Jerusalem, 94
Background of Christ's life, 101-114
Ban on certain meats among Jews, 106-107
Baptism
  and the Kingdom of God, 293
  ritual of, 217
Baptism of Christ, 151-152
Baptism of repentance enjoined by John the Baptist, 150
Baptist; *see* John the Baptist
Barnabas, St., witness to authenticity of Gospels, 55
Baur, Ferdinand C., rationalistic critic of Gospels, 67
Beatific Vision and Christ's sufferings reconciled, 285
Beatific Vision, enjoyed by Christ, 284-285
Beatitudes, 181-182
Benedict XV, xviii
*Benedictus,* Messianic ideas of the Just shown in, 127-129
Bethany, home of Mary, Martha and Lazarus, 242
  supper at, 246-247
Bethsaida, "woe" to, 229
Bethsaidas, two, 218

[ 310 ]

## INDEX

Bible, the, 1-9
  canon of, 78-80
  derivation of the term, 1
  inerrancy of, 73-78
  inspiration of; see Inspiration of Bible
  language of, 3
  manuscripts of, 4-6
  translations of, 6-8
"Bind and loose," power to, 220
  given to Apostles, 228
Birth of Christ, date of, 135-136
Blasphemy against Son of Man forgivable;
    against Holy Spirit not forgivable, 193-194
Blind man cured, 237-239
Blind men, cure of, 201-202
Blood of New Covenant foreshadowed by
  blood of Covenant between God and
  Israel, 90
"Boanerges," meaning of, 44
Body of Christ, 278
Books, Ancient, 3-4
Books of New Testament, 2-3
Books of Old Testament, 2
Bread of life, 50
  discourse on, 210-213
"Bridegroom," title assumed by Christ, 175-176

Caesar, tribute to, 256-258
Caesarea Philippi, Peter's confession at, 219-221
Call of the four, 170-171
Calming of storm, 30, 199
Cana, marriage feast at, 160
Canaanite woman, 217
Canisius College, vii
Canon of Bible
  defined by the Church, 79
  Jewish canon of the Old Testament, 80
  meaning of, 78
  Protestant canon, 80
"Canticles of the Incarnation," 126-130
Capharnaum, Christ's discourse in the
  synagogue at, 138
Capharnaum, "woe" to, 229
Captivity of Jews in Babylon, 95
Castigation of incredulity, 235-236
Catechesis, Apostolic, 11
Catechesis of Peter and order of Mark's
  Gospel, 28
Cathechetical instruction, purpose of, xi
"Catholic" letters, 2
Catholicity, mark of the Church, 307
Causality in inspiration of Bible, 73-75
Center of our religious life, Christ claims to be, 277
Centurion, Servant of, 188
Ceremonial law of the Jews, 105
Cerinthus, Gnostic heretic, witness to
  authenticity of Gospels, 59
Chalcedon, council of, condemns
  Monophysism, 281
Change in original text of Gospels, no
  substantial, 60-61
Characteristics of the Church, 301
Characteristics of the Kingdom, 292-294
"Chester Beatty Papyri" discovered, 62-63
Chief priests challenge Christ, 252
Christ
  as fulfillment of a promise made at the Fall
    of Adam, 85
  as King, xvi-xvii, 144, 289
  as Master of the Law, 216

as Messias; see Messianic prophecies and
  Messias
as Priest, xvi-xvii
as Prophet, xvi, 141-142
called "the lion of the tribe of Juda," 89
divinity of, explained, 213-214
essential message of, 141
is God, a key idea in John's Gospel, 49
false views about, 142-143
life of men, 46
  a key idea in John's Gospel, 50
light of the world, 46
  a key idea in John's Gospel, 49-50
natural, not adopted Son of God, 220
Son of David, 201
Son of God, 46,220
stands at center of Christianity, xii
Christian education, aim of, ix-xi
Christian family, Gospel of, 40
Christian morality, xviii
  basic principle of, 185
  not fully promulgated in the Sermon on
    the Mount, 184
Christian writers, early, witnesses to integrity
  of Gospels, 61
Christianity, Christ stands at center of, xii
Christianity, "idea" of, sought in theology
  course, xii
Christology, 276-290
Chronology, Luke not preoccupied with, 39
Chronology of life of Christ, 135-136
Church and Gospels, relationship between, 14
Church, the
  apostolicity of, 301-303
  as outward institution in John's Gospel, 50
  as visible society, 291-292
  "authoritarianism" of, 300
  Catholicity of, 307
  founded upon Peter and the Apostles, 160
  Gospels belong to, 15
  membership in, 292-293
  summary of doctrine on, 291-309
  testifies to fact of inspiration of Bible, 70-72
  unicity of, 294
Church Militant prophesied by Isaias, 124
Church of Christ
  indefectibility and perpetuity of, 220
  a spiritual Kingdom, 294
Church Triumphant prophesied by Isaias, 124
Circumcision, effects of, 87
Civic regulations of the Jews, 105
Criticism of Gospels, rationalistic, 66-68
Classes of people with whom Christ is
  confronted, 194
Cleansing of the Temple, 163
  Christ's first public act in Judea, 137
    second time, 252
Clement of Alexandria, witness to authenticity
  of Gospels, 57
Clement of Rome, St., witness to authenticity of
  the Gospels, 55
Climactic point of public ministry, 219
Codex Alenandrinus, 6
Codex Ephraemi, 6
Codex Sinaiticus, 5
Codex Vaticanus, 6
Coercive power of the Church, 297
Collapse of Israelite Nation, 93-96
Coming of an individual King and Saviour
  promised to Jacob, 89

[ 311 ]

# INDEX

Satan; *see also* Devil
  Christ charged by Pharisees to be tool of, 193-194
  tempts Christ, 152-156
Saturday before Christ's Passion, 246
Saul, first king of Israelites, 93
Scandal, sin of, 228
Scribes
  inner core of Pharisaic party, 104
  power of, 104
Scriptures; *see also* Bible
  testify to Christ's divinity, 215
  testify to fact of their own inspiration, 69-70
Scythopolis, 101
Second coming of Christ, 262
Secrecy about Christ's identity, Apostles commanded to maintain, 221
Self-denial of Christ's followers, 222
Semites, descendants of Sem, 86
Separatism of the Pharisees, 108-109
  reprobated by Christ, 109
*Septuagint*, 6
Sermon on the Mount, 180-186
  general theme of, 180
  not the whole of Christ's message, 184
  related to rest of Christ's message, 184
  versions by Matthew and Luke differ considerably, 181
Servant of the Centurion, 188
Seth, son of Adam, 86
Sex and legal uncleanness in Bible regulations, 107
Shema, the, 115-116
"Shepherd" of Hermas, witness to authenticity of Gospels, 55
Sign
  demanded by Pharisees, 218
  asked for by people at Nazareth and refused by Christ, 203
  demanded by crowd, 210-211
  of Jonas given to Pharisees, 218
Simon the leper, 246
Sin against the Holy Spirit, 192-195
Sin, "the unforgiveable," 193-194
Sinaitic Manuscript of the Bible, 5
Sinful woman, 190-191
Sinners not excluded from Kingdom of God, 293-294
"Sion" and "Jerusalem," references to, in prophecies misinterpreted by Jews, 124
Social situation in Palestine, 103-113
Society, Church as visible, 291-292
Society, definition of a, 292
Solitude sought by Christ, 172
Solomon, king of Israelites, 93
Solomon's Porch, Christ teaches in, 241
"Son of David," 217, 259-260
"Son of David," clear Messianic title, 201
Son of God, 46
  Martha confesses Christ to be, 243
  Peter confesses Christ to be, 220
"Son of Man"
  Messianic meaning of Daniel's prophecy of, 177
  reasons for Christ's use of the title, 176
  title assumed by Christ as official designation, 175
Son of widow of Naim, raising of, 188-189
Soul of Christ, 278
Sources of Church's teaching on inspiration, 71-72

Sources of error in text of Bible, 76-77
Source of Life, Christ the, 233-234
Sower, parable of the, 114, 195
Specially privileged apostles, Peter, James, and John, 170
Spirit of Christ contrasted with spirit of Jewish religion as taught by Pharisees, 180
Spiritual Kingdom, Church of Christ as, 294
Spiritual relationship between members of Christ's Church, 192
Statements of Christ about His Divinity, 276-277
Storm, calming of, 199, 209
Stranger Exorcist, 227-228
Strategy of Christ, 170
**Strauss, D. F., rationalistic critic of Gospels,** 66-67
Submission to Church not a loss of freedom, 300
Submission to God's will affirmed by Christ, 153
Substantial change in original text of Gospels, absence of, 60-61
Succession, apostolic, 302
Suffering and sacrifice, 222
Suffering Messias
  foretold by Isaias, 125
  hinted at in *Psalm 109*, 123
  Jews reject idea of, 121
Summary of Christian doctrine not found in Sermon on the Mount, 184
Summary of Christian morality not found in Sermon on the Mount, 184-185
Sunday before the Passion, 247-250
Supper at Bethany, 246-247
Supplements by John to the synoptic narratives, 48
Supremacy of Peter and successors, 297-298
Supreme jurisdiction of the Pope, 299-300
Survey of Christ's life and teaching (Apostolic Catechesis), 11
Symbolism of blind man's cure, 239
Sympathy and gentleness of Christ, 171
Sympathy for the poor, 40
Synagogue the cradle of the Church, 169
Synopsis of public life of Christ, 268-273
Synoptic Gospels, 16-18
  only a selective history of Christ's life, 17
  peculiarities of, 17
  purpose of, 16-17
Syrian Kings of Palestine, 96

Tabernacles, feast of, 231-232
Tatian, heretic, witness to Integrity of Gospels, 62
Taxes and Pharisees, 107
Teaching power of the Church, 295
Tears over Jerusalem, 247
Temple
  cleansed, 137, 163
  cleansed for second time, 252
  Christ predicts destruction of, 261
  destroyed by Babylonians, 94
  rebuilt by Jews, 95
Temptation in the desert, 152-156
"Ten Cities," 101
  Christ travels into, 217
Ten Virgins, parable of, 263-264
Tendency theory, rationalistic attack on Gospels, 67
Tertullian of Carthage, witness to authenticity of Gospels, 57-58
Test questions put to Christ, 256-257
Testament, meaning of the term, 1
Testimony in behalf of Christ's divinity, 214-215

# INDEX

Testimony to Christ at Transfiguration, 224
Text of New Testament, modern knowledge of, 77-78
Textual criticism of Bible and correction of error in texts, 77-78
Textual criticism of Gospels, 53, 61
Themes in John's Gospel, 49-51
Theological scheme of conversation with Nicodemus, 164
Theological truth of blind man's cure, 238-239
Theology, aims of course in, ix-xi
Theology in John's Gospel, 46-47
Theophany at the baptism of Christ, 152
Theophilus, Luke's Gospel dedicated to, 38
Third missionary tour, 203-204
Three classes with whom Christ is confronted, 194
"Tolerance," idea of, clarified, 110-111
"Tolerance" of Christ for individual Pharisees, 190
*Torah, the,* 105
Tradition of the Ancients imposed on the Jews by Scribes, 107
Traditions, Pharisaic, 215-216
Tragedy of His life foreseen by Christ in His struggle with Satan in desert, 154
Transfiguration, 223-224
Translations of the Bible, 6-8
Treasure, parable of the, 196
Tribute to Caesar, lawfulness of, 256-258
Trinitarian heresies, 279
Trinity
   disbelieved by Jews, 116-117
   not explicitly revealed in Old Testament, 116
   revealed at the baptism of Christ, 151
   revealed by Christ, 116-117
Truth, Christ the, in John's Gospel, 46
Truth will make disciples free, 235-236
Tuesday before the Passion, 253-267
Twelve apostles; *see* Apostles
Twelve, symbolism of the number, 178
Two sons, parable of, 254

Uncleanness and purification among Jews, 105-107
"Unforgiveable" sin, 193-194
Unicity of the Church, 294
Uniformity of belief and practice in the Church, 295
Union, Hypostatic, 282-283
Union of the mystical body in John's Gospel, 50
Unity in Christ, mystery of, 280
Unity, mark of the Church, 303-304
Universality of the Church, 307
Universality of the Kingdom, 292-293
Universal, other Churches not, 307
Universal redeeming mission of Christ, a key idea in Luke's Gospel, 39

Unmerciful servant, 228-229
Unselfishness, dominant trait of the Baptist, 159

Valentinus, early heretic, witness to authenticity of Gospels, 59-60
Vatican Council defines papal infallibility, 221
Vatican Manuscript of the Bible, 6
"Verbal inspiration," theory of, 74-75
Vine-dressers, parable of, 254-255
Virtues, discourse on Christian, 227-229
Visit of mother and relatives of Christ, 191-192
Voice of Heavenly Father at Transfiguration, 224
Vulgate, Latin, 7

Walking of Christ upon the waters, 209
Warnings uttered by Christ in Sermon on the Mount, 184
Watchfulness, need of, 263
Water springing up and divine life, 50
Way, the truth, and the life, Christ as the, 50
Weeds, parable of the, 195-196
"Westminster" translation of Bible, 8
Whole of Christ's message not found in Sermon on the Mount, 184
Widow of Naim, raising of son of, 188-189
Widow's mite, 261
Wisdom and holiness of Christ proofs of His divinity, 278
Witnesses, Peter, James and John as privileged, 201
Witnesses to Christ, Apostles as, 11
Witnesses to divinity of Christ, 214-215
Witness of Christ's life, John the Apostle as, 47
Witness of Father to Christ, 235
Witness of John the Baptist, 159
"Who is God?", answer to, xviii
"Woe," to Corozain, Bethsaida and Capharnaum, 229
"Woe," to Scribes and Pharisees, 260
Woman of Samaria, 50, 166
Woman, the sinful, 190-191
Woman with hemorrhage, 201
Women, Gospel of, 40
Women in Christ's entourage, 191
Women who give their lives to Christ's Church, 191
Worship, Christian, xviii
Worship of the Word Incarnate, 284
Wrath, Christ's capacity for, 163

"Yahweh," 237

Zachary, canticle of, 127-129
Zebedee, sons of, 43
Zeal for religion among Jews, 102
Zealots, 101-102

[ 321 ]

The student will find this index helpful in looking up explanations of Scripture texts. Only those texts are listed here which concern the chronological treatment of the Life of Christ. Casual Scripture references are not listed because it is unlikely that the places cited would contain an exegesis of the text.